The Story of the World

THE STORY OF THE WORLD: HISTORY FOR THE CLASSICAL CHILD
#1: ANCIENT TIMES by Susan Wise Bauer
Copyright ⓒ 2001, 2006 by Susan Wise Bauer
All rights reserved.

This Korean edition was published by Will Books in 2015
by arrangement with Susan Wise Bauer c/o InkWell Management, LLC
through KCC(Korea Copyright Center Inc.), Seoul.

이 책의 저작권은 (주)한국저작권센터(KCC)를 통한 저작권자와의 독점계약으로 월북에 있습니다.
저작권법에 의해 한국 내에서 보호를 받는 저작물이므로
무단전재와 무단복제를 금합니다.

The Story of the World

세계 역사 이야기
영어 리딩 훈련

고대 2

윌북

한국의 독자들에게

Why do we read about history?
우리는 왜 역사를 읽어야 하는가?

이 책은 까마득히 먼 옛날이야기로 시작된다. 인류가 농사를 짓고 가축을 기르기 시작하기 전, 도시를 건설하기 전, 왕을 뽑거나 지도자를 선출하기 이전의 시절부터 이야기가 시작된다. 첫 번째 장에 나오는 남자들과 여자들은 아직 지중해 해안을 여기저기 떠돌아다니던 유랑민들이다. 《The Story of the World》는 이 유랑민들이 어떻게 서서히 여러 민족으로 성장하게 되는지, 이들 민족에게 무슨 일이 일어났는지 이야기해준다.

여러분이 이 책에서 만날 이집트인들, 아카디아인들, 수메르인들, 그리고 여러 다른 민족들은 아주 먼 과거에 흥망을 겪은 사람들이다. 이들은 여러분이 사는 곳에서 아주 멀리 떨어져 살았다. 또한 그들은 여러분이 쓰는 언어와는 전혀 다른 언어를 사용했다. 그 언어들 중 상당수는 이제 더 이상 존재하지도 않으며 그 언어들을 사용한 사람들도 수천, 수만 년 전에 세상을 떠났다.

그럼 왜 우리는 굳이 이 사람들에 대한 이야기를 읽어야 할까? 두 가지 중요한 이유가 있다. 첫 번째 이유는 간단하다. 그동안 사람들이 그다지 많이 변하지 않았기 때문이다! 만 년 전에 살았던 사람들도 오늘날의 남자와 여자들이 원하는 것과 똑같은 것들을 갖고 싶어 했다. 그들 역시 먹을 음식, 마실 물과 술, 안락하게 살 수 있는 곳, 사랑하는 사람을 원했던 것이다. 만 년 전에 살았던 남자와 여자들도 힘을 갈구했다. 오늘날과 다를 바가 없다. 그들도 자신의 부모님을 사랑했고, 의견 충돌을 빚기도 했다. 그들도 자기 자식들을 걱정했다. 그들도 사는 동안 뭔가 훌륭하고 의미 있는 일을 하고자 열망했다. 그들도 우리처럼 죽음을 두려워했다. 이 과거의 사람들에 대해 공부할 때, 사실 우리는 '인간'을 공부하고 있는 셈이다. 우린 우리 자신에 대해 공부하고 있는 것이다.

두 번째 이유 역시 단순하다. 과거에 대해 알지 못하면, 현재를 온전히 이해할 수 없다. 여러분이 어디에서 태어났고, 여러분의 부모와 조부모는 누구이며, 그분들이 중요하다고 여기며 여러분에게 가르친 중요한 가치들이 무엇인지 등등, 아주 어린 시절에 겪은 여러분의 경험은 바로 여러분의 일부이다. 여러분의 부모와 조부모에 대해 모른다면, 여러분의 조상이 누구인지 모른다면, 여러분은 자신에 대해 온전히 알 수 없는 것이다. 고대의 민족들은 바로 오늘날에 존재하는 현대의 국가를 구성하고 있는 사람들의 조상들이기 때문에 우리는 그들이 누구인지 알아야만 비로소 우리 자신을 알 수 있는 것이다.

여러분은 모국어로 고대의 역사에 대해 읽을 수도 있다. 그런데 왜 이 책을 영어로 읽어야 할까? 생각해보자. 영어로 쓰인 세계의 역사에 대해 읽을 때, 여러분은 다음 세 가지 측면에서 여러분의 세계를 확장하고 있는 것이다.

첫째, 여러분은 시간을 초월하게 된다. 이 책을 읽으면서 아주 먼 과거 속으로 들어가 그 시대를 경험함으로써 여러분은 시간 여행자가 되는 것이다!
둘째, 여러분은 공간을 초월하게 된다. 여러분이 살고 있는 친숙한 나라의 경계에서 아주 멀리 떨어져 있는 것을 이해하는 사람이 되는 것이다.
셋째, 여러분은 또 다른 한계, 즉 언어의 한계를 뛰어넘게 된다.

언어마다 생각을 표현하는 방식이 다르다. 한국어로 어떤 사고에 대해 읽으면, 그것을 하나의 방식으로 이해하게 된다. 똑같은 생각에 대해 영어로 읽게 되면, 그것을 새로운 방식으로 이해하게 된다. 미국의 작가인 닐 포스트만(Neil Postman)은 이런 말을 했다. 외국어에 대해 잘 알아서 그 외국어로 쓰인 글을 읽을 수 있다면, "자신의 세계관과는 다른, 또 하나의 세계관을 가질 기회를 얻게 된다". 역사를 영어로 읽으면 여러분이 지금 알고 있는 것을 뛰어넘어, 여러분의 세계관을 훨씬 더 넓힐 수 있다!
이 책을 읽다 보면, 아마 여러분이 모르는 단어들, 이해하지 못하는 개념들도 접하게 될 것이다. 그러나 너무 걱정할 것 없다. 걱정하지 말고, 우선 이 책을 빠짐없이 한 번 이상 읽겠다고 마음먹자.

처음 읽을 때에는 그냥 '이야기' 속에 빠져들면 된다. 즐기자! 그런 다음, 다시 한 번 읽으면서 익숙하지 않은 단어들과 개념들을 확실히 이해하도록 노력하자. 그리고 마지막으로, 앞에서부터 다시 읽어보자. 읽으면서 자문해보자. 이 사람들은 왜 이렇게 행동했을까? 그들이 원한 것은 무엇일까? 그들은 어떻게 그것을 얻으려 했는가? 그들을 '이해하기' 위해 최선을 다하기 바란다.

수잔 와이즈 바우어
2014년 12월

차례

한국의 독자들에게 4 이 책의 구성 및 활용법 10

고대 2

Chapter 22	Sparta and Athens	19
Chapter 23	The Greek Gods	33
Chapter 24	The Wars of the Greeks	41
Chapter 25	Alexander the Great	55
Chapter 26	The People of the Americas	73
Chapter 27	The Rise of Rome	91
Chapter 28	The Roman Empire	103
Chapter 29	Rome's War With Carthage	125
Chapter 30	The Aryans of India	135
Chapter 31	The Mauryan Empire of India	155
Chapter 32	China: Writing and the Qin	167
Chapter 33	Confucius	191
Chapter 34	The Rise of Julius Caesar	199
Chapter 35	Caesar the Hero	217
Chapter 36	The First Roman Prince	239
Chapter 37	The Beginning of Christianity	247
Chapter 38	The End of the Ancient Jewish Nation	261
Chapter 39	Rome and the Christians	267
Chapter 40	Rome Begins to Weaken	285
Chapter 41	The Attacking Barbarians	297
Chapter 42	The End of Rome	313

Sentence Review 325
세계 역사 연대표 · 고대 353
저자의 말 356

*고대 1은 전 권에서 만날 수 있습니다

고대 1

Introduction	How Do We Know What Happened?
Chapter 1	The Earliest People
Chapter 2	Egyptians Lived on the Nile River
Chapter 3	The First Writing
Chapter 4	The Old Kingdom of Egypt
Chapter 5	The First Sumerian Dictator
Chapter 6	The Jewish People
Chapter 7	Hammurabi and the Babylonians
Chapter 8	The Assyrians
Chapter 9	The First Cities of India
Chapter 10	The Far East: Ancient China
Chapter 11	Ancient Africa
Chapter 12	The Middle Kingdom of Egypt
Chapter 13	The New Kingdom of Egypt
Chapter 14	The Israelites Leave Egypt
Chapter 15	The Phoenicians
Chapter 16	The Return of Assyria
Chapter 17	Babylon Takes Over Again!
Chapter 18	Life in Early Crete
Chapter 19	The Early Greeks
Chapter 20	Greece Gets Civilized Again
Chapter 21	The Medes and the Persians

이 책의 구성

영어 학습판
세계 역사의 흐름과 원서 읽는 재미를 동시에 잡은 우리 시대 최고의 텍스트입니다. 함께 읽기를 위한 Read-aloud 기법에 따라 이야기체로 서술되어 있어 기초 문법만 알면 누구나 부담 없이 읽을 수 있습니다. 영단어 설명과 역사 속 Q&A, 구문 해설을 첨부하여 보다 정확한 이해를 도왔습니다.

오리지널 오디오 파일
CNN이 '황금의 목소리'로 경탄한 북텔러, Jim Weiss의 오디오북을 MP3 파일에 담았습니다. 영어 텍스트 전체를 한 편의 소설처럼 실감 나게 읽어줍니다. 귀 기울여 듣다 보면 어느새 역사적 사건들이 하나의 줄기로 이어지며 전체적인 그림을 그리게 됩니다.

셀프 스터디북 Tests and Answer Key
영어 학습판의 영어 문장들과 역사적 내용을 제대로 이해했는지 스스로 파악할 수 있는 익힘책입니다. 100퍼센트 영어로 묻고 대답하면서 영어로 생각하는 법을 익힐 수 있습니다. 별도로 판매하고 있으며 자기주도로 학습할 수 있는 힘이 커집니다.

이 책의 활용법

단어 익히기

중요 영단어를 엄선하여 재치 있는 설명과 예문을 달았습니다.
단순 암기가 아닌 이미지 연상 방식을 채택하여 중고등학교 과정의
필수 어휘들을 완전히 자기 것으로 만들 수 있습니다.

문장 이해하기

대부분 중학교 1학년 수준의 쉬운 영어로 서술되어 있지만 간혹 해석이
어려운 문장은 Sentence Review에서 별도 해설하였습니다.
문법과 숙어를 자연스럽게 익힐 수 있으므로 꼼꼼히 읽어둡니다.

영어 원문 읽기

역사임에도 술술 읽을 수 있는 스토리 중심의 텍스트입니다.
100퍼센트 영어로 되어 있지만 한 문장씩 읽어나갈수록 영어 읽는
재미는 물론 역사적 지식과 생각하는 힘이 점점 커집니다.

오디오 파일 듣기

읽기에만 멈추지 말고 듣기를 반복하여
꾸준히 듣다 보면 직청직해 능력이 향상됩니다. 영어임에도 우리말처럼
편안하게 귀에 쏙쏙 들리는 놀라운 일이 벌어집니다.

Introduction
How Do We Know What Happened?

What Is History?

Do you know where you were born? Were you born at a hospital, or at home? How much did you weigh when you were born? What did you have to eat for your first birthday?

You don't remember being born, do you? And you probably don't remember your first birthday party! So how can you find the answers to these questions?

You can ask your parents. They can tell you about things that happened long ago, before you were old enough to remember. They can tell you stories about when you were a baby.

These stories are your "history." Your history is the story of what happened to you from the moment you were born, all the way up to the present. You can learn this history by listening to your parents. They remember what happened when you were born. And they probably took pictures of you when you were a baby. You can learn even more about your history from these pictures. Did you have hair? Were you fat or thin? Are you smiling or frowning? What are you wearing? Do you remember those clothes?

You have a history—and so do your parents. Where were they born? Were they born at home, or at a hospital? Where did they go to school? What did they like to eat? Who were their best friends? How can you find the answers to these questions? You can ask your parents. And if they don't remember, you can ask *their* parents—your grandparents.

Now let's ask a harder question. Your grandmother was once a little girl. What is *her* history like? How much did she weigh when she was born? Did she cry a lot? When did she cut her first tooth? What was her favorite thing to eat?

You would have to ask *her* mother—your *great*-grandmother. And you could look at baby pictures of your grandmother. But what if you can't talk to your great-grandmother, and what if you don't have any baby pictures of your grandmother? Is there another way you could find out about your grandmother's history?

There might be. Perhaps your grandmother's mother wrote a letter to a friend when she was born. "Dear Elizabeth," she might write. "My baby was born at home on September 13. She weighed seven pounds, and she has a lot of fuzzy black hair. She certainly cries a lot! I hope she'll sleep through the night soon."

Now, suppose you find this letter, years later. Even though you can't talk to your great-grandmother, you can learn the *history* of your grandmother from her letter. You could also learn *history* if your great-grandmother kept a diary or a journal, where she wrote about things that happened to her long ago.

In this book, we're going to learn about the *history* of people who lived a long time ago, in all different countries around the world. We're going to learn about the stories they told, the battles they fought, and the way they lived—even what they ate and drank, and what they wore.

How do we know these things about people who lived many,

many years in the past? After all, we can't ask them.

We learn about the history of long–ago people in two different ways. The first way is through the letters, journals, and other written records that they left behind. Suppose a woman who lived in ancient times wrote a letter to a friend who lived in another village. She might say, "There hasn't been very much rain here recently! All our crops are dying. The wheat is especially bad. If it doesn't rain soon, we'll have to move to another village!"

Hundreds of years later, we find this letter. What can we learn about the history of ancient times from this letter? We can learn that people in ancient times grew wheat for food. They depended on rain to keep the wheat healthy. And if it didn't rain enough, they moved somewhere else.

Other kinds of written records tell us about what kings and armies did in ancient times. When a king won a great victory, he often ordered a monument built. On the monument, he would have the story of his victory engraved in stone letters. Or a king might order someone in his court to write down the story of his reign, so that everyone would know what an important and powerful king he was. Thousands of years later, we can read the stone letters or the stories and learn more about the king.

People who read letters, journals, other documents, and monuments to find out what happened in the past are called *historians*. And the story they write about the past is called *history*.

What Is Archaeology?

We can learn about what people did in the past through

reading the letters and other writings that they left behind. But this is only one way of doing history.

Long, long ago, many people didn't know how to write. They didn't write letters to each other. The kings didn't carve the stories of their great deeds on monuments. How can a historian learn the story of people who didn't know how to write?

Imagine that a whole village full of people lived near a river, long ago. These people don't know how to write. They don't send letters to their friends, or write diaries about their daily life. But as they go about their duties every day, they drop things on the ground. A farmer, out working in his wheat field, loses the iron blade from the knife he's using to cut wheat from the stalks. He can't find it, so he goes to get another knife—leaving the blade on the ground.

Back in the village, his wife drops a clay pot by accident, just outside the back steps of her house. It breaks into pieces. She sighs, and kicks the pieces under the house. Her little boy is playing in the dirt, just beyond the back steps. He has a little clay model of an ox, hitched to a cart. He runs the cart through the dirt and says, "Moo! Moo!" until his mother calls him to come inside. He leaves the cart where it is and runs into the house. His mother has a new toy for him! He's so excited that he forgets all about his ox and cart. Next day, his father goes out into the yard and accidentally kicks dirt over the clay ox and cart. The toy stays in the yard, with dirt covering it.

Now let's imagine that the summer gets drier and drier. The wheat starts to die. The people who live in the village have less and less to eat. They get together and decide that they will pack up their belongings and take a journey to another place, where there is more rain. So they collect their things and start off down the river. They leave behind the things that they don't want any more—cracked jars, dull knives, and stores of wheat kernels that are too hard and dry to use.

The deserted village stands by the river for years. Slowly, the buildings start to fall down. Dust blows overtop of the ruins. One year, the river floods and washes mud over the dust. Grass starts to grow in the mud. Eventually, you can barely see the village any more. Dirt and grass cover the ruins from sight. It just looks like a field by a river.

But one day a man comes along to look at the field. He sees a little bit of wood poking up from the grass. He bends down and starts to brush dirt away from the wood. It is the corner of a building. When he sees this, he thinks to himself, "People used to live here!"

The next day he comes back with special tools—tiny shovels, brushes, and special knives. He starts to dig down into the field. When he finds the remains of houses and tools, he brushes the dirt away from them. He writes down exactly where he found them. And then he examines them carefully. He wants to discover more about the people who used to live in the village.

One day, he finds the iron knife blade that the farmer lost in the field. He thinks to himself, "These people knew how to make iron. They knew how to grow wheat and harvest it for food. And they used iron tools to harvest their grain."

Another day, he finds the clay pot that the farmer's wife broke. Now he knows that the people of the village knew how to make dishes from clay. And when he finds the little ox and cart that the little boy lost in the yard, he knows that the people of the village used cows, harnessed to wagons, to help them in their farm work.

He might even find out that the people left their village because there was no rain. He discovers the remains of the hard, spoiled wheat that the people left behind. When he looks at the wheat, he can tell that it was ruined by lack of rain. So he thinks to himself, "I'll bet that these people left their village during a dry season. They probably went to find a place where it was rainy."

This man is doing history—even though he doesn't haveany written letters or other documents. He is discovering the story of the people of the village from the things that they left behind them. This kind of history is called *archaeology*. Historians who dig objects out of the ground and learn from them are called *archaeologists*.

The Story of the World

Chapter 22
Sparta and Athens

1 Life in Sparta

🌐 스파르타 사람들의 조상은 기원전 1200년경에 그리스로 남하한 도리아인들로, 라코니아 지역의 원주민들을 굴복시키고 도시 국가 스파르타를 세웠다. 그런데 스파르타인들의 인구 수는 원주민들의 10분의 1에 불과했다. 따라서 피지배민들의 반란을 막으려면 군사적으로 강해질 수밖에 없었다. 중앙 집권적 국가 운영과 스파르타식 교육은 존립을 위해 불가피했던 것이다. 스파르타는 기원전 5세기에 펠로폰네소스 전쟁에서 아테네를 누르고 그리스의 패권을 차지하지만, 100년도 지나지 않아 그리스의 다른 도시 국가들과 마찬가지로 북쪽에서 침공한 마케도니아에게 멸망하고 만다.

The Persian empire was a huge country ruled by just one man—Cyrus the Great. Cyrus made the laws for Persia to follow. He decided when the army would attack another country. He decided how much tax the people would pay. He was a good king, but he expected to be in charge, and to have people obey him.

Greece, across the Aegean Sea, was a completely different kind of country. The Greeks all spoke the same language, dressed the same way, and worshipped the same gods. They all came to the Olympic Games and feasted together. But the Greeks didn't all obey a single king. Instead, each Greek city made its own laws. Each Greek city had its own army. And each Greek city had its own way of living. *The Greeks were horrified by the thought of obeying one, single, powerful ruler. They liked their independence.

Athens and Sparta were the two largest Greek cities, but the people of these two cities lived in very different ways. Sparta was ruled by warrior kings, and all Spartan men were required to be soldiers. Boys went to school, but they didn't learn philosophy, art, and music. Instead, when they were seven, they were sent away to special camps where they learned how to be obedient, disciplined fighters. They were taught to exercise so that their bodies would be strong. They were made to march long distances without socks or shoes, so that their feet would be tough. They weren't given very much to eat. And they were never allowed to complain. Spartan boys were expected to be tough and silent.

One story from Spartan times tells of a boy who was away at military camp, learning how to be a soldier. He was so hungry that he stole a live fox from someone else at the camp. He was planning on cooking and eating the fox! But just as he was getting ready to kill the fox, he saw some Spartan soldiers walking over to talk to him. He knew that they would beat him for stealing the fox, so he quickly hid the fox underneath his shirt. The fox immediately started biting him. But rather than admit that he had stolen the fox, the boy stood up and talked to the soldiers without showing any pain—even though the fox was chewing on his stomach. He suffered without showing it until the soldiers went away. All Spartan boys were supposed to be this brave and silent.

When they were twenty, boys had to pass a special test of fitness and bravery. If they passed, they were allowed to join the army. They would stay in the army until they were old men! Even if they got married, they weren't allowed to live with their families. Instead, they lived with the other soldiers in barracks. Boys who didn't pass the test weren't allowed to vote. They could never be full citizens of Sparta.

But what about the girls?

Girls were taught to exercise and be strong too, so that they could be the mothers of more boys who would fight for Sparta. In the ancient world of the Spartans, only fighters were truly important. And the Spartans thought that women were weaker and more timid than men. So the women of Sparta were less important than the men.

Spartan mothers were supposed to praise their sons for warlike behavior, and reward them for bravery. One Spartan mother told her son, who was leaving for battle, "Come back with your shield, or on it!" Since the losers of battles were forced to give up their shields, here's what she was really saying: "Either win the battle, or come back dead!" Spartans would rather die than lose a fight.

Sparta wasn't known for its art or storytelling, but the Spartan army was known and feared all over the world for its bravery and toughness. Today, we still call someone *spartan* if they suffer pain or disappointment without complaining.

Spartan Warrior

2 Life in Athens

🌐 그리스의 도시 국가 아테네는 직접 민주 정치로 운영된 것으로 유명하다. 그러나 처음에는 왕이 다스리는 왕정이었고, 이후 왕권이 약화되면서 소수의 귀족들이 국가를 운영하는 귀족정 국가로 변모했다. 귀족 회의인 '아레오파고스'에서 선출된 '아르콘'들이 권력을 쥐고서 국가를 운영했던 것이다. 아테네의 민주 정치는 기원전 6세기에 아르콘으로 선출된 솔론이 재산에 따른 정치 참여를 허용하면서부터 시작되었다. 이때부터 귀족 이외의 계층에 속한 성인 남자들이 민회에 참석해 국가의 중요한 일들을 논의하고 결정할 수 있게 된 것이다.

Spartans were expected to obey their king. But the Greeks who lived in Athens had a different way of doing things. *Everyone who lived in Athens had a say in how the city was run, because Athens was a *democracy*. That means that whenever a new law was written, the people of Athens could *vote* on whether or not it should actually be followed. Each citizen would have the chance to say, "Yes, this is a good law!" or "No, this is not a good law!" If more people voted Yes than voted No, the law would pass! They also voted on their leaders, on how much tax they should pay, and on whether they should go to war. *Whenever it was time for the citizens to vote about something, they would gather in the middle of the city, at a special meeting place called a *forum*. *There, they would argue about whether to vote yes or no. After the arguments, they would make up their minds and then vote.

*So that they could understand how to vote properly, the citizens had to be educated. They needed to know why taxes were important, and whether leaders were good or bad. They had to understand the laws of the city. *If they were ignorant, they wouldn't be able to argue properly about the government of the city. And they wouldn't be able to make up their minds about how to vote.

So education in Athens looked very different from education in Sparta. The Spartans were expected to obey their king and to fight for him, so they were taught how to be brave, strong, and obedient. But Athenians had to learn about taxes, laws, and government. Athenian boys went to school, just like Spartan boys. But they didn't learn how to fight. Instead, they were taught how to read and how to write on wax tablets. *They learned mathematics, so that they could count and add and subtract. They memorized the poetry of Homer. They learned how to play the flute and the lyre (an ancient Greek instrument that looked like a small harp). Like the Spartans, the Athenians were expected to be strong. But they exercised by wrestling and by racing with each other on foot.

Athenian girls were also different from Spartan girls. Athenian girls were taught to be housewives. Some girls learned how to read and write. But *all* girls learned, from their mothers, how to be *domestic*—how to manage a home, sew, raise a garden, take care of children, and manage slaves. Athenian women weren't allowed to vote. But they were expected to keep their homes running smoothly, while their husbands were away arguing in the forum and voting about laws and leaders.

One of the most famous men in Athens was named Plato. Plato told the Athenians that a democracy had to have educated people in it! If they are ignorant, he said, people who know more than they do will become tyrants and tell them what to do.

Was Plato right?

Well, let's think about this. Imagine that you've never been taught anything about stealing or about ownership. You don't know that people have a right to own things and to keep them. And no one has ever told you what stealing is. You're completely ignorant.

Now imagine that you're on your way to the store with five dollars to buy a LEGO set. Along comes your neighbor. She's bigger and older than you are, and she decides that she'd really like to have that five dollars.

"Hey!" she says. "Don't you know that it's Wednesday?"

"Why is that important?" you say.

"Well," she says, "on Wednesday, all smaller children are supposed to give their money away to larger children. It's a law! If you don't give me your money, you'll be breaking the law and you'll go to jail."

You want to do the right thing. And no one ever taught you that there was no such law! So you hand over your money, and your neighbor walks off with it.

Athenian Philosopher Plato

chapter 22 Sparta and Athens 25

That's just what Plato meant when he said that ignorant people will always obey tyrants. If you don't know what the law is, anyone can tell you what to do. The Athenians didn't want tyrants to be in charge. So they were careful to educate themselves and their children. The Spartans wanted to be strong and victorious, but the Athenians wanted to be wise and educated. These two Greek cities were very different.

Note to Parent: The Greek city-states began to arise in the mid 800s BC/BCE. The Athenian and Spartan lifestyles described here date from the 600s.

The Story of the Words

Chapter 22 Sparta and Athens

1 Life in Sparta

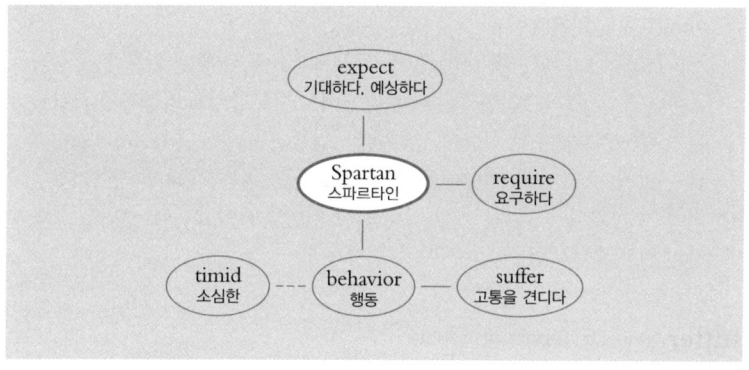

expect ⓥ to feel sure that something will happen

expect는 '밖(out)'을 뜻하는 ex-와 '바라보다(look)'를 뜻하는 spect가 합쳐진 것이다. 즉 뭔가를 기다리며 밖을 내다보는 것이다. 그래서 창문을 자꾸 내다보는 사람에게 Are you expecting someone?(누구 오기로 한 사람 있어요?)이라고 묻는다. expect는 '기대하다, 예상하다, 당연하게 여기다'라는 뜻으로, 명사형은 expectation(기대, 예상)이다.

He was a good king, but he expected to be in charge, and to have people obey him. 그는 좋은 왕이었지만, 자신이 모든 것을 결정하고 백성들이 자신에게 복종하는 것이 당연하다고 여겼다.

require ⓥ must do something

require에서 re-는 '강한, 강하게'를 뜻하고, quire는 '요구하다(seek)'이다. 어떤 행동을 하지 않을 수 없도록 강하게 요구하는 것이어서 require는 '요구하다, 필요로 하다'라는 뜻이다. 수동태로 쓰면 '~하지 않을 수 없다, 반드시 ~해야 한다'로 법에 의해, 권력에 의해 의무적으로 해야 하는 행동을 표현할 때 쓴다.

Sparta was ruled by warrior kings, and all Spartan men were required to be soldiers. 스파르타는 전사인 왕에 의해 통치되었고, 모든 스파르타의 남자는 군인이 되어야 했다.

> **Q** 스파르타에서 '스파르타식 교육'이 왜 필요했을까요?
> **A** 우선 트로이 전쟁의 원인이었던 절세의 미녀 헬레나는 스파르타 왕 메넬라오스의 부인이었어. 트로이의 왕자 파리스에게 부인을 뺏긴 메넬라오스는 화가 나서 형인 미케네 왕 아가멤논에게 달려갔지. 그 지역은 미케네 문명이었는데, 그들이 전쟁에서 이기고 돌아오니 사정이 달라져 도리아인이 북쪽에서 내려왔어.
> 스파르타는 도리아인의 나라이지만, 전사의 수에 비해 원주민 수가 훨씬 늘어난 거야. 스파르타인들은 정복 과정에서 자신들에게 반항하던 사람들은 노예(헤일로타이)로 삼았고, 협조한 사람들은 반자유인(페리오이코이)으로 두었지. 오로지 도리아인만 시민이었고, 나머지는 전부 전사로 키웠던 거야. 스파르타식 교육은 언제라도 들고 일어날지 모르는 원주민을 장악하기 위한 훈련이었던 거지.

suffer ⓥ to be in pain or trouble

suffer의 기본적인 의미는 '밑에서 견디다'이다. 가난, 고통, 질병 등이 위에서 누르면 '힘들고 괴롭다'. 그래서 suffer는 '고통 받다, (나쁜 일을) 견디다, 겪다'라는 뜻의 동사로 쓰인다. He suffered severe pain은 그는 '극심한 고통을 겪었다'라는 것이고, She suffered from depression은 그녀는 '우울증으로 고생했다'라는 의미이다. 질병 앞에는 from을 쓴다.

He suffered without showing it until the soldiers went away. 그는 병사들이 갈 때까지 내색하지 않고 고통을 견뎠다.

timid ⓐ not brave; shy

timid는 '두려워하다(to fear)'를 뜻하는 라틴어에서 왔다. 두려워하면 용기도 없어지고 소심해지므로 형용사 timid는 '소심한(shy), 용기[자신감] 없는'을 뜻한다. I was too timid to ask for what I wanted(나는 너무 소심해서 내가 원하는 것을 요구할 수 없었다)처럼 쓸 수 있다.

And the Spartans thought that women were weaker and more timid than men. 또한 스파르타인들은 여성이 남성보다 힘이 약하고 더 소심하다고 생각했다.

behavior ⓝ the way someone behaves

'생긴 대로 논다'라는 속된 말이 있다. 자신의 타고난 성향대로 행동한다는 의미인데, 이 말뜻을 고스란히 담고 있는 영어 단어가 바로 behave이다. behave는 be와 have가 합쳐진 말로 to have oneself를 뜻한다. 자기의 '본모습(oneself)'을 갖고 있다(have)'라는 의미이다. 행동이 본성을 투영한다는 것이다. 그래서 behave는 '행동하다'라는 뜻의 동사형이고, behavior는 명사형으로 '행동'이다.

Spartan mothers were supposed to praise their sons for warlike behavior, and reward them for bravery. 스파르타의 어머니들은 아들이 호전적인 행동을 하면 칭찬했고, 용기에 대해 보상했다.

Spartan ⓝ someone who is very tough, strict or simple

Spartan은 '스파르타인'을 뜻하는 말이다. 스파르타인은 강인하고(tough), 자신과 세상에 대해 엄격하며(strict), 검소(simple)했다. 그래서 지금도 그런 사람을 비유적으로 spartan이라고 부르면서 생활방식도 spartan lifestyle이라고 표현한다.

Today, we still call someone spartan if they suffer pain or disappointment without complaining. 오늘날에도 어떤 사람이 불평 없이 고통이나 실망을 견뎌내면 그런 사람을 '스파르타인'이라고 부른다.

> **Q 스파르타의 시민은 누구였나요?**
> **A** 스파르타에서는 기원전 6세기경부터 두 명의 왕, 60세 이상의 덕이 있는 시민 중에서 선택한 원로원, 20세 이상의 성인 남성으로 이루어진 민회, 시민 중에서 뽑은 다섯 명의 감독관이 정치를 담당했어. 주민은 앞에서 말한 대로 3계층으로 이루어졌는데 시민권을 가진 지배층은 '동등자'라고 불렸지. 이들이 바로 전체 인구의 10퍼센트에 해당하는 도리아인이었지만, 여성에겐 참정권이 없었으니 실제 정치에 참여하는 도리아인의 수는 훨씬 적었겠지?
> 그리고 자유 신분이었으나 참정권이 없었던 페리오이코이, 마지막이 노예 신분의 선주민인 헤일로타이야. 그들은 자신의 땅에서 전쟁에 졌다는 이유로 노예로 살아가야 했지.

2 Life in Athens

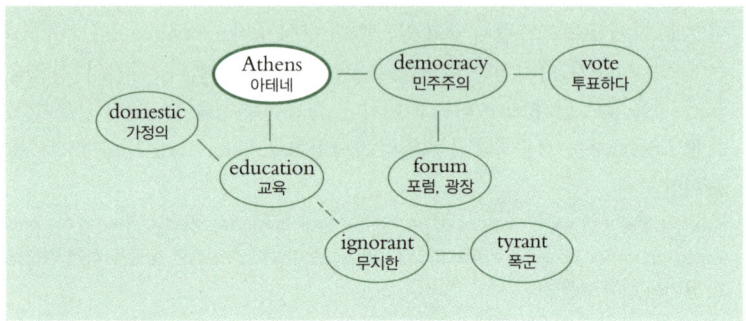

democracy ⓝ a country where everyone has an equal right to vote and choose the leaders

democracy는 '민족, 국민(the people)'을 뜻하는 demo와 '권력(power), 통치(rule)'를 뜻하는 cracy가 합쳐진 것이다. 국민이 권력을 갖고 스스로 통치하는 체제, 즉 '민주주의(民主主義)'가 democracy이다. Athens was a democracy(아테네는 민주국가였다)에서처럼 '민주주의로 운영되는 국가'를 뜻하기도 한다. 형용사형 democratic은 '민주주의의, 민주적인'을 뜻한다.

Everyone who lived in Athens had a say in how the city was run, because Athens was a *democracy*. 아테네에 사는 사람들은 누구나 도시가 운영되는 방식을 결정할 권리를 갖고 있었는데, 아테네가 민주주의 국가이었기 때문이다.

vote ⓥ to show who you want to elect or which plan you support

민주 사회의 구성원이라면 반드시 신중하게 고민해서 '투표해야' 한다. 왜냐하면 '투표, 투표하다'를 뜻하는 vote는 '맹세하다, 서약하다(vow)'라는 뜻의 라틴어에서 온 단어이기 때문에 그만큼 vote는 엄중한 것이다w. 대개 민주 사회 사람들은 새로운 법을 결정하거나 지도자를 뽑을 때 투표하는데(People vote on a new law, or on their leaders) 사람을 뽑는 선거는 election이라고 하고, 법을 직접 정하는 국민투표는 referendum이나 plebiscite라고 한다.

That means that whenever a new law was written, the people of Athens could vote on whether or not it should actually be followed. 그것은 새로운 법이 작성될 때마다, 아테네 국민들이 그 법을 실제로 따라야 하는지를 두고 투표를 할 수 있었다는 것을 의미한다.

forum ⓝ a place or meeting where ideas and views on issues are exchanged
forum은 what is out of doors(문밖에 있는 것)을 뜻하는 라틴어에서 온 것으로, 말 그대로 '마당'이 된다. 지금처럼 '사람들이 모여 의견을 주고받는 장소나 모임'을 뜻하는 '포럼(forum)'의 효시는 고대 아테네의 '광장'이었다. 지금은 주로 '토론회'의 의미로 쓴다.

Whenever it was time for the citizens to vote about something, they would gather in the middle of the city, at a special meeting place called a *forum*. 시민들이 어떤 일에 대해 투표를 할 때면 도시 중앙에 있는, '포럼'이라고 부르는 특별한 회의 장소에 모이곤 했다.

Q 아테네가 처음부터 민주 정치를 했던 것은 아니었다면서요?
A 아테네하면 직접 민주주의! 그러나 처음부터 이 제도가 확립된 것은 아니었어. 아테네에도 왕이 다스리던 시절이 있었거든. 귀족들이 권력을 차지했지만, 상업이 번창하면서 부유한 시민들도 정치 참여를 원하게 되었지. 한편 농민들이 빚 때문에 노예가 되는 경우도 늘었어. 한마디로 사회가 크게 변하고 있었던 거야.
그 시기에 등장한 사람이 솔론이었어. 기원전 594년 솔론은 시민들을 수입에 따라 4계급으로 나누고 돈이 많은 사람들에게는 더 많은 정치 참여의 기회를 허용하는 법을 만들었단다. 지금 보면 재산에 따라 정치 참여의 기회가 달라지는 것이 말도 안 되지만, 당시에는 귀족들만의 권리가 부유한 사람들에게도 허용되었다는 점에서 발전한 거야.
기원전 510년에는 클레이스테네스가 법을 고쳐 아테네와 주변에 사는 자유 시민이라면 누구라도 민회에 참석할 수 있게 했단다. 물론 자유 시민에는 여성과 외국인, 노예는 포함되지 않았어. 그러나 재산과 관계없이 시민이라면 누구라도 정치에 참여할 수 있게 되었다는 점에서 커다란 발전이었지. 아테네 민주 정치의 원형이 만들어진 시기도 바로 이때였어.

education ⓝ teaching and learning
education은 동사 educate의 명사형이다. educate는 '이끌어내다(to lead out)'라는 뜻의 라틴어에서 왔는데, 어근에 해당하는 educe는 지금도 '잠재된 어떤 성질이나 능력을 끌어내다'라는 뜻으로 쓰인다. 즉 '능력을 이끌어내다'라는 말의 의미는 '교육하다(educate)'이다. 선생님은 학생들의 능력을, 학생들은 선생님의 능력을 이끌어내는 것이 '교육(education)'의 본질이다.

So education in Athens looked very different from education in Sparta. 그래서 아테네의 교육은 스파르타의 교육과 상당히 달라 보였다.

domestic ⓐ in the home or about the home

domestic은 house(집)를 뜻하는 라틴어 domus에서 온 것이다. 그래서 형용사인 domestic은 '집과 관련된, 집안의, 가정의'를 뜻한다. domestic life는 '가정생활'이고, domestic chores는 집안에서 하는 '가사일'이다. domesticate는 집에서 애완동물로 기를 수 있게 '동물을 길들이다'라는 뜻이다. domestic은 foreign(해외의, 타국의)과 상대되는 개념으로, '국내의'라는 뜻도 있어서 domestic affairs(국내 문제)처럼 쓸 수 있다.

But *all* girls learned, from their mothers, how to be *domestic*—how to manage a home, sew, raise a garden, take care of children, and manage slaves. 그러나 모든 소녀들은 어머니로부터 가정적으로 되는 법, 즉 가정을 운영하고, 바느질하고, 정원을 가꾸고, 자식을 돌보고, 노예를 부리는 방법을 배웠다.

ignorant ⓐ not knowing very much; not educated

ignorant에서 맨 앞의 i는 not을 gnorant는 knowing(알고 있는)을 뜻한다. 라틴어 어근 gnore 자체가 know의 어원이다. 그래서 ignorant는 '무지한, 무식한'이고, ignore는 '무시하다, 모른 척하다'라는 뜻이다. 무지 중에 최악은 자신이 모른다는 사실조차 모르는 것이다. 소크라테스는 '무지의 자각'을 강조하며 '너 자신을 알라!(Know yourself!)'라는 말을 했다.

If they are ignorant, he said, people who know more than they do will become tyrants and tell them what to do. 그(플라톤)는 시민들이 무지하면 그들보다 더 많이 알고 있는 사람들이 폭군이 되어 시민들에게 명령을 하게 될 거라고 말했다.

tyrant ⓝ a ruler who has complete power and uses it in a cruel and unfair way

tyrant는 '독재자, 폭군'을 뜻한다. 국가 권력을 손에 쥐고 폭정을 일삼는 군주를 의미하는데, 20세기에는 이런 지도자가 많았다. 물론 지금도 선거로 뽑혔어도 당선 후에 권력을 독점하고 국민을 억압하면 tyrant이다. '독재[폭압] 정치, 독재 국가'를 의미하는 단어는 tyranny로, democracy의 반대 개념이다. 플라톤의 말대로, 무지한 국민은 폭군을 섬길 자격이 충분하다.

That's just what Plato meant when he said that ignorant people will always obey tyrants. 무지한 사람들은 항상 폭군들에게 복종하게 될 것이라는 플라톤의 말은 바로 그런 의미이다.

The Story of the World

Chapter 23
The Greek Gods

1 The Golden Apple

🌐 올림포스 산(Mount Olympus)은 그리스에서 가장 높고 큰 산이다. 그리스 북부 테살리아의 해안에 위치하며, 해발 2,919미터인 최고봉 미티카스를 비롯해 2,000 미터가 넘는 웅장한 봉우리들이 여덟 개나 모여 있다. 올림포스 산은 에게 해에 접해 있기 때문에 거의 항상 안개와 구름에 가려 있다. 고대 그리스인들은 이 장엄하고 비밀스러운 산에 제우스를 비롯한 신들이 살고 있다고 믿었다.

The ancient Greeks may have lived in very different ways, but they all spoke the same language—Greek. And they all worshipped the same gods. The Greeks were polytheists. Remember: Polytheists believed in many gods. Monotheists, like the Jews, only believed in one god.

The Greeks believed in a whole family of gods. They thought that these gods lived up on the top of Mount Olympus, the highest mountain in Greece. And they also thought that the gods were very interested in what men were doing.

Sometimes the Greek gods were kind and helpful to men. But at other times, they were cruel. As a matter of fact, the chief god of the Greeks, Zeus, started a horrible war down on earth:

Zeus sat on the top of Mount Olympus and looked down over Greece. All over the countryside, he could see men, swarming like ants. Men cutting down trees, men building houses all over the beautiful green fields, men pulling fish out of the sea. Men killing deer for food, shooting birds for fun, and blocking up streams for water. Zeus sighed.

"There are too many people on the earth," he said gloomily. "I should get rid of some of them." He thought and thought. And finally he came up with a plan. He knew that

Zeus

the gods were all going to a big wedding, and that it would be the perfect time to start a fight. So he made a golden apple, so beautiful that it made the sun look dim, and wrote around the top, "For the Most Beautiful." Then he called Eris, the goddess of strife. "Here," he said, "take this apple to the wedding, and drop it on the floor in front of my wife Hera."

Eris liked to cause trouble. So she took the apple to the wedding, and waited until Hera and two other goddesses were standing next to each other, chatting. Then she rolled the apple over to Hera. It bumped against Hera's toes, and she picked it up.

"For the Most Beautiful!" she read. "Why, thank you! That's obviously me!"

But the two goddesses with her disagreed. Aphrodite, the goddess of love, twirled her shining golden hair around one hand and blinked her huge blue eyes.

"Hera, my dear," she said sweetly, "I think the apple must be for me."

"Oh, no," put in Athena, the goddess of war. She reached for the apple. "The apple is obviously for me."

"No!" Hera snapped, clutching the apple. "It's mine!"

chapter 23 The Greek Gods 35

The wedding guests all started to argue about which of the goddesses was the most beautiful. But then Hera said, "I know. Let's ask my husband to judge which of us deserves the apple. After all, he is the chief of the gods."

Zeus was standing innocently by the punch bowl. "What?" he said. "How can I judge my own wife? No, no. You must ask a mortal man to judge you. Ask Paris, the prince of Troy. He's the handsomest man on earth, so surely he can decide who is most beautiful among the goddesses."

Paris was lying happily on a mountainside, staring at the sky without a care in the world, when the three goddesses suddenly appeared in front of him with the apple in hand. They demanded that he judge them. Which was the most beautiful?

"Hmm," Paris said, wondering whether one of them would strike him dead if he chose the wrong goddess. "Well, let me see …"

"Pick me," whispered Hera, "and I'll make you the king of the whole world of men."

"Really?" Paris said.

"No, no," hissed Athena. "Pick me, and I'll give you victory in every battle you ever fight!"

"That would be wonderful!" Paris said.

"Wait!" said Aphrodite. "Pick me, Paris, and I will give you the most beautiful woman on earth."

Paris's eyes lit up. "That's what I want!" he said, and gave the apple to Aphrodite.

Aphrodite went back to Mount Olympus, with Hera and Athena behind her, grumbling and complaining. There, Aphrodite made Helen, the most beautiful woman in the world, fall in love with Paris. As soon as she saw him, she was

Aphrodite

his forever. And she ran away to live with him in Troy.

Unfortunately, Helen was already married—to Menelaus, the king of the Greeks! Menelaus was furious. And he called on the gods to help him fight against Troy, defeat Paris, and get his wife back. Hera was still angry with Paris, so she chose to fight against Troy. Aphrodite was on Troy's side. The sun god decided to be on Troy's side as well. Poseidon, the god of the sea, wanted to see Troy destroyed. And so it went; all of the gods lined up for or against Troy, as the Greeks sailed to attack it. And so the Trojan War began, and lasted for years and years of bloodshed and death—all because of Zeus and his golden apple. 📖

The Story of the Words

Chapter 23 The Greek Gods

1 The Golden Apple

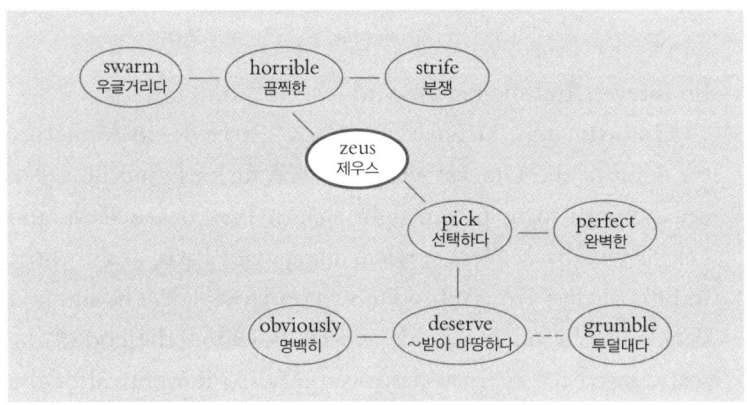

horrible ⓐ very unpleasant, frightening or shocking

horrible은 '공포, 두려움'을 뜻하는 horror의 형용사형이다. '공포 영화'를 horror movie라고 한다. horror는 '떨다(tremble)'라는 뜻의 라틴어에서 온 것으로, 부르르 몸서리를 치거나 떨릴 만큼 무서운 것, 끔찍하게 싫은 것에 모두 쓸 수 있다. a horrible war는 끔찍하고 잔혹한 전쟁을 의미하고, 어떤 음식의 맛이 몸서리칠 만큼 싫으면 This food tastes horrible이라고 한다.

As a matter of fact, the chief god of the Greeks, Zeus, started a horrible war down on earth. 사실 그리스인들의 최고 신인 제우스는 지상에서 끔찍한 전쟁을 일으키기도 했다.

swarm ⓥ to move in a large group

개미나 바퀴벌레, 구더기 같은 벌레들이 많이 모여 있으면 '바글바글, 우글우글' 하다고 말하는데, 그런 느낌의 단어가 바로 swarm이다. swarm은 '떼를 지어 움직이다', '무리, 떼'를 뜻한다. 아주 높은 올림포스 산의 꼭대기에서 아래를 내려다보면, 사람들이 벌레처럼 우글대는 듯 보였을 것이다.

All over the countryside, he could see men, swarming like ants. 사람들이 교외 여기 저기에서 개미떼처럼 움직이는 모습이 제우스의 눈에 들어왔다.

perfect ⓐ exactly right for a particular purpose
perfect는 '완전히, 완벽히(completely)'를 뜻하는 접두사 per-와 '하다(do)'를 뜻하는 fect가 합쳐진 것이다. 즉 일을 완전하게, 완벽하게 하는 것이다. 그래서 perfect는 형용사로 '완벽한, 완전한, 더할 나위 없이 좋은[알맞은]'을 뜻한다.
He knew that the gods were all going to a big wedding, and that it would be the perfect time to start a fight. 제우스는 신들이 모두 성대한 결혼식에 갈 것이고, 그때가 싸움을 시작하기에 완벽한 시간임을 알고 있었다.

strife ⓝ fighting or strong disagreement between people or groups
그리스 신화의 에리스(Eris)는 분쟁의 여신(the goddess of strife)이다. eris라는 말 자체가 그리스어로 '분쟁, 투쟁'이다. '분투하다'라는 뜻의 동사형 strive와 어원이 같다. strife는 '갈등, 불화, 다툼'을 뜻하는 명사형으로, conflict와 동의어이다. political strife(정치적 갈등)나 religious strife(종교적 분쟁)처럼 쓴다.
Then he called Eris, the goddess of strife. 그런 다음 제우스는 '분쟁의 여신'인 에리스를 불렀다.

obviously ⓐd in a way that is clear for almost anyone to see or understand
obviously는 obvious의 부사형이다. obvious는 ob viam이라는 라틴어 어구에서 유래했다. in the way(가는 길에서)라는 의미인데, 항상 다니는 길에서 마주치는 풍경과 사람들은 낯이 익어 어디인지, 누구인지 알 것이다. 이런 의미에서 obvious는 '분명한, 확실한, 너무 뻔한'이고, 부사형 obviously는 '확실히, 분명히, 명백히'라는 뜻이다.
That's obviously me! 누가 봐도 그건 나지!

deserve ⓥ to be worthy of something
deserve는 de-와 serve가 합쳐진 말이다. de-는 '강조'의 의미가 있고, serve는 '적합하다'라는 의미이다. 따라서 deserve는 '~에 아주 적합하다, 잘 맞다'라는 뜻이다. You deserve the prize(넌 그 상을 받을 만해)나 You deserve the punishment(넌 그 벌을 받아 마땅해) 모두 상과 벌에 '아주 적합하다'라는 의미이다. '~을 받아 마땅하다, ~을 받아도 싸다'라는 뜻으로, 좋고 나쁜 것 둘 다에 목적어로 쓸 수 있다.

chapter 23 The Greek Gods 39

Let's ask my husband to judge which of us deserves the apple. 우리들 중에 누가 그 사과를 받아야 마땅한지 우리 남편에게 판정해 달라고 합시다.

pick ⓥ to choose someone or something

pick의 기본적인 의미는 '손으로 뭔가를 집다'이다. 그런데 여럿 중에 하나를 집는다는 것은 그것을 '선택했다'라는 의미가 된다. 열매를 따더라도 잘 익은 것을 '골라서' 따지 않는가? 그래서 pick은 '고르다, 선택하다'이다. 이 경우에는 choose와 의미가 같다.

"Pick me," whispered Hera, "and I'll make you the king of the whole world of men. 헤라가 속삭였다. "날 선택해. 그러면 내가 너를 인간 세상의 왕으로 만들어줄 테니까."

grumble ⓥ to complain in a quiet, but slightly angry way

우리말에 '구시렁거리다'는 말이 있는데, 여기에 딱 적당한 단어가 바로 grumble이다. 뭔가 불만스러워서 자꾸 중얼거리는 모습을 표현한 단어이다. 즉 '투덜대다, 구시렁거리다'라는 뜻이다. 그런데 grumble하면 상대가 정확히 무슨 말을 하는지 못 알아듣는다. 정확히 자신의 불만을 말하는 complain과는 다르다.

Aphrodite went back to Mount Olympus, with Hera and Athena behind her, grumbling and complaining. 아프로디테는 올림포스 산으로 돌아갔고, 헤라와 아테나는 구시렁대고 불만을 토로하면서 그 뒤를 따랐다.

Q 황금 사과 말고도 유명한 사과가 있다면서요?
A 트로이 전쟁의 원인이 되었다는 황금 사과는 그 후에도 화가들의 상상력을 불러일으켰어. 지금도 미술관에 가면 황금 사과로 벌어진 이야기들이 그림으로 남아 있지. 그러나 그 황금 사과만이 유명한 것은 아니야. 성서에 아담과 이브의 선악과를 사과로 소개한 이야기도 있고, 빌헬름 텔의 사과도 유명하지. 뉴턴은 사과가 떨어지는 것을 보고 만유인력의 법칙을 발견했어. 마지막으로 세잔은 '사과 하나로 세상을 정복하겠노라!'라는 유명한 말을 남겼지. 세잔은 화가니까 사과로 세상을 정복하겠다는 것은 사과를 그리는 방식을 새롭게 보여주겠다는 의미라고 할 수 있어.

The Story of the World

Chapter 24
The Wars of the Greeks

1 Greece's War With Persia

🌐 기원전 6세기에 오리엔트 지역을 모두 차지한 페르시아는 점차 서쪽으로 세력을 확장해 그리스 원정에 나서는데, 이 전쟁을 '페르시아 전쟁'이라고 부른다. 아테네와 스파르타를 중심으로 연합한 그리스의 도시 국가들은 대규모의 페르시아 군대를 성공적으로 막아냈고, 결국 기원전 492년부터 448년까지 3차에 걸쳐 이루어진 페르시아의 그리스 원정은 실패한다. 마라톤의 기원이 된 마라톤 전투(Battle of Marathon)와 영화 〈300〉의 배경이 된 테르모필레 전투(Battle of Thermopylae), 그리고 제3차 원정에 나선 페르시아 해군을 살라미스 해협에서 괴멸시킨, 살라미스 전투(Battle of Salamis) 등이 이 전쟁에서 치러진 유명한 전투이다.

•Athens and Sparta didn't have much in common except for their language and their gods. As a matter of fact, they fought with each other. Sometimes the Athenians attacked Sparta. Sometimes Sparta attacked Athens. They went on fighting, off and on, for years.

But then something frightening happened. The Persians started to invade Greece. After all, the Persians had conquered almost all the rest of the land around them! Greece was one of the few countries that didn't obey the Persian empire. And the Persians wanted Greece too.

At first, the Persians just sent messengers to Greece. The messengers came to Athens and Sparta and announced, "We are from the great king of the Persians! He wants you to be part of his empire. If you agree, send him back some earth and some water from your cities. Then he won't attack you."

The Athenians and the Spartans were furious. How dare the king of the Persians demand that they surrender without even a fight? So they grabbed the messengers and threw them down a well. "There!" they said. "There's plenty of earth and water for

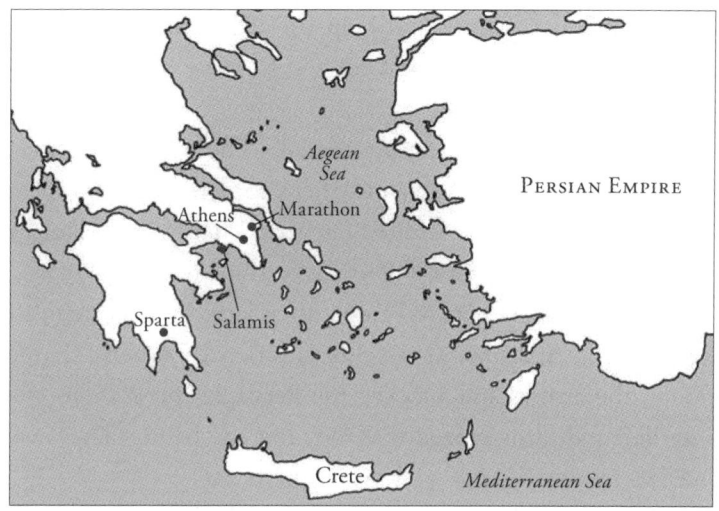

Greece's War With Persia

you down there!"

After that, Persia was determined to attack. The Persian army advanced on Greece. Athens and Sparta decided that they had better stop fighting each other, and become friends and allies so that they could defend themselves against the Persians.

The war against Persia began around 500 BC/BCE. It dragged on for years and years. Athens and Sparta fought battle after battle against the Persian invasion.

One of the most famous battles of the war was the Battle of Marathon. Marathon was a little village near the coast of Greece, close to the Aegean Sea.

One day in the year 490 BC/BCE, a ship came to Athens with frightening news: The Persians were coming! They were sailing from Asia Minor across the Aegean Sea, straight for the village of Marathon. The Athenians knew that if the Persians could land all of their soldiers at Marathon, they could march into Athens and destroy it. So the Athenian army sent a message to Sparta, saying "Come and help us!" But the Spartans were having a religious festival, and refused to leave Sparta until the festival was over.

•The Athenians were outnumbered. •There were too many Persian soldiers for the army of Athens to defeat alone. But the men of Athens had no choice. They marched from Athens to Marathon and waited for the Persians to land.

When the Persian army landed, they launched thousands of arrows at the Athenian army. But the men of Athens charged through the arrows and attacked the Persians. The Persians were so startled and disorganized that they lost the battle. •They were forced to retreat.

•When the Athenians saw that they had won the battle, they sent a runner back to Athens, to tell the people who were anxiously waiting at home that the Persian threat had been driven back. •The runner, Pheidippides, ran over twenty-six miles, up steep hills and through rough country, to reach Athens. When he arrived at the city, he gasped out, "We have won!" And then—according to legend—he died of exhaustion.

Today we have a race named after the village of Marathon. The race is a little over twenty-six miles long, and it is called the *marathon*. •It is run in the Olympics in honor of the brave Athenian who ran from Marathon to Athens with the good news of victory.

The Battle of Marathon didn't end the war, though. •The Persians and Greeks went on fighting until the Greeks finally defeated the Persians, once and for all, in a great sea battle at a place called Salamis. After the Battle of Salamis (which took place in 480 BC/BCE) the Persians finally gave up attacking Greece. The Greek cities would remain free and independent from Persia.

2 The Greeks Fight Each Other

기원전 431년부터 404년까지 27년 동안 그리스의 양대 세력인 아테네와 스파르타가 벌인 전쟁을 '펠로폰네소스 전쟁'이라고 부른다. 페르시아의 침입을 막아낸 후 아테네는 그리스의 맹주로서 다른 도시 국가들의 내정에 간섭하며 '보호비' 명목의 돈을 걷었고, 반발하는 도시 국가들은 군사력으로 제압하기도 했다. 아테네의 세력이 확장되자 스파르타가 견제에 나섰고, 결국 431년에 아테네 중심의 델로스 동맹과 스파르타가 결성한 펠로폰네소스 동맹이 그리스의 패권을 놓고 전쟁을 벌이게 되었다. 3차에 걸친 전쟁에서 아테네가 패해 스파르타가 그리스의 패권을 쥐게 되었지만, 전쟁의 여파로 국력이 쇠해 북쪽에서 침공한 마케도니아에 의해 그리스의 도시 국가들이 모두 정복되고 만다.

Now Greece was at peace. Instead of putting all their time and energy into fighting the Persians, the Greeks were able to do other things. *They became famous for their *architecture*—the way they designed and built buildings. The Greeks built enormous buildings from marble. One of the most famous Greek buildings is called the Parthenon. The Parthenon was a temple built in honor of Athena, the Greek goddess of war. Its ruins still stand in Greece, in the city of Athens, on a hill called the Acropolis.

*Inside the Parthenon were pictures, carved in marble, of different Greek battles. These pictures were called *friezes*. One of the friezes shows a legendary battle between the Greeks and an army of centaurs. Centaurs were imaginary creatures that were half man and half horse.

The soldiers and centaurs on the friezes look very real. You can see the muscles in the arms of the soldiers, and the expression on the faces of the soldiers. *The Greeks tried very hard to make their pictures and statues look like real people. The faces of their statues look like the faces of real men and women. And the folds of their clothing look like they are made from real cloth. It is hard to believe that they are carved from stone.

With the Persians defeated, Athens and Sparta no longer had to fight. The Greeks could have gone on making their beautiful buildings and creating their statues in peace.

But they didn't. Sparta and Athens were both afraid that the other city would become too powerful. So instead of remaining on friendly terms, Sparta and Athens began to fight with each other again. The war between Sparta and Athens began in 431 BC/BCE. It had a very long name—the Peloponnesian War. And the Peloponnesian War went on for a long time, over 25 years.

At first, Sparta gathered all its armies together and marched towards Athens to invade it. But the Athenians decided that the Spartan soldiers were too strong to fight. They didn't march out to meet the Spartan army. Instead, they stayed inside the walls of Athens and waited for the Spartan army to go away. "We will fight with the 'Long Walls' of Athens!" the people said. Instead of fighting with swords, they would let the strong walls of the city protect them.

The Athenians waited and waited. Maybe their strategy would have worked—if something terrible hadn't happened. The plague broke out, inside the city walls.

The plague was a sickness spread by the fleas that lived on rats. But the Athenians didn't know this. They just knew that people were getting sick and dying all over the city. They couldn't leave the city, because of the Spartan army camped outside. And inside the city, sickness was everywhere. The greatest Athenian general, a man named Pericles, and many of the strongest young men of Athens died. The Athenians panicked. How could they defeat the Spartans now?

Finally one Athenian decided that he was tired of waiting for the siege to end. His name was Alcibiades, and he wanted to be the king of Athens. He thought to himself, "If I can defeat the Spartans, the Athenians will want to follow me!" So he called out to the Athenians, "Follow me! Let's get rid of these Spartans once and for all. We'll attack the Spartan army and defeat it!"

Alcibiades led the Athenians outside the city walls and attacked the Spartan camp. But the men of Athens were sick and weak, and the Spartans defeated them. *The survivors straggled back into Athens, angry and embarrassed. "Let's get rid of Alcibiades!" they shouted. "He led us into defeat!"

*But Alcibiades was nowhere to be found. When he saw how angry the Athenians were, he deserted the city and went over to the Spartan camp. "Follow me back into Athens!" he told the Spartan general. "I know a secret passageway into the city. We can sneak in after dark and take over before the Athenians know what has happened to them!"

The Ruins of the Acropolis

The Spartans agreed to follow Alcibiades. So late one night, the traitor led the Spartans into his own city. The Spartan army captured Athens and took over. Sparta became the strongest city in Greece.

But most of the Athenian men and many of the Spartan soldiers had died in the long, long Peloponnesian War. *Now Greece no longer had the men they needed to keep other invaders away. *The Greeks had spent all their energy fighting each other; they had none left to defend themselves.

And soon, invaders would come. 📖

Note to Parent: The Peloponnesian Wars were fought 431–404 BC/BCE, with a brief peace in the middle.

The Story of the Words

Chapter 24 **The Wars of the Greeks**

1 Greece's War With Persia

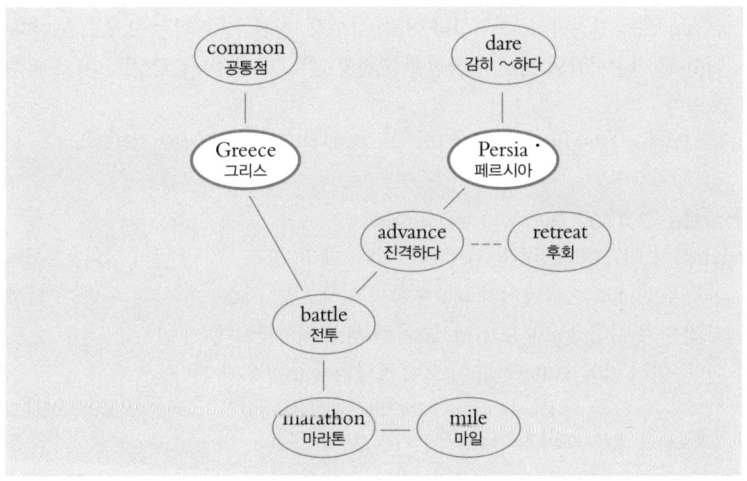

common Ⓝ the same things such as aims, beliefs, ideas that are shared by several people or groups

com-은 together(함께)라는 의미이다. common은 '함께 하는'을 뜻하는 프랑스어 comun에서 온 것이다. 그래서 common은 '공동의, 공통의, 보통의, 흔한'의 뜻이다. 명사형으로는 생각, 태도, 목표, 방식 등이 같다는 의미로 '공통점'이고, in common은 '공통적으로'를 뜻한다.

Athens and Sparta didn't have much in common except for their language and their gods. 아테네와 스파르타는 언어와 신들을 제외하면 공통점이 별로 없었다.

dare Ⓥ to be brave enough to do something dangerous or afraid to do

하룻강아지가 호랑이에게 덤빈다면 하룻강아지 입장에서는 대단히 '용감한' 행동이고, 호랑이의 입장에서는 '어처구니없고 가소로운' 행동일 것이다. 이 둘의

chapter 24 The Wars of the Greeks **49**

입장을 모두 표현할 수 있는 말이 dare로, '감히 ~하다, ~할 용기가 있다'라는 뜻이다. 위의 상황은 The puppy dared to bark at the tiger(강아지는 무모하게도[용감하게도] 호랑이에게 짖었다)처럼 표현할 수 있다.

How dare the king of the Persians demand that they surrender without even a fight? 어떻게 감히 페르시아 왕이 한 번도 싸우지도 않고, 그리스인들에게 항복하라고 요구할 수 있단 말인가?

advance ⓥ to move forward

advance는 advantage와 같은 어원에서 유래하여 모두 '앞으로'라는 뜻이다. advance는 '전진하다, 진격하다'이고, 명사형 '전진, 진군'의 뜻으로도 쓰인다. 어떤 일이나 사람의 성공과 발전을 표현할 때도 '발전[하다], 향상[하다]'로 자주 쓰인다.

The Persian army advanced on Greece. 페르시아 군대는 그리스로 진격했다.

battle ⓝ a fight between two armies

battle의 어근에 해당하는 bat에는 '치다, 때리다(beat)'라는 뜻이 있다. 그래서 야구공을 때리는 방망이가 bat(배트)이고, 동사형 batter는 '세게 치다, 구타하다'라는 뜻이다. battle도 combat처럼 서로 치고받고 함께 싸우는 '전투'를 뜻한다. 여러 번의 battle(전투)이 모여 하나의 war(전쟁)가 된다.

Athens and Sparta fought battle after battle against the Persian invasion. 아테네와 스파르타는 페르시아의 침략에 맞서 연거푸 전투를 치렀다.

Q 그리스는 대제국 페르시아를 어떻게 이길 수 있었을까요?

A 헤로도토스는 페르시아 전쟁에서 어떻게 그리스가 승리할 수 있었을까 생각했어. 그가 내린 결론은 그리스의 자유 정신이 페르시아의 전제 정치를 이겼다는 것이었어. 막상 페르시아가 쳐들어오자 병력 면에서는 그리스가 압도적으로 불리했지만, 그리스인들은 이 전쟁에서 지게 되면 자신들이 누리던 자유는 끝이라는 것을 알았지. 그러니 필사적으로 이길 방법을 생각했겠지?

반면에 페르시아군은 연합군이어서 그들에겐 이 전쟁이 그리스인들만큼 절박하지 않았을 거야. 또한 역사가들은 대군으로 움직이는 페르시아가 불리했을 수도 있었다고 해. 한 가지 더 생각해볼 점은 이 전쟁을 기록한 사람들이 그리스인이었다는 점! 페르시아가 진 것은 확실하지만, 어느 정도 규모의 병력을 보내어 어떻게 싸웠는지에 대해 우리가 알고 있는 모든 사실은 그리스인의 시각에서 쓰여진 거란다.

retreat ⓥ to go back or move away from something or someone

retreat에서 접두사 re-는 '뒤에서, 뒤로(back)'를, treat는 '당기다(pull)'를 뜻한다. 뒤에서 잡아당기면 뒤로 갈 수밖에 없다. 그래서 retreat는 '뒤로 물러나다, 후퇴하다'이고, 명사형으로 '뒤로 물러섬, 후퇴, 철수'를 뜻한다. 어떤 원인이나 힘에 의해 후퇴하는 것이다.

They were forced to retreat. 페르시아인들은 후퇴할 수밖에 없었다.

mile ⓝ a measure of length equal to 1.6 kilometers

mile은 원래 '1000, 천(thousand)'을 뜻하는 라틴어 mille에서 온 것이다. 그래서 '천년'의 시간을 millennium(밀레니엄)이라고 한다. 통일된 규격이 없던 시절에 로마인들은 평균적인 '보폭'을 활용해 거리를 쟀다. 한 걸음의 최대 길이가 대략 160센티미터정도였다. mile은 '천 걸음'이어서 1마일은 약 1.6킬로미터이다. 그럼 승리를 전하기 위해 페이디피데스가 달린, 마라톤에서 아테네까지의 거리 26마일은 몇 킬로미터쯤 될까?

The runner, Pheidippides, ran over twenty-six miles, up steep hills and through rough country, to reach Athens. 전령 주자인 페이디피데스는 가파른 언덕을 오르고 거친 황야를 지나며 26마일이 넘는 거리를 달려서 아테네에 도착했다.

marathon ⓝ a long race of 42.195 kilometers

지금 마라톤 선수들은 42.195킬로미터를 달린다. 본문에도 있듯이 marathon 용어와 경주 거리는 마라톤에서 아테네까지 달린 페이디피데스의 이야기에서 유래한 것이다. 페이디피데스는 철인적인 달리기 선수였던 것 같다. 고대 그리스의 역사가 헤로도토스의 기록에 따르면, 페르시아의 침략 직전에 아테네에서 스파르타까지 150마일(240킬로미터)을 달려 도움을 청한 것도 페이디피데스였다고 한다. marathon은 1896년 제1회 아테네 올림픽에서 정식 종목으로 채택되었는데, 그때 구간이 마라톤에서 아테네 경기장까지였다.

The race is a little over twenty-six miles long, and it is called the *marathon*. 그 경주 거리가 26마일이 조금 넘으며, '마라톤'이라고 불린다.

2 The Greeks Fight Each Other

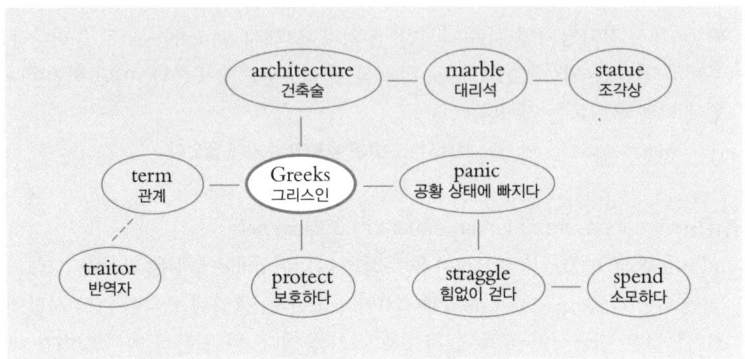

architecture ⓝ the shape and style of buildings

architecture는 architect에 명사형 접미사 -ure가 붙은 형태이다. architect는 희랍어에서 유래했는데, arch는 chief(우두머리)를 뜻하고 tect는 builder(건설자)이다. 쉽게 말하면 '건설 책임자'이다. 건설하는 건물의 설계, 재료, 규모 등의 모든 것에 대해 알고 결정하는 사람이다. 즉 architect는 전문적인 '건축가'를 뜻하고, architecture는 '건축가의 일, 기술', '건축학, 건축술'이다.

They became famous for their *architecture*—the way they designed and built buildings. 그들은 건물을 설계하고 건설하는 방식, 즉 건축술로 유명해졌다.

marble ⓝ a hard white rock that can be made smooth and shiny and is used in building things

고대 그리스의 건축물들이 2,500년이 지난 지금까지 건재할 수 있었던 것은 marble 덕분이다. marble은 '대리석'인데, shining stone(반짝이는 돌)을 뜻하는 희랍어에서 온 단어이다. 그리스에는 질 좋은 대리석이 풍부하게 매장되어 있기 때문에 marble로 웅장한 건물들을 짓고 아름다운 조각상을 만들 수 있었다. 아이들이 갖고 노는 '구슬'도 marble이라고 한다.

The Greeks built enormous buildings from marble. 그리스인들은 대리석으로 거대한 건물들을 지었다.

statue ⓝ a shape of a person or animal made of stone, metal, or wood

statue는 라틴어에서 유래한 것으로, 어근인 sta에는 '서다, 세우다'라는 뜻이 있다. 그래서 stand가 '서다, 서 있다'이고, stable이 가만히 서 있듯 '안정된, 안정적인'을 뜻한다. 광화문에 이순신 장군 동상은 항상 그 자리에 가만히 서 있다. statue가 '조각상, 동상, 석상'이다.
The Greeks tried very hard to make their pictures and statues look like real people. 그리스인들은 그림과 동상들이 진짜 사람처럼 보이도록 만들기 위해 무척 애썼다.

term ⓝ relationship

term은 '끝(end), 경계(boundary), 한계(limit)'를 뜻하는 라틴어 terminus에서 온 것이다. 버스 '터미널(terminal)'이나 영화 터미네이터(Terminator)에도 term이 있다. 인간관계를 말할 때 term을 쓰면 '관계, 사이'를 뜻한다. 부모와 자식, 친구, 선후배 등의 관계는 경계가 정해져 있으므로 term은 '범위, 경계'를 뜻한다. friendly terms는 '우호적인 관계'이다.
So instead of remaining on friendly terms, Sparta and Athens began to fight with each other again. 그래서 스파르타와 아테네는 우호적인 관계를 유지하지 않고, 다시 서로 싸우기 시작했다.

protect ⓥ to keep someone or something from being harmed or damaged

protect는 '앞으로(forward)'를 뜻하는 접두사 pro-와 '덮다, 가리다(cover)'를 뜻하는 tect가 합쳐진 것이다. 새 둥지로 뱀이 다가오면 어미 새가 '앞으로(pro)' 나서 둥지를 '덮듯(tect)' 날개를 편다. 새끼를 보호하기 위해서다. 그래서 protect는 '보호하다, 지키다'라는 뜻이다. 명사형 protection은 '보호, 수호'이고, protector는 '보호자'이다.
Instead of fighting with swords, they would let the strong walls of the city protect them. 칼로 싸우는 대신에 그들은 튼튼한 도시의 성벽이 자신들을 보호하게 했다.

panic ⓥ to feel sudden fear which makes you do things quickly without thinking

풀지 못한 수학 문제가 열 개나 남았는데 시험 시간이 1분밖에 남지 않았다면, '패닉(panic)' 상태에 빠질 수밖에 없다. panic은 '두렵고 의식이 희미해진다'라는 의미이다. panic은 그리스 신화에서 들판 수풀에 숨어 있다가 소리를 지르며 갑자기 뛰어나와 사람들을 겁주는 '목신(牧神)'인 판(Pan)의 이름에서 온 것이다. panic을 동사형으로 쓰면 '겁에 질려 어쩔 줄 모르다, 공황 상태에 빠지다'이다.
The Athenians panicked. 아테네인들은 공황 상태에 빠졌다.

straggle ⓥ to go in a group slowly and untidily

전쟁 영화에서 전투에 지고 후퇴하는 패잔병들의 행렬을 보면 활기는커녕 군기도 없는 모습이다. 삐뚤빼뚤 줄도 안 맞고, 하나같이 고개는 푹 숙인 채 터벅터벅 느리게 걷는다. 이런 패잔병들의 모습을 가장 잘 표현하는 단어가 바로 straggle이다. '여럿이 무질서하게 힘없이 걷다'라는 뜻이다.

The survivors straggled back into Athens, angry and embarrassed. 살아남은 자들은 패잔병의 모습으로 터벅터벅 걸어서 아테네로 돌아왔다. 화가 치밀었고 수치스러웠다.

traitor ⓝ someone who is not loyal to their country, friends or beliefs

traitor는 trait 행위를 한 '사람(-or)'을 뜻한다. trait는 '넘겨주다(to hand over)'를 뜻하는 라틴어에서 온 것이다. 따라서 traitor는 '넘겨주는 사람'이라는 뜻인데, 적에게 우리의 비밀이나 중요한 정보를 넘겨주는 '배신자, 반역자'를 일컫는다. trait를 동사형으로 쓰지는 않고, '배신하다, 반역하다'는 betray로 쓴다.

So late one night, the traitor led the Spartans into his own city. 그래서 어느 늦은 밤, 그 배신자는 스파르타인들을 이끌고 자신의 도시로 들어갔다.

spend ⓥ to use something like money, time, or energy to do something

spend는 '지불하다(to pay out)'라는 뜻의 라틴어에서 유래해 쓰면 없어지는 것을 '사용하다, 쓰다'라는 뜻이다. 돈, 시간, 에너지는 쓰면 없어지므로 to spend money/time/energy라는 표현이 가능하다. 예를 들어 사용한 후에도 망치는 그대로 남아 있으므로 to spend a hammer와 같은 표현은 쓰지 않는다.

The Greeks had spent all their energy fighting each other; they had none left to defend themselves. 그리스인들은 서로 싸우느라 힘을 모두 써버려서 자신들을 방어할 힘이 전혀 남아 있지 않았다.

> **Q** 펠로폰네소스 전쟁을 기록한 역사가는 누구인가요?
>
> **A** 역사의 아버지로 불리는 헤로도토스가 그리스와 페르시아의 전쟁을 기록했다면 델로스 동맹과 펠로폰네소스 동맹 간의 싸움인 펠로폰네소스 전쟁을 기록한 역사가는 '투키디데스'야. 투키디데스는 사실에 입각하여 역사를 썼다는 점에서 '역사학의 아버지'라고 불려. 투키디데스 본인이 직접 펠로폰네소스 전쟁에 전사로 참여하여 전쟁 전반에 걸친 세세한 사실들을 기록한 덕분에 우리는 지금도 페르시아 전쟁에서 이긴 후 그리스 반도에서 무슨 일이 있었고, 그 결과 어떻게 그들은 전쟁에 끌려갔는지, 전쟁 중에 발생한 다양한 사건과 사람들의 동향에 대해 알 수 있게 되었지.

The Story of the World

Chapter 25
Alexander the Great

1 Philip and His Son

🌐 마케도니아 왕국은 도리아인들이 그리스의 북쪽에 세운 고대 왕국이다. 페르시아 전쟁 후에 그리스의 문화를 적극적으로 받아들이고, 군사력을 키워 강국으로 부상한다. 기원전 4세기에 필리포스 2세가 적극적인 정복 전쟁을 벌여 영토를 확장했고, 마침내 기원전 338년에 그리스의 도시 국가들을 정복하게 된다. 필리포스의 아들인 알렉산드로스는 왕위에 오르자마자 동쪽 페르시아 정벌에 나섰고, 기원전 330년에 페르시아, 이집트, 인도의 북서부를 정복해 광대한 제국을 건설했다. 그러나 알렉산드로스 대왕의 사후에 분열되어 기원전 2세기에 로마에 의해 멸망한다.

*If the Greek cities had stayed friends and allies, like they were when they fought against the Persians, Greece would have been a strong country. But instead, Sparta and Athens fought. *They were like brothers who were too busy arguing with each other to notice that a bully is coming.

In this case, the bully was a king named Philip, who ruled a country called Macedonia. Philip noticed that Athens and Sparta had become weaker and weaker after years of battle. And so he came down into Greece with his army and conquered the Greek cities. They barely had enough energy to resist.

Now Philip ruled Macedonia and Greece. But he wanted even more cities. He wanted to sail across the Aegean Sea to Asia Minor and take over the Persian Empire as well. But before he could attack Persia, Philip died. And his son Alexander took over his throne.

Do you know what the name *Alexander* means? It means "ruler of men." Alexander became the most famous "ruler of men" ever. He was known by the whole world as "Alexander the Great."

Alexander had always been an unusual boy. Even as a child, he was strong and brave. Nothing scared him. When he was still a small boy, he went with his father Philip to look at a warhorse that Philip wanted to buy. The horse, a huge black stallion named Bucephalus, bucked and kicked constantly. No one could ride him.

"He's too wild," King Philip said. "I don't want him. I would never be able to manage him."

"I can ride him!" Alexander said.

"Nonsense!" Philip said. "You're too little."

"But I can!" Alexander insisted.

"If you can ride him, I'll buy him for you," Philip promised.

Alexander had been watching Bucephalus carefully. He noticed the horse kicked and reared whenever the sun threw his shadow on the ground in front of him. Alexander thought that the huge stallion was frightened of his shadow. So he walked, fearlessly up to the horse, took his bridle, and turned him so that he couldn't see his shadow. Instantly, Bucephalus stood still. He allowed Alexander to mount him and ride him around.

Philip bought the horse for Alexander. And when Alexander became king after his father's death, the great black stallion Bucephalus always carried him into battle. He even named a city after his horse. He called it Bucephela!

Alexander had many opportunities to ride his warhorse into battle. His father Philip had conquered Greece, but Alexander had even larger goals in mind. He wanted to rule Persia. The Persians had given up trying to conquer Greece, but their empire was still the largest in the world. It stretched all the way from Asia Minor to India. And Alexander wanted it.

When Alexander met the Persian army in Asia Minor, he used his cavalry—soldiers riding on horseback—to push the Persians back. Asia Minor was now his. But could he conquer the rest of the Persian Empire?

According to one story, Alexander stopped at a city in Asia Minor and saw there, in the city's center, a chariot tied to its axle with a huge, complicated knot of rope, larger than a man's head. "What is that?" he asked.

"That is the Gordian Knot," the people told him. "We have a legend about it. The man who loosens that knot will rule all the rest of Asia. But it is impossible to untie the knot. Hundreds of men have tried, and no one has ever succeeded!"

Alexander studied the knot carefully. Then he took out his sword and sliced the knot in half.

"There," he said. "I have loosened the knot."

No one had ever thought of doing that before. But the

Alexander and Bucephalus

prophecy of the knot came true. Alexander conquered all the rest of Asia. He went south into Egypt and was crowned the pharaoh of Egypt. And then he came back up into Mesopotamia and took over the rest of the Persian Empire.

Now Alexander was king of more land than anyone else had ever ruled. He was truly "Alexander the Great"—the ruler of the largest empire the world had ever seen.

2 Alexander's Invasions

영어로 '알렉산더(Alexander)'라고 불리는 알렉산드로스는 기원전 356년에 그리스 북쪽 마케도니아(Macedonia) 왕국의 왕자로 태어났다. 아버지인 필리포스 왕은 펠로폰네소스 전쟁으로 힘이 약해진 그리스 도시 국가들을 정복한 후 페르시아 정복의 꿈을 아들인 알렉산드로스에게 유산으로 물려주었다. 알렉산드로스는 왕위를 물려받은 후 페르시아 정복에 나선다. 기원전 334년, 20세의 나이에 소아시아 정복을 시작으로 10여 년 동안 끊임없이 정복 전쟁을 벌여, 페르시아를 포함해 인도의 펀자브 지역과 이집트까지 진출했다. 비록 30대 초반에 사망했지만, 대제국을 건설했기 때문에 그의 이름에 대왕(the Great)이라는 칭호가 붙게 되었다.

When Alexander the Great arrived at the edge of the Persian Empire, he wanted to keep going. He wanted to conquer all of India.

Alexander's army began to invade India. Alexander learned how to use elephants in combat. And his soldiers won most of their battles.

But the Indians who fought against Alexander were fierce warriors as well. Even though the soldiers from Macedonia won many battles, more and more of them died claiming these victories. Finally, Alexander's army mutinied. After a particularly difficult battle, in which over a thousand soldiers were killed or badly wounded, the army refused to go any further. "Be content with what you have!" they told Alexander. "We don't want to go on dying to make your empire bigger."

Alexander didn't want to stop. He stayed in his tent, sulking. He refused to see anyone, hoping that his army would change its mind. But the men were firm: They would not fight in India any longer.

Finally Alexander agreed. He gave up trying to take over the rest of India. Instead, he put his energy into running the huge kingdom he already had.

Alexander wanted the people of the future to remember what a great ruler he was. And he knew that cities last for years and years. So he built new cities all over his empire. He named many of these cities after himself: Alexandria. Some of these cities still stand today. Just as Alexander intended, they remind us that Alexander the Great was the greatest conqueror of ancient times—and ruled over the hugest empire that the world had ever seen.

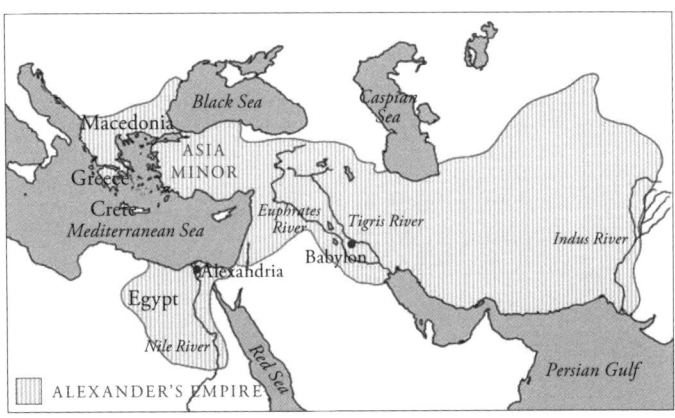

The Empire of Alexander the Great

The most famous city called Alexandria is in Egypt. Alexandria was built near the Nile River and the Mediterranean Sea, so that merchants could reach it easily by ship. Alexander himself marked out the city's walls, but he died before he could see any of the city's buildings. But after his death, Alexandria became the greatest city in the world. Many famous scholars and writers lived in Alexandria. It became a center for art, music, and learning. Today, Alexandria is still a big and important city.

Just outside Alexandria was the biggest lighthouse in the world. It was called the Pharos, and it was 330 feet tall. Ships could see it from miles away. They used its light to sail safely into the harbor of Alexandria.

Do you remember reading about the Seven Wonders of the Ancient World? These were seven amazing sights of ancient times. We learned that the Hanging Gardens of Babylon and the Great Pyramid are two of the Seven Wonders. The Pharos is the third. No one had ever seen a lighthouse as large as this one.

The Pharos was destroyed long, long ago. No pictures of the Pharos survive from ancient times. But only a few years ago, divers found huge chunks of stone at the bottom of Alexandria's harbor. This stone may be all that is left of the Pharos.

3 The Death of Alexander

알렉산드로스 대왕이 죽은 후 마케도니아 제국은 시리아, 이집트, 마케도니아, 세 왕국으로 분열된다. 이때부터 로마가 지중해를 제패한 기원전 31년까지 약 300년 동안 그리스의 문화가 유럽, 서아시아, 아프리카 북부까지 전파되어 많은 영향을 미쳤기 때문에 이 시기를 '헬레니즘 시대'라고 부른다. 천문학, 수학을 중심으로 과학이 크게 발달했으며 정신적 쾌락을 중시한 에피쿠로스 학파와 금욕을 통한 자연 순응적인 삶을 강조한 스토아 학파 등이 등장하며 철학이 발달했다. 헬레니즘의 영향은 미술에도 나타나 현실적인 아름다움이 표현된 조각상들이 많이 만들어졌는데, 불상을 비롯한 인도의 불교 미술에서도 헬레니즘의 특징을 엿볼 수 있다.

Alexander the Great became king when he was only twenty. Most people today haven't even finished college when they are twenty. But at this young age, Alexander inherited a throne and all the responsibilities of a ruler.

It only took Alexander eleven years to spread his empire all across the ancient world. One story tells us that when Alexander was still young, he burst into tears one day because there was no more of the world left to conquer. He had already conquered it all.

What would Alexander the Great have done next? We will never know, because Alexander died suddenly when he was only thirty-two. He was planning on taking an expedition with his army when he began to feel weak. He decided to wait a day or two until he felt better. "Go ahead and make all the preparations," he told his generals. "We will go as soon as I feel better."

But that day never came. Alexander got weaker and weaker. Finally, he was too weak to speak. His generals came to see him, but Alexander could only move his eyes. The next day he died.

No one knows exactly why he died. Some people think he might have been poisoned by one of his generals who wanted his power. Others say that he probably died of malaria—a fever caused by mosquitoes who carry certain kinds of germs. We will never know for sure. Alexander's body was put into a glass coffin and taken back to the city of Alexandria. The coffin was placed into a stone sarcophagus, there in Alexandria.

Alexander's generals knew that no one else could keep control of Alexander's large empire. Only Alexander could manage to rule such a huge kingdom. So they divided it up. One of the generals took Macedonia and the northern part of Alexander's kingdom in Asia Minor. Another general, named Ptolemy I, took over Egypt. His family would rule Egypt for three hundred years. Ptolemy was responsible for finishing the city of Alexandria; he built a huge library in Alexandria and filled it with books. A third general, named Seleucus, took over the southern part of Asia Minor and Alexander's lands in Asia, almost all the way over to India. The descendents of Seleucus were called the Seleucids, or the Syrians.

Now Alexander's great empire had become three separate kingdoms, with three kings fighting for power. Alexander had brought a very brief time of peace by uniting different cities and nations into one country. But that time of peace was over. Alexander's three generals and their descendents would spend the next hundred years fighting over control of different parts of Alexander's old kingdom.

Note to Parent: Philip conquered the Greek city states in 338 BC/BCE. Alexander the Great ruled from 336–323 BC/BCE.

The Story of the Words
Chapter 25 Alexander the Great

1 Philip and His Son

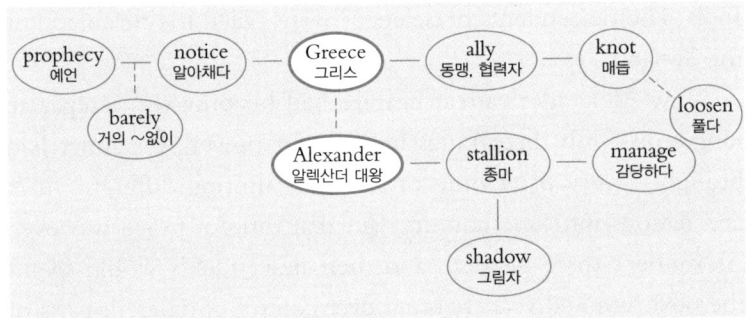

ally ⓝ someone who helps you or supports you in a fight, argument or war
　ally는 '함께 묶다(bind together)'를 뜻하는 라틴어에서 와서 약속과 맹세의 끈으로 함께 묶인 관계를 말한다. 즉 '동맹(同盟), 협력자'를 뜻한다. 특정한 목적을 위해 서로 연합해 돕는 조력자인데, 흔히 전쟁에서 공동의 적에 대항해 함께 싸우는 나라를 일컫는 말로 쓰인다. 그래서 제1차, 2차 세계대전에서 승리한 미국의 연합국을 the Allies라고 표현한다.
　If the Greek cities had stayed friends and allies, like they were when they fought against the Persians, Greece would have been a strong country. 만약 그리스 도시들이 페르시아에 대항해 싸웠을 때처럼 계속 친구와 동맹국으로 남았다면, 그리스는 힘이 센 나라였을 것이다.

notice ⓥ to see, hear or smell something
　notice는 '알려진(being known)'을 뜻하는 라틴어에서 온 것이다. 보고 듣고 냄새를 맡아서 안다는 의미이므로 notice는 '인식하다, 알고 있다'라는 뜻이다. I didn't notice him leaving은 '그가 떠나는 것을 (보지 못해서) 알지 못했다'이다. notice는 '사람들이 꼭 알아야 하는' 내용을 담은 '공고문, 안내문'의 명사형으로도 쓰인다.
They were like brothers who were too busy arguing with each other to notice that a bully is coming. 그들은 서로 다투느라 바쁜 나머지 불량배가 다가오고 있는 것을 알아채지 못한 형제들과 같았다.

barely ⓐ almost not

barely는 bare의 부사형이다. bare는 '덮여 있지 않은(uncovered)'을 뜻하므로, '맨발'은 bare feet, '잎이 다 떨어진 나무'는 a bare tree, '식물이 자라지 않은 맨땅'은 bare ground로 표현할 수 있다. 부사형 barely는 '거의 ~없이, 아닌'의 부정적인 의미를 표현할 때 쓴다. hardly, scarcely와 동의어이다.
They barely had enough energy to resist. 그들에겐 저항할 수 있을 만큼의 힘이 거의 남아 있지 않았다.

> **Q** 마케도니아 사람들이 '바르바로이'라고 불렸다면서요?
> **A** 마케도니아는 발칸 반도에 위치한 나라로, 그리스의 북쪽에 있었어. 그들도 역시 그리스어의 한 갈래를 썼고, 그리스 신들을 섬겼지. 그러나 그리스 도시 국가 사람들은 그들을 같은 민족이라고 생각하지 않았단다. 처음에는 단순히 다른 민족이라는 의미로 '바르바로이'라고 불렀는데, 자신들보다 문화 수준이 떨어지는 민족을 일컫는 의미로 변했어. 그렇게 무시당하던 마케도니아에도 변화가 시작되었는데, 강한 나라를 만들기 위해 군대를 키우면서 왕이 등장한거야. 그가 바로 알렉산드로스의 아버지인 필리포스 왕이야.

stallion ⓝ a fully grown male horse that is kept for breeding

stallion은 '종마(種馬)'이다. 말 중에서 가장 몸집이 크고 잘 달리는 수컷의 번식을 목적으로 키우는데, 이 수컷 말을 stallion이라고 한다. 앞에서 statue를 공부하며 배웠듯이, 어근 sta는 '서다(stand)'를 의미한다. stallion은 늠름하게 서 있어야 한다. 자꾸 주저앉으면 '종마'가 아니다. 그리고 '마구간'을 뜻하는 stall과 어원이 같다.
The horse, a huge black stallion named Bucephalus, bucked and kicked constantly. 털이 검은 커다란 '부세팔라스'라는 이름의 종마가 계속 껑충껑충 뛰면서 발길질을 하고 있었다.

manage ⓥ to control or direct something or someone

manage는 원래 '손(hand)'을 뜻하는 라틴어 manus에서 유래하여 '손으로 다루다'라는 의미가 있다. 손으로 다룰 수 있으므로 manage는 '통제하다, 처리하다, 관리하다, 감당하다'라는 뜻이다.

I would never be able to manage him. 난 저 말을 감당할 수 없을 것이다.

shadow ⓝ a dark shape made when something is between a surface and the light

shadow와 shade는 같은 고대 영어에서 유래한 친척이다. 둘 다 '그늘'의 뜻을 갖고 있는데, 개념은 좀 다르다. shade는 뜨거운 햇볕을 피할 수 있는 '그늘진 곳'을 의미하며 긍정적 느낌을 담고 있다. 반면 shadow는 햇빛이 비추는 사물의 반대쪽에 생기는 '그림자'를 뜻한다. 누군가의 그림자 뒤에 계속 있으면 빛을 보지 못하므로 부정적인 '영향'의 뜻으로도 쓰인다.

Alexander thought that the huge stallion was frightened of his shadow. 알렉산더는 몸집이 큰 종마가 자신의 그림자를 무서워한다고 생각했다.

knot ⓝ a place where two ends of string or rope are tied together

신발 끈의 양쪽 끝을 잡고 묶으면 가운데에 매듭이 생긴다. 이런 '매듭'이 knot이다. to tie a knot는 '매듭을 묶다'인데, 남녀가 결혼하는 것은 둘이 하나의 매듭처럼 묶이는 것이므로 We decided to tie the knot(우리 결혼하기로 결정했다)의 문장에서처럼 '결혼하다'라는 의미로 쓰인다. 알렉산더의 전설에 등장하는 '고르디우스의 매듭(Gordian Knot)'은 '아주 해결하기 힘든 문제'라는 의미로 종종 쓰이는 관용어이다.

"That is the Gordian Knot," the people told him. 그 사람들이 알렉산더에게 말했다. "저것은 고르디우스의 매듭입니다."

loosen ⓥ to make something become less tight; untie

loosen은 '묶여 있지 않은, 풀린, 느슨한'을 뜻하는 형용사 loose와 동사형 어미 -en이 합쳐진 형태이다. 뭔가 묶여 있는 것을 '풀다, 느슨하게 하다'라는 뜻의 동사형이다. to loosen the bolt는 '볼트를 풀다'이고, He loosened his tie라고 하면 '그는 넥타이를 풀었다'이다.

The man who loosens that knot will rule all the rest of Asia. 저 매듭을 푸는 사람이 아시아의 나머지 전부를 통치하게 될 것이다.

prophecy ⓝ a statement that tells what will happen in the future

prophecy는 prophet의 파생어이다. prophet에서 pro-는 '~을 위해(for)'이고, phet는 '말하다(speak)'라는 의미이다. 원래 그리스의 신들을 '대변하는(speak for)' 제사장을 부르는 희랍어에서 유래했다. 신을 대변하는 '예언자'가 prophet 이므로 파생된 명사형 prophecy는 '예언'이고, prophesy는 '예언하다'이다.
But the prophecy of the knot came true. 그러나 그 매듭의 예언은 현실이 되었다.

2 Alexander's Invasions

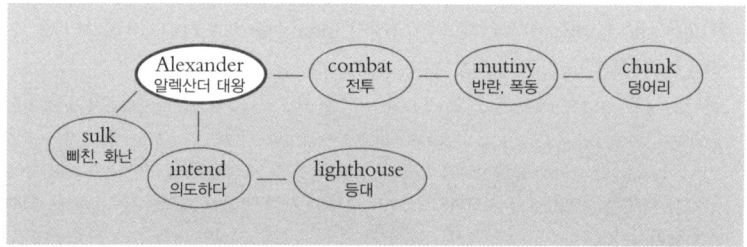

combat ⓝ fighting during a war

combat에서 com-은 '~와 함께(together with)'이고, bat는 '싸우다(to fight)'라는 뜻이다. bat는 원래 '치다, 때리다'라는 의미이므로, 서로 치고받고 싸우는 '전투'가 combat이다. 파생어인 combatant는 '전투병, 전투부대'이고, 형용사 combative는 '전투적인, 투지 넘치는'의 뜻이다.
Alexander learned how to use elephants in combat. 알렉산더는 전투에서 코끼리를 활용하는 법을 배웠다.

mutiny ⓥ to refuse to obey the person in charge

mutiny는 '이동하다(to move)'를 뜻하는 라틴어에서 온 것이다. '힘과 권력의 이동'을 의미하는 말로 발전해 '반란을 일으키다'가 되었다. 군대에서 졸병들이 상관의 명령을 거역하거나 항해 중인 배 위에서 선원들이 선장을 몰아내고 배를 장악하는 행위 등이 mutiny이다. 명사형으로는 '반란, 폭동'을 뜻한다.
Finally, Alexander's army mutinied. 결국 알렉산더의 군대가 반란을 일으켰다.

sulk ⓥ to show that you are angry by looking unhappy and not talking to anyone

한동안 인상을 구긴 채 아무 말도 하지 않고 삐쳐 있는 친구의 모습을 떠올려보자. 이런 모습을 표현한 동사가 sulk로, '화가 나서 부루퉁해 있다'라는 뜻이다. 그렇게 삐쳐 있는 상태를 나타내는 형용사형은 sulky이다.
He stayed in his tent, sulking. 알렉산더는 삐쳐서 말도 안 하면서 천막 속에 있었다.

intend ⓥ to plan to do something

intend는 '~쪽으로(toward)'를 뜻하는 접두사 in-과 '뻗다(stretch)'를 뜻하는 tend가 합쳐진 것이다. 어떤 일을 해야겠다고 계획을 세우면 마음이 '그쪽으로 쏠리기(stretch toward)' 마련이다. 그래서 intend는 '의도하다, 작정하다'를 뜻한다. 명사형은 intention(의도, 작정, 목적)이다.
Just as Alexander intended, they remind us that Alexander the Great was the greatest conqueror of ancient times—and ruled over the hugest empire that the world had ever seen. 알렉산더가 의도했던 것처럼, 그 도시들은 알렉산더 대왕이 고대의 가장 위대한 정복자로서 그때까지 세계가 목격한 가장 광대한 제국을 통치했음을 우리에게 상기시킨다.

> **Q** 이집트 사람들은 왜 알렉산더를 환영했을까요?
>
> **A** 이집트는 당시 페르시아 제국의 지배하에 있었단다. 키루스 사후에 아들 캄비세스가 이집트를 수중에 넣었고, 그 이후 페르시아의 통치를 받던 중이었어. 알렉산더의 군대가 이집트에 들어왔을 때 이집트 사람들은 페르시아의 통치에 불만을 잔뜩 품고 있던 중이었지. 덕분에 알렉산더는 정복자인데도 환영을 받을 수 있었던 거야. 심지어 그는 기원전 332년 이집트의 파라오 자리까지 올랐어. 이집트 사제들은 그를 '아몬의 아들'이라 불렀고, 이 말에 깊은 인상을 받은 알렉산더는 자신을 더욱더 특별한 인간으로 생각하게 되었지.

lighthouse ⓝ a tall building near the ocean with a powerful light at the top that warns ships of danger

lighthouse는 말 그대로 '빛나는 집, 빛이 머무는 집'을 뜻한다. 바다를 항해하는 배들에게 길잡이 역할을 하는 '등대(燈臺)'이다. 등대의 불빛을 보고 해안의 암초를 피할 수 있고, 부두를 찾아올 수 있다. 등대의 불이 꺼지지 않도록 관리하는 '등대지기'를 lighthouse keeper라고 한다. 형태는 등대와 비슷하지만,

light tower는 '조명탑'이다.
Just outside Alexandria was the biggest lighthouse in the world. 알렉산드리아의 바로 외곽에 세계에서 가장 큰 등대가 있었다.

chunk ⓝ a large piece of something
chunk는 '소의 어깨뼈'를 뜻하는 chuck의 형태가 변해 생성된 것이다. 소의 어깨뼈는 크고 살점이 많이 붙어 있으므로 chunk는 '큰 덩어리'를 의미한다. huge chunks of stone은 '큰 돌덩어리'이고, a chunk of meat는 '큰 고깃 덩어리'이다.
But only a few years ago, divers found huge chunks of stone at the bottom of Alexandria's harbor. 그런데 바로 몇 해 전에 잠수부들이 알렉산드리아 항구의 해저에서 거대한 돌덩어리를 발견했다.

3 The Death of Alexander

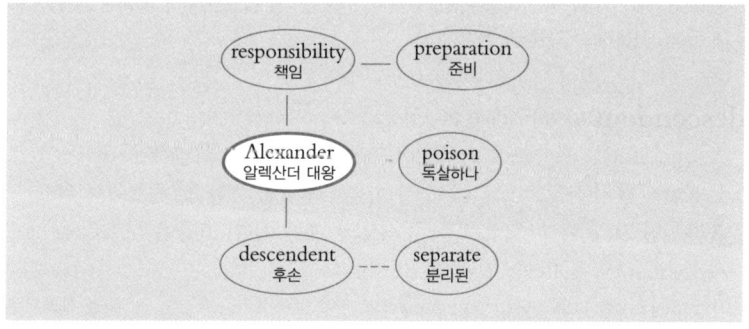

responsibility ⓝ a duty that you have to do or to take care of
responsibility에서 어근에 해당하는 spons는 '약속하다(promise), 맹세하다(pledge)'를 뜻한다. 물음과 다짐에 대해 '그렇게 하겠노라' 하고 응답하는 것이다. 그래서 respond가 '응답하다, 반응하다'라는 뜻이다. 자신이 한 말에 대해 책임을 져야 하기 때문에 responsible은 '책임이 있는, 책임을 져야 하는'이고, responsibility는 '책임'이다.
But at this young age, Alexander inherited a throne and all the responsibilities of a ruler. 그러나 이런 젊은 나이에 알렉산더는 왕위와 통치자로서의 모든 책임도 함께 물려받았다.

preparation ⓝ the act of getting something ready

preparation은 prepare의 명사형이다. prepare에서 접두사 pre-는 '미리(before)'를 뜻하고, pare는 '갖추다(make ready)'를 뜻한다. 즉 '미리 준비하다'이다. 예를 들어 해외 여행을 떠나기 전에 항공편도 예약하고 짐도 꾸리고 돈도 환전해야 하는데, 이런 모든 '준비'가 preparation이다.
"Go ahead and make all the preparations," he told his generals. 알렉산더가 장군들에게 말했다. "가서 만반의 준비를 하여라."

poison ⓥ to kill or harm someone or an animal using poison

poison은 '물약(potion)'을 뜻하는 라틴어에서 유래하여 '마법의 물약'을 뜻하는 말로 발전했고, 중세 시대부터 '독약'을 뜻하는 말로 쓰이게 되었다. poison은 '독살하다', '독을 넣다[바르다]'라는 뜻으로도 쓸 수 있다. 백설 공주가 먹은 '독이 든 사과'가 a poisoned apple이다. 형용사형 poisonous는 '독[독성]이 있는'을 뜻한다.
Some people think he might have been poisoned by one of his generals who wanted his power. 어떤 이들은 알렉산더가 그의 권력을 탐했던 부하 장수 중 한 명에 의해 독살되었을지도 모른다고 생각한다.

descendent ⓝ a relative of a person who lived in the past

descendent는 '후손'으로 ancestor(조상)와 반대되는 개념이다. de-는 '밑으로(down)'를 뜻하고, scend는 '수직 이동(climb)'을 뜻한다. 족보에서 위로 쭉 올라가면 '조상'이고, 밑으로 쭉 내려오면 '후손'이다. 요즘은 descendent를 descendant로 표기하는 것이 더 일반적이다.
The descendents of Seleucus were called the Seleucids, or the Syrians. 셀레우쿠스의 후손들은 셀레우시드 또는 시리아인들로 불린다.

separate ⓐ different; apart

separate에서 se-는 apart(따로, 분리해)를 뜻하는 접두사이고, parate는 prepare(준비하다)를 뜻한다. 즉 따로 '분리해서 준비해야' 한다는 의미이다. We separated last year(우린 작년에 헤어졌다)의 문장 속에서 '분리하다, 가르다, 이별하다'라는 의미로 쓰였다. three separate kingdoms(세 개의 서로 다른[분리된 왕국)처럼 형용사형은 '분리된, 서로 다른'을 뜻한다.
Now Alexander's great empire had become three separate kingdoms, with three kings fighting for power. 이제 알렉산더 대제국은 세 명의 왕들이 권력을 차지하기 위해 싸우는, 세 개의 다른[분리된] 왕국이 되었다.

Q 알렉산더 사후에 넓은 제국은 어떻게 되었나요?

A 알렉산더는 후계자가 누구라고 정확히 정하지 않고, '가장 힘센 자'에게 란 말만 남긴 채 너무 급작스럽게 죽었어. 당시의 장군들은 서로 힘이 세다고 주장했겠지? 결국 최후에는 영토가 셋으로 나뉘었어.

마케도니아와 그리스 지역은 알렉산더의 이복형제인 아리다이오스와 알렉산더의 아들이 공동 통치하는 것으로 결정되었지만 결국 나중에는 살해되고 말았어. 정복자라는 별명을 지닌 셀레우코스에게 돌아간 영토는 페르시아와 시리아였고 셀레우코스 왕조는 240여 년 동안 이어졌단다. 다른 하나가 바로 알렉산드리아를 수도로 하는 프톨레마이오스 왕조인데, 장군 프톨레마이오스가 세운 왕조라서 이런 이름이 붙었지. 이 왕조의 마지막 여왕이 바로 클레오파트라야. 이들 세 지역에서 꽃핀 문화를 헬레니즘 문화라고 부른단다. 알렉산더 사후 300여 년간 헬레니즘 문화의 중심이 된 도시가 바로 알렉산드리아야.

The Story of the World

Chapter 26
The People of the Americas

1 The Nazca Drawings

🌐 남아메리카 페루의 나스카 평원에는 거대한 그림들이 존재한다. 사막 기후의 메마른 땅 위에 누군가 돌과 흙을 이용해 길이 100~300미터 정도의 선으로 이루어진 그림들을 그렸는데, 이들은 기원전 2000년경 나스카 문명을 이룬 사람들일 것으로 추정한다. 벌새, 원숭이, 고래, 개, 거미 등 30여 개의 동물 그림과 소용돌이, 삼각형 등 기하학적 문양 약 200여 개가 그려져 있다. 왜 이 그림들을 그렸는지 이유는 알 수 없지만, 종교적인 이유나 천문학적 목적으로 그렸을 것으로 추정하고 있다.

We have been reading about the people who live in Europe, Africa, and Asia. But over on the other side of the world, other ancient civilizations lived. Like the people of ancient Africa, the people of the Americas didn't leave written records behind them. So we don't know as much about them as we know about the Egyptians, the Babylonians, the Assyrians, and the Greeks. ⸰But the people of the Americas did leave artifacts behind them— ancient buildings, ruined villages, and mysterious earth mounds.

If you put your finger on the Fertile Crescent again, and this time go *left*, you'll go across the Mediterranean Sea and out into the Atlantic Ocean. ⸰And if you keep going across the Atlantic Ocean, you'll come to two continents (big masses of land) linked together in the middle by a narrower strip. These are the Americas. The top continent is called North America, and the bottom continent is called South America. We call the strip in the middle *Central America*.

South America has mountains all along one edge and flat, fertile land in the middle. Tribes of ancient people lived both in the mountains and down in the jungles of the flat lands. Like the people of ancient Mesopotamia, the people of ancient South America grew crops, kept animals, hunted, and caught fish. ⸰They ate cassava, just like the people of ancient Africa. As a matter of fact, they learned how to dry cassava roots and grind them up into a powder. They used this powder to make a kind of pudding that you've probably eaten yourself—tapioca pudding.

One of these South American tribes was called the Nazca. They lived along the rivers of South America in a place that is now called Peru. The Nazca left behind them one of the strangest mysteries of ancient times.

More than two thousand years after the Nazca lived in South America, an airplane flew over Peru. The pilot looked down. He saw a drawing of a monkey—a drawing that covered hundreds of miles of ground. The lines of the drawing were scraped into the earth. From down on the ground, the drawings couldn't be seen. The lines just looked like old roads, or gashes in the ground. But from up in the air, those lines made pictures.

Soon, flyers discovered more enormous pictures: a spider, a pelican more than one thousand feet tall, a hummingbird, and flowers. They also found spirals, squares, and other patterns carved into the ground. There were over three hundred line drawings and patterns there on the earth.

Because there is very little rain in the area where the Nazca drawings were made, the lines have lasted for over a thousand years. A highway was built across some of the drawings, and others have been damaged by cars driving across them or by people scuffing at the lines with their feet. But many of the drawings are still intact. Look on the next page for a map of the drawings. Can you tell what they are?

So how did the Nazca people make these drawings? After all, they couldn't fly. They couldn't get up in the air to see what their finished drawings looked like. Making a line drawing on the ground must have been like drawing with your eyes closed. Do

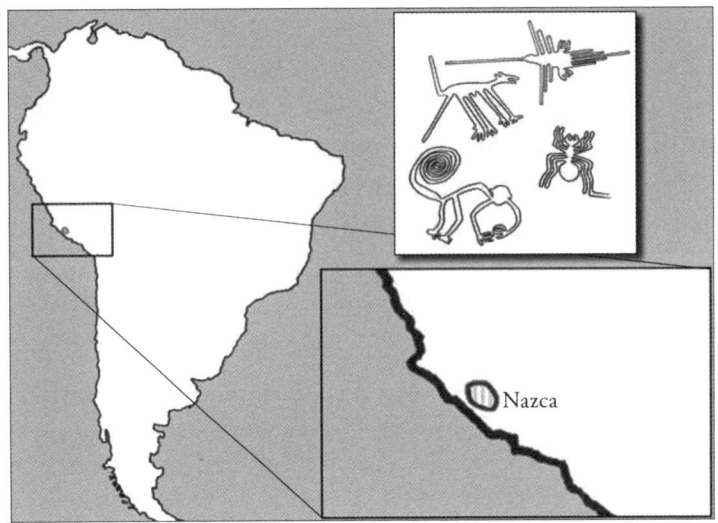

Nazca Line Drawings in South America

you think you could draw these pictures with your eyes closed? *It probably wouldn't look much like a bird when you were finished.

No one has been able to solve the mystery of the Nazca drawings. The best guess we can make is that the Nazca people were very good at mathematics. They could figure out how long each line should be, where it should turn, and where it should meet the next line through doing calculations. Another theory is that the Nazca artists used the position of the stars to help them with their drawings. But the Nazca civilization ended about 1500 years ago. So we will never know the answer to this question.

2 The Heads of the Olmecs

올메 문명은 기원전 1500년경부터 멕시코 동쪽의 멕시코만(灣) 유역에서 형성된 고대 문명으로, 중앙아메리카에서 가장 오래된 문명이다. 올메(Olmec)은 원주민 말로 '고무가 나는 곳에 사는 사람들'이라는 뜻이다. 거대한 피라미드와 거두상(巨頭像) 등의 유적이 발견되어 발달된 문화가 존재했음을 짐작케 한다. 올멕인들은 촌락을 이루고 농사를 지었으며 재규어를 비롯해 야생의 동물들을 믿는 토템 신앙을 가지고 있었다. 올멕 문명은 이후에 등장하는 마야 문명과 아즈텍 문명의 원류로 추정된다.

Just above South America is Central America, which is sometimes called *Mesoamerica*. Earlier, we read that *Mesopotamia* means "between the rivers" because *potamia* means "rivers" and *meso* means "between." (Remember the hippopotamus? *Hippo* means "horse" and *potamus* means "river," so a *hippopotamus* is a "river horse"!) Well, since *meso* means "between," *Mesoamerica* means "between the Americas." Central America is between North America and South America.

The Olmecs were the first civilization in Central America. They built a big city, now called San Lorenzo, in the country that we now call Mexico. The city stood up on top of a huge hill. The most important people—leaders, priests, and rich men—lived up in the city. Poor people and farmers lived down at the foot of the hill, on the plain. They grew crops on the plain and sent them up for the important people to eat. If you were an Olmec, it was much more fun to be rich than to be poor.

At the center of the city, on top of the hill, the Olmecs built a huge pyramid of dirt and clay. The platform was so high that it could be seen by someone standing miles away. Every single bit of clay that was used to build the pyramid had to be hauled up the hill in baskets. The Olmecs built the dirt pyramid basketful by basketful, just like the Egyptians, who built their stone pyramids by hauling stone blocks one by one.

Up on top of this clay and dirt pyramid, the Olmecs built a

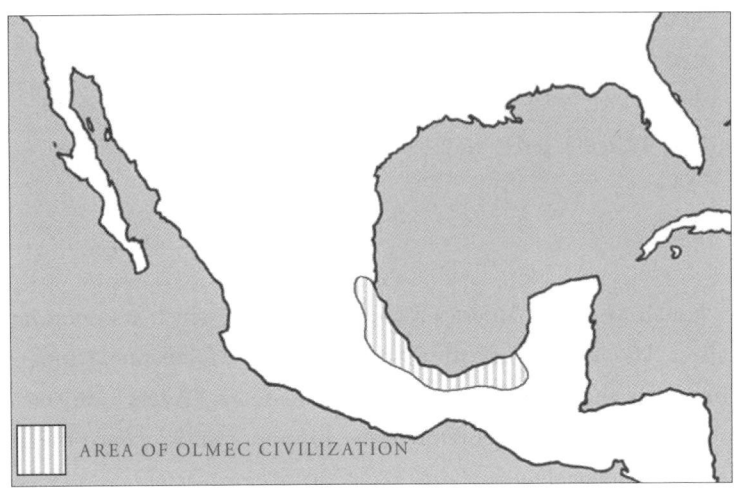

Mesoamerica

temple to their gods. That means that the temple was the highest place in the whole city. We don't know what the Olmec gods were called, but we know what they looked like. One was a snake with feathers. Another was half-human, half-jaguar. A third was a dwarf-like **creature** who lived in waterfalls.

The temple of the Olmecs disappeared long, long ago. But the statues that stood around the temple still exist. They aren't statues of people. They're just statues of heads.

The Olmec heads are probably **sculptures** of important rulers. But none of these stone rulers has a body. The heads sit directly on the ground, as though an enormous stone person had been buried in the dirt up to his neck. And the heads are enormous— as big as nine feet tall. That's taller than the biggest person you know, and probably higher than your ceiling. The eyes of the heads are bigger than your whole head. You could put your entire hand up their noses! If you were standing next to one, your head would only come up to its cheek.

What if these huge heads had bodies? They would be stone

giants, as tall as a four-story building. Their hands would be big enough for you to sit in. A grown-up's head wouldn't even reach to one of their knees.

The huge heads sat in a circle around the temple on top of the clay pyramid. What were they for? No one really knows. Perhaps the Olmecs, like the Egyptians, thought that their rulers were gods and wanted to honor them. Maybe they carved the giant heads to remember their rulers, the same way that we name airports and roads and buildings after our own leaders. Some archaeologists have suggested that the giant heads were used for altars, or for thrones. But we will never know the answer. The Olmec heads, like the Nazca drawings, will remain mysterious.

An Olmec Head

3 Rabbit Shoots the Sun

북아메리카의 원주민을 흔히 인디언(Indian)이라고 부르는데, 정확히 말하면 아메리칸 인디언(American Indian)이라고 해야 한다. 콜럼버스가 북아메리카를 인도(India)로 착각하면서 잘못 붙여진 명칭이다. 북아메리카의 원주민들은 빙하기에 얼어붙은 바다를 건너 시베리아에서 알래스카로 이동한 것으로 추정한다. 인종학적으로 보더라도, 아메리카 인디언들은 몽골 인종에 가깝다. 아메리카 인디언들은 유럽인들이 넘어와 정착할 때까지도 부족 단위로 각자의 영역 안에서 이동을 하며 살았다.

Now let's travel up from Central America into Northern America. Today, North America contains the countries of Canada and the United States. But back in ancient times, tribes of people roamed all through this big continent.

Way, way up north, where the weather is very cold, ancient North American people hunted and fished to survive. It was too cold to grow crops, so they lived by trapping the animals all around them—seals, polar bears, birds, and caribou. (Caribou are like elk or antelopes.) They gathered and ate the special kinds of mosses and lichens that grow in the cold north. Some of the bravest even went out onto the icy seas in boats that were made out of skins. They fished and chased whales. A whale could provide enough meat for an entire village. And its blubber, or fat, made good oil for oil lamps.

In the middle of North America, ancient tribes grew corn and wheat. They followed the huge herds of buffalo that roamed around from meadow to meadow. They ate buffalo meat (the tongue was one of their favorite parts!). They used buffalo skins for clothes and for blankets and tents, and sharpened the buffalo's horns into knives. Tribes who lived near the oceans and rivers also fished and trapped.

The ancient North Americans didn't settle down in one place and own houses. Instead, they lived like nomads. They moved from place to place, eating whatever the land could give them. They didn't make written records, or leave great stone buildings behind them. Instead, they left us stories that were passed down from fathers and mothers to children for hundreds and hundreds of years. Many of these stories try to explain something about nature. "Rabbit Shoots the Sun" tells us why rabbits are so timid:

> It was the hottest day of summer. The rays of the sun beat down on the ground and turned it brown and dry. The grass withered in the heat. The animals were too hot and weary to run, hunt, or play. They lay in the shade, gasping for breath and wishing that the sun would set.
>
> Rabbit had been trying to find water all day. Every puddle he came to was dried up into hard, black mud; even the stream had trickled away into dust. His throat was sore and dry. Even his eyes were dry! He sat down in the middle of the dry stream bed and yelled up at the sun, "Stop shining! Stop drying everything up! We need to cool off!"
>
> But Sun paid no attention to Rabbit. He went on shining. The ground kept right on drying up, and Rabbit got hotter and hotter and thirstier and thirstier.
>
> "Sun needs to learn a lesson," Rabbit grumbled. "I know what I'll do. I'll take my bow and arrows and go east, to the place where the Sun comes up every morning. And when Sun puts his head up tomorrow morning, I'll shoot him!"
>
> Now, in those days, the Sun did not rise slowly, coming up over the edge of the world a little at a time. Instead, he jumped up into the sky with a great bound. And Rabbit knew that he could shoot an arrow directly into the middle of the Sun. So he grabbed his bow and arrows and loped off towards the east. As he ran, he sang:
>
> *Rabbit, great Rabbit,*

Rabbit, enemy of the Sun.
The Sun will learn my strength.
Ho! Rabbit is coming!

When he reached the edge of the world, he sat down under a tree and waited. The sky grew dark. Rabbit waited all night long with his bow in his hands.

In the morning, Sun sprang up over the edge of the world. He laughed out loud and stood looking around him. At once, Rabbit jumped to his feet and shot an arrow straight into Sun's center.

•At once, the arrow ripped a great hole in the Sun. •Fire poured out all over the world. The tree above Rabbit's head began to smoke and crackle. •The grass at his feet went up into flames. Rabbit's fur began to scorch. •In a panic, he threw down his bow and arrow and ran away. As he ran, he called out,

Rabbit has shot the Sun!
Fire is over the world!
Watch out, watch out for the flames,
Ho! The fire is coming!

"Over here!" a little voice called. "Quick! Jump under me and you will be safe! I am so little that the fire will sweep right overtop of me!"

Rabbit looked and saw a tiny green bush. At once he jumped beneath it, buried his head beneath his paws and put his nose into the ground. The fire swept over him with a huge roar. When it had died away, Rabbit put his nose out from underneath the bush and looked around him. The fire was gone, but the world was brown and burnt. And the bush was no longer green. Now it was yellow, scorched by the fire. We still call it the yellow bush, because although it is green when it first grows, it turns yellow when the sun sweeps over it.

Rabbit crept quietly away. To this day, Rabbit runs and hides when the light of the sun falls over him. As for the Sun, he was never as bold as before. Instead of leaping up over the edge of the world, he creeps carefully up, little by little, looking all around him for Rabbit and his bow.

Note to Parent: Most of our detailed knowledge of South, Central, and North American native peoples dates from medieval times. The Mayans, the Aztecs, the Incas, the Native American tribes of North America, and the native peoples of South America will be covered in more detail in the second volume of The Story of the World, since in most cases their civilizations reached their highest points after AD/CE 400. This chapter is a first introduction to the Americas and highlights (slightly out of chronological order) the most memorable tribe of each of the Americas in order to lay a foundation for later learning.

The Nazca civilization flourished around 200 BC/BCE. The Olmec civilization flourished between 1200–900 BC/BCE (roughly corresponding to the Assyrian expansion, the Greek Dark Ages, and the New Kingdom of Egypt).

The Story of the Words

Chapter 26 The People of the Americas

1 The Nazca Drawings

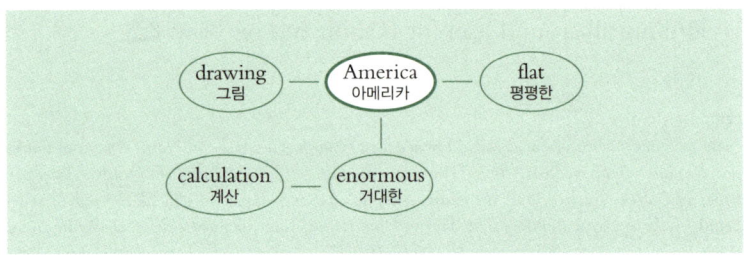

America ⓝ a land mass between the Pacific Ocean and the Atlantic Ocean

　America는 현재 '미국(the United States of America)'을 뜻하기도 하지만, 원래 의미는 '아메리카 대륙'이었다. '아메리카' 명칭은 16세기 초에 수차례 유럽에서 아메리카 대륙까지 항해했던 이탈리아의 탐험가 '아메리고 베스푸치(Amerigo Vespucci)'의 이름에서 온 것이다. 아메리카 대륙은 미국과 캐나다가 속한 북아메리카와 브라질과 아르헨티나 등이 속한 남아메리카, 그 사이의 좁은 땅과 섬들로 구성된 중앙아메리카로 나뉜다.

Like the people of ancient Africa, the people of the Americas didn't leave written records behind them. 고대 아프리카 사람들과 마찬가지로, 아메리카의 사람들도 글로 쓴 기록을 남기지 않았다.

flat ⓐ smooth and level

　flat은 면이 울퉁불퉁하지 않고 '매끄럽고 평평한' 모양을 나타낸다. 화면 가운데가 불룩 나와 있었던 브라운관 TV와는 달리, 디지털 텔레비전은 화면이 평평해서 a flat (screen) TV라고 한다. 먼 옛날 사람들은 The earth is flat(지구가 평평하다)이라고 생각했다. 본문에 나온 flat, fertile land는 농사짓기 좋은 '평평하고 비옥한 땅'이다.

South America has mountains all along one edge and flat, fertile land in the middle. 남아메리카에는 한쪽 끝을 따라 온통 산이 있으며 가운데에 평평하고 비옥한 땅이 있다.

drawing ⓝ a picture that you draw with a pencil, pen, etc.
drawing과 painting 모두 '그림(picture)'에 속하지만, 미술에서는 엄밀히 구분된다. drawing은 연필이나 펜을 이용해 단색으로 그린 그림이고, painting은 여러 색으로 그린 '채색화'를 말한다. 그래서 미술에서 drawing은 '소묘, 데생'이라고 한다. 나스카의 그림(The Nazca Drawings)은 땅을 파거나 돌과 흙을 쌓아 선을 이어 표현했기 때문에 공중에서 보면 단색의 drawing으로 보인다. 그래서 비행사가 본 것은 a painting of a monkey가 아니라 a drawing of a monkey이다.
He saw a drawing of a monkey—a drawing that covered hundreds of miles of ground. 그는 원숭이 그림을 보았는데, 땅 위로 수백 마일에 걸쳐 있는 그림이었다.

enormous ⓐ very large
enormous에서 e-는 '벗어난(out of)'을, 어근인 norm은 '척도(rule), 기준'을 뜻한다. 크기가 척도인 '자(rule)'의 범위를 벗어났으니 그만큼 크다는 의미이다. 즉 enormous는 크기나 양, 세기 등이 '막대한, 거대한'이라는 뜻이다.
Soon, flyers discovered more enormous pictures: a spider, a pelican more than one hundred feet tall, a hummingbird, and flowers. 곧이어 비행사들은 거대한 그림을 더 발견했는데, 거미와 100피트가 넘는 크기의 펠리컨, 벌새, 꽃 그림이었다.

calculation ⓝ using numbers to find an answer or to measure something
고대 로마의 상인들은 작은 돌을 지니고 있었는데, 그 돌로 더하고 빼면서 장사의 '셈'을 하기 위해서였다. '셈하다, 계산하다'라는 뜻의 calculate는 '조약돌, 자갈(pebble)'을 뜻하는 라틴어 calculus에서 온 것이다. calculus는 지금도 골치 아픈 수학의 '미적분학'을 뜻하는 용어로도 쓰인다. calculation은 calculate의 명사형으로 '계산, 셈'이다.
They could figure out how long each line should be, where it should turn, and where it should meet the next line through doing calculations. 그들은 각각의 선이 얼마나 길어야 하는지, 어디에서 꺾여야 하는지, 어디에서 다음 선과 이어져야 하는지 계산을 통해 파악할 수 있었다.

2 The Heads of the Olmecs

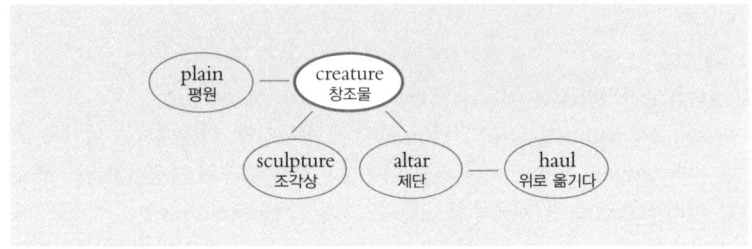

plain ⓝ a large area of flat land
　plain은 flat(평평한)을 뜻하는 라틴어에서 유래하여 명사형으로 쓰면 바닥이 평평한 땅, 즉 '평원, 평지, 평야'를 뜻한다. plain을 형용사로 쓰면 '있는 그대로'의 모습인 아무런 꾸밈도 없고, 평범하고, 굴곡 없는 모습을 표현한다. 그래서 과일이나 설탕을 첨가하지 않은 발효 요구르트가 플레인 요구르트(plain yogurt)이다.
　Poor people and farmers lived down at the foot of the hill, on the plain. 가난한 사람들과 농부들은 언덕 밑의 평원에 살았다.

haul ⓥ to carry or pull something heavy
　haul은 상당히 '무거운 것을 계속 잡아당기거나 옮기는' 행동을 표현한 동사이다. 가볍거나 힘이 들지 않을 때에는 haul을 쓸 수 없다. haul up은 '위로 끌어당기다, 옮기다'라는 뜻이다. 많은 양의 흙, 돌, 물, 나무 등을 옮기려면 힘이 들어서 haul을 쓴다.
　Every single bit of clay that was used to build the pyramid had to be hauled up the hill in baskets. 피라미드를 짓는 데 쓰인 찰흙은 전부 바구니에 담아 언덕 위로 옮겨야 했다.

creature ⓝ an imaginary animal or person that looks very strange
　creature는 동사형 create에서 파생된 명사형이다. create는 '만들다, 창조하다'이고, creature는 만들어진 결과물, 즉 '창조물'을 뜻한다. 영어권[기독교] 사회에서는 하느님이 인간을 비롯한 모든 생물을 창조했다고 믿었는데, 바로 creature가 '생물'을 뜻하기도 한다.
　A third was a dwarf-like creature who lived in waterfalls. 세 번째는 폭포에 살았던 난쟁이처럼 생긴 창조물이었다.

sculpture ⓝ an object made from wood, stone, or metal by an artist
sculpture는 sculpt의 명사형이다. sculpt는 carve(조각하다, 새기다)라는 뜻의 라틴어에서 유래하여 뭔가를 '깎고 새겨서 원하는 모양으로 만들다'라는 뜻이다. 그래서 sculpture는 '조각, 조각품[상]'을 뜻하고, '조각가'는 sculptor라고 한다. 올맥의 거두상(巨頭像)도 거대한 돌을 깎아서 만든 것이기 때문에 sculpture이다.
The Olmec heads are probably sculptures of important rulers. 올멕의 거두상들은 어쩌면 중요한 통치자들의 조각상일 수도 있다.

altar ⓝ a raised table used in a religious place
altar는 '높은(high)'을 뜻하는 라틴어에서 유래했다. 신은 대개 '높은' 곳에 존재한다고 믿어서 산꼭대기나 피라미드의 꼭대기처럼 높은 곳, 신과 가장 가까운 곳에서 제사를 지냈다. altar는 신에게 제사를 지내는 높은 곳의 평평한 땅[장소], 즉 '제단(祭壇)'이다.
Some archaeologists have suggested that the giant heads were used for altars, or for thrones. 일부 고고학자들은 그 거두상이 제단이나 왕좌로 사용되었다는 의견을 내놓았다.

> **Q** 올멕 거두상 외에도 발견된 조각상이 있나요?
> **A** 아메리카 내륙에서 가장 오래된 문명이 올멕 문명이야. 기원전 14세기에서 3세기까지 지속되었던 이 문명이 왜 갑자기 끝나게 되었는지 기록이 없으니 알 수 없단다.
> 올멕 문명의 대표적인 작품인 올멕 두상은 높이가 3미터에 달하는 현무암 조각인데, 채석장에서 돌을 나르는 것도 쉬운 일은 아니었겠지? 돌을 운반하고, 조각상을 만드는 일을 지휘하는 조직이 있었을 거야. 17개나 발견된 거대한 조각의 얼굴이 각각 다르게 조각된 것을 보면 능숙하게 훈련된 조각가들이었겠지. 신관으로 추측되는 조각상 외에도 표범과 사람의 특징을 동시에 보여주는 조각상, 어린아이의 모습을 한 조각상, 레슬링을 하는 남자 조각상도 발견되었지.

3 Rabbit Shoots the Sun

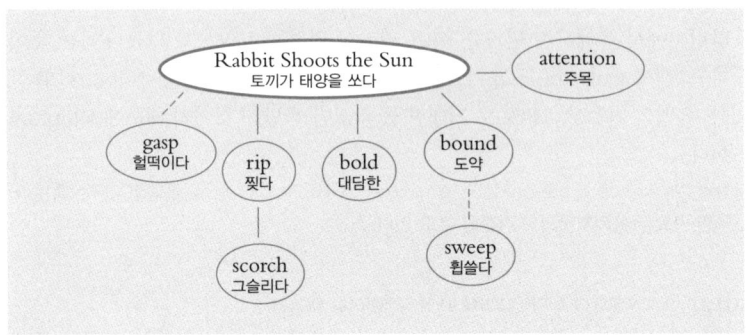

gasp ⓥ to take quick, short breaths
북유럽 언어에서 영어로 유입된 gasp는 원래 '하품하다(yawn)'라는 뜻이었다. 하품은 몸 안에 산소가 부족할 때 나타나는 생리적인 현상이다. 산소가 아주 많이 부족하여 숨이 차면, 헐떡이게 된다. 그래서 gasp는 '헐떡이다, 숨을 짧게 자주 쉬다'라는 뜻이다. 뭔가에 놀라거나 갑자기 통증을 느낄 때 '짧고 굵게' 숨을 들이마시는 것도 gasp라고 할 수 있다.
They lay in the shade, gasping for breath and wishing that the sun would set. 동물들은 그늘에 누워서 숨을 헐떡이며 해가 지기만을 바라고 있었다.

attention ⓝ special care or interest that you give to someone or something
attention은 동사 attend에서 파생된 명사형이다. attend는 '~쪽으로 (마음을) 뻗다'라는 라틴어에서 유래하여 마음이 쏠리면 그곳으로 가게 되니까, '참석하다, 수행하다'라는 뜻이다. 명사형 attention도 마음이 쏠리는 것, 즉 '주의, 주목, 관심'이다. to pay attention to A(A에게 주목하다, 관심을 집중하다)의 구문으로 자주 쓰인다.
But Sun paid no attention to Rabbit. 태양은 토끼에게 전혀 신경 쓰지 않았다.

> **Q** 나스카 유적 이전에도 문명이 있었나요?
> **A** 안데스 산맥을 중심으로 발생한 첫 문명을 '차빈 문명'이라고 부른단다. 이들은 유목 생활을 하다 기원전 3500년경부터 이 지역에서 옥수수를 재배하고 라마를 기르는 데 성공하면서 정착을 하게 되었어.
> 기원전 2000년경에는 지금의 리마 지역에서 토기를 만들었고, 기원전 800

> 넌경에는 아도베(햇볕에 말린 벽돌)로 피라미드를 만들었지. 기원전 500년
> 경에는 아도베가 아니라 돌로 종교적인 공간을 만들기도 했어.
> 농경 생활의 시작과 도시화에 대한 공식은 이곳에서도 마찬가지로 적용되
> 어 이루어졌어. 도시가 생기면 신관을 비롯한 행정 관료들이 그곳에 살게
> 되고, 이들을 먹여 살릴 필요 때문에 다양한 물품이 만들어진단다. 또한
> 농산물이 도시까지 운반되어야 했겠지? 도시가 형성된다는 것은 농촌과
> 의 연계가 더욱 필요해진다는 의미야.

bound ⓥ a big jump

bound는 원래 '메아리'를 뜻하는 단어에서 유래했다. 첩첩산중이나 동굴 안에서 소리를 지르면 '그 소리가 다시 울려서(resound) 들리는 현상을 나타낸다. 나중에 소리뿐만 아니라 반사되어 나오는 모든 것에 쓰이게 되었고, '땅을 박차고 뛰어오르는 동작' 즉 '도약'을 뜻하는 명사형으로도 발전했다.

Instead, he jumped up into the sky with a great bound. 그러지 않고, 태양은 힘차게 도약하며 하늘로 뛰어올랐다.

rip ⓥ to tear something quickly and violently

rip은 '당기다(pull)'를 뜻하는 네덜란드어에서 유래한 것으로 추정한다. 종이나 천을 세게 잡아당기면 찢어진다. 이렇게 뭔가를 '거칠게 찢는' 동작을 표현하는 동사가 바로 rip이다. rip-ripped-ripped

At once, the arrow ripped a great hole in the Sun. 순식간에 화살은 태양에 커다란 구멍을 냈다.

scorch ⓥ to burn something's surface and change its color

It's scorching today!라고 하면 어떤 날씨일까? scorch는 불이나 열 때문에 '쪼그라들다, 시들다'라는 뜻의 바이킹어에서 온 것이다. 동사형 scorch는 '열에 의해 그슬리다, 살짝 타다'라는 뜻으로, scorching한 날씨는 '타는 듯 햇볕이 따갑고 더운' 상태를 말한다.

Rabbit's fur began to scorch. 토끼의 털이 그슬리기 시작했다.

sweep ⓥ to move quickly

축구에서 '스위퍼(sweeper)'라고 부르는 포지션이 있다. 중앙에 위치한 최종수비수인데, 이 선수의 임무는 상대팀 공격수가 공을 몰고 오면 '청소부(sweeper)'

가 쓰레기를 치우듯 공을 다른 곳으로 차버리는 것이다. 이처럼 sweep의 기본적인 의미는 '빗자루로 쓸다, 청소하다'이다. 이 의미에서 확장되어 바람이나 파도, 불길 등이 마치 '비질하듯' 획획 쓸고 지나가는 것도 sweep이다. sweep-swept-swept

The fire swept over him with a huge roar. 불은 커다란 굉음을 내며 그의 위로 휙 지나갔다.

bold ⓐ not afraid to do dangerous things

bold는 '대담한, 용감한'을 뜻하는 형용사이다. 가끔 너무 대담하면 '건방지고 뻔뻔한' 사람으로 보일 수도 있으므로, bold는 부정적인 의미로도 쓰인다.

As for the Sun, he was never as bold as before. 태양에 관한 이야기를 하자면, 그는 예전만큼 결코 대담하지 못했다.

The Story of the World

Chapter 27
The Rise of Rome

1 Romulus and Remus

세계에서 가장 오래된 박물관인 이탈리아 로마의 카피톨리노 박물관에는 루파 카피톨리나(Lupa Capitolina)라는 청동상이 있다. '카피톨리나의 암늑대상'이라는 뜻의 이 동상은 쌍둥이 사내 아기들이 암늑대의 젖을 빠는 모습을 형상화한 것인데, 이 쌍둥이들이 로마의 건국 시조로 전해지는 로물루스(Romulus)와 레무스(Remus)이다. 버려진 아기들을 늑대가 거두어 길렀고, 이들이 성장해서 로마를 건설했다는 내용의 건국 신화를 상징적으로 그리고 있다.

Assyria was a great kingdom, but it was conquered by Babylon. Babylon was a great empire, but it was conquered by Persia. Persia and Greece were great empires, but they were conquered by Alexander the Great. Alexander the Great built his own huge kingdom, but then he died and his generals broke the kingdom up into pieces.

That is what the story of the ancient world is like. One king comes along, wins battles, and builds a big empire. His empire lasts for a little while, but the kings who come after him slowly lose control of it. Then another king from another country does the same thing and builds another empire. After a little while, that empire too falls apart. This happens over and over again.

So you won't be surprised to learn that we're going to learn now about *another* big empire. But this one was bigger and stronger than any empire we've read about before. It grew to be bigger than Alexander's empire, and it lasted much longer. As a matter of fact, it lasted for hundreds and hundreds of years. Over a thousand years after this empire fell, people were still learning its language, reading its books, and copying its government. This empire was called Rome.

At first, Rome was just a tiny village in the hills of Italy. Go

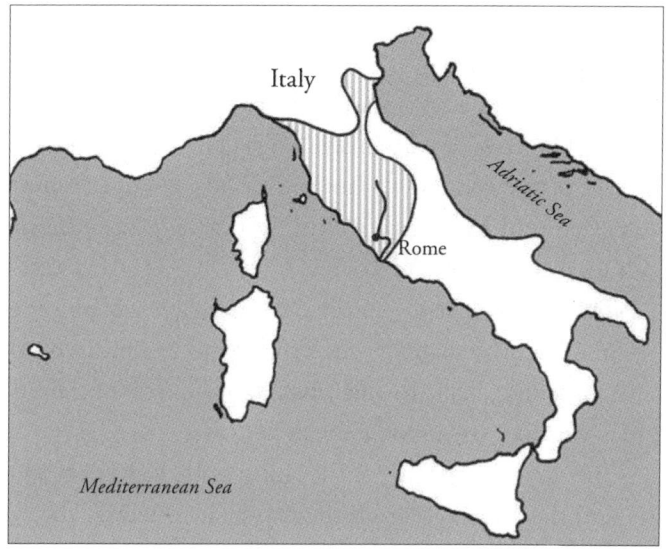

Rome and the Area Under Etruscan Rule

west from Greece and you'll see a piece of land that looks like a boot, jutting down into the Mediterranean Sea. This is called a *peninsula*, because it sticks out into the water. This peninsula is Italy.

The people who lived in Rome told this story about the village's beginning:

Once upon a time a great king named Numitor had twin grandsons—strong, healthy baby boys, named Romulus and Remus. But Numitor also had a wicked younger brother who plotted against him and stole his throne. The new, evil king wanted to get rid of anyone who might claim to be the rightful king.

"Those babies might grow up to take my crown!" he said. "Go put them in the Tiber River!"

So a servant took the boys down to the Tiber River. But

chapter 27 The Rise of Rome 93

she felt sorry for them, and put them into a basket and pushed it out into the current.

The basket floated along the river until it got stuck in the root of a fig tree at the river's edge. That might have been the end of the two boys—but a wolf heard them crying. She peered around the trunk of the fig tree, and saw the basket with the babies in it.

Now, this wolf had cubs of her own. She felt pity for the two hungry babies, and so she tugged the basket up onto the bank and then back to her own den. There, she raised the babies with her own wolf cubs, as her own.

One day a shepherd, out looking for a lost lamb, heard a coo and then a gurgle from the brush surrounding the wolf's den. He pushed some branches aside—and there saw two fat, happy baby boys, playing naked among the wolf cubs. The shepherd and his wife had no children of their own. So he took the boys home, and the two of them raised the babies to be tall, handsome young men.

When Romulus and Remus were grown, they went back to the fig tree where their basket had landed, so many years

Romulus and Remus

ago. They looked around and saw seven hills. "This is the perfect place to build a town," they said to each other. "A town on top of these seven hills would be strong and hard to attack!" So they began to build a town.

And Romulus declared himself the king of this new town. He put himself in charge of building a wall around it. "*This wall will keep us safe!" he declared. "Anyone who climbs over my wall will instantly be killed!"

But Remus was angry with his brother. He thought to himself: "We built this town together! Why should Romulus be the ruler of it? I want to be the leader." So he walked up to the wall and vaulted easily over it.

"What kind of a wall is that?" he sneered.

"Anyone can climb over it! How can *you* keep this town safe?"

Romulus was so angry that he drew his sword, charged at his brother, and killed him on the spot. Then he named the town Rome, after himself. He was Rome's first king.

*What does this story remind you of? Do you remember the story of Sargon, the ruler of one of the very first kingdoms we studied? He floated down the river in a basket until someone rescued him. And do you remember Cyrus? He was also raised by shepherds in the woods. Ancient people liked these stories about their kings. The stories made the kings seem even more legendary—like great fairy-tale heroes who could do anything!

2 The Power of Rome

로마는 건국 이래 약 200년 동안 왕정(王政)을 이어가다가 기원전 509년에 귀족들이 왕정을 무너뜨리고 새로운 정치 체계인 공화정을 세운다. 귀족들은 입법을 담당하는 원로원(senatus) 의원 300명과 행정부의 대표 격인 집정관(consul) 2명을 뽑았다. 집정관들은 임기 1년 동안 서로 견제하며 독재를 막았다. 끊임없는 전쟁으로 전투를 담당하는 평민들의 역할이 중요해지자 기원전 494년에 평민들은 평민회를 조직하고 호민관(tribune) 10명을 뽑아 정치에 참여하게 된다. 이후 약 200년 동안 로마는 집정관, 원로원, 호민관과 평민회가 서로 권력을 견제하면서 공화정(res publica)을 기반으로 삼아 제국으로 발돋움하게 된다.

The legend of Romulus and Remus tells us that Romulus was the first king of Rome. Other stories about ancient Rome say that he was the first of seven kings of Rome. These kings fought with other tribes of people who lived in Italy. The kings wanted to take over more and more land, so that Rome would get larger and stronger.

The most important Italian tribe was called the Etruscans. *The Etruscans lived north of Rome, in the hills and mountains of Italy. They liked music and art, and painted pictures that we can still see today. The Etruscans also grew crops, made weapons and jewelry out of metal, and sailed back and forth between Greece and Italy, trading with the Greeks. On these trips, the Etruscans learned how to use the Greek alphabet and worship the Greek gods.

The Roman kings fought with the Etruscans. But they also traded with them, and learned from them. The Etruscans taught the Romans how to dress like Greeks. They told the Romans about the Greek gods. The Romans learned about painting and music from the Etruscans as well. And they borrowed the customs of the Etruscan kings, who wore special robes called *togas*, with purple borders. *The purple showed everyone how important the king was.

The Etruscan kings also carried a bundle of rods with an axe blade in it, as a symbol of royal power. The rods showed that the king had the power to punish anyone who did wrong. The axe blade showed that he could execute people who did very evil things. The Romans liked this symbol of power, which was called the *fasces*. Soon Roman kings, like Etruscan kings, wore special purple-bordered togas and carried fasces. Do you have an old dime? Look on the back of it and you will see a picture of the fasces.

American courtrooms and government offices sometimes copy this Roman symbol, even today. They have a fasces in them to show that the judges have the power to punish criminals. The courtroom in the United States Capitol building has two fasces on the wall, one on each side of the American flag.

The fasces showed how powerful the king was. But after seven kings, the people of Rome decided that the king had too much power. They didn't like living in a monarchy—a country where the king was in charge. Instead, they wanted Rome to be a place where the people could help make the laws and choose the leaders.

Do you remember the Greek city that wanted the people to help make laws and choose leaders? The city of Athens was a democracy, where the people voted on their laws and leaders. But Rome didn't become a democracy like Athens, though. In Athens, all the men who weren't slaves could vote about laws and leaders. But in Rome, only rich and powerful men called *patricians* were allowed to have a say in the government. Two of these patricians were appointed by the other patricians to be the leaders of the city. They were called *consuls*. The Romans thought that having two leaders, instead of one king, would keep any one man from getting too much power. The two consuls were supposed to keep an eye on each other! Neither one could do exactly what he pleased.

The Story of the Words

Chapter 27 The Rise of Rome

1 Romulus and Remus

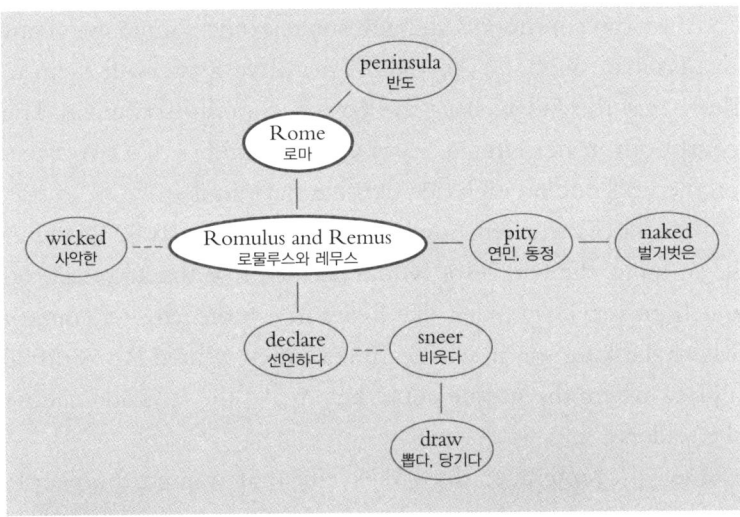

peninsula ⓝ a piece of land mostly surrounded by water but joined to a larger area of land

대한민국 지도를 보면 동아시아 대륙에서 남쪽으로 길게 바다를 향해 나와 있고, 삼면이 바다로 둘러싸여 있다. 남북한이 위치한 지형을 한반도(the Korean Peninsula)라고 부른다. peninsula는 '거의(almost)'를 뜻하는 pen-과 '섬(island)'을 뜻하는 insula가 합쳐진 것이다. 영어나 한자나 모두 '반도(半島)'를 '섬이나 다름없는 곳'으로 표현하고 있다. 로마 제국의 본거지였던 장화(a boot) 모양의 반도는 이탈리아 반도(the Italian Peninsula)이다.

This is called a *peninsula*, because it sticks out into the water. 이런 곳을 '반도'라고 부르는데, 바다 쪽으로 돌출되어 있기 때문이다.

wicked ⓐ very bad; evil

wicked는 witch(마녀)에 형용사형 어미 -ed가 붙어 변형되었다. 동화 속에 자주 등장해 친숙해진 단어로, 심술궂고 멍청한 캐릭터로 등장하기도 하지만, witch의 본모습은 사람의 영혼을 지배하고 조종하는 악한 존재였다. 형용사형 wicked는 그런 마녀의 성격을 담고 있기 때문에 '사악한, 못된'을 의미한다. 《신데렐라》와 《헨젤과 그레텔》에 나오는 계모도 wicked stepmother이다.

But Numitor also had a wicked younger brother who plotted against him and stole his throne. 그러나 누미토르에게는 사악한 남동생도 있었는데, 그 남동생은 음모를 꾸며서 형의 왕좌를 빼앗았다.

pity ⓝ the sadness that you feel when someone else is hurt or unhappy

르네상스 시대의 이탈리아 예술가 미켈란젤로의 작품 중에 피에타(Pieta)라는 대리석 조각상이 있다. 성모 마리아가 죽은 예수를 안고 있는 모습을 표현한 것인데, 이 작품명인 라틴어 pieta가 바로 pity의 어원이다. 우리를 불쌍히 여겨달라고 하느님께 빈다는 의미이다. 그래서 pity는 '연민, 동정, 측은지심'을 뜻하고 What a pity!는 '참 불쌍하구나!'라는 표현이며 Poor thing!과 같은 의미로 쓰인다.

She felt pity for the two hungry babies, and so she tugged the basket up onto the bank and then back to her own den. 암컷 늑대는 굶주린 두 아기들에게 동정을 느꼈고, 그래서 바구니를 강둑으로 끌어올린 다음 자신이 사는 굴로 끌고 갔다.

naked ⓐ not wearing any clothes

Adam and Eve were naked at first처럼 태초의 인간 아담과 이브에게는 '수치'의 개념이 없었기 때문에 옷을 입지 않았다. 모든 인간은 평등하게 naked한 모습으로 태어난다. 이렇게 몸에 실오라기 하나 걸치지 않은 상태가 naked이다. '벌거벗은, 나체의'를 뜻한다.

He pushed some branches aside—and there saw two fat, happy baby boys, playing naked among the wolf cubs. 양치기가 나뭇가지를 옆으로 밀자 알몸으로 새끼 늑대들과 어울려 놀고 있는 통통하고 해맑은 사내 아기들이 눈에 들어왔다.

declare ⓥ to say in public what you think or decide

declare는 '완전히(thoroughly, fully)'를 뜻하는 접두사 de-와 '분명한, 확실한 (clear)'을 뜻하는 clare가 합쳐진 말이다. 누구나 알 수 있게 확실하게 한다는 의미로, 자신의 주장을 공개적으로 밝힐 때 쓴다. 즉 '분명하게 말하다, 선언하다,

chapter 27 The Rise of Rome 99

공표하다'라는 뜻이다. 명사형은 declaration이다. 독립을 대외적으로 공표하는 '독립 선언'을 the Declaration of Independence라고 한다.
And Romulus declared himself the king of this new town. 그리고 로물루스는 자신이 새로운 도시의 왕이라고 선언했다.

sneer ⓥ to smile or talk about someone in a way that shows you have no respect for them

기분 나쁘게 피식 웃거나, 다른 사람을 노골적으로 놀리면서 '참 잘나셨어!' 하고 반어법을 써서 대꾸하는 행동과 태도를 sneer라고 할 수 있다. 한마디로 '비웃다, 조롱하다'라는 뜻이다.
"What kind of a wall is that?" he sneered. 그는 조롱하듯 말했다. "저게 무슨 성벽이람?"

draw ⓥ to take something from its place

동사 draw의 기본적인 의미는 '당기다(pull)'이다. 펜을 원하는 방향으로 '당겨야' drawing(그림)이 그려진다. '서랍'도 '당겨야' 열 수 있기 때문에 drawer이다. 즉 draw는 '그림을 그리다'라는 의미도 있고 '당겨서 빼다, 뽑다'라는 뜻도 지닌다. draw-drew-drawn
Romulus was so angry that he drew his sword, charged at his brother, and killed him on the spot. 로물루스는 너무 화가 난 나머지, 검을 뽑아들고서 동생에게 달려들어 그 자리에서 죽여버렸다.

2 The Power of Rome

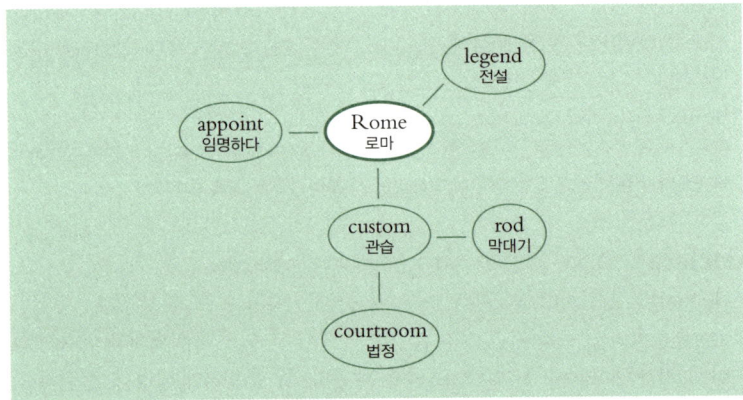

legend ⓝ an old story about people and the things they did in the past, which may not be true

legend의 어원은 '읽을거리(things to be read)'를 뜻하는 라틴어 legenda이다. 문자가 발전하면서 사람들은 '전해져 내려오는 이야기'를 기록해 책에 담았다. 어떤 이야기가 사라지지 않고 전해 내려온다는 것은 그만큼 가치가 있고, 꼭 읽어야 한다는 의미이다. legend는 전해져 내려온 이야기, 즉 '전설(傳說)'을 뜻한다. Pele is a soccer legend(펠레는 축구의 전설이다)처럼 앞으로 기억될 '전설적인 인물'을 뜻하기도 한다. legend의 형용사형은 legendary(전설적인)이다.

The legend of Romulus and Remus tells us that Romulus was the first king of Rome. 로물루스와 레무스의 전설은 로물루스가 로마의 첫 번째 왕이었음을 우리에게 말해준다.

> **Q** 로마의 왕 중에 에트루리아인도 있었다면서요?
> **A** 로물루스가 로마를 세웠을 때 이탈리아 반도에는 여러 나라가 있었단다. 특히 기억해야 할 나라가 이탈리아 북쪽의 에트루리아와 남쪽의 그리스 식민시(대 그리스)야. 로마의 왕 중에서 마지막 3명의 왕이 에트루리아인이었고, 그들이 로마에 끼친 영향이 아주 컸어. 그들은 로마를 지배하면서 도시를 확장하고, 기반 시설을 만들었단다. 그러니 로마의 초기 역사에서 에트루리아인의 역할을 제대로 평가해야겠지? 에트루리아인은 그리스 식민시들과 무역을 통해 만나면서 자연스럽게 상대방 문화도 흡수하게 되었어.

custom ⓝ a special way of doing something by a person or group

라틴어에서 유래한 custom은 '매우 익숙해지다'라는 뜻을 담고 있다. 어떤 일을 반복적으로 하거나 자주 접해서 익숙해지면 하나의 습관이 된다. 그래서 custom은 개인이나 조직, 사회가 갖고 있는 '관습, 풍습, 습관'을 뜻하며 the customs of the Etruscan kings는 '에트루리아 왕들의 관습'이다.

And they borrowed the customs of the Etruscan kings, who wore special robes called *togas*, with purple borders. 또한 그들은 가장자리가 자주색으로 장식된 특별한 가운인 '토가'를 입는 에트루리아 왕들의 관습을 차용했다.

rod ⓝ a long thin pole or stick

지금은 많이 사라졌지만, 여전히 학교에서 체벌이 행해지고 있다. 옛날에는 선생님이 '막대기'로 학생들의 손바닥이나 엉덩이를 때리기도 했는데, 바로 그

chapter 27 The Rise of Rome

'막대기'가 rod이다. 그런 선생님들의 신조는 Spare the rod, and spoil the child(매를 아끼면 아이를 망친다)라는 유명한 영어 속담 때문이었을지도 모른다. The Etruscan kings also carried a bundle of rods with an axe blade in it, as a symbol of royal power. 또한 에트루리아의 왕들은 왕권의 상징으로 도끼날이 안에 들어있는 막대 묶음을 들고 다녔다.

courtroom ⓝ a room in a law court where cases are judged

courtroom은 당연히 court와 room이 합쳐진 것이다. court는 원래 '사방이 막힌 곳(an enclosed place)'을 뜻하는 라틴어에서 유래했다. 옛날에는 사법권을 갖고 있는 왕의 궁궐이나 지방 관청에서 재판이 열렸는데, 그곳은 모두 사방이 담이나 벽으로 막혀 있었다. 그래서 court가 '법원, 재판소'를 뜻한다. courtroom은 재판이 행해지는 법원에 있는 방, 즉 '법정, 재판정'이다.
American courtrooms and government offices sometimes copy this Roman symbol, even today. 오늘날까지도 미국의 법정과 정부 사무실들은 때때로 이 로마의 상징물을 모방하기도 한다.

Q 왜 로마인들은 왕을 몰아내고 공화정을 택했나요?

A 로마의 마지막 왕은 오만왕 '타르퀴니우스'라고 불렸어. 오만왕이라니! 백성과의 충돌이 눈에 보이지 않니? 결국 뜻이 맞는 사람들끼리 그를 몰아내고, 로마를 다시는 왕이 지배할 수 없는 나라로 만들겠다고 선언했어. 두 명의 집정관을 뽑아 서로 견제하면서 1년 동안 나라를 운영하게 하자는 거였지. 왕처럼 권력을 휘두르지 않게 하기 위해서였지. 그러나 왕도 순순히 물러나지는 않았단다. 추방당한 뒤에 귀족의 아들들과 반란을 일으킨 거야. 왕을 쫓아낸 당사자 루시우스 브루투스(로마 공화정의 아버지)의 두 아들도 그 음모에 가담했고, 이 사실이 적발되자 브루투스는 냉정하게 두 아들을 사형에 선고했지.

appoint ⓥ to choose someone for a job

appoint는 to a point(어느 지점으로)를 의미한다. 권력자가 아랫사람에게 '너는 이쪽으로, 너는 저쪽으로' 가라고 지시하는 것이 appoint이다. 즉 '임명하다, 지명하다, 정하다'이다. 투표로 뽑는 선출직에는 쓰지 않고, 임명직에만 쓴다. 예를 들어 He was appointed as the principal of the school(그는 그 학교의 교장으로 임명되었다)처럼 쓸 수 있다. appoint의 명사형은 appointment이다.
Two of these patricians were appointed by the other patricians to be the leader of the city. 이 귀족들 중에서 두 명이 다른 귀족들에 의해 도시 지도자로 임명되었다.

The Story of the World

Chapter 28
The Roman Empire

1 The Roman Gods

🌏 로마인들은 그리스 신화를 차용해 자신들의 신으로 삼으면서 이름을 바꾸었다. 그리스 신화의 최고의 신인 '제우스(Zeus)'는 로마의 '주피터(Jupiter)'가 되었고, 부인인 '헤라(Hera)'는 '주노(Juno)'가 되었다. 또한 태양계의 행성들에는 로마 신들의 이름이 붙여졌는데, 다음과 같다.

- 머큐리(Mercury) : 수성
- 비너스(Venus) : 금성
- 마스(Mars) : 화성
- 주피터(Jupiter) : 목성
- 새턴(Saturn) : 토성
- 유래너스(Uranus) : 천왕성
- 넵튠(Neptune) : 해왕성

We learned earlier that the Etruscan tribes of Italy went to Greece to buy and sell. In Greece, they learned about the Greek gods, and heard Greek myths. And when they came back to Italy, they passed these stories along to the Romans.

The Romans took the Greek gods as their own. They worshipped the gods of Greece. But they called these Greek gods by their own, Roman names.

Do you remember Zeus, the king of the Greek gods? He made the golden apple so that he could start the Trojan War on earth. In Rome, Zeus was called Jupiter. He controlled the sky, the moon, and the weather: wind, rain, and thunder. Today, we call one of the planets in our solar system Jupiter, after the Roman name of the king of the gods. The planet Mars is also named after a Roman god—the god of war. And do you remember the god of the sea, Poseidon, who tried to keep Odysseus from getting home? The Romans called this sea god Neptune. Our solar system also has a planet named Neptune.

The Romans told stories of their gods to explain the natural world. One story, about Ceres and her daughter Proserpine, tries to show why winter and summer come every year.

One day Ceres, the goddess of the harvest, and her daughter Proserpine were roaming through the woods. Wherever Ceres stepped, ripe grain sprang up; whenever she touched a tree, fruit blossomed beneath her hands. Her daughter followed along behind her, as beautiful as springtime, with long golden hair.

Ceres stopped for a moment to drink from a cool stream. While she drank, Proserpine wandered away to a beautiful clump of lilies nearby. As she bent down to pick them, the ground suddenly opened beneath her and she disappeared! When Ceres looked up, Proserpine was gone. "Proserpine!" Ceres called. "Proserpine! Where are you?" But there was no answer.

For fourteen days, Ceres wandered the earth, looking for her lost daughter. Finally, Ceres met a nymph who whispered, "I have just come from the Underworld, land of the dead. I saw your daughter there! She was stolen by Hades, the king of the underworld, to be his wife! When he saw her, he fell in love with her, and the ground opened up beneath her so that she could walk through it into the land underground."

When Ceres heard this, she was furious. "I have helped the ground to bear crops!" she shouted. "And this is how it rewards me! I will curse it until it is dry and empty of all life!" Instantly the trees around her began to turn brown, and the leaves fell from them. The grass died, and the flowers withered. In great rage, Ceres turned and climbed up into the heavens, all the way to the palace of Jupiter, king of the gods.

"Jupiter!" she said. "Force Hades to return my daughter to me! If you don't, I will never again let spring come to the

Pluto stole Ceres away

earth. There will never be fruit, or grain, or grass again. The earth will always be as dead and hard as my heart without my daughter!"

Jupiter thought about this.

"Very well," he said at last. "I will tell Hades to let your daughter go—on one condition. She can leave the underworld as long as she hasn't eaten or drunk anything in the palace of Hades. But if she ate or drank with him there, she will have to stay."

Suddenly the earth cracked open. There stood Proserpine, beside a tall dark man in a black cloak—Hades, lord of the underworld.

"My daughter!" Ceres exclaimed.

"Wait," Jupiter said. "Proserpine, have you eaten or drunk anything in the underworld?"

"Hardly anything," the girl said. "I only ate six seeds from a pomegranate, just a few minutes ago."

"Then you must stay with Hades," Jupiter said.

But Ceres refused to give in. "If I don't get my daughter back," she warned, "spring will never come again."

Jupiter considered the case carefully. At last he said, "She only ate six seeds. So for six months—half of the year—she must stay in the underworld with Hades. But for the other six months, she can come and live with her mother in the world above."

And so Proserpine spends six months of every year in the underworld. When she is in the palace of Hades, her mother Ceres mourns and weeps. The leaves fall from the trees, the grass turns brown, and the flowers die. But when Proserpine comes back to her mother each spring, Ceres rejoices. The leaves of the trees begin to grow; the grass turns green again, and flowers begin to bud and bloom.

2 The Roman Builders

한때 유럽의 거의 모든 땅이 로마 제국의 것이었다. 로마 제국은 이탈리아는 물론 점령지의 대도시들을 잇는 도로를 건설했는데, 심지어 바다 건너 잉글랜드 브리튼 섬에도 로마가 건설한 도로가 아직 남아 있다. 모든 길은 로마로 통한다(All roads lead to Rome)라는 속담은 거뭇망처럼 뻗은 로마 제국의 도로 시스템에서 유래한 것이다. 기원전 312년부터 건설된 아피아 가도(The Appian Roads)는 로마와 브린디 시를 잇는 총 길이 50킬로미터, 폭 8미터의 도로로, 지금도 일부 원형이 보존되어 있어 로마의 도로 건설 기술을 잘 보여주고 있다.

The Romans weren't content just to stay in their little city of Rome. *The bigger the city got, the more land the Romans wanted. And the best way to get land was to take it from other towns and tribes. So the Romans attacked their neighbors and conquered them. *The more land they conquered, the richer they got. Soon, Rome controlled the whole Italian peninsula.

*Now that Rome ruled all of Italy, the Romans needed to be

able to travel easily from one end of the peninsula to the others. So they began to build roads.

Most roads in the ancient world were rough, muddy tracks filled with holes and blocked by rocks and fallen trees. But the Romans built roads that were easy to travel on. First, they dug a wide ditch and filled the ditch with sand. Then they poured small stones on top of the sand. Next, they poured concrete over top of the stones. Finally, they laid wide, smooth paving stones on top of the concrete. Along the road, the Romans put up stone pillars and carved on them the distance between towns. A traveler on a Roman road could look at these *mile stones* and know exactly how much farther he had to go!

The Romans became famous for their beautiful roads. The most famous of all Roman roads was called the Appian Way. It led from Rome to several large Roman cities in Italy. The Appian Way can still be used today. Roman roads were so well built that they lasted for hundreds of years. Today, many roads in Italy still follow the tracks of the old Roman roads. The Romans were the first ancient people to use concrete. They discovered that if they mixed volcanic ash, water, and lime, the soupy mixture would dry as hard as stone. They used this concrete to cement large stones together into buildings and roads.

The Romans built whole apartment buildings out of concrete. Some of these ancient apartment buildings were five stories high. One Roman writer tells the true story of an ox who escaped from his owner on market day and ran into an apartment building. It kept climbing up higher and higher and higher, until it reached the top floor. And then it jumped out of a window.

Unfortunately, some of the apartment buildings weren't very well built—and they collapsed, sometimes killing the people who lived inside. Others were slums, without any water or toilets.

Whole families lived in one room. They dumped their waste out the windows into the streets.

As the Roman cities grew larger and larger, the people who lived in them needed more and more fresh water. So the Romans designed special channels for water, called *aqueducts*. The aqueducts were like narrow stone bridges with water pipes that ran across the top of them. *Through these aqueducts, the Romans could bring water into the cities from springs thirty miles away.

The Romans needed water for drinking and cooking, but also for taking baths. Baths were very important to the ancient Romans! Most of them took a bath every day. But they didn't bathe in a bathtub, like you do. Instead, they went to the public baths, which were more like swimming pools. People gathered at the public baths to get clean. They rubbed soap made from animal fat on their skin, and then scraped themselves clean with special curved blades. Then they could swim in cold or hot water, brought in by the aqueducts.

Today, the ruins of Roman roads, buildings, baths, and aqueducts can still be found in the places where the Romans lived—even though they were built more than two thousand years ago.

3 The Roman Gladiators

로마의 검투 경기는 에트루리아에서 전래된 것으로 알려져 있다. 처음에는 귀족들의 장례식 중에 치러지는 한 행사로 시작되었다가 점점 대중적인 오락으로 퍼졌다. 전쟁 포로, 죄수, 노예 중에 검투사를 뽑아 훈련소에서 일정 기간 동안 훈련을 시켰는데, 이 검투사(劍鬪士)들을 '글라디아토르(gladiator)'라고 불렀다. 로마인들은 로마와 여러 대도시에 설치된 콜로세움에서 검투 경기를 관람했는데, 검투사들은 다른 검투사들과 대결을 펼치거나 사자 같은 맹수들과도 싸워야 했다. 승자는 많은 돈을 받거나 자유인으로 풀려날 수도 있었지만, 대부분의 패자는 경기장에서 죽음을 맞아야 했다.

Today we're going to read a story about a man who became a Roman gladiator—someone who fought with other men as a game. The man in the story, Servius, is imaginary. But there were thousands of men just like him in ancient Rome.

Servius lived in a small village near the sea. He spent his days working with metal—he made plows and hoes for the farmers who lived near him, and fishhooks for the fishermen. He liked his work. At night, he would sit with his friends around a fire and talk, sing songs and tell stories. Servius was happy.

One day, as Servius was heating the metal to make a new hoe, he heard a thundering noise. *He looked up, wondering if it were about to rain. But the noise wasn't thunder! It was the sound of horses' hooves. *Around the corner of the peaceful village rode a group of men with swords, shields and spears. They wore helmets and red cloaks.

"We are Romans!" the biggest man shouted. "We claim this village for Rome! Now you must obey us!"

Servius looked around for a weapon, but all he could see was a hoe, hanging on the wall! He grabbed it and swung it at the man, but he missed. Two other Roman soldiers leaped from their horses and seized Servius from behind.

"You are our prisoner!" the big man said. "You'll return with us to Rome."

They put Servius on a horse and made him ride with them for days and days down a broad, wide road of stone. Finally Servius saw the wall of a city ahead. *It was the highest wall he had ever seen. A man standing on another man's shoulders couldn't even see over it.

The soldiers took him through a small gate in the city wall. When they came out the other side, Servius found himself in a narrow, crowded street full of people. Little wooden booths lined both sides of the street. Inside the booths, men and women were selling fruit, pieces of cooked meat, bread, cabbages and carrots, and jugs of cheap wine. Children ran down the middle of the street, chasing a mangy dog. Women hung laundry out on wooden balconies above the street. He could hear babies crying, men shouting, women talking to each other, horses and donkeys neighing. He had never seen so many people in one place at the same time.

Soon, the street grew wider, and the houses grew bigger. Servius began to see green gardens, fountains, and houses made out of white marble. There were fewer people here, and they were dressed in fancier clothes—white togas with borders of red and blue. They were approaching the center of Rome.

"Where are you taking me?" Servius asked one of the soldiers who rode beside him.

"To the gladiator school," the soldier said. You're big and strong, and you have courage. You'll make a great fighter, once the trainers at the school have taught you what to do."

Servius felt his mouth go dry with fright. He had heard about the notorious gladiators of Rome—fierce men who fought with each other and with wild animals while a cheering crowd looked on. "But what if I don't want to be a gladiator?" he said.

"You don't have any choice," the soldier answered. "You're our prisoner. Go to the gladiator school, or be executed."

They stopped at a high stone wall, and two Romans took

Servius through the gate. Inside, a large courtyard was full of men, training for their gladiator matches. At the center, a man wearing only a loincloth and a belt was trying to throw a fishnet over his opponent. He brandished a three-pointed spear in his other hand. The man who fought against him was waving a short sword and defending himself with a large round shield. His helmet was covered with pictures of fish.

"The man with the net is called a net-fighter," one of the soldiers told Servius. "The other one is a fish man. The net-fighter is trying to catch him in the net and stab him. Maybe, if you're lucky, you'll learn how to be a net-fighter!"

Servius' knees were shaking with terror. If this was just the training camp, what would it be like to fight a real gladiator fight, in the arena? How could he ever survive?

4 The Gladiator School

'로마' 하면 떠오르는 관광 명소가 바로 콜로세움이다. 콜로세움의 정식 명칭은 플라비우스 원형경기장(Amphitheatrum Flavium)이다. 로마의 콜로세움은 5만 명을 수용할 수 있는 대규모 타원형 경기장으로, 플라비우스 왕조 때인 서기 80년에 완성되었다. 4층으로 된 계단식 관람석을 갖추고 있고, 가운데에는 모래가 깔린 아레나(arena)가 있다. 검투사들의 시합과 맹수들과 인간의 혈투, 모의 해전 등이 열렸으며 기독교 박해 시대에는 기독교도들이 학살되기도 했다. 콜로세움은 이후 400년 넘게 로마인들에게 오락을 제공하는 장소로 이용되었다.

At the gladiator school, Servius lived in a cell just like a prison cell. But he was taken out every day for gladiator training. First, he had to pass a test to see how fit he was. Two trainers—big men with scars on their faces, wearing armor and carrying short, sharp swords—walked all around him. They poked him and squeezed his arms. Then they pointed to a post, a hundred feet away. "How quickly can you run to that post and back?" one asked.

Servius scowled at the man. He didn't want to learn how to fight, but if he didn't, he would be killed. Finally he turned around and ran to the post and back.

"Very good," the trainer said. "Now let's see how you do for endurance."

For the rest of the day, the two trainers forced Servius to run, jump, wrestle, and climb. By night, he was covered with sweat and mud, and was so tired he could hardly drag himself back to his cell. But he had passed the test. The next day, Servius stood in the courtyard along with five other new prisoners.

"You will be gladiators!" one of the trainers shouted. "Repeat after me the oath of the gladiator! 'I undertake to be burnt by fire, to be bound in chains, to be beaten by rods, and to die by the sword.' To be a gladiator is a wonderful privilege! You are indeed lucky!"

Servius swallowed nervously. He didn't feel lucky. But all around him, the other prisoners were repeating the gladiator's oath. So he took the oath as well. The next thing he knew, they were being marched off to their first training exercise—swinging wooden swords at straw men, propped up against the gladiator school wall.

The trainers had once been gladiators. They taught Servius and the other new recruits swordfighting moves. When Servius had learned the moves, he then fought against one of the other gladiator students. They both had wooden swords, so no one got killed. But Servius didn't parry quickly enough, and the other student's wooden sword crashed against his side. He was sore for days, but the trainers just laughed at him. "You'd better learn to be tough," one of them said. "We don't care if it hurts. Just keep fighting. You'll get hurt worse than that when you fight in the arena."

In the arena! Servius' heart sank. He already knew that his first fight in the arena was only a week away. He was to be a *secutor*, a gladiator who chased net-fighters around the arena. He had already practiced fighting with his real weapons and armor—a short, strong sword, a large shield, and a metal legguard that covered his left leg. On his head he wore a round helmet with two tiny eye-holes. He could barely see out of the helmet! How would he ever catch a net-fighter? What if the net-fighter caught him first?

On the day of the fight, Servius was taken to the arena—a large bare space near the outer walls of Rome. Wooden seats had been built all around it. They were filled with men and women, and even children. All of them were cheering and shouting. They were enjoying this!

Servius' trainer put his helmet on and tightened his armor. "Go get him!" he said, and pushed Servius into the arena. The metal helmet was hot and tight. Servius felt like he could barely breathe. He turned his head and caught sight of his opponent—a net-fighter, creeping towards him from the other side of the arena. The net-fighter threw his net. Servius felt it strike against his shield. He advanced forward, waving his sword. The net-fighter backed away. Suddenly he turned and began to run.

"He's as frightened as I am!" Servius thought. He started to chase the net-fighter. His heavy armor slowed him down. The net-fighter wasn't wearing armor. He was getting away.

Suddenly the net-fighter tripped and stumbled. Before he knew it, Servius was standing right over top of him. He could hardly believe it. He had won the match! He put his foot on the net-fighter's chest and looked around him. The crowd was booing and making the thumbs-down sign. Servius knew what that meant. They wanted him to kill his opponent. If the net-fighter had been brave and bold, the crowd might have had pity on him and turned their thumbs up. Then, Servius could show mercy and let the other man live. But he was supposed to do whatever the crowd said.

Servius looked down. The net-fighter knew what the thumbs-down meant. He had closed his eyes. He thought he was about to die.

Servius stepped back and put his sword back in its sheath. "Get up," he said. "I can't kill you. I am not an animal! I know that it would be wrong to kill a man for sport."

The net-fighter scrambled away from him, hardly able to believe his ears. The crowd was booing louder and louder. They wanted to see blood! But Servius turned around and walked back towards his trainer. He knew he would be punished. Maybe he would even be killed. But he knew now that he could not kill another man.

The Romans were great, powerful people, but they were also bloodthirsty. They liked to see men hurt. They enjoyed seeing blood.

Some of the historians who lived in Rome thought that this bloodthirstiness was wrong and evil. They wrote about men like Servius who refused to kill their opponents in the arena. Some even killed themselves so that they would not be forced to kill other men. The Roman philosopher Seneca wrote, in a letter to a friend, "The show was even better to watch when this happened—because the men in the audience learned that it is more decent to die than to kill."

The Story of the Words

Chapter 28 The Roman Empire

1 The Roman Gods

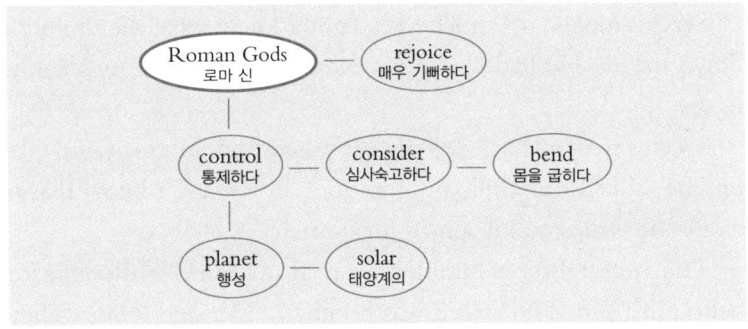

control Ⓥ to make someone or something do what you want

control은 원래 against a roll을 의미하는데, roll은 두루마리 문서이다. control은 원본과 사본을 대조하며 기록이 맞는지 확인하는 의미로 발전하여 '통제하다, 지배하다'라는 뜻으로 쓰이게 되었다.

He controlled the sky, the moon, and the weather: wind, rain, and thunder. 주피터는 하늘과 달 그리고 바람, 비, 천둥의 날씨를 지배했다.

planet Ⓝ a very large round object that moves around the sun in space

희랍어에서 유래한 planet에는 wander(배회하다, 돌아다니다)라는 뜻이 담겨 있다. 밤하늘을 보다가 여기저기 왔다 갔다 하는 듯 보이는 별들을 발견하고 '배회하는 별들'이라는 의미로 planet이라고 한 것이다. 물론 그 별들의 정체는 수성(Mercury), 금성(Venus), 지구(Earth), 화성(Mars), 목성(Jupiter), 토성(Saturn), 천왕성(Uranus), 해왕성(Neptune)의 태양계 행성들이다.

Today, we call one of the planets in our solar system Jupiter, after the Roman name of the king of the gods. 오늘날, 우리는 신들의 왕을 부르는 로마 이름을 따서 우리 태양계의 행성 중 하나를 '주피터(목성)'라고 부른다.

solar ⓐ relating to the sun or the sun's power
라틴어에서 sol은 태양(sun)이다. 이 단어의 형용사형이 영어에 유입되어 solar로 변형되었다. solar는 '태양의, 태양 에너지를 이용하는'을 뜻한다. our solar system은 '우리 (지구가 속해 있는) 태양계'라는 의미로, 태양과 그 위성들의 존재와 현상을 모두 포함하는 개념이다.
Our solar system also has a planet named Neptune. 우리 태양계에는 '넵튠(해왕성)'이라는 행성도 있다.

bend ⓥ to move the top part of your body down toward the ground
바닥에 떨어진 물건을 주울 때나 어른에게 인사를 할 때 상체를 굽히게 되는데, 이런 동작을 표현하는 것이 바로 bend이다. 즉 '몸을 굽히다'이다. bend에는 '자신을 낮추거나 복종하다'는 의미도 있는데, Better bend than break(부러지는 것보다는 휘어지는 게 낫다)라는 의미의 유명한 격언도 있다.
As she bent down to pick them, the ground suddenly opened beneath her and she disappeared! 그녀가 꽃을 꺾기 위해 몸을 굽히자, 갑자기 밑에서 땅이 열리더니 그녀가 사라졌다!

consider ⓥ to think carefully about something
consider에서 con은 with(~로, ~와 함께)를 의미하고, sider는 stars(별들)를 의미하는 것으로 추정한다. 천체의 별을 보고서 운명과 미래의 일을 판단하는 점성술에서 유래한 것이다. 별로 세상일을 예측하려면 정확한 관찰과 더불어 '신중한 사고와 판단'이 필요하므로 consider가 '숙고하다, 고려하다'라는 뜻이 되었다. 명사형은 consideration이다.
Jupiter considered the case carefully. 주피터가 그 사건에 대해 신중하게 고려했다.

rejoice ⓥ to feel or be very happy
rejoice에서 re-는 '강조'를 의미하는 접두사이고, joice는 '기쁨을 느끼다'라는 뜻이다. 즉 '매우 기뻐하다'라는 의미이다. 보통 Ceres rejoiced at her daughter's returning(케레스는 딸이 돌아와서 무척 기뻤다)처럼 rejoice 다음에 전치사 at을 붙여 표현한다.
But when Proserpine comes back to her mother each spring, Ceres rejoices. 그러나 프로세르피나가 매년 봄에 자신의 어머니에게 돌아올 때, 케레스는 무척 기뻐했다.

Q 성산 사건이 무엇인가요?

A 로마가 왕을 몰아내고 공화정을 실시하게 된 것은 기원전 509년의 일이야. 그때까지만 해도 로마는 아주 작은 지역에 불과했고, 인구가 적어서 다른 지역에서 오는 사람들을 환영했지. 아직 귀족과 평민의 차별도 엄격하지 않았어. 로마 하면 훈련된 군대가 떠오를 정도로 로마는 싸움을 통해서 영역을 넓혀가고 있었단다.

영토를 나누는 과정에서 귀족이 절대적으로 유리하자 평민들 사이에 불만이 커졌어. 평민들은 싸우러 나간 사이에 자신의 농토를 제대로 돌보지 못해 곤란을 겪었고, 전투 중에 죽어도 제대로 보상도 못 받았지. 싸워 이긴다고 해도 그들에게 돌아오는 몫은 거의 없고, 정치적으로 좋은 자리는 모두 귀족이 차지하니 도대체 왜 우리는 나라를 위해서 싸워야 하는 거지? 하고 의구심을 품게 되었어.

결국 화가 난 평민들이 기원전 494년 로마를 떠나 성산(Mons Sarcer, 성스러운 산이라는 뜻)으로 몰려가게 되었단다. 그런데 마침 적이 로마에 쳐들어와서 군사의 출동이 꼭 필요한 때였어. 성산으로 평민들이 몰려가는 바람에 군대를 소집할 수 없게 된 귀족들은 그때서야 평민이 없으면 국가가 성립되지 않는다는 사실을 깨닫게 되었어. 기원전 493년 귀족들은 양보 조건을 내걸고, 성산에 있던 평민들을 다시 로마로 불러들였어. 평민들만의 모임인 '평민 회의'를 구성하고, 이들이 뽑은 평민 대표 호민관을 정식으로 인정한다는 조건이었어.

2 The Roman Builders

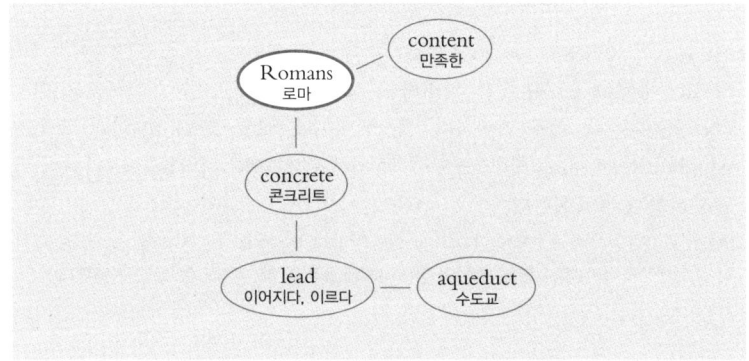

content ⓐ satisfied and happy

content는 형용사로 '만족한, 흡족한'이라는 뜻이다. content에서 con-은 altogether(모두 함께)이고, tent는 to hold(쥐다, 보유하다)를 뜻한다. 즉 모든 것을 다 갖고 있는 상태이다. 앞에서 배운 동사 contain과 어원이 같다. 창고에 곡식이 가득하고, 부와 명예와 건강을 다 갖고 있으면 만족스러울 수밖에 없을 것이다.
The Romans weren't content just to stay in their little city of Rome. 로마인들은 자신들의 작은 도시인 로마에만 머물러 있는 것에 만족하지 않았다.

concrete ⓝ a substance mixed with cement, sand, small stones and water, which becomes hard and is used for building

concrete는 지금 우리가 사용하는 거의 모든 건물의 주재료인 '콘크리트'를 말한다. 시멘트와 모래, 자갈, 물 등을 섞으면 일정 시간 후에 단단해진다. concrete에서 con-은 '함께(together)'를 뜻하고, crete는 'to grow(커지다)'를 뜻한다. 커진다는 것은 '단단하게 만들어지고 세워진다'라는 의미이다. 그래서 concrete가 건설에 쓰이는 것이다. 이미 만들어져 세워졌으면 그 모습이 구체적으로 보이므로 concrete는 '구체적인, 명백한'이라는 뜻도 지닌다.
Next, they poured concrete over top of stones. 그다음에 그들은 쌓인 돌 위로 콘크리트를 부었다.

lead ⓥ to go to a place

lead의 기본적인 의미는 '손을 잡고 데려가다'이다. 아이의 손을 잡고 어딘가로 이끌고 가니까 '인도하다'라는 뜻이고, 그 어른 역할을 하는 사람이 leader가 되는 것이다. 아이 입장에서는 어른을 따라가면 '어떤 곳에 이르게 된다.' 그래서 lead에는 '~로 길이 이어지다, 이르다'라는 뜻이 있다. This road leads from Seoul to Busan(이 길은 서울에서 부산까지 이어진다)처럼 쓸 수 있다.
It led from Rome to several large Roman cities in Italy. 그 길은 로마에서 이탈리아에 있는 로마의 몇몇 대도시들로 이어진다.

aqueduct ⓝ a structure like a bridge, that carries water across a river or valley

aqueduct에서 aque는 물(water)을 뜻하는 aqua(아쿠아)에서 온 것이다. duct는 to lead(이끌다)라는 뜻을 담고 있어서 aqueducts는 '물을 한 곳에서 다른 곳으로 흐르게 하다'라는 의미이다. 로마 제국은 다리처럼 생긴 수로를 만들어 강이나 호수에서 물을 끌어다가 도시 용수와 농업 용수로 사용했는데, 바로 이 '수도교(水道橋)'를 aqueduct라고 한다.
So the Romans designed special channels for water, called aqueducts. 그래서 로마인들은 물을 얻기 위한 특별한 수로 즉 수도교를 고안했다.

3 The Roman Gladiators

gladiator ⓝ someone who fought against other men or wild animals as a game in ancient Rome

고대 로마의 콜로세움에서 목숨을 걸고 결투를 하거나 맹수들과 싸우던 사람들을 '검투사(劍鬪士)'라고 하는데, gladiator를 글자 그대로 정확하게 이해한 것이다. gladiator는 sword(검)을 뜻하는 라틴어 gladius에서 유래했기 때문이다. 즉 gladiator는 '검을 쓰는 사람'이다.

Today we're going to read a story about a man who became a Roman gladiator—someone who fought with other men as a game. 오늘 우리는 로마의 검투사가 된 어떤 남자에 대한 이야기를 읽을 것인데, 검투사란 일종의 경기로 다른 남자들과 싸우던 사람을 말한다.

metal ⓝ hard substance such as iron, gold or bronze

metal은 철, 금, 은, 동, 알루미늄 등의 '금속'을 통칭한다. 본문의 이야기 속 주인공 Servius는 금속으로 일을 하는 사람이다. metal로 쟁기(plow)도 만들고, 괭이(hoe)도 만든다. 그럼 직업이 뭘까? 답은 '대장장이(blacksmith)'이다.

He spent his days working with metal—he made plows and hoes for the farmers who lived near him, and fishhooks for the fishermen. 그는 금속으로 일을 하며 살았다. 근방에 사는 농부들을 위해 쟁기와 괭이, 어부들이 쓸 낚시 바늘도 만들었다.

claim ⓥ to ask for something that you think belongs to you
claim은 to call out(큰 소리로 부르다, 외치다)을 뜻하는 라틴어에서 온 것이다. 큰 소리를 내는 데에는 목적이 있다. 무역 용어인 '클레임(claim)'은 계약을 위반한 상대에게 보상을 요구하는 행위이다. 이런 개념에서 동사 claim은 '~이 자기의 것이라고 주장하다, 사실이라고 주장하다'라는 뜻으로 쓰인다.
We claim this village for Rome! 이 마을은 로마의 것이다!

prisoner ⓝ someone who is taken by force and kept somewhere
prisoner는 prison(감옥)에 갇혀 있는 사람, 즉 '죄수'이다. 전쟁에서 적에게 잡혀 한동안 감옥에 갇혀 있으면 prisoner는 '포로'라는 뜻이다. 군대 용어로 '전쟁 포로'는 POW(Prisoner of War)라고 한다. Servius는 로마군의 정복지에서 잡혔으므로 '포로'이다.
"You are our prisoner!" the big man said. 덩치 큰 사내가 말했다. "넌 우리 포로다!"

approach ⓥ to move closer to someone or something
approach는 어딘가로 '다가가다, 다가오다, 접근하다'를 뜻한다. 이미 단어 안에 '~로, ~를 향해(ap-)'라는 말이 담겨 있기 때문에 approach와 목적어 사이에 전치사를 넣으면 안 된다. I approached the house(나는 그 집으로 다가갔다)처럼 써야 한다.
They were approaching the center of Rome. 그들은 로마의 중심부로 다가가고 있었다.

notorious ⓐ famous for doing something bad
notorious에서 notori는 '알려진(known)'을, -ous는 형용사형 접미사이어서 '알려진, 유명한'이라는 뜻이다. 공부를 잘하고 선행을 많이 해서 유명할 수도 있지만, 악행을 저질러서 유명할 수도 있다. notorious는 '부정적인 이유로 유명한' 경우에 써서 '악명 높은'이라는 뜻이다. notorious의 동의어는 famous(유명한) 앞에 in-이 붙은 infamous이다.
He had heard about the notorious gladiators of Rome—fierce men who fought with each other and with wild animals while cheering crowd looked on. 세르비우스는 악명 높은 로마의 검투사들에 대해 들은 적이 있었다. 그들은 환호하는 관중들이 구경하는 동안 서로 싸우거나 야수들과 싸우는 사나운 사내들이었다.

execute ⓥ to kill someone as a punishment decided by law
out을 뜻하는 ex-와 follow를 뜻하는 sequor가 합쳐져 execute가 생겨났다.

법, 명령, 규칙을 '끝까지(out) 따라서(follow) 수행한다'라는 의미이다. 그래서 execute는 '실행하다'와 '사형을 집행하다, 처형하다'라는 뜻으로도 쓰인다.
Go to the gladiator school, or be executed. 검투사 학교에 가든가 아니면 처형되든가.

> **Q** 로마법은 하루아침에 이루어지지 않았다고요?
> **A** 기원전 493년에 귀족들의 양보로 평민들이 돌아와 평민회, 호민관 제도가 만들어졌어. 그러나 이것으로 귀족과 평민이 대등한 입장에 서게 된 것은 아니었단다. 평민들은 로마 살림에 보탬을 주는 만큼 자신들도 제대로 대접받기를 원했어.
> 이러한 노력의 결과로 12표법이 만들어졌는데, 이것이 로마 최초의 성문법이야. 성문법은 말 그대로 문서로 작성된 법이라는 뜻이야. 그전에는 불문법 혹은 관습법만 존재하고 기록된 법이 없었으니 아무래도 힘 있는 귀족의 뜻대로 움직여졌지. 이제 문서화된 법이 만들어졌으니 평민 입장에서는 도움이 되었어.

opponent ⓝ someone who tries to defeat someone else in a game or competition

TV 토론 프로그램을 보면, 서로 입장과 생각이 반대인 토론자들이 양쪽으로 앉아 있다. opponent라는 말도 원래 그렇게 생겼다. 학술 회의나 정치 토론장에서 '반대 입장에 있는 사람'을 opponent라고 불렀다. opponent는 against(반대, 맞은 편)를 뜻하는 op-와 place(자리, 입장)를 뜻하는 어근 pon, 명사형 접미사 -ent가 합쳐진 말이다. 즉 '반대편에 있는 사람'이다.
At the center, a man wearing only a loincloth and a belt was trying to throw a fishnet over his opponent. 한가운데에 허리에 천과 벨트만 찬 한 사내가 상대에게 그물을 던져 씌우려고 하고 있었다.

4 The Gladiator School

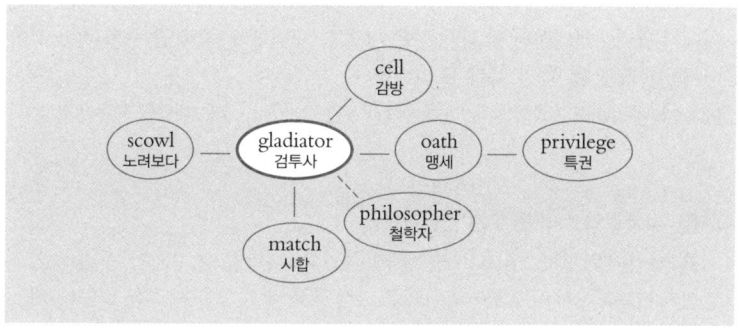

cell ⓝ a small room where a prisoner is kept
cell은 작은 방이다. 주로 칸칸이 나누어진 감옥의 '감방'이나, 수도원의 '방' 등을 cell이라고 부른다. 동물과 식물의 '세포'도 현미경으로 보면 아주 작은 방처럼 나누어져 있어서 cell이라고 한다. cell phone(휴대 전화기)도 전파의 기지국을 '방'을 나누듯이 송수신할 수 있게 만든 시스템이기 때문에 붙여진 것이다.
At the gladiator school, Servius lived in a cell just like a prison cell. 검투사 학교에서 세르비우스는 감방처럼 생긴 작은 방에서 살았다.

scowl ⓥ to look at someone in an angry way
다른 사람을 바라보는 모습에는 여러 가지가 있는데, scowl은 가장 무서운 표정을 지으며 '분노, 혐오'의 눈빛으로 보는 것이다. '노려보다, 째려보다'라는 뜻이다. 그 시선이 상대에게 딱 닿기 때문에 look이나 glance처럼 뒤에 전치사 at을 붙인다.
Servius scowled at the man. 세르비우스는 그 남자를 무섭게 노려보았다.

oath ⓝ a very serious promise
oath는 지극히 엄중한 약속이다. 그 약속을 지키지 않으면 법적인 책임을 져야 한다. 그래서 미국 대통령 취임식에서 신임 대통령이 성경책 위에 손을 얹고 '맹세'를 하는데, 이를 Bible oath라고 부른다. oath는 공식적인 '맹세, 서약'을 뜻한다. '맹세하다'는 to take[swear] an oath라고 표현한다. The witness took an oath on the Bible(그 증인은 성경에 손을 얹고 맹세했다)처럼 쓸 수 있다.
Repeat after me the oath of the gladiator! 나를 따라 검투사의 맹세를 말하거라!

chapter 28 The Roman Empire 123

privilege ⓝ a special advantage given only to one person or group
privilege에서 privi는 '개인적인(private)'이고, lege는 '법(law)'를 뜻하는 라틴어에서 왔다. '개인적인 법'의 목적은 대개 한 개인에게 '특혜'를 주기 위한 것이어서 privilege는 '특권, 특혜'를 의미한다.
To be a gladiator is a wonderful privilege! 검투사가 되는 것은 대단한 특권이다!

Q '피로스의 승리'는 무슨 뜻인가요?
A 리키니우스-섹스티우스 법(귀족과 평민의 대립 해소를 위한 법. 두 명의 호민관 이름을 따서 이렇게 불린다)으로 다시 국내의 갈등을 해결한 로마는 에트루리아에 이어 이탈리아 남부의 그리스 식민시들을 정복하기 시작했어. 그리스 식민시들이 계속 패하자 타렌툼에서는 마케도니아의 에페이로스 왕 '피로스'에게 도움을 청했어. 이때는 이미 알렉산더 왕이 죽고, 커다란 제국이 셋으로 나누어진 상태였단다.
피로스는 제2의 알렉산더가 되고 싶다는 야망을 지닌 왕으로 실제로 실력도 있었어. 피로스는 타렌툼의 원조 요청에 즉각 대군을 이끌고 이탈리아 반도에 왔어. 긴 창을 지닌 군인들과 전투용 코끼리까지 등장했어. 로마군들은 코끼리를 큰 소로 잘못 보고 허둥대다가 참패했단다. 피로스 군의 승리도 상당한 손실을 겪고 나서 얻은 것이라 '피로스의 승리'는 승리했지만 이득은 별로 없는 상황을 가리키는 말로 쓰이게 되었어.

philosopher ⓝ someone who studies life and its meaning, how we should live, or what knowledge is
philosopher는 philosophy를 연구하는 사람이다. philosophy는 love of wisdom(지혜에 대한 사랑)을 뜻하는 희랍어에서 온 것이다. '지적인 탐구, 갈구'를 의미하는 philosophy는 우리말로 '철학'이고, philosopher는 '철학자'이다. 세네카는 로마 제정 초기의 철학자이자 정치가로, 네로 황제의 스승이었다. 편지 형식의 《도덕서간》 20권을 집필했다.
The Roman philosopher Seneca wrote, in a letter to a friend, "The show was even better to watch when this happened—because the men in the audience learned that it is more decent to die than to kill." 로마의 철학자 세네카는 친구에게 보낸 편지에 이렇게 썼다. "그 구경거리는 이런 일이 일어나는 것을 볼 때가 훨씬 더 좋지. 왜냐하면 다른 사람을 죽이는 것보다 스스로 죽는 편이 더 훌륭하다는 사실을 관중 속의 사람들도 배웠기 때문이야."

The Story of the World

Chapter 29
Rome's War With Carthage

1 The Punic Wars

🌏 포에니 전쟁은 기원전 264년부터 기원전 146년까지 로마 제국과 카르타고 간에 벌어진 세 차례의 전쟁을 말한다. 첫 번째 전쟁에서는 로마가 승리해 지중해의 시칠리아 섬을 차지했다. 제2차 전쟁에서는 카르타고의 한니발 장군이 대군을 이끌고, 알프스를 넘어 이탈리아 반도로 침입해 연승을 거두면서 로마를 위기로 몰아넣었다. 그러나 로마의 스키피오 장군이 북아프리카를 침공하고, 기원전 202년 자마 전투에서 한니발 군대가 대패하면서 로마의 승리로 돌아간다. 기원전 149년에 로마군이 카르타고를 점령하고 철저히 파괴하면서 오랜 전쟁의 마침표를 찍었다. 이로써 카르타고는 멸망하고, 로마는 제국으로 발돋움하게 된다.

•Rome took over all of Italy. But the Romans still weren't happy. They wanted more!

Unfortunately, another city, Carthage, also wanted more. Do you remember reading about Carthage? The Phoenicians built the city of Carthage on the northern coast of Africa. They sailed their trading ships in and out of Carthage for hundreds of years.

Carthage made a lot of money trading with cities all around the Mediterranean Sea. •They wanted to keep on trading with these cities, and they didn't want Rome to get in the way! But the Romans also wanted to trade with these cities without Carthage interfering. So Rome and Carthage began to fight. They fought for years and years and years. These wars were called the Punic Wars. They began in 264 BC/BCE. And they didn't finally end until 146 BC/BCE, over a hundred years later.

At first, Carthage had the advantage because it had a navy— soldiers who knew how to sail ships. Rome didn't have a navy. •But when a Carthaginian ship wrecked on the coast of Italy, the Romans took it apart and figured out how to copy it. They built ships of their own and learned how to sail them. Soon the

Rome and Carthage

Romans could match the Carthaginians in a sea battle.

But Carthage was a tough enemy. The Romans had to work hard to beat them. They made lots of sacrifices to their gods, asking for victory. One Roman general named Claudius Pulcher actually took sacred chickens with him on his ship! He hoped that the sacred chickens would give him good fortune in battle. And he also thought that he could foretell the future by watching the way the chickens ate.

Unfortunately, the chickens got seasick and wouldn't eat at all. This was a very bad sign. The Roman soldiers on Claudius Pulcher's boat got more and more nervous. "The gods are against us!" they whispered. "We can tell, because the chickens aren't eating! We are doomed to fail!"

Claudius Pulcher got more and more irritated. Nothing he could do would make those chickens eat. So finally he ordered, "Throw the chickens overboard!"

Sure enough, he got badly beaten in the next battle. And all of his soldiers thought that they were defeated because they had thrown the sacred chickens into the sea.

The Carthaginians and Romans fought back and forth for a long time. Neither side could win. And then, one of the Carthaginian generals got a wonderful idea. Instead of attacking the Romans with ships, he would attack them with elephants.

Roman soldiers were camping near the Alps, up in the north of Italy, when they heard strange noises. They peered out of their tents into the swirling snow and mist. Suddenly, huge dark shapes loomed up in the snow. The ground shook. A herd of wild elephants was charging through the camp.

The Roman soldiers fled in terror. Many of them had never seen an elephant before. And these were no ordinary elephants. They were specially trained for battle. When they were told to attack, they spread their ears wide out to make their heads even larger. Their heads and ears were painted red, white and yellow, to make them look even more terrifying. Some of them were pulling carts full of armed Carthaginian soldiers, shooting arrows at the Roman troops. Others were carrying wooden boxes that contained even more attacking soldiers.

Some of the Romans did try to fight back. They ran for their horses and mounted, ready to attack the thundering beasts head on. But the horses were stricken with terror. They bolted, carrying the Roman soldiers off into the dark.

The Carthaginian general who planned this attack was named Hannibal. Hannibal saw that the battle between Carthage and Rome at sea was a stalemate—no one was winning. So while the two navies fought with each other, Hannibal took his army and forty elephants around the Mediterranean Sea by land. He surprised the Romans by coming down over the mountains into Italy. His invasion took place in 218 BC/BCE.

Once Hannibal had gotten into Italy with his elephants, he

roamed up and down Italy, burning villages and leaving Roman soldiers dead all through the countryside. The Romans were terrified. And they were afraid that Hannibal would come all the way to the city of Rome and burn it too.

Then a Roman general named Scipio thought of a plan to defeat Hannibal and his men. He gathered together the best Roman soldiers, sailed down to Carthage, and attacked the city itself. The city of Carthage wasn't expecting to be attacked! And all the best Carthaginian soldiers were over in Italy. So the people of Carthage sent a message to Hannibal: "Come back to Carthage and help us!"

Hannibal left Italy and sailed across the African Sea to defend his home town. But his soldiers were so worn out from burning and sacking towns in Italy that they were defeated! Hannibal himself ran away and hid, in Asia Minor.

Hannibal, the Carthaginian General

Finally, the city of Carthage was forced to surrender to Rome. When Hannibal heard this news, over in Asia Minor, he drank poison. He could not bear to think that his great city, Carthage, had been beaten by the Romans who were afraid of his elephants.

Note to Parent: The First Punic War was fought 264–241 BC/BCE; the Second Punic War took place 218–202 BC/BCE.

The Story of the Words
Chapter 29 Rome's War With Carthage

1 The Punic Wars

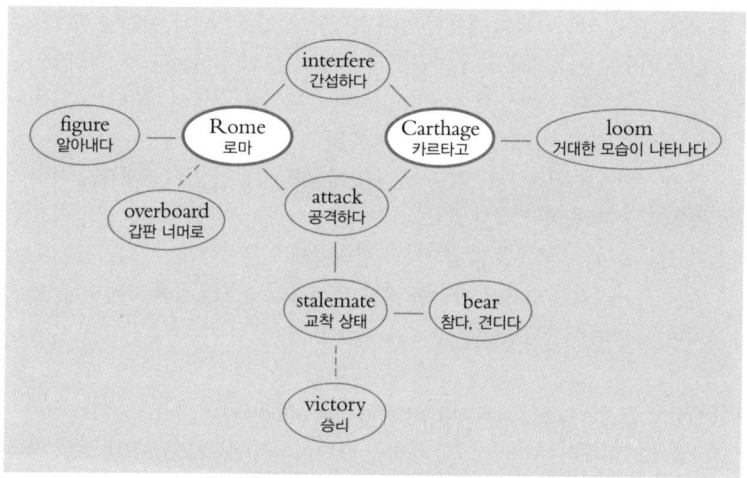

interfere ⓥ to get involved in a situation when you are not wanted
interfere에서 inter-는 '사이(between)'를, fere는 '때리다(strike)'를 뜻한다. 둘 사이를 때리면 연결이 끊어지거나 깨진다. 이렇게 사이에 끼어들어 영향을 미치는 것이 interfere로, '간섭하다, 개입하다, 방해하다'라는 뜻이다. 명사형은 interference이다.
But the Romans also wanted to trade with these cities without Carthage interfering.
그러나 로마인들 역시 카르타고의 간섭 없이 이 도시들과 무역을 하고 싶어 했다.

figure ⓥ to recognize or understand something
만화와 영화 캐릭터의 작은 인형을 '피규어(figure)'라고 하는데, 피규어를 보면 그 캐릭터를 즉시 떠올릴 수 있다. figure는 '모양, 형태'를 뜻하는 라틴어에서 와서 동사형으로 '형상이나 모양을 알아내다, 실체를 이해하다'라는 뜻이다. to

figure out은 '(완전히) 이해하거나 알아내다'이다.
But when a Carthaginian ship wrecked on the coast of Italy, the Romans took it apart and figured out how to copy it. 그러나 카르타고의 배 한 척이 이탈리아의 해안에서 좌초되었을 때 로마인들은 그 배를 분해해서 똑같이 만드는 법을 알아냈다.

> **Q** 로마와 카르타고의 싸움은 어떻게 시작되었나요?
> **A** 지중해를 사이에 두고 무역을 하던 나라 중에서 에트루리아와 그리스 식민시가 로마에 의해 무너졌어. 로마가 이탈리아 전체를 통일하자 아프리카 북부의 카르타고와 로마는 시칠리아 섬을 가운데 두고 마주보게 되었지. 시칠리아는 카르타고의 영향력 안에 있었단다. 당시 농업국이었던 로마가 힘을 키우자 지중해에 눈독을 들이게 되었어. 그러나 카르타고는 배 만드는 기술이 뛰어난 해상 왕국이었어. 바다에 나가본 경험이 없는 로마인들은 새로운 것을 배우는 일에 겁을 내지 않고 적한테서도 배운다는 긍정적인 정신이 있었단다. 지중해를 노리고 기회를 엿보던 로마인에게도 기회가 왔어. 시칠리아 섬에서 카르타고 용병의 반란이 일어난 거야. 카르타고가 진압을 위해 군대를 파견하자 시칠리아에서 로마에게 도움을 청했지. 얼씨구나 기회가 왔다고 판단한 로마도 시칠리아에 군대를 보내면서 '포에니 전쟁'이 시작되었단다.

victory ⓝ the act of winning a battle or competition

victory는 '정복하다(conquer)'를 뜻하는 라틴어에서 온 것으로, 고대 로마 제국에서 승리한다는 것은 곧 정복한다는 것을 의미했다. 지금은 전쟁뿐만 아니라 스포츠 경기나 선거 등의 경쟁에서 이기는 것을 모두 victory, 즉 '승리'로 표현한다. 검지와 중지 손가락을 벌려 V자를 만드는 것도 Victory의 앞 글자를 상징하는 것이다.
They made lots of sacrifices to their gods, asking for victory. 그들은 자신들이 믿는 신에게 승리를 빌며 많은 제물을 바쳤다.

overboard ⓐ over the side of a boat into the water

board는 나무판이다. 특히 갑판은 board를 이어서 평평하게 만들었기 때문에 board 자체가 '갑판'을 뜻한다. over는 '너머'이므로 overboard는 '갑판 너머'이다. 항해하는 배의 '갑판 너머'에는 뭐가 있을까? '물'이다. 누군가 갑판에서 떨어져 물에 빠졌다면 A man fell overboard!라고 소리쳐야 한다.
Throw the chickens overboard! 저 닭들을 갑판 너머로 던져라!

loom ⓥ to appear as a large unclear shape, usually in a threatening way
loom은 '도구(tool)'를 뜻하는 고대 영어에서 온 것이다. 산업 혁명 시기에 실과 천을 만드는 '도구'인 방적 기계(loom)는 크기가 커서 마치 어떤 커다란 존재가 그림자를 드리우며 나타나는 듯했는데, 이 모습을 loom을 써서 표현할 수 있다. '커다란 형상이 모습을 나타내다, 어렴풋이 보이다, 위험이 닥치다'의 뜻으로 쓰인다.
Suddenly, huge dark shapes loomed up in the snow. 갑자기 눈 속에서 거대하고 시커먼 형상들이 모습을 드러냈다.

stalemate ⓝ a situation of war in which neither side is winning
stalemate에서 stale은 '위치(position), 자리하다(be placed)'를, mate는 '둘, 쌍(pair)'을 뜻한다. 둘이 한 자리를 차지하고 있는 것이 stalemate의 기본적인 의미이다. 전쟁에서 양측이 한곳에 계속 머물러 있으면 어떤 상태일까? 이기지도 지지도 않고 버티는 상황, 즉 어느 쪽도 이기지 못하는 '교착 상태'이다. 그래서 체스(chess)에서도 승부가 나지 못하는 상태를 stalemate라고 한다.
Hannibal saw that the battle between Carthage and Rome at sea was a stalemate—no one was winning. 한니발은 바다에서 카르타고와 로마의 전투가 교착 상태임을 알았다. 어느 쪽도 이기고 있지 않았다.

> **Q** 한니발의 연전연승에도 로마가 무너지지 않은 이유는 무엇이었나요?
> **A** 피레네 산맥과 알프스 산맥마서도 넘은 한니발의 군대가 이탈리아 반도에 들어왔어. 트라시메노 호수와 칸나에 전투에서 한니발의 군대는 로마군을 막다른 궁지까지 몰아넣었지. 칸나에 전투에서는 8만 명 군사 중에서 살아 돌아간 사람이 1만 4천여 명뿐이었다니!
> 이제 로마가 공격받는 것도 시간문제라고 생각했던 사람들은 공포에 떨었지만, 한니발은 로마 공격을 하지 않았어. 진격을 하자고 주장하는 부하들에게 한니발은 3만 명도 안 되는 병력으로 로마를 공략하는 것은 무리이니 카르타고 본국에 병력을 요청하고 기다리자고 했지.
> 그러나 본국에서는 원군을 파견하는 일에 반대하는 세력이 있었어. 왜냐고? 승승장구하는 한니발을 시기하면서 그가 왕이 되려는 야심이 있다는 근거 없는 소문을 퍼뜨렸지. 결국 원군이 왔지만 기병 4,000명과 코끼리 40마리로는 전력에 크게 도움이 되지 않았어.

attack ⓥ to use violence against a person or place, often with weapons
attack은 동사형 '공격하다'와 명사형 '공격'으로 쓰인다. attack에는 '힘'이 실리기 때문에 He attacked me라고 하면 '폭행을 당했다'라는 의미가 된다. '군대를 동원해 공격하다, 폭력을 써서 공격하다, 맹비난하다'의 뜻을 attack으로 표현한다.

He gathered together the best Roman soldiers, sailed down to Carthage, and attacked the city itself. 그는 로마의 최정예 병사들을 모아 배를 타고 카르타고로 가서 그 도시 자체를 공격했다.

bear ⓥ to accept a bad situation
동사형 bear는 어떤 것을 '안에 품고 있다'라는 의미를 갖고 있는데, 책임감과 인내심이 따르는 것을 품고 있는 경우에 자주 쓰인다. 그래서 '참다, 견디다'라는 뜻이다. I can't bear it any longer(나는 그것을 더는 참을 수 없다)에서 bear는 take나 stand로 바꿔 쓸 수 있다. bear-bore-born

He could not bear to think that his great city, Carthage, had been beaten by the Romans who were afraid of his elephants. 한니발은 코끼리들을 두려워하는 로마인들에 의해 자신의 위대한 도시인 카르타고가 패했다는 사실을 생각하면 견딜 수 없었다.

> **Q** 해상 왕국 카르타고를 로마는 어떻게 이길 수 있었나요?
> **A** 시칠리아 섬 남쪽을 정복했다고 전쟁이 끝난 것이 아니었어. 겨우 시작에 불과했지. 로마에게 꼭 필요한 것은 배 만드는 기술과 바다에서 싸우는 전략이었어. 그들은 난파한 카르타고 배를 분해해서 몇 번이나 시행착오를 거치면서 다시 만드는 법을 배웠단다.
> 그러나 항해 기술을 익힌다는 것이 그리 간단한 것이 아니지. 그렇다고 포기할 수는 없는 법! 여기서 등장하는 것이 까마귀야. 진짜 까마귀냐고? 그건 아니고 crow(까마귀)라고 불리는 갈고리를 이용해 카르타고 배를 가까이 끌어오는 거야. 그리고 배와 배 사이에 갑판을 설치해 군인들이 카르타고 배로 올라갈 수 있게 하여 그때부터 지상전과 똑같이 해상전을 진행하는 것이었지. 카르타고인들에게는 상상도 하지 못한 전투 방식이었으니 얼마나 당황했을까? 그렇다고 까마귀 전법으로 로마가 금방 카르타고를 이긴 것은 아니었어. 20년 넘게 전장이 카르타고로 다시 시칠리아로 옮겨가면서 지속되었는데 결국 로마가 승리했단다.

The Story of the World

Chapter 30
The Aryans of India

1 Life on the Ganges River

🌐 인도의 지도를 보면 두 개의 거대한 강이 인도의 북쪽에서 동서로 흐르고 있다. 서쪽의 강은 인더스 문명이 시작된 '인더스 강(Indus River)'이고, 동쪽의 강은 '갠지스 강(Ganges River)'이다. 갠지스 강은 히말라야에서 발원해 벵골 만으로 흐르는, 총 길이 약 2,460킬로미터의 긴 강이다. 갠지스 강 유역은 비옥한 곡창 지대로, 고대부터 힌두 문화의 중심지였다. 인도의 힌두교도들은 지금도 갠지스 강의 물을 성스러운 물로 여겨 죄를 씻는 의미로 목욕을 하고 죽은 자를 화장해 강물에 뿌려 '극락'으로 보낸다. 힌두교(Hinduism)라는 말도 갠지스 강 유역에 살던 사람들을 일컫는 Hindus에서 유래했다.

While the Romans were building their power in Italy, another great civilization was growing in another part of the world—the Indus Valley.

Do you remember reading about Mohenjo-Daro, the mysterious deserted city of the Indus Valley? The citadel cities of the Indus Valley were deserted long, long ago. Maybe the cities were attacked by invaders. Maybe a long drought killed all the crops and forced the people to move away. Perhaps an earthquake destroyed the citadels. •We'll never know for sure.

•But India didn't just sit empty! After the people of the Indus Valley disappeared, new settlers came into India. They were called the *Aryans*, and they came down into India from the north, from the area we call *Asia*.

At first, the Aryans were nomads. But they soon settled down along the two big rivers of India, the Indus River and the Ganges River. They became farmers, just like the people who lived in the first villages of Mesopotamia. They grew crops for food. And like the people of ancient Mesopotamia, the Aryans raised animals, especially horses and cows.

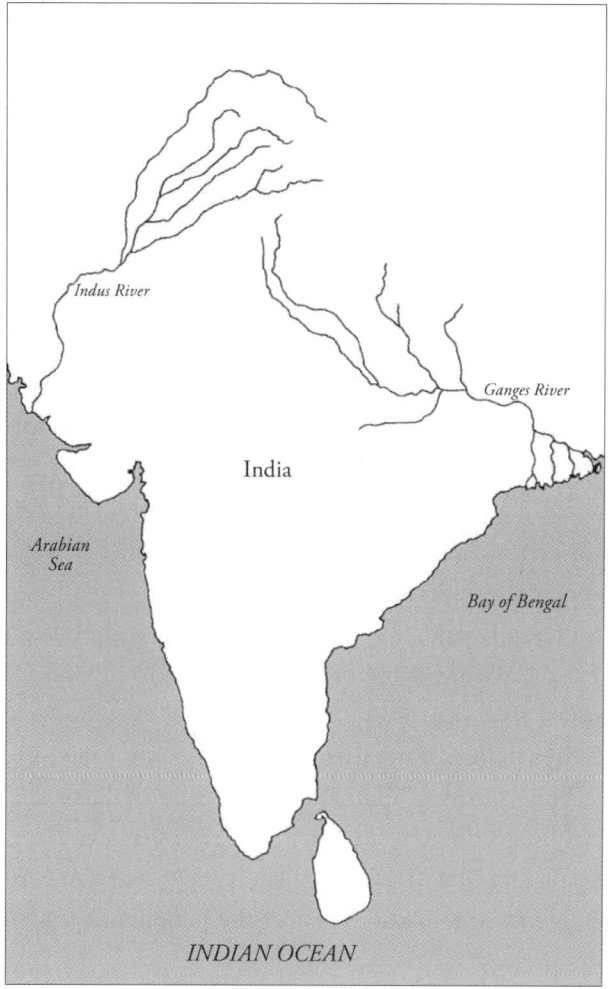

India

Every year, the Ganges River overflowed its banks and left rich, dark soil all over the fields nearby, just like the Nile River in Egypt. The people of ancient India grew wonderful crops in the dirt left by the Ganges River floods. They grew wheat, like the Mesopotamians, and rice, like the Chinese. Without the Ganges

River, the people of India wouldn't have been able to survive. They believed that the river had been provided by their chief god, Shiva, the god of life. Here is the story that the people of ancient India told about Shiva and the Ganges:

Once, the river-goddess Ganga lived in the heavens. She never came down to earth at all; instead, she danced through the skies, bringing water to all who lived in the clouds, but ignoring the ground down below.

The good king of India, King Bhagiratha, grew more and more worried. How could his people survive without water? Surely Ganga would come down from the heavens and bring water to the people who lived on earth. But Ganga refused to come down. She stayed up in the skies with her water—and the people of India were thirsty.

So King Bhagiratha called to Shiva, the god of life. "Shiva!" he cried. "We are dying of thirst! Please, please send Ganga to earth for us."

When Shiva heard Bhagiratha's cries, he called Ganga to his throne. "Ganga," he said, "the people of earth are thirsty. You must go down to the earth and take water to them!"

Ganga refused. "I will not!" she said. "I will stay here in the skies, my favorite place to be. Let the people of earth take care of themselves.

"But I command you!" Shiva answered, "and you must obey me."

At that, Ganga became furious. "Go to earth?" she yelled. "I'll go to earth all right—and drown everyone on it!" She balanced on the top of a cloud, ready to throw herself down to the earth with such violence that water would flood the entire surface of the ground.

But when Shiva saw what she was about to do, he leaped down to earth ahead of her. When Ganga came crashing down, she landed on his head, and her full weight came down on Shiva, instead of on the unhappy people of earth. Water flowed down Shiva's head in seven streams, down onto the thirsty ground beneath him. The seven streams came together into one mighty river—the Ganges River. *And the Ganges River brought life and plenty to all the people who lived along its banks.

The people who believed in Shiva and Ganga were called *Hindus*. Their religion was called *Hinduism*. Like the ancient Egyptians, the Hindus worshipped many different gods. But all Hindu believers worshipped the Ganges River! Today, Hindu pilgrims still come to the banks of the Ganges. *At dusk, they float lighted candles on the water and pray to the river-goddess, Ganga.

2 The Castes of Ancient India

인도의 오래된 신분 제도를 '카스트'라고 부르지만, Caste라는 말 자체는 인도어가 아니다. caste는 16세기에 '혈통'을 뜻하는 스페인어가 영어로 유입된 것이고, 원래는 라틴어에서 유래했다. 인도의 카스트 계급은 크게 네 그룹으로 나뉜다. 제1계급은 '브라만'으로, 힌두교 성직자이다. 제2계급은 '크샤트리아'인 무사 계급인데, 왕족과 귀족이 이에 속한다. 제3계급은 농업, 상업, 공업 등을 담당하는 생산 계급인 '바이샤'라고 부른다. 제4계급은 피정복민, 하인에 해당되는 '수드라'라고 한다. 그리고 그 밑에 어느 계층에도 속하지 못하는 '불가촉천민'이 있다. 자유가 거의 없는 노예들이다. 이는 카스트가 정립될 당시의 신분 기준인데, 이 신분은 자손에게 그대로 상속되어 현재까지 이어지고 있다.

The people of ancient India worshipped Shiva, Ganga, and many other gods. Their religion, called "Hinduism," taught that these gods had created life on earth. Their holy book, the Rig Veda, told the Hindus a story about how life began. The Rig Veda says:

Long, long ago, there was only one gigantic man who lived in the whole universe. His name was Purusha. He had a thousand heads, a thousand eyes, and a thousand feet. The gods looked at Purusha and said, "Let's make a world from this enormous man!"

So the gods turned Purusha's head into the sky, and his eyes into the sun. They turned his legs into the Earth. His breath became the wind. And out of his body, they made four different kinds of people.

The first and most important people were the priests— the *brahmin*. They came out of Purusha's mouth. They were intelligent and wise; as they walked out onto the Earth, they became the most honored people in India. They were given the most delicious food, the finest clothing, and the biggest houses.

Out of Purusha's arms, the gods made the second kind of people—the noble warriors. They rode out onto the Earth on strong, beautiful horses. Their job was to protect the priests from enemies and to rule India. They too had good food and fine clothing, but not quite as fine as that of the priests.

Then the gods made traders and farmers out of Purusha's knees. The traders bought and sold goods; the farmers grew crops and raised their animals. They worked hard every day. They had enough food to keep them from going hungry, warm clothes, and dry houses. Their lives were harder than the lives of warriors and priests.

Finally the gods came to the bottoms of Purusha's feet. Out of his feet, they made a humble group of people—the servants. Servants were not allowed to learn how to read and write. Instead, they spent their lives taking care of the priests, the warriors, and the traders and farmers.

These four groups of people became known as *castes*. If your family belonged to the farmer caste, you could only grow up to be a farmer. You could only marry someone who was also born to be a farmer. You could never be a warrior or a priest. And if your parents were servants, you were doomed to be a servant. Priests, warriors, farmers and traders expected you to serve them for the rest of your life. You would never learn how to read, or to write. You would spend the rest of your life cooking, washing, and cleaning for someone else!

But the poorest people in India were those who didn't belong to the caste system at all. They were called "Untouchables." They weren't priests, or warriors, or farmers and traders, or even servants. They belonged to the poorest, most miserable families in India. The "Untouchables" did all the dirtiest jobs in ancient India. They buried dead animals, cleaned the streets, worked in the fields, and picked up trash. They weren't allowed to drink water from public wells, or to use the same dishes as people from the four castes. The Hindus believed that touching an Untouchable would make them unclean. And they didn't even want to look at the Untouchables who did the dirtiest jobs! These Untouchables were called Unseeables. They were only allowed to do their work at night.

It was a terrible thing to be born into an Untouchable family! Untouchables were poor and badly treated. They weren't allowed to go to the doctor when they were sick. Children from Untouchable families couldn't go to school, or grow up to do jobs that they liked. They had to collect garbage and work in the fields, like their parents. Thousands and thousands of people were Untouchables in ancient India—with no chance ever to be anything else.

3 Siddhartha

🌐 싯다르타는 보리수 그늘에 앉아 오랜 기간 생각을 하며 깨달음을 얻고 부처(Buddha)로 거듭났다. 그래서 불교에서는 보리수를 신성한 나무로 여긴다. 열매가 무화과(fig)처럼 생겼기 때문에 '보리수'를 a wild fig tree로 표현하기도 하는데, 실제로 인도의 보리수는 무화과 나무와는 달리 높이가 30미터나 자랄 만큼 큰 나무이다. 그늘에 앉아 있을 만하다. '보리수(菩提樹)'라는 말 자체는 인도의 나무 이름을 한자로 번역하면서 만들어졌는데 '깨달음의 나무'라는 뜻이다.

The priests, warriors, and rulers of ancient India lived well. They had good food and drink, soft beds to sleep in, beautiful clothes, and servants to do anything they asked. The traders and farmers of India weren't quite as well off—but they also had food to eat, decent houses to live in, and enough money to take care of themselves and their families.

But the servants who belonged to the lowest caste of India worked hard for very little money. They had to do the jobs that the priests, warriors, rulers, traders, and farmers didn't want to do. Servants didn't have nice houses or clothes. They weren't even allowed to learn how to read. And the Untouchables were even more miserable than the servants. Untouchables couldn't even be friends with servants. They were only allowed to talk to each other. They spent their days doing dirty, disgusting jobs. And at the end of the day, they weren't even paid enough money to eat properly or to buy warm clothes.

Long ago, a prince named Siddhartha lived in India. He didn't know how miserable the servants and Untouchables were, because he was surrounded by beauty and luxury every moment of his life. His proud father, King Suddhodana, built three palaces for his son! He gave Siddhartha a thousand servants to wait on him hand and foot. He hired the best tutors to teach his son how to write poetry, play music, fence, and wrestle. At night, Siddhartha slept on rich, soft sheets, while musicians played beautiful music to lull him to sleep. In the morning, servants brought him his meals in bed, while poets read to him and other servants burned incense to make his room smell sweet and fragrant.

But in time, Siddhartha became curious about the world outside. "What is outside the palace walls?" he asked his father. "I want to go and see the city around me."

"There's nothing that you need to see out there," his father answered. "Stay here in the palace. Eat the good food I've provided for you. Enjoy the music and the poetry!"

But Siddhartha kept begging his father to let him go outside. Finally, Suddhodana agreed. But he told Siddhartha's chariot driver to stay only in the streets near the palace. He ordered all of these streets swept, and the fronts of the buildings scrubbed and repainted. He drove all the sick and poor away, into other parts of the city. At last, he allowed his son to go out.

At first Siddhartha was delighted. "The city is as beautiful as my palace!" he exclaimed. "How wonderful it must be to live in this city! And how fortunate its people are!"

But as his chariot turned a corner, Siddhartha saw an old, old man, dragging himself along with the help of two sticks. "Who is that?" he asked his chariot driver. "What is wrong with him?"

"That is an old, poor man," the chariot driver said. "He can barely see or walk, and the only food he is given is the food that he can beg from generous people passing by. Everyone will grow old and feeble in time. Even you, Siddhartha."

Siddhartha had never before seen an old person. He was horrified. But he was even more distressed a few minutes later, when they passed a man sitting on the sidewalk, bent double in pain and pleading for help.

"What is wrong with that man?" he asked.

"He is sick," the chariot driver said, "and no one will help him, because he is an Untouchable. Soon he will die."

"What is death?" Siddhartha asked.

"Death is the end of life," the chariot driver told him. "We will all die. Even you, Siddhartha!"

A Statue of the Buddha

Siddhartha returned to his palace, struck with grief and misery. He had never known that people lived in pain and suffering, or that all men will die. The luxuries all around him seemed false and wrong. So he took off his fine clothes, put on the poor clothes of a beggar, and went out into the world.

For years and years, Siddhartha lived the life of a beggar. He spent his time trying to find out why people must grow old and sick, and finally die.

One day, Siddhartha was sitting beneath a wild fig tree, thinking about the mysteries of life. Suddenly, he exclaimed, "I understand! Everyone, no matter how poor, sick, or miserable, can find happiness by leading a good life!"

From then on, Siddhartha was known as the Buddha. He taught his followers that they should be honest, make peace with their enemies, and avoid violence. The followers of the Buddha became known as *Buddhists*. Soon, many people in ancient India were Buddhists. Today, Buddhism is followed by many, many people, both in India and in other countries around the world.

Note to Parent: The Aryan people probably came into India around 1500 BC/BCE; their civilization reached a high point around 500 BC/BCE, when sixteen separate kingdoms existed in the northern part of India. Siddhartha Gautama (the Buddha) lived around 563–483 BC/BCE.

The Story of the Words

Chapter 30 The Aryans of India

1 Life on the Ganges River

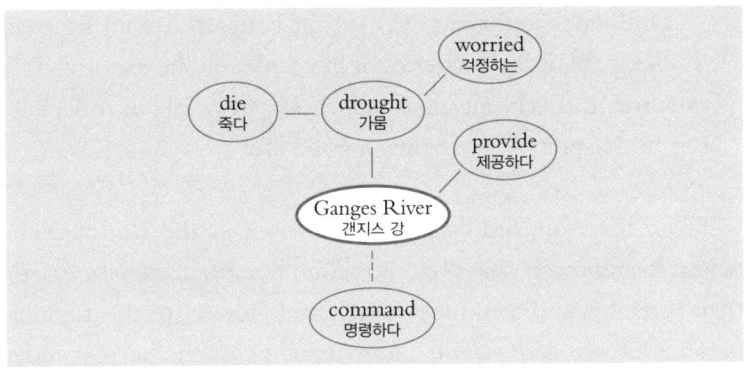

drought ⓝ a time when no rain falls and the land becomes very dry

drought는 '가뭄'이다. 오랫동안 비가 오지 않아 메마른 상태인 dryness를 의미한다. dry(마른, 건조한)와 어원이 같다. '가뭄을 겪다'는 to have a drought로써 We are having a long drought in our region(우리 지역은 오랜 가뭄을 겪고 있다)처럼 쓸 수 있다.

Maybe a long drought killed all the crops and forced the people to move away. 아마도 오랜 가뭄으로 농작물이 모두 죽고 사람들이 다른 곳으로 이주할 수밖에 없었을 것이다.

provide ⓥ to give something to someone

provide는 '제공하다, 공급하다'라는 뜻이다. 흔히 provide A for B=provide B with A의 형태로 써서 'B에게 A를 공급하다'라는 뜻이다. We provide food for hungry children=We provide hungry children with food(우리는 굶주린 아이들에게 음식을 제공한다)처럼 쓸 수 있다. 그런데 provide에서 pro-는 '미리'를, vide는 '보다(see)'를 뜻한다. 즉 미리 예상하고 대비해서 뭔가를 주는 것이 provide의 의미이다.

They believed that the river had been provided by their chief god, Shiva, the god of life. 그들은 가장 위대한 신인 생명의 신 시바가 그 강을 준 것이라고 믿었다.

worried ⓐ unhappy or anxious because of something bad
worry는 '걱정하다, 걱정하게 만들다'라는 동사이다. 걱정을 하고 있는 상태를 표현하는 형용사는 worried로 표현한다. 그래서 걱정 많은 엄마는 자식에게 I'm worried about you(난 네가 걱정 돼)라는 말을 자주 한다. 지금 내가 걱정하고 있는 상태라는 의미이다.
The good king of India, King Bhagiratha, grew more and more worried. 인도의 선한 왕인 바기라타 왕은 점점 더 걱정이 커졌다.

die ⓥ to stop living
We are dying of thirst!에서 dying은 동사 die의 진행형이다. die는 이승에서 저승으로 이동하는 찰나의 동작, 변화를 표현하는 것이다. 즉 '죽다, 사망하다'이다. 물을 마시지 못해 그 사람들이 실제로 죽었으면 They died of thirst라고 표현할 수 있다. 이처럼 die of 뒤에는 죽음의 원인이 온다. die from도 같은 용법으로 He died of[from] cancer(그는 암으로 사망했다)처럼 쓸 수 있다.
We are dying of thirst! 우린 물이 없어 죽어가고 있어요!

command ⓥ to order someone to do something
command에서 com-은 '세게, 강하게'의 뜻을 갖는 강조 접두사이다. 그리고 mand에는 '손 안에 주다(give into one's hand)'라는 뜻이 담겨 있다. 돈이나 먹을 것을 준다는 의미가 아니라 반드시 실행해야 할 임무를 준다는 의미이다. 그래서 command는 '명령하다'라는 뜻이고, 명사형으로 '명령'이 된다. 기독교 성경에서 하느님이 모세에게 반드시 실행하라고 준 '십계명'도 영어로 The Ten Commandments이다.
"But I command you! Shiva answered, "and you must obey me." 시바가 대답했다. "그러나 내가 너에게 명령하면 넌 나에게 복종해야 한다."

> **Q** 인도인들은 갠지스 강을 아직도 신성하게 여긴다면서요?
> **A** 이 책에 소개된 강의 여신 '강가'와 생명의 신 '시바' 이야기를 재미있게 읽었니? 아리아인이 처음 도착한 곳이 인더스 강 근처였는데, 그들은 계속 동쪽으로 이동했어. 지리적으로 보면 인더스 강보다 갠지스 강 유역이 더 비옥했지만, 인더스 강의 문제는 강우량이 많아서 홍수가 자주 일어나고

농사짓기 힘든 땅이었다는 거야.
철을 잘 다루던 인도인들은 농사를 지으면서도 자신들의 그 기술을 적극적으로 활용했어. 덕분에 갠지스 강의 불리한 조건을 극복하고 정착하게 되었지. 이제 인도인들은 갠지스 강 주변에 살게 되었단다. 그들은 물이 인간의 몸과 마음을 맑게 해주는 것으로 생각했어. 그러니 그들이 나중에 정착해서 살게 된 갠지스 강을 신성시하는 것은 당연한 것이었지. 가장 신성한 장소는 강과 강이 합쳐지는 지점인 '바라나시'였어. 지금도 이곳에서는 인도인들이 물을 긷고, 목욕을 하고, 심지어는 죽은 사람을 화장한 재를 흘려보내고 있단다.

2 The Castes of Ancient India

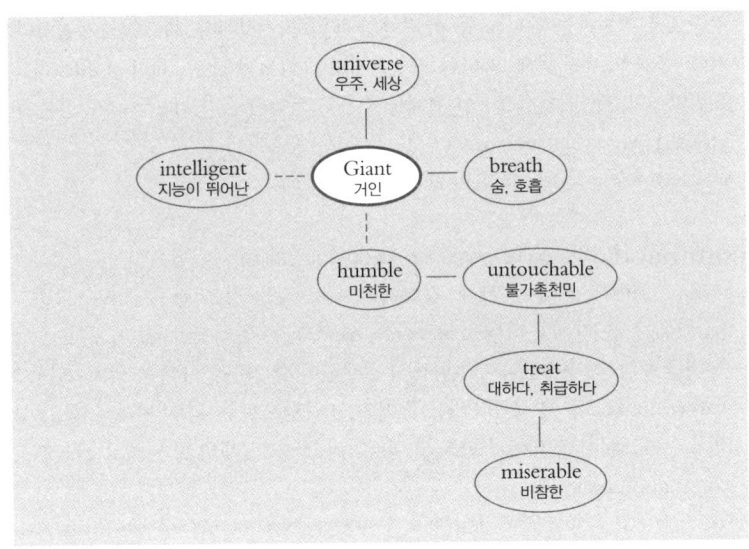

universe ⓝ all the space, stars etc. that exist

 universe에서 uni-는 '다 함께(all together)'이고, verse는 '돌다(turn)'라는 뜻이다. 즉 '다 함께 돈다'라는 의미이다. 그럼 무엇이 다 함께 어디를 돈다는 것일까? 처음에 유럽 사람들은 지구가 우주의 중심이라고 믿었다. 그래서 태양, 달, 별 등 우주의 모든 것이 다 함께 지구의 둘레를 돈다고 생각했다. 물론 사실은 아니었지만 universe는 그때부터 '우주, 세상'이라는 의미가 되었다.

148

Long, long ago, there was only one gigantic man who lived in the whole universe. 아주 오래 전에, 전 우주에는 단 한 명의 거인만이 살고 있었다.

breath ⓝ the air that you take in and let out through your nose or mouth
breath는 '숨, 호흡, 입김'이다. 공기를 코와 입으로 흡입하면 폐를 거쳐서 산소를 혈액에 공급하게 되고, 다시 몸 안의 이산화탄소를 공기 중으로 배출하게 된다. 이런 공기의 흐름이 breath이다. '숨을 쉬다, 호흡하다'라는 동사형은 breathe이다.
His breath became the wind. 그의 숨은 바람이 되었다.

intelligent ⓐ able to learn and understand things quickly
intelligent는 라틴어에서 유래한 말로, '~중에(between)'와 '선택하다(choose)'라는 말이 합쳐진 것이다. 여기서 '선택'은 찍는 것과는 차원이 다른, 올바르게 선택한다는 의미이다. 즉 여럿 중에 올바른 것을 선택하는 능력을 갖춰야 intelligent라는 말을 붙일 수 있다. intelligent는 '똑똑한, 지능이 뛰어난'이고, 명사형인 intelligence는 '지능'이다.
They were intelligent and wise; as they walked out onto the Earth, they became the most honored people in India. 그들은 지능이 뛰어났고 현명했다. 그래서 그들은 세상으로 걸어 나오면서 인도에서 가장 존귀한 사람들이 되었다.

humble ⓐ having a low social class or position
hum은 '땅(ground), 흙(earth)'을 의미한다. humble은 라틴어에서 유래하여 '땅에 가까운'을 뜻한다. 머리와 몸을 땅 쪽으로 가깝게 숙이는 모습을 표현한 것이다. 긍정적 의미로는 '겸손한, 겸허한'을 뜻하고, 부정적인 의미로는 '미천한, 보잘것없는'을 뜻한다. 본문 내용에 따르면 하인들(servants)은 거인의 몸 중에서 '땅에 닿는' 발로 만들었으니 humble이라는 표현이 잘 어울린다.
Out of his feet, they made a humble group of people—the servants. 그들은 거인의 발로 미천한 사람들인 하인들을 만들었다.

untouchable ⓝ the lowest social class in the Indian Caste
인도의 카스트에서 최하층민인 '불가촉천민'을 영어로 Untouchable이라고 한다. 이들은 상위 계층 사람의 몸에 손을 대서는 안 된다. 또한 상위 계층의 사람들도 이들이 더럽고 천하다고 느껴 접촉을 하지 않아서 '만질 수 없는'이라는 의미로 Untouchable이라고 부르는 것이다. 그런데 이 의미를 제외하고 영어에서 untouchable은 대단히 '막강한'이라는 뜻을 지닌 단어이다. 왕의 몸에 함부로 손을 대면 엄벌에 처해진다. 왜냐하면 The king is untouchable(왕은 막강하다)이기 때문이다.
They were called "Untouchables." 그들은 '불가촉천민'으로 불렸다.

> **Q 카스트가 아니라 '바르나'고요?**
> **A** 우리가 카스트 제도라고 알고 있는 인도의 계급 구분은 바르나(피부색)에서 시작되었어. 우선 카스트라는 단어는 포르투갈인이 인도에 온 이후 포르투갈어에서 유래되었어. 피부색 구분으로 시작된 이 제도는 인도인의 생활을 규제하는 강력한 힘을 발휘하게 되었어. 계급 간의 결혼은 허용되지 않았고, 지위는 세습되었어.
> 이렇게 불합리한 제도가 오래 유지될 수 있었던 것은 왜일까? 그들은 카르마(업)를 믿었거든. 자신이 태어난 카스트는 전생의 업 때문이지, 남탓이 아니라고 생각한 거야. 또한 지금 이 세상에서 열심히 살면 다음 생에서 다른 존재가 될 수 있다고 믿었으니 저항 없이 유지될 수 있었던 거지.

miserable ⓐ very unhappy or uncomfortable

19세기 프랑스의 대문호인 빅토르 위고(Victor Hugo)의 작품 《레미제라블(Les Miserables)》을 기억할 것이다. 주인공 장발장이 빵을 훔친 죄로 감옥에 가면서 파란만장한 인생을 산다는 내용이다. 이 작품의 제목 Les Miserables은 '비참한[불쌍한] 사람들'이라는 뜻이다. miserable은 프랑스어에서 영어로 유입되었다. 외부의 환경에 의해 물질적, 정신적으로 비참해진 상태를 표현하는 형용사가 바로 miserable이다. 명사형 misery는 '고통, 비참함, 빈곤'을 뜻한다.
They belonged to the poorest, most miserable families in India. 불가촉천민들은 인도에서 가장 가난하고 가장 비참한 집안의 사람들이었다.

treat ⓥ to behave toward someone in a particular way

로큰롤의 제왕으로 불린 엘비스 프레슬리(Elvis Presley)의 노래 중에 Treat me like a fool이 있는데, 이 노래를 잠깐 불러볼까? Treat me like a fool(절 바보로 대해 주세요) Treat me mean and cruel(절 야비하고 잔인하게 다뤄 주세요) But love me(하지만 사랑해주세요). 어떻게 '대하든(treat)' 사랑만 해달라는 내용이다. 이렇게 동사형 treat은 사람이나 동물, 물건 등을 '대하다, 다루다, 취급하다'라는 뜻이다.

Untouchables were poor and badly treated. 불가촉천민들은 가난했으며 나쁜 대우를 받았다.

3 Siddhartha

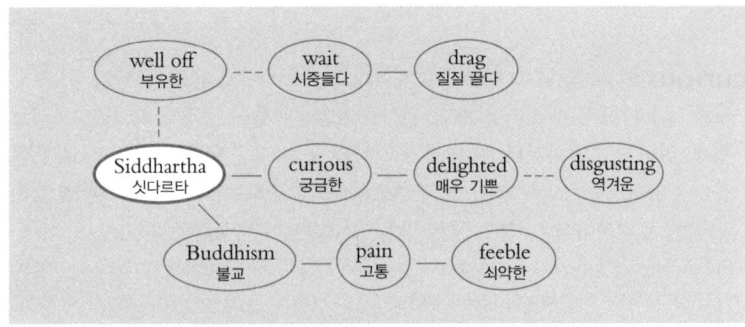

well off ⓐ having enough money to live in comfort
well-off로 표기하고 한 단어로 취급하기도 한다. 이 단어에서 핵심은 off인데 '단절, 분리'를 뜻한다. 그럼 well-off는 무엇과의 단절을 했다는 의미일까? 바로 '가난, 돈 걱정'이다. 먹고 살 걱정, 돈 걱정 없는 넉넉한 상태가 바로 well-off이다. 즉 '잘사는, 부유한, 유복한'이라는 뜻이다.
The traders and farmers of India weren't quite as well off—but they also had food to eat, decent houses to live in, and enough money to take care of themselves and their families. 상인들과 농부들은 그만큼 잘살지는 못했다. 그러나 그들 역시 먹을 음식과 살 수 있는 괜찮은 집, 자신과 가족을 돌보기에 충분한 돈이 있었다.

disgusting ⓐ very unhappy or uncomfortable
disgusting에서 앞의 dis-는 '반대, 역(逆)'을 뜻하는데, '맛이 역겹다'는 의미에서 발전하여, disgust는 명사형 '역겨움'과 동사형 '역겹게 만들다'라는 뜻이다. 형용사형 disgusting은 '역겨운, 구역질 나는'으로 쓰인다.
They spent their days doing dirty, disgusting jobs. 그들은 더럽고 역겨운 일을 하면서 살았다.

wait ⓥ to serve someone
웨이터(waiter)나 웨이트리스(waitress)는 항상 손님이 부를 수 있는 거리에서

'기다리고(wait)' 있어야 한다. 그래야 손님의 요구를 바로 들어줄 수 있기 때문이다. 옛날 하인들도 마찬가지였다. 즉시 시중을 들 수 있게 주인이 부르기를 '기다리고' 있어야 했다. 그래서 '기다리다'라는 뜻의 동사 wait에 on이 붙으면 '시중들다, 서빙하다'라는 뜻이 된다.
He gave Siddhartha a thousand servants to wait on him hand and foot. 왕은 싯다르타에게 천 명의 하인들을 주어 충실하게 그를 시중들게 했다.

curious ⓐ wanting to know something or learn about something
사람이나 어떤 물건을 처음 보면 '뭘까?' 하고 궁금증이 생긴다. 그리고 '조심스럽게' 접근해서 알아본다. 이렇게 호기심을 품는 것을 형용사 curious로 표현한다. curious는 '조심스러운, 신중한(careful)'을 뜻하는 라틴어에서 온 것으로, '궁금한, 호기심이 많은, 알고 싶은'이다. 명사형 '호기심, 궁금증'은 curiosity이다.
But in time, Siddhartha became curious about the world outside. 그러나 시간이 지나자 싯다르타는 바깥세상이 궁금해졌다.

delighted ⓐ very pleased or happy
delight는 명사형으로 '큰 기쁨, 대단한 즐거움'을 뜻하고, 동사형으로는 '큰 기쁨을 주다, 무척 즐겁게 하다'이다. 감정을 움직이는 동사는 모두 타동사이고, delight도 예외가 아니다. 예를 들어 The news delighted him → He was delighted by the news(그는 그 소식을 듣고 무척 기뻤다)처럼 주어의 감정 상태는 수동형으로 표현한다. 이처럼 delighted는 '무척 기쁜' 감정 상태를 표현하는 형용사로 쓰인다.
At first Siddhartha was delighted. 처음에 싯다르타는 될 듯이 기뻤다.

drag ⓥ to pull something heavy along behind you
drag의 기본적인 의미는 저항력을 갖고 있는 어떤 물체를 '잡아끌다(draw, pull)'이다. 그래서 컴퓨터를 사용할 때 마우스 버튼을 누르고 한 방향으로 '끌어서' 원하는 글자나 이미지, 아이콘 등을 움직이는 동작을 '드래깅(dragging)'이라고 한다. 이처럼 신경을 써서, 힘을 주어 뭔가를 끄는 것이 drag이다. 노쇠하고 병약한 사람들에게는 자기 몸이 천근만근이어서 to drag oneself(자기 몸을 질질 끌다)라는 표현도 쓸 수 있다.
But as his chariot turned a corner, Siddhartha saw an old, old man, dragging himself along with the help of two sticks. 그러나 마차가 모퉁이를 돌자, 지팡이 두 개에 의지해 자신의 몸을 끌다시피 움직이는 늙은, 아주 늙은 노인이 싯다르타의 눈에 들어왔다.

feeble ⓐ very weak

feeble은 병이 들거나 늙어서 '쇠약한' 상태를 뜻한다. 원래 '비통한 (lamentable)'을 뜻하는 라틴어에서 왔다. 병이 들거나 늙으면, 과거의 인생과 자신의 현재 모습을 비교하며 한탄하기도 한다. 눈도 침침하고, 귀도 멀고, 다리에 힘도 없고, 병치레도 자주 한다. 이런 상태가 바로 feeble이다.

Everyone will grow old and feeble in time. 시간이 지나면 결국 모두 늙고 쇠약해진다.

pain ⓝ the feeling that you are hurt physically or emotionally

Pain is the proof of existence(고통은 존재의 증거다)라는 말이 있다. 삶 자체가 고통이라는 의미이다. 이 문장에서 pain이 바로 '고통'이라는 뜻이다. I have a pain in my chest(가슴에 통증이 있어요)처럼 육체적인 '통증, 아픔'을 표현할 수도 있고, Divorce causes great pain for children(이혼은 자녀들에게 큰 고통을 준다)처럼 정신적 '고통'을 표현할 수도 있다.

He had never known that people lived in pain and suffering, or that all men will die. 그는 이제껏 사람들이 고통과 역경 속에서 살아간다는 사실도, 모든 사람이 죽게 된다는 사실도 알지 못했다.

Buddhism ⓝ the religion based on the teachings of Buddha

부처의 가르침을 진리로 믿고 그에 따라 삶을 사는 것이 Buddhism이다. 흔히 내세관이 결합된 종교로서의 '불교(佛敎)'도 Buddhism이라고 한다. 불교를 믿는 사람은 Buddhist이다. 두 단어 모두 '부처'의 영어 이름인 Buddha에서 온 것이다. 부처는 '깨달음을 얻은 자'라는 뜻이다.

Today, Buddhism is followed by many, many people, both in India and in other countries around the world. 오늘날 불교는 인도를 비롯해 전 세계 여러 나라에서 아주 많은 사람들이 믿고 있다

> **Q** 종교 발생이 '브라만교-불교-힌두교'의 순서라고요?
>
> **A** 이 책에서는 힌두교 다음에 불교를 소개하고 있지만, 좀 더 정확하게 말하면 '브라만교-불교-힌두교'의 순서로 종교가 생겼어. 브라만의 특권에 의문을 갖는 사람들이 늘면서 생긴 것이 우파니샤드야. 우파니샤드란 '비밀스런 지혜'란 뜻인데, 이런 지혜를 여러 이야기에 담아 전해 주는 경전이야. 우파니샤드에 관심을 갖는 사람들은 주로 자신의 내면, 즉 나란 무엇인가에 몰두했어.

기원전 6세기 중반이 되자 계급 차별에 반대하는 신흥 종교가 생겼는데, 그것이 바로 불교야. 불교는 당시 갠지스 강 주변에 세워진 신흥 도시 국가들에게서 상당한 지원을 받았어. 왜냐고? 도시 국가를 다스리게 된 크샤트리아 계급, 상공업으로 돈을 번 바이샤 계급에겐 브라만교의 교리가 장애물로 느껴졌거든. 카스트 제도에 반대하는 불교는 이들에게 신선하게 받아들여져 부처와 제자들이 머무를 수 있는 장소, 설법할 수 있는 기회를 기꺼이 제공했어.

자, 이어서 브라만의 입장에서 생각해보자. 이런 현상이 더욱 확대되면 자신들의 위치가 위험하다고 느끼지 않았을까? 브라만들도 필사적으로 대중 속으로 들어가려고 했지. 토착 신앙의 신까지 받아들이려고 노력한 결과 리그베다(고대 인도의 힌두교 성전(聖殿) 중의 하나)에서는 존재감이 약하던 신 비슈누와 시바를 앞에 내세우게 되었어. 이러한 노력을 하기 전의 종교가 브라만교라면, 오랜 기간의 노력으로 불교의 부처마저 자신들의 신으로 흡수한 종교가 힌두교란다.

The Story of the World

Chapter 31
The Mauryan Empire of India

1 The Empire United

기원전 3세기 인도 마우리아 왕조의 제3대 왕인 아소카(Asoka)는 남부의 정복 전쟁을 마친 후, 전쟁의 참상을 직접 보고서 깊은 생각에 잠긴다. 그리고 부처의 가르침을 받아들이고 불교를 국교로 삼아 불교의 발전과 보급에 힘쓴다. 아소카 왕은 인도 곳곳에 높이가 10~13미터에 이르는 거대한 돌기둥을 세우고 부처의 가르침에 기초한 자신의 세계관과 통치관 등을 새겨 놓았는데, 이 돌기둥들을 '아소카 왕의 석주(The Pillars of Asoka)'라고 부른다. 여기에는 '종교들 사이의 소통은 선한 것이다. 다른 이들이 따르는 가르침에도 귀 기울이고 그것을 존중하라' 같은 문구들이 새겨져 있다.

When we read about Egypt, we learned that Egypt was divided into two parts—Lower Egypt and Upper Egypt. The Lower and Upper Egyptians fought each other until King Narmer made them all into one country. After the Egyptians stopped fighting each other, Egypt grew to be rich and strong.

When we read about the Akkadian Empire, we learned that Sumer was full of lots of independent cities. Each one had its own army, its own king, and its own way of doing things. But Sargon, the first great Akkadian king, united all the cities into one empire with one king and one set of laws. Sargon and King Narmer did the same thing! *They made people who were quarrelling and fighting with each other be friends and allies.

We also read about two cities that refused to be allies. Two great Greek cities, Athens and Sparta, fought with each other for years and years, until both cities were weak and tired. After Athens and Sparta were finished fighting each other, the Macedonians came down and conquered both cities! Athens and Sparta were too worn out to resist.

All of these countries were weak when they were divided, and strong when they were united. India was no different. When the Aryans first settled in India, they built lots of different cities. The cities belonged to many different small kingdoms. Each kingdom was independent, and the kings of these little kingdoms spent many years fighting each other.

But one family of Indian kings wanted India to be a strong, unified country. They united the different Indian cities together into one empire—the Mauryan Empire. This empire covered the whole northern part of India.

The most famous Mauryan emperor was named Asoka. He became king around 268 BC/BCE. Asoka conquered cities through India in a war that killed thousands of people. But when Asoka visited the defeated cities after his great victories, he saw the suffering that his soldiers had caused.

"I will no longer fight with an army," he announced. "Instead, I will draw people into my empire through honesty, truthfulness, and mercy. I will follow the teachings of the Buddha and give up violence from now on!"

Asoka renounced war after seeing the suffering it caused

Asoka carved these ideas on stone monuments and pillars and set them up all around his empire. We can still read them today. *He tried to reason with his subjects, rather than giving out strict, harsh commands. He tried to act kindly and mercifully to all his people. He had trees planted along the roads, so that travelers could walk in the shade. He built hospitals for sick people and for sick animals as well. He even made laws to keep people from being cruel to animals, and he became a vegetarian (someone who doesn't eat meat) so that no animals would be killed for his food. Asoka became famous for his ideas and for his just, merciful rule.

2 The Jakata Tales

자카타 이야기(The Jakata Tales)는 오랜 세월 동안 인도에서 전래된 불교 설화를 모아 부처의 전생을 우화의 형식에 대입해 풀어낸 것이다. 자카타(Jakata)라는 말은 '전생(前生)'을 뜻한다. 자카타 이야기는 본생경(本生經)이나 본생담(本生譚)으로 불리기도 한다. 이 이야기들에서 부처는 전생에서 왕, 수행자, 상인 등 인간의 모습이나 원숭이, 비둘기, 코끼리 등의 동물의 모습으로 등장하기도 한다. 불교에서 가장 중요한 개념 중 하나인 윤회(輪廻)를 바탕으로 지금 세상에서 어떻게 살아야 다음 생에서 복된 인간으로 태어날 수 있는지, 부처의 가르침이 무엇인지 잘 보여주고 있다.

King Asoka gave up fighting and stopped eating meat because of the teachings of the Buddha. Many of these teachings are written down in one of India's most famous books. It has a very long name—the Mahayana Tripitaka. This book contains all sorts of writings, but some of the best-known writings are called the Jakata Tales. According to legend, these tales were told by the Buddha to show the people of ancient India how to live. The stories explain that goodness, patience, mercy, honesty, and friendship will bring happiness.

One of these stories, called "The Hare," teaches that generosity will be rewarded. Here is how the story goes:

Once upon a time, a hare, an otter, a jackal, and a monkey lived together in a deep wood near a village. Through the deep wood wound a long, dark path. Many travelers walked along the path, traveling to the village on the forest's other side.

One night, the hare, the otter, the jackal, and the monkey sat together around their evening meal. "Tomorrow is a special day in the village on the other side of the forest," the hare said. "We should be ready to give food to anyone who is traveling to the village. Let's be generous and give our best to any traveler who asks."

The otter, the jackal, and the monkey agreed. The next morning, the otter went out to the river nearby to hunt for food. Now, that same morning a fisherman had caught seven red fish and buried them in the damp sand to keep them fresh. Then he had gone off downstream to fish some more. The otter smelled the fish and dug them up. "Whose are these?" he asked, looking around. "I don't see anyone to claim them. I'll take them home and eat them myself."

The jackal went out to the edge of the village on the other side of the forest and sniffed around a poor man's hut. In the poor man's kitchen, he found two pieces of meat and a jar of milk. "Well, I don't see anyone in this hut!" he said. "So I'll just take these home and eat them myself."

The monkey climbed up a forest tree and picked mangoes for himself. He scurried back down the tree and hid the mangoes in his own bed. "Later," he said, "I'll eat these myself."

The hare went out into the field and started to pick grass. Grass was his favorite food. But then he stopped and thought, "A traveler will not want to eat grass! What else can I feed a hungry man who asks for food? I have nothing else! If someone begs me for a meal, I will offer myself for his dinner."

From up above, the god Sakka heard the hare's promise. "Can this be true?" he said to himself. "Will this hare really be so generous and unselfish as to give his own life? I will go down to the earth and see."

So Sakka disguised himself as a priest and went down to the earth. He walked along the forest path. Soon he saw the monkey. "Monkey, monkey," he cried, "I am so hungry! Will you give me food?"

"I could share a mango or two," the monkey offered.

"Thank you," said Sakka. "I'll come back for it tomorrow."

Next he saw the jackal. "Jackal, jackal," he cried, "I am so hungry! Will you give me food?"

"Well," the jackal said, "you can have one of my pieces of meat, and a drink of my milk."

"Thank you," said Sakka, "I'll come back for it tomorrow."

A little further along the way, he saw the otter. "Otter, otter," he cried, "I am so hungry! Will you give me food?"

"You can have two or three of my fish," the otter suggested.

"Thank you," said Sakka. "I'll come back for it tomorrow."

Finally, Sakka met the hare. "Hare, hare," he said, "I am so hungry! Will you give me food?"

"All I have is myself," said the hare, "but you are welcome to eat me."

"But I am a follower of the Buddha!" Sakka objected. "I cannot kill an animal for food!"

"Then light a fire," the hare said, "and I will jump into it myself. Then I will be roasted for you to eat—and you won't have to kill me."

So Sakka built a fire. The hare shook himself, crouched down, and jumped into the flames. But although the fire licked at his fur, he felt no heat.

"Why isn't this fire hot?" the hare asked. "It won't roast me so that you can eat!"

"Because I am no priest," Sakka said. "I am the god Sakka, come down to earth to see whether you would be as generous as you promised. Now, good and generous hare, live happily the rest of your life with my blessing." And he made the hare a nest of soft grass, and returned to his place in the sky. The hare lived happily ever after, and when he died he was rewarded for his kindness.

Note to Parent: The Mauryan Empire lasted from 321–233 BC/BCE. Asoka ruled from 268–233 BC/BCE; the Mauryan empire began to disintegrate after his death.

The Story of the Words
Chapter 31 The Mauryan Empire of India

1 The Empire United

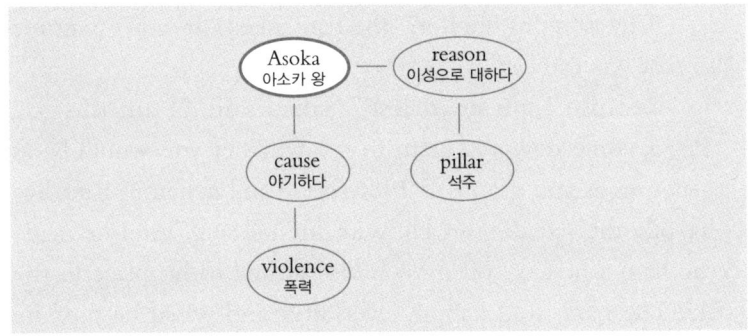

cause ⓥ to make something happen

    cause는 '원인, 이유'라는 뜻의 명사형과 '원인을 제공하다'의 동사형으로도 쓰인다. 동사 cause가 쓰인 문장에는 항상 '원인과 결과(cause and effect)'가 명시된다. A careless driver caused the accident(한 부주의한 운전자가 그 사고를 일으켰다)에서 원인은 a careless driver이고, 결과는 the accident이다. 이렇게 cause는 '~을 일으키다, ~을 발생하게 하다, ~의 원인이다'라는 뜻이다.
But when Asoka visited the defeated cities after his great victories, he saw the suffering that his soldiers had caused. 그러나 대승을 거둔 후 아소카가 패한 도시들을 방문했을 때, 자신의 병사들이 일으킨 고통을 보게 되었다.

violence ⓝ behavior that hurts someone in a physical way

    violence는 '폭력, 폭력 행위'이다. 물리적인 힘을 사용해 다른 사람을 제압하고 자신의 뜻을 관철시키는 것이 violence이다. 형용사형 violent는 '폭력적인, 난폭한'을 뜻하는데, 어떤 반응이나 현상이 '격렬한, 맹렬한' 상태를 표현하기도 한다. 폭력은 폭력을 낳는다(Violence begets violence). 그래서 부처는 비폭력(non-violence)을 강조했고, 아소카 왕도 부처의 뜻을 따르기로 결심했다.

I will follow the teachings of the Buddha and give up violence from now on! 나는 지금부터 부처의 가르침을 따라 폭력을 쓰지 않을 것이다!

> **Q** 아소카 왕은 어떤 계기로 불교에 귀의하게 되었나요?
>
> **A** 아버지에 이어 정복 활동을 마무리한 아소카 왕은 잔인한 성격으로, 처음부터 다르마(불교의 법)를 중히 여기는 사람은 아니었단다. 탁실라 지역에서 총독으로 근무하다 아버지의 병이 위독하다는 소식을 듣고 수도로 돌아왔지. 그때 그는 99명의 형제를 살해하고 왕이 되었어.
> 즉위한 후 정치적으로 안정되자 기원전 261년, 그는 군대를 이끌고 칼링가 왕국에 쳐들어갔어. 칼링가 왕국은 작은 나라임에도 불구하고 마우리아 제국에 굴복하지 않았지. 본때를 보여주리라 결심한 아소카 왕은 무자비할 정도로 칼링가 왕국 사람들을 죽였단다. 전투가 끝나고 환호하는 군사들을 뒤로 한 채, 전장에 누워 있는 사람들을 보다가 아소카 왕은 갑자기 진저리를 쳤대. 왜 자신이 이렇게까지 했을까? 후회하며 칼링가 전투를 계기로 그는 힘에 의한 지배를 포기했어. 그리고 앞으로는 '다르마'에 의한 통치를 펴기로 결심하여 각 지역에 석주(돌기둥)를 세워 내용을 알렸단다.

pillar ⓝ a tall upright round post, used as a support for a building or as a monument

pillar는 '긴 원기둥'이다. 건축에 쓰면 다리 상판이나 건물의 지붕을 받치는 '지주(支柱), 대들보'를 뜻한다. 본체를 떠받치는 중요한 역할을 하는 것이 pillar이다. 우뚝 서 있는 pillar는 멀리서도 잘 보이고, 주변 사람들이 우러러볼 수 있으므로 왕이나 황제의 업적을 기리거나 중요한 기록을 새겨서 후대 사람들에게 알리는 기념비로도 쓰였다. 아소카 왕의 석주(The pillars of Asoka)도 그런 것이다. Asoka carved these ideas on stone monuments and pillars and set them up all around his empire. 아소카는 이런 생각들을 돌 기념비와 기둥에 새겨서 그것들을 제국 전역에 세웠다.

reason ⓥ to try to persuade someone to do something by explaining why it is sensible

reason에는 '깊이 생각하다(consider)'라는 의미가 담겨 있다. 깊이 생각해야 사물의 이치를 알 수 있고, 원인과 결과의 관계를 파악할 수 있다. 그래서 명사형 reason에는 '이유, 근거'와 '이성(理性), 사리분별'이라는 뜻도 있다. reason을 동사형으로 쓰면 '이성적으로 근거를 대면서 설명하다'라는 뜻이 된다. 쉽게 말해 힘으로 억누르고 자기 마음대로 하는 것이 아니라 '이성적으로 대하다, 이성적으로 처리하다'라는 의미이다.
He tried to reason with his subjects, rather than giving out strict, harsh commands. 그는 엄격하고 가혹한 명령을 내리기보다는 백성들을 이성적으로 대하려고 했다.

2 The Jakata Tales

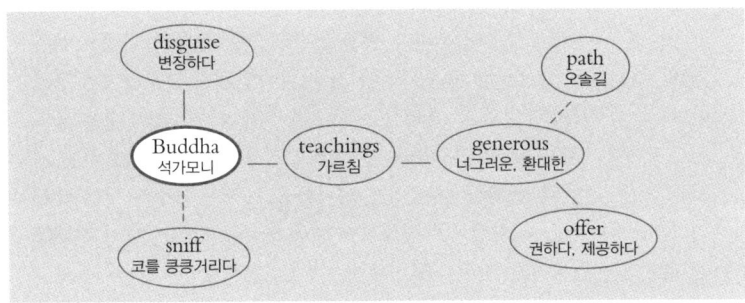

teachings ⓝ the ideas of a great person
'가르치다'라는 뜻의 teach에 -ing를 붙이면 '가르치는 일, 교편(the work of a teacher)'과 '가르침'이라는 뜻도 된다. '배운 사람은 가르칠 의무가 있다'라는 말이 있듯이 누구나 teaching을 전할 수 있지만, 대개는 성인(聖人), 사상가, 종교 지도자 등의 사상이나 교리(敎理) 등을 말할 때 teachings로 표현한다. 가르친 내용이 한두 가지가 아니므로 복수형을 쓴다. the teachings of the Buddha는 '부처의 가르침'이다.
King Asoka gave up fighting and stopped eating meat because of the teachings of the Buddha. 아소카 왕은 부처의 가르침 때문에 싸움을 포기했고, 고기를 먹지 않았다.

path ⓝ a narrow road you can walk on
'길'을 표현하는 단어 중에서 path는 사람이 다니기 위해 일부러 닦아 놓은 길, 오랜 세월 동안 사람들이 지나다녀서 생긴 길을 뜻한다. path는 '폭이 좁은 길'로 산이나 숲에 나 있으면 '오솔길(trail)'이다. 앞으로 죽 이어진 길을 따라가게 되어 있으므로 '진로, 진행 방향'의 의미로도 쓰인다. the path of the typhoon(태풍의 진로)처럼 쓸 수도 있다.
Through the deep wood wound a long, dark path. 깊은 숲속으로 길고 어두운 오솔길이 굽이굽이 나 있었다.

generous ⓐ willing to give money, help, or time to someone
부모를 닮은 모습으로 '태어나게' 하는 '유전자'가 영어로 gene이다. generous 에서 gener는 '귀족이나 명문 가문에서 태어난'을 뜻하는데, 넉넉한 집안에서 태어나 마음 씀씀이가 넉넉하다는 의미이다. 즉 generous는 '관대한, 너그러운, 인색하지 않은'을 뜻한다. 명사형은 generosity이다.
Let's be generous and give our best to any traveler who asks. 청하는 여행자가 있으면 누구에게든 인색하게 굴지 말고, 우리가 가진 가장 좋은 것을 주자.

sniff ⓥ to smell something by taking air into your nose
개를 키워본 사람이라면 sniff가 어떤 의미인지 정확히 알 것이다. 개는 하루에도 수십 번 코를 킁킁거리며 여기저기 냄새를 맡는다. sniff에는 '코를 킁킁대며 냄새 맡다' 외에도 '코를 훌쩍이다, 콧방귀를 뀌다'라는 뜻도 있다. 어떤 의미든지 코에서 소리가 난다는 공통점이 있다.
The jackal went out to the edge of the village on the other side of the forest and sniffed around a poor man's hut. 자칼은 숲 반대편에 있는 마을 외곽으로 가서는 가난한 사람의 오두막 주변을 코를 킁킁거리며 냄새 맡았다.

disguise ⓥ to make yourself look like someone else so that people do not know who you are
disguise는 '반대, 부정'을 뜻하는 접두사 dis-와 '겉모습'을 뜻하는 guise가 합쳐진 것이다. 옷차림, 머리 모양, 목소리, 걸음걸이처럼 밖으로 드러나는 특징을 다르게 바꾸는 것이 바로 disguise이다. 겉모습을 바꿔 자신을 숨기는 것으로 '가장하다, 변장하다'라는 뜻이다. 명사형 '가장, 변장'으로도 쓰인다.
So Sakka disguised himself as a priest and went down to the earth. 그래서 사카는 승려로 변장하고 지상에 내려왔다.

offer ⓥ to say that you are willing to give something to someone
offer는 뭔가를 자신이 하겠다고 '제안하다', 뭔가를 '주려고 내놓다'라는 뜻으로 쓰인다. 그런데 이때 겸손함과 공손함이 느껴져야 한다. 왜냐하면 원래 offer는 '신께 바치다'라는 뜻에서 유래했기 때문이다. 예를 들어 The monkey offered a mango to Sakka(원숭이는 사카에게 망고 하나를 먹으라고 내놓았다)에서 원숭이는 망고를 '드십시오'라고 공손하게 주는 것이다.
"I could share a mango or two," the monkey offered. 원숭이는 "제가 망고를 한두 개 같이 먹도록 해드릴게요"라고 권했다.

The Story of the World

Chapter 32
China: Writing and the Qin

1 Calligraphy in China

🌐 1899년에 약 3,000년 전에 존재했던 중국 상(商)왕조의 유적이 은허(殷墟)에서 발굴되었는데, 이 유적에서 문자의 형태가 발견되었다. 거북 '등껍데기(甲)'와 소의 '뼈(骨)'에 새겨져 있었기 때문에 이 문자를 '갑골 문자(甲骨文字)'라고 부른다. 그림 문자에서 발전된 상형 문자의 모습을 하고 있는데, 길흉화복을 점치는 내용을 담고 있다. 또한 산둥 성의 태안(泰安)에서 발굴된 신석기 유적에서도 한자의 원류로 추정되는 문자가 발견되었으며 중국 고전인 《순자(荀子)》와 《여씨 춘추(呂氏春秋)》에는 고대 황제(黃帝) 때 '창힐(倉頡)'이라는 인물이 한자를 처음 만들었다는 기록이 있다. 정확한 기원은 아직 알 수 없으나 지금까지의 발견으로 볼 때 한자는 4,000년 전에 이미 그림 문자의 형태로 존재했음을 짐작할 수 있다.

The Aryans came to India from Asia. If you were to put your finger on India, on your map, and then move it up to the north, you would be in Asia. And if you move your finger right on the map, you'll go into the eastern part of Asia—China. We've already learned a little bit about the farmers of ancient China, and about the pictograms used by the ancient Chinese.

Pictograms were picture-words that looked almost exactly like the words they represented.

But as Chinese writing continued to develop, pictograms looked less and less like the words they stood for. In later Chinese writing, you can often still see a picture. But the picture is harder to find. This kind of Chinese writing is called *calligraphy*, and the pictures are called *characters*. Here are some modern Chinese characters. Do they look like the words they stand for?

Mountain (can you see the peaks of the mountain?)

Fire (can you see the flames leaping up?)

Man (he has two sets of arms!)

馬

Horse (does this look like a horse to you?)

Writing Chinese characters is more like drawing a picture than writing a word. Chinese *calligraphers*—people who spent many years learning how to write in Chinese—used seven different kinds of lines to write their characters. They called these lines the "Seven Mysteries." The first three lines are easy:

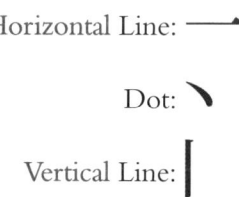

Can you draw these lines?

The next three lines that belong to the Seven Mysteries are a little more difficult:

Downward Stroke 1: This line is like a mountain slope.

Downward Stroke 2: This line has a little point at the top.

Sweeping Downward Stroke: This line goes the other way!

Can you draw these three lines?

The very last line is a Hook that can be drawn two different ways:

like this: 乙

or like this, like a big "L": 凵

Chinese calligraphers put these lines together to form Chinese characters. This character, for "field," uses three Horizontal Lines and three Vertical Lines:

It represents a farmer's field. Can you see the rows in the field?

Here is a character that uses a Vertical Line, a Horizontal Line, a Downward Stroke, and a Sweeping Downward Stroke. Can you guess what it is?

It's a tree. The Chinese word for "forest" is three trees, put together like this:

Now let's look at one last character. It uses a Horizontal Line, a Sweeping Downward Stroke, and a Hook:

女

This is the character for "Woman." It is supposed to look like a mother with a baby on her lap. Do you see anything that looks like a baby? Remember, Chinese characters aren't the same as pictures. Sometimes it is very difficult to see a picture in them.

In ancient China, calligraphy was done with a special sharp paintbrush, made out of animal hairs. Calligraphers made their own brushes by tying the hairs together into a little bundle with a silk thread. Then they glued the hairs into the end of a tube made out of a tiny piece of bamboo. If the calligrapher wanted to paint very small, thin lines, he made his brush out of mouse hair, because the hairs are so little! If he wanted to paint medium-thick lines, he would use rabbit hair. And if he wanted to paint big, broad lines, he would use sheep hair—or wolf hair.

Painting each Chinese character took a long, long time. Can you imagine writing a whole book this way? Eventually, the Chinese people decided to find a quicker way to write books. They carved their characters into blocks of wood. First, the calligrapher would write the character on the block of wood. Then, a craftsman would carve away the wood from around the character, so that it stood out. Then the calligrapher would coat the raised Chinese character with ink, turn the wood block over, and press it down on a piece of paper. Now he could copy the character over and over in seconds, just by dipping the wood into ink and pressing it down.

This process is called "printing." With printing, books can be made quickly and cheaply. The Chinese were the first ancient people to use printing. The oldest printed book in the world is a Chinese book called the *Diamond Sutra*. It was printed over a thousand years ago, but we can still read it today!

2 Warring States

중국 고대 역사의 한 시대를 일컫는 춘추전국(春秋戰國) 시대는 춘추 시대와 전국 시대를 합친 말이다. 춘추 시대는 주(周) 왕조가 수도를 낙양으로 옮긴 기원전 770년부터 진(晉)나라가 한, 위, 조 세 개의 제후국으로 분할된 기원전 403년까지의 시기이다. 전국 시대는 그 이후부터 '전국 7웅'으로 불린 일곱 나라들이 중국의 통일을 꿈꾸며 전쟁을 벌이다가 진(秦)이 통일한 기원전 221년까지의 기간을 말한다. 공자를 비롯한 '제자백가(諸子百家)' 사상가들이 등장한 시기이다.

We've learned about several different countries that had to be united by strong kings. King Narmer made Upper and Lower Egypt into one country. Over in Sumer, Sargon the Great united all the different, fighting Sumerian cities into one country. And in India, the different cities were all independent until the Mauryan Empire united them all into one country.

Exactly the same thing happened in China. China was ruled by strong warriors called "warlords." Each warlord had his own, separate kingdom and his own army. There were at least six strong warlords in ancient China—and at least six different Chinese kingdoms. This time in China is called "The Period of the Warring States," because China wasn't one country. It was a whole handful of different countries, all fighting with each other! And like Egypt, Sumer, and India, the Warring States of China all became part of one country.

The Warring State all the way to the East was called Qin (pronounced "Chin"). Its warlord, Qin Zheng, had an army with one million men in it.

The other Warring States didn't like the Qin. They thought the Qin people were barbarians, uncivilized people who didn't care about reading, writing, or art. But the Qin army was the strongest army in China. The Qin conquered the other Warring States, one at a time, until Qin Zheng ruled all of China!

Qin Zheng became the first emperor of all China. And this new, united country, was named after Qin Zheng and his tribe. The word "China" comes from the word *Qin*.

Qin Zheng knew that the conquered warlords would try to rebel against him. So he forced all the warlords and former rulers of the Warring States to move into his capital city. As long as they lived near him, he could keep an eye on them and make sure they weren't planning to overthrow him. He took all their weapons away, melted them down, and turned the metal into twelve enormous statues, which he put in his own palace. He built wide, straight roads so that his soldiers could travel quickly to fight anyone who might try to rebel against him. He executed anyone who might be planning treason. And because he was afraid that Chinese writers might encourage the Chinese people to get rid of him, he ordered thousands and thousands of books burned.

Some of these books were printed. But many were written by hand. Calligraphers had spent years and years laboring over their pages. But Qin Zheng didn't care. He wanted those books destroyed, so that no one would get rebellious ideas from them.

His prime minister even announced that anyone who discussed books in public would be executed in the marketplace.

Qin Zheng kept his new empire together. But he used burning, destroying, and killing to keep his power. Even though he gave his name to the country of China, many Chinese people despised him for his cruelty.

3 The First Emperor and the Great Wall

만리장성(萬里長城)을 처음으로 쌓기 시작한 것은 춘추전국 시대에 북쪽에 위치한 나라들이었다. 이후 중국을 통일한 진이 흉노족의 침입을 막기 위해 기존의 성벽을 연결하고 새로 지어 약 1,500킬로미터에 달하는 방어벽, '장성(長城)'을 완성했다. 중국의 역대 왕조들에게 이 성벽은 대단히 중요했기 때문에 지속적으로 증축되었는데, 특히 명나라 때 몽골의 침입에 대비해 성벽을 대규모로 증축해서 총 길이 6,000킬로미터가 넘는 만리장성을 완성하게 된다.

When Qin Zheng became the emperor of all China in 221 BC/BCE, he changed his name. From now on, he would be known as "Shi Huangdi." In Chinese, this name means "First Emperor." Qin Zheng, now called Shi Huangdi, wanted his subjects to remember his power every time they spoke his name!

One day Shi Huangdi sat on his throne, thinking about his new empire. He had been careful to stamp out rebellion inside his borders. All of his enemies lived near his palace, and Shi Huangdi had sent his soldiers to guard them and to report on all their activities. He had burned the books that might encourage his people to rebel. He was safe from revolt.

But his kingdom wasn't secure yet. Outside the borders of China, ferocious tribes roved through the wild mountains and

Shi Huangdi, China's "First Emperor"

plains of the north. For years, these northern barbarians had attacked the Warring States, trying to take over their land. They were the earliest of the tribes which were later called Mongols.

The Mongols rode swift horses, and shot arrows with deadly precision. So some of the Warring States had built walls to keep the Mongols out. These walls were still standing, but parts of them had crumbled away into dust. And between the walls were huge gaps.

"The Mongols could come through those gaps at any time," Shi Huangdi thought. "They could sweep down and take over parts of my empire. How can I protect China from the Mongols? If only I could build a wall along the whole northern side of my empire!"

Then Shi Huangdi had an idea: a stupendous, incredible idea. "Perhaps I *can* build a wall along China's northern border!" he exclaimed. "A wall thousands of miles long! A *Great* Wall!"

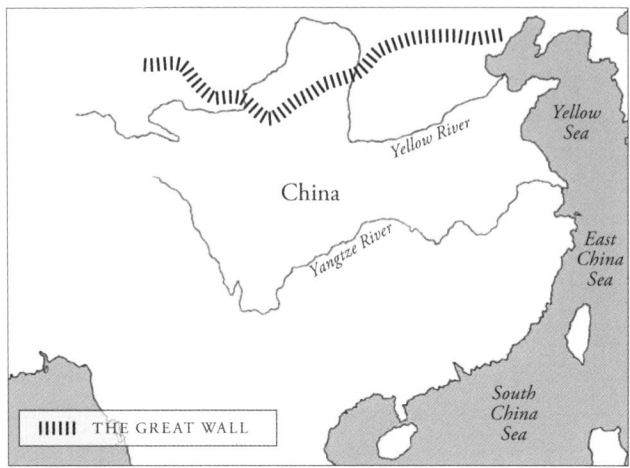

The Great Wall of China

So Shi Huangdi summoned his architects and builders. "All along the northern part of my empire," he told them, "old walls are falling down. I want to repair these walls. And then I want to build a new wall, connecting all the old walls together into one huge barrier that will keep the Mongols out of my kingdom."

"But, Emperor," the architects and builders protested, "there is not enough stone in the far reaches of your kingdom to build a Great Wall!"

"Then think of another way to do it," Shi Huangdi ordered.

The builders and architects labored for weeks, trying to think of a way to build the wall in places where stone was scarce. Finally, they discovered a way. The builders made a wooden frame, as high as a man's waist and as wide as a wall. They set this frame upon the ground and filled it with loose dirt. Then workers stamped and packed the earth until it was only four inches high and as hard as concrete. They lifted the frame up, set it on top of the packed dirt, and filled it again. They could build a dirt wall as hard as stone, four inches at a time!

When Shi Huangdi saw the dirt wall, he was pleased. "Now it is time to build!" he commanded. And he ordered thousands and thousands of men out to work on the Great Wall. He sent peasants who had no choice but to obey. He sent his enemies and his prisoners out to work on the Wall, forcing them to labor day and night. He declared that every grown man in China must work on the Wall for one month out of the year. And he sent his armies out to guard the workers from attack as they built the Wall.

For years, the people of China worked to finish the Wall. They built up over mountain ridges and down into valleys. As the Wall grew higher and higher, they were forced to haul dirt up to the top in small baskets. It took days and days to complete even one section of the Great Wall.

When Shi Huangdi died, the Wall was still unfinished. But over the next few hundred years, each Chinese emperor who came to the throne sent men to work on the Wall. Guard towers were built every few miles, so that watchmen on top could see the Mongols coming long before they reached the Wall. Brick and rock reinforcements were added to the dirt sections. Eventually, the Wall was almost three thousand miles long, almost long enough to reach from one side of the United States to the other!

Today, long stretches of the Great Wall of China still stand. Although some parts of it have collapsed, others are still strong and high enough to walk along. People come from all over the world to walk on the Great Wall of China.

4 The First Emperor's Grave

🌐 1974년, 중국 서안의 진시황릉에서 약 1.5킬로미터 떨어진 곳에서 '병마용갱(兵馬俑坑)'이 발굴되었다. 20~30미터 간격으로 총 4곳의 용갱이 발견되었는데, 길이가 100미터에 너비가 80미터에 이르는 엄청난 규모였다. 그중 세 군데의 용갱에는 흙을 빚어서 구운 실물 크기의 병사들과 각종 무기들, 전차 등이 전투 대형으로서 있었다. 현재까지도 발굴 작업이 진행되고 있어서 실제 규모를 다 파악할 수는 없지만, 진시황의 친위 부대를 그대로 땅속에 재현한 것으로 추정한다.

Almost thirty years ago, two men were digging a well. They were farmers who lived near the city of Xi'an, in the middle of China. The morning was hot; the sun beat down, and the two men were sweating and thirsty.

"Let's stop for a drink," one of the farmers said to his friend. "Oh, let's just dig a little longer," his friend answered. "We're bound to hit water soon."

So they kept digging. The ground was hard, and the dirt they turned up was red and rocky. Soon their shovels began to turn up pieces of broken pottery.

"Someone broke a pot here," the first farmer said.

"Those pieces are too big for a pot!" his friend said. "And look. That piece looks like … an arm!"

The two friends kept digging. They found broken arms and legs made out of clay—and even a head, wearing a helmet! Soon, word of their discoveries spread to the city of Xi'an. Archaeologists living in the city hurried out to see what the farmers had found. They began to dig deeper and deeper.

They found a huge underground pit filled with three thousand soldiers, made out of clay baked hard. The soldiers were life-size! And buried along with the soldiers were sharp shining weapons, full-sized horses also made out of clay, and wooden war chariots! The horses wore clay saddles, and harnesses made from gold and bronze. As the archaeologists uncovered each soldier, they saw that every single face was different—molded to look like a real person. No two soldiers were the same! *And all the soldiers were facing east, as though they were guarding something behind them. What were they guarding?

They were guarding the tomb of Shi Huangdi.

You see, the First Emperor of China wanted to live forever. He spent the last part of his life looking for the Water of Eternal Life, a legendary drink that would keep him from dying. He made five different trips into the mountains of China, looking for this Water.

But he never found it. And when he knew that his death was near, he ordered a great underground city, more than nine miles wide, built for his tomb. He hoped that his body would stay forever in this city. Shi Huangdi ordered his crown, robe, and royal bed placed in one of the chambers. He commanded his servants to enter the chamber every day, even after his death, to make the bed and bring water and food—just as though he were still alive!

So far, archaeologists have found three pits filled with clay soldiers. At the center of the underground city, a huge burial mound rises up above the ground. Underneath this burial mound, archaeologists hope to find the body of Shi Huangdi itself. But the mound still hasn't been excavated. Ancient Chinese writers, describing Shi Huangdi's underground city, tell us that the tomb itself is far, far below the mound—almost a hundred feet below the surface of the ground. The tomb is made of stone, covered with melted copper to keep the water out.

What is inside the burial mound? We don't know for sure.

But shortly after the death of Shi Huangdi, an ancient Chinese historian described the burial chamber like this:

Rare treasures and jewels, removed from various palaces, towers and halls, filled the grave. Craftsmen were ordered to set arrows on crossbows, which would shoot automatically at anyone breaking in. Rivers and seas in miniature were dug and filled with mercury, made to flow by mechanical devices. On the ceiling, stars and planets were set. Candles were lighted, burning fish fat, so that they might keep the grave chambers lit for a long time.

Does the burial mound really contain all of these wonders? Well, archaeologists have already discovered that the ground around the mound contains mercury—a silver metal that flows like water. This mercury must have come from inside the mound.

One day, archaeologists will open the mound and look inside. Let's hope that they watch out for those automatic crossbows!

Note to Parent: The "Period of the Warring States" began around 500 BC/BCE. Qin Zheng's forced unification began around 230 BC/BCE; the first united Chinese empire dates from 221 BC/BCE. The burning of the books took place in 212 BC/BCE. Construction of the Great Wall of China began in 214 BC/BCE and continued for several centuries.

The Story of the Words
Chapter 32 China: Writing and the Qin

1 Calligraphy in China

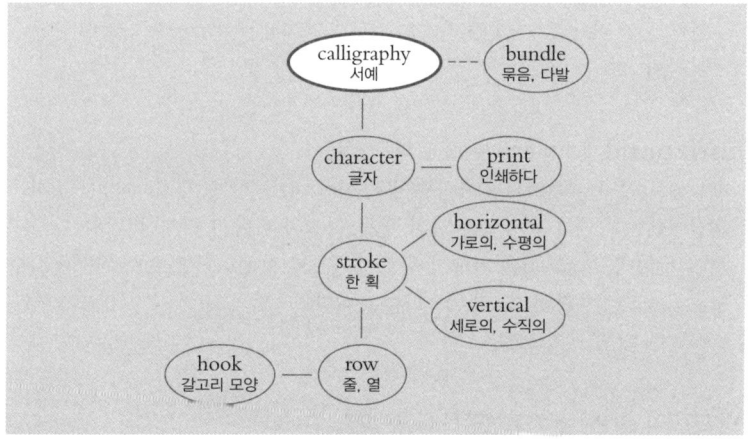

calligraphy ⓝ the art of producing beautiful writing using special brushes or pens

    calligraphy는 희랍어에서 유래하여, calli는 '미, 아름다움(beauty)'을 뜻하고, graphy는 '글씨 쓰기(writing)'를 뜻한다. 즉 글씨를 아름답게, 예술적으로 쓰는 것이 바로 calligraphy이다. 문장 속에서 '서예, 서도'를 의미한다. calligrapher는 '서예가'이다.

This kind of Chinese writing is called *calligraphy*, and the pictures are called characters. 이런 종류의 중국 글씨 쓰기를 '서예', 그 그림들을 '글자'라고 부른다.

character ⓝ a letter, number or symbol that is written or printed

    character는 '눌러서 표시를 남기는 도구'를 뜻하는 희랍어에서 유래했다. 낙인이나 도장에는 특정한 글자나 문양이 새겨져 있어서 찍으면 그 이미지가 남기 때문에 character가 '글자, 숫자, 상징'을 의미한다.

Here are some modern Chinese characters. 다음은 몇몇 중국 현대 글자들이다.

> **Q** 간자체는 왜 만들어졌나요?
> **A** 중국인이 쓰는 글자를 한자라고 하는데, 지금은 한자에서 달라진 간자체를 쓰고 있지. 1949년 중화인민 공화국이 생길 당시 인구가 8억 명이 넘었는데, 이들 중에는 문맹이 많았단다. 금세 익힐 수 있는 한글과는 달리 한자는 글자 수가 너무 많았어. 한자의 총수가 5만자니까 최소한 3,800에서 3,500자는 익혀야 일상에서 문자 생활이 가능해. 국민의 문맹률을 줄이기 위해 고심한 당국에서는 '간자체'를 만들었단다. 말 그대로 한자를 간단하게 줄인 거야. 그러니 옛 한자와 지금의 간자체를 똑같이 생각하면 곤란하겠지?

horizontal ⓐ flat and level to the ground
horizontal은 horizon의 형용사형이다. horizon은 '한계, 경계(limit)'를 뜻하는 희랍어에서 유래하여 하늘과 땅의 경계, 하늘과 바다의 경계인 '지평선, 수평선'을 뜻한다. horizon은 좌에서 우로 수평으로 형성되어 있으므로, 형용사형 horizontal은 '수평(선)의, 가로의'라는 뜻이다.
Horizontal Line: ― 가로 선: ―

vertical ⓐ pointing straight up; upright
vertical은 '바로 머리 위로(directly overhead)'라는 뜻의 라틴어에서 온 것이다. 똑바로 서서 고개를 들고 위를 보면 직선상의 모든 것이 보여서 '수직의, 세로의'라는 뜻이 된다. 앞에 the를 붙여 the vertical이라고 하면 '수직(선/면)'을 뜻하는 명사형이다.
Vertical Line: | 세로 선: |

stroke ⓝ a single movement of a pen or brush, or a line made by this
stroke은 '가볍게 문지르다, 쓰다듬다'라는 뜻의 고대 영어에서 유래했다. strike(치다)와 어원이 같다. 지금도 stroke은 '쓰다듬다, 문지르다'라는 뜻으로 쓰인다. 세월이 흐르면서 stroke은 점차 어떤 목적을 위해 '손과 팔을 한 번 움직이다'라는 뜻으로 발전하여 '공을 한 번 치기, 노를 한 번 젓기, 필기구를 한 번 긋기'의 뜻이 되었다.
Downward Stroke 1: This line is like a mountain slope. 하향 획 1: 이 선은 산비탈 모양이다.

hook ⓝ a curved object for hanging things on, or for catching fish
hook은 '휘어진, 구부러진 것'이다. 대개는 특정 목적을 위해 구부리는 것으로, 물고기를 낚기 위해 철사를 '구부린' 낚싯바늘이 hook이고, 권투에서 팔을 '구부려' 상대 선수를 세게 치는 것도 hook이다. 한자의 획 중에 '갈고리' 모양으로 끝이 구부러진 것도 hook이다.
The very last line is a Hook that can be drawn two different ways: 마지막 선은 '갈고리' 형태로, 다른 두 방향으로 그을 수 있다.

row ⓝ series of things arranged in a straight line
row는 '일렬로 늘어선 줄'을 뜻한다. 학교에서 체육 시간이나 조회 시간에 '앉아 번호!'라는 지시에 따라 동시에 앉는 그 '한 줄'이 row이다. 또 극장에서 스크린을 기준으로 가로줄에 해당하는 좌석들도 row이다. 세로줄은 column이라고 부른다. 그러나 가로 세로의 구분 없이 '일렬로 늘어선 사물이나 사람'을 표현할 때 row를 쓰기도 한다.
Can you see the rows in the field? 밭에 있는 줄들이 보이는가?

bundle ⓝ a group of things such as papers or clothes that are tied together
bundle은 '묶음, 다발'이다. 요즘은 비닐 포장을 많이 하지만 옛날에는 생선, 달걀, 얼음, 종이, 천 등을 주로 끈이나 실로 묶어서 한 단위로 구분하고 운반했다. 컴퓨터 프로그램을 구입할 때 '번들'로 판다는 말을 들어봤을 것이다. 이때 '번들'이 바로 bundle이다. 여러 개의 프로그램을 패키지(package)로 '묶어서' 같이 판다는 의미이다.
Calligraphers made their own brushes by tying the hairs together into a little bundle with a silk thread. 서예가들은 털들을 비단실로 동여매어 작은 다발로 묶어 자신만의 붓을 만들었다.

print ⓥ to put words or pictures on paper or clothes using a machine
print는 '누르다(press)'라는 뜻의 라틴어에서 유래했다. 누르면 자국이 남기 때문에 '도장이나 인장을 찍다'라는 뜻이다. 같은 원리로 활자에 잉크를 발라 종이에 찍는 '인쇄'도 print, printing으로 표현할 수 있다. press에도 '인쇄'라는 뜻이 있다.
With printing, books can be made quickly and cheaply. 인쇄를 하면, 책을 빠르고 싸게 만들 수 있다.

2 Warning States

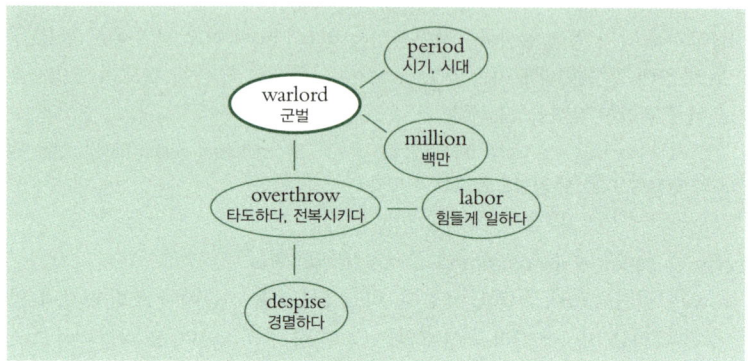

warlord ⓝ the leader of any group involved in fighting

중국 고대사를 공부하다 보면 '군벌(軍閥)'이라는 용어가 자주 등장하는데, 영어로 warlord라고 표현한다. war(전쟁)와 lord(주인, 군주)가 합쳐진 것으로, '군사력을 기반으로 일정 영역을 세력권에 둔 지배자'를 뜻한다. 중국 각지에서 많은 세력들이 영토를 넓히기 위해 끊임없이 '전쟁'을 벌였기 때문에 warlord라고 표현할 수 있다.

China was ruled by strong warriors called "warlords." 중국은 '군벌'이라고 불리는 힘이 센 전사들이 지배했다.

period ⓝ a particular time in history

period에서 peri-는 '한 바퀴, 빙 둘러(around)'이고, -od는 '길(way), 코스(course)'를 뜻한다. 원래는 시간이 지나 다시 제자리로 오는 주기(cycle)를 뜻하다가 '시작과 끝 사이의 시간'의 의미로 쓰이게 되었다. 즉 '시기, 시대, 기간'을 뜻한다. The Period of the Warring States는 중국 역사에서 기원전 8세기부터 3세기까지 약 500년 동안 이어진 춘추전국 시대(春秋戰國時代)를 말한다.

This time in China is called "The Period of the Warring States," because China wasn't one country. 중국에서 이 시대를 '춘추전국 시대'라고 부르는데, 그 이유는 중국이 하나의 나라가 아니었기 때문이다.

million ⓝ the number 1,000,000

million의 어원은 라틴어 millione이다. 여기에서 milli는 '천(thousand)'을 뜻하고, one은 '하나 더' 첨가하라는 의미이다. 1,000에 영을 세 개 더 붙이면

1,000,000(백 만)이다. 옛날에는 million이 어마어마하게 큰 수였기 때문에 '수많은'을 뜻하기도 한다.
Its warlord, Qin Zheng, had an army with one million men in it. 그곳 군벌인 진정은 1백만 대군을 갖고 있었다.

> **Q** 춘추전국 시대는 무엇을 기준으로 나눈 것인가요?
> **A** 이 책에서 warring states라고 표현한 시기가 춘추전국 시대를 말하는 거야. 춘추전국 시대는 동주가 약해지면서 주왕에게 도전하는 제후국들이 늘어난 상황을 알려주는 표지판 역할을 했어. 주나라 초기만 해도 1,800여 개의 도시 국가가 있었는데, 제후들이 영토를 차지하기 위해 전쟁에 돌입했어. 수도를 동쪽으로 옮겼을 때 이미 도시 국가가 200개 정도로 줄었단다.
> 기원전 453년(다른 책에서는 403년으로도 표기) 제후국인 진나라가 한, 위, 조 셋으로 나뉘게 되는 사건이 발생했어. 주나라로부터 제후로 봉건된 나라가 셋으로 나뉘었다는 사실 자체가 주나라 왕의 권위가 땅에 떨어졌다는 사실을 증명한 것이지. 이 사건 이전을 춘추 시대, 이후를 전국 시대라고 불러. 춘추 시대에는 제후들이 최소한 겉으로라도 주나라 왕실을 받들었지만, 전국 시대에는 그런 체면치레도 벗어던지고 전쟁에 돌입한 시대야. 춘추 시대는 공자의 역사서 《춘추》를, 전국 시대는 유향의 《전국책》이라는 책 제목에서 온 명칭이야.

overthrow ⓥ to force a leader or government out of the position of power
뭔가를 '저 높이, 저 너머로(over) 던지면(throw)' 어떻게 될까? 높이, 멀리 던졌으니 시야에서 사라진다. overthrow는 이렇게 세게 던져서 없앤다는 의미에서 권력자를 '타도하다, 전복시키다'라는 뜻이다. overthrow-overthrew-overthrown
As long as they lived near him, he could keep an eye on them and make sure they weren't planning to overthrow him. 그들이 그와 가까이에 사는 한, 그가 그들을 감시할 수 있었으며 그들이 그를 타도할 계획을 세우지 않을 거라고 확신할 수 있었다.

labor ⓥ to work very hard
일, 공부, 살림을 labor라고 하고, 이 행위에 해당하는 이들(노동자)을 laborer라고 할 수 있다. '힘든 일(toil), 곤경(trouble)'을 뜻하는 라틴어가 labor의 어원이어서 labor는 '힘든 일, 노동'과 '힘들게 일하다'라는 뜻으로 쓰인다.

Calligraphers had spent years and years laboring over their pages. 서예가들은 오랜 세월 한 장 한 장 힘들게 책을 써왔다.

despise ⓥ to dislike and have a low opinion of someone

despise에서 de-는 '아래, 밑(down)'을 뜻하는 접두사이고, spise는 '쳐다보다(look at)'를 뜻한다. 즉 '다른 사람을 내려다보는' 것이므로, '경멸하다, 욕하며 깔보다'라는 뜻으로 쓰인다.

Even though he gave his name to the country of China, many Chinese people despised him for his cruelty. 비록 그가 자신의 이름을 중국이라는 나라에 주었지만, 많은 중국인들이 잔인함 때문에 그를 경멸했다.

> **Q** 중화 사상은 무슨 뜻인가요?
>
> **A** 주나라는 넓어진 영토를 다스리기 위해 봉건제를 실시했단다. 봉건제는 주나라 왕이 나라를 세우는 데 도움을 준 제후들과 주나라 왕실의 가족들에게 수도에서 가까운 곳에 토지를 나눠주는 거야. 토지를 받은 사람들은 주나라의 제사에 참여하고, 나라에 위급한 일이 있으면 군대를 이끌고 도와줬지.
> 봉건제 하에서 주나라의 수도는 아주 특별한 의미를 갖게 되었어. 수도에는 하늘의 상제로부터 천명을 받은 하늘의 아들이 살면서 하늘과 사람, 땅을 이어주는 신성한 일을 한다고 당시 사람들은 생각했단다. 수도에서 멀어질수록 문화의 혜택을 덜 받은 야만족이 살아서 그들에게 문화의 향기를 나눠주는 것이 문명인이 할 일이라고 생각하는 것이 바로 '중화 사상'의 핵심이란다. 그들은 자신들의 수도를 중심으로 동쪽에는 동이, 서쪽에는 서융, 남쪽에는 남만, 북쪽에는 북적이 산다고 생각했어. 이, 융, 만, 적은 다 오랑캐라는 뜻이야.

3 The First Emperor and the Great Wall

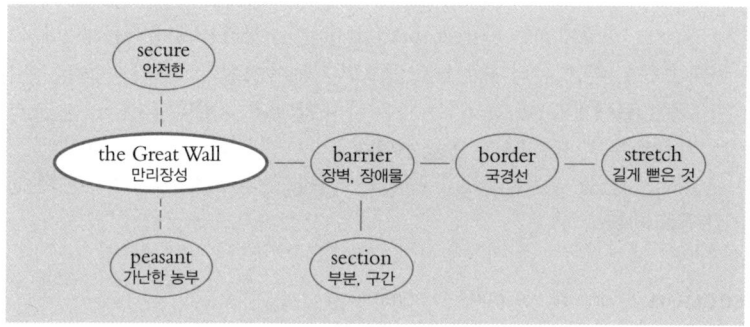

secure ⓐ safe; not likely to be harmed
  secure는 라틴어에서 유래하여 se-는 without(없는), cure는 care(걱정)를 뜻한다. 즉 '걱정이 없는 상태'를 의미한다. 형용사 secure는 '안정적인, 안전한, 튼튼한'이고, 동사형으로 쓰면 '안전하게 지키다, 튼튼하게 고정하다'의 뜻이다. 명사형 security는 '안보, 보안, 경비, 보장'이다.
  But his kingdom wasn't secure yet. 그러나 그의 왕국은 아직 안전하지 않았다.

border ⓝ the dividing line between countries
  나라마다 자국 영토를 정하는 선은 다른 나라의 국경선과 맞닿아 있다. 나라와 나라의 경계인 이 '국경선'을 border라고 한다. 원래 '가장자리(edge)'를 뜻했는데, 지리상의, 지도상의 국경선은 border line으로 표현하기도 한다.
  "Perhaps I can build a wall along China's northern border!" he exclaimed. 그가 소리쳤다. "내가 중국의 북쪽 국경을 따라 성벽을 건설할 수도 있을 것이다!"

barrier ⓝ a wall or fence that stops people from going through a place
  bar는 '막대, 봉'인데, 빗장으로 썼다. 출입하지 못하게 막는 것이다. He was behind the bar라고 하면 '그가 감옥에 갇혀 있었다'라는 의미이다. barrier도 이런 뜻을 갖고 있는데, '장벽, 장애물'이다. 만리장성도 성벽 너머로 들어오지 못하게 막는 것이므로 barrier에 속한다.
  And then I want to build a new wall, connecting all the old walls together into one huge barrier that will keep the Mongols out of my kingdom. 그런 다음 나는 몽골인이 내 왕국으로 들어오지 못하도록 오래된 성벽들을 하나의 거대한 장벽으로 연결하는 새로운 성벽을 건설하고자 한다.

peasant ⓝ someone who is poor and does farm work on a small piece of land

peasant는 '시골에 사는 사람(a country dweller)'을 뜻하는 말에서 유래했다. 그런데 요즘도 '촌놈, 촌티' 같은 말을 들으면 기분이 나쁘거나 화가 나듯이, 옛날 지주(地主)들에게도 peasant라는 말은 하지 않았던 것 같다. peasant는 '소작농, 가난한 농부'만을 뜻하는 말로 쓰였다.
He sent peasants who had no choice but to obey. 그는 복종할 수밖에 없는 가난한 농부들을 보냈다.

section ⓝ one of the parts of something

영미권 책을 읽다보면, section이라는 단어를 자주 접한다. 한 챕터(chapter)나 파트(part)를 부르는 말이다. section에서 sect는 '자르다(cut)'라는 뜻이 있다. 즉 '자른 부분'이 section으로 '부분, 구역, 구간'을 뜻한다.
It took days and days to complete even one section of the Great Wall. 만리장성의 한 구간을 완성하는 데에도 여러 날[많은 시간]이 걸렸다.

stretch ⓝ a long and narrow area of land or water

'기지개'를 켜면 몸이 죽 늘어나 길어 보인다. '기지개'가 영어로 stretch이다. 본 운동을 하기 전에 준비 운동으로 몸을 '늘이는' 운동도 '스트레칭(stretching)'이다. stretch는 '늘이다, 뻗다, 길게 이어지다'라는 뜻이고, 명사형으로는 '기지개, 신축성' 외에도 '길게 뻗어 있는 지형, 오래 지속되는 시간'을 뜻한다. '길게 뻗어 있는 모양에 해당하는 것'에 stretch라는 말을 쓸 수 있다.
Today, long stretches of the Great Wall of China still stand. 오늘날에도 중국 만리장성의 긴 성벽들이 아직 서 있다.

4 The First Emperor's Grave

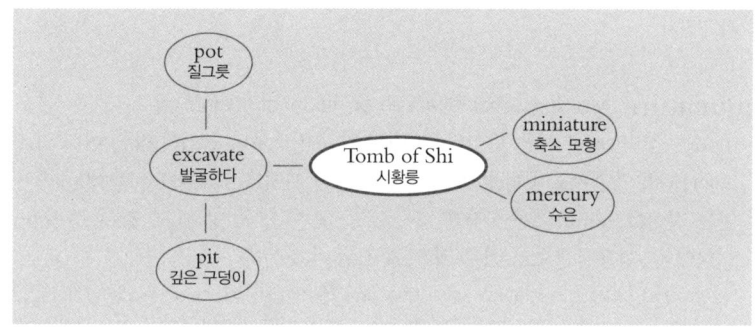

pot ⓝ a round container, used for cooking or pouring water
pot은 '솥, 냄비'와 같은 주방용품을 뜻하는데, 원래는 흙을 빚어 만든 그릇이었다. 진시황릉을 발견한 중국 농부들은 땅을 파다가 도자기나 질그릇 조각을 발견했을 것이다. pottery는 흙으로 만든 그릇 종류를 통칭하며 pieces of broken pottery가 '깨진 도자기 조각들'이다. pot이 들어간 재미있는 속담이 있다. The pot calls the kettle black(솥이 주전자 보고 검다고 한다)은 제 잘못은 모르고 남을 비난한다는 뜻으로, '똥 묻은 개가 겨 묻은 개 나무란다'나 '오십보소백보(五十步 笑百步)'와 같은 의미이다.
"Someone broke a pot here," the first farmer said. 첫 번째 농부가 말했다. "누가 여기에 그릇을 깼네."

pit ⓝ a large, deep hole in the ground
자동차 정비소나 세차장에 가면 직사각형으로 깊게 파놓은 구멍이 있는데, 이것을 pit이라고 한다. 탄광의 갱도도 pit이라고 한다. 모두 땅을 파서 만들었다는 공통점이 있다. 즉 pit은 '땅을 파서 만든 크고 깊은 구멍'이라는 뜻이다. 진시황릉의 병마용갱(兵馬俑坑)도 땅을 깊게 파서 만든 것이므로 pit이라고 할 수 있다.
They found a huge underground pit filled with three thousand soldiers, made out of clay baked hard. 그들은 거대한 지하 구멍을 발견했는데, 그곳에는 점토를 구워서 단단하게 만든 3천 명의 병사들로 가득 차 있었다.

excavate ⓥ to dig in the ground in order to find things from the past
excavate에서 ex-는 '밖으로(out)'를 뜻하는 접두사이고, cavate는 '구멍을 파다'라는 뜻이다. 즉 파서 뭔가를 밖으로 꺼내는 것이다. 고고학자들이 유적이나 유물을 발굴할 때 '발굴하다, 출토하다'의 뜻이다. 명사형은 excavation이다.
But the mound still hasn't been excavated. 그러나 이 능은 아직까지도 완전히 발굴되지 않았다.

miniature ⓝ a very small example or model of something

mini는 '작다(small)'라는 뜻이다. 그래서 일반 버스보다 크기가 작은 미니 버스(mini bus), 연속극보다 방영 기간이 짧은 미니 시리즈(mini series) 등에 mini가 붙는 것이고, miniature는 '작게 만든 것'을 뜻한다. 즉 명사형으로 '축소 모형, 미니어처', 형용사형으로 '아주 작은, 축소된'의 뜻이다.
Rivers and seas in miniature were dug and filled with mercury, made to flow by mechanical devices. 땅을 파서 축소 모형의 강과 바다를 만들어 수은을 가득 채웠으며, 기계 장치로 수은이 흐르도록 만들었다.

mercury ⓝ a silver liquid metal

mercury는 유일하게, 상온에서 액체 상태로 존재하는 금속 원소인 '수은(水銀)'이다. 연금술사들이 이 신비로운 액체 금속을 행성인 '수성(Mercury)'과 연결해 부르면서 이름 붙여졌다. 수은과 수성 모두 로마 신화의 메르쿠리우스(Mercurius) 신의 이름에서 유래한 말이다. 인체에 대단히 해로운 물질이지만, 고대 사람들에게는 신비로운 힘을 갖고 있는 물질로 여겨졌다.
Well, archaeologists have already discovered that the ground around the mound contains mercury—a silver metal that flows like water. 글쎄, 고고학자들은 능 주변의 땅에 수은이 함유되어 있다는 사실을 이미 알아냈다. 수은은 물처럼 흐르는 은빛 금속이다.

The Story of the World

Chapter 33
Confucius

1 China's Wise Teacher

🌐 제자백가(諸子百家) 중 한 사람인 유가(儒家)의 '공자(孔子)' 영어 이름이 Confucius이다. 공자는 기원전 551년에 노(魯)나라에서 서자(庶子)로 태어났다. 가난 속에서도 학문에 매진해 20대에 이미 제자들을 거느린 사상가로 이름을 떨치기 시작했다. 공자는 '인(仁)'의 실천을 통해 바람직한 사회를 이루고, 도덕적 이상국가를 세워야 한다고 가르쳤다. 그의 사상과 그가 제자들과 나눈 언행이 기록된 책이 《논어(論語)》이다.

When we studied India, we read about a prince who left his palace to wander through the world and look for the secret of happiness. He was named Siddhartha, but he became known as the Buddha. His followers were called Buddhists.

The Buddha taught that a good, virtuous man could be happy, even if he were poor. He taught his followers to be peaceful, honest and kind, and to avoid doing any kind of violence, even to animals or insects.

At the same time that the Buddha was teaching people in India, another man in China was teaching the Chinese people that they too could learn to be happy, even if they were poor. His name was Confucius.

Confucius was born to a noble Chinese family. He had the chance to go to school, where he learned music and archery. But his family was poor. And all around him, Confucius saw war and turmoil. He lived during the Period of the Warring States, before the Qin made China into one country.

Confucius hated war. He wanted the Chinese people to live in peace. He offered to work for the government of his own Warring State. He wanted to help the rulers make peace. But the rulers rejected his advice.

So Confucius became a teacher. He told all those around him his ideas for bringing peace and happiness. More and more people listened to his teachings.

Confucius taught his followers that each person should respect the authority of those who are greater. Children ought to listen to and obey their parents. Women should obey their husbands. Husbands should do whatever the rulers tell them to do. Rulers should obey the laws of the gods.

He also taught that people in authority should be kind to those who are beneath them! So rulers should be kind to men, men should treat their wives well, and parents should take care of their children.

Confucius told his followers that if they behaved properly, their lives would be peaceful. His sayings were collected together into a book called *The Analects of Confucius*. Here are some of his most famous sayings:

*Do not do unto others what you
would not want others to do to you.*

Can you think of something you would not want done to you? Should you do it to someone else? Here is another saying:

*If you make a mistake and do not correct it,
this is called a mistake.*

This means that, whenever you make a mistake, you should try to fix it. If you don't, you have actually made two mistakes! Can you think of a mistake you made recently? Did you try to fix it?

It is the wiser person who

gives rather than takes.

Giving is more fun than getting! Do you enjoy watching other people open the gifts that you give them?

*He who aims to be a man of complete virtue
does not seek to gratify his appetite in his food.*

Good people are not greedy! Eating whatever you want whenever you want it shows that you don't have self control.

Note to parent: Confucius lived around 551–479 BC/BCE.

The Story of the Words
Chapter 33 Confucius

1 China's Wise Teacher

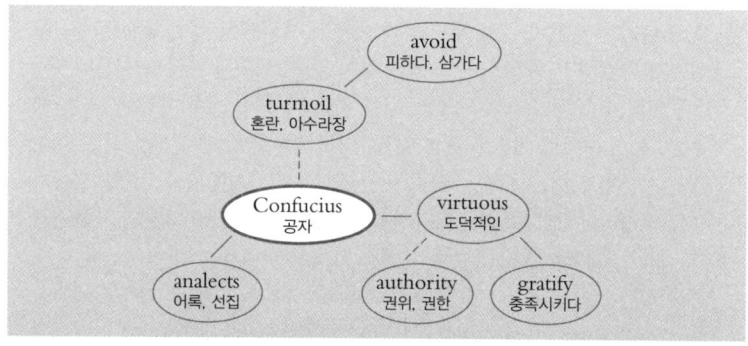

virtuous ⓐ behaving in a very honest and moral way

virtuous는 '선(善), 선행, 미덕'을 뜻하는 virtue의 형용사형으로, '정직하고 도덕적으로 행동하는'이라는 뜻이다. vir는 라틴어로 '사나이, 남자(man)'를 나타내는데, 당시의 관념으로 '남성'은 여성에 비해 우월하고 도덕적인 존재였다. 물론 지금은 아니지만, 그 당시에는 남자다우려면 '도덕적'이어야 한다고 여겨지기도 했다.

The Buddha taught that a good, virtuous man could be happy, even if he were poor. 부처는 착하고 도덕적인 사람은, 비록 가난하더라고 행복할 수 있다고 가르쳤다.

avoid ⓥ to stay away from a person, place or thing

avoid에서 a는 '밖으로(out)'이고, void는 '비우다(empty)'를 뜻한다. 어떤 일을 하지 않거나 무엇과 마주치지 않기 위해, 자리를 비우고 나간다는 의미로 이해할 수 있다. avoid는 '피하다, 면하다, 방지하다'를 뜻한다.

He taught his followers to be peaceful, honest and kind, and to avoid doing any kind of violence, even to animals or insects. 부처는 추종자들에게 평화적이고, 정직하고 친절하며, 어떤 폭력도, 심지어 동물이나 벌레에게도, 폭력을 삼가라고 가르쳤다.

turmoil ⓝ a state of confusion, anxiety or uncontrolled activity

turmoil의 어원은 '곤경(trouble)'을 뜻하는 turb와 '힘들게 움직이다'는 뜻의 moil이 합쳐진 것으로 추정된다. 흔히 무질서하고 혼란에 빠진 곳을 '아수라장'이라고 표현하는데, 이 말에 적합한 단어가 바로 turmoil이다. 전쟁이 끊이지 않았던 중국의 춘추전국 시대가 그런 상황이었을 것이다.
And all around him, Confucius saw war and turmoil. 그리고 공자는 사방에서 전쟁과 혼란을 보았다.

> **Q 제자백가는 어떤 상황에서 출현했나요?**
>
> **A** 주나라는 봉건제, 종법제에 의해 지탱된 사회였어. 종법제에서는 신분 질서가 확실했지. 주나라 수도에는 왕이 있고, 제후의 나라에서는 제후가 우두머리였어. 왕도 제후도 큰아들이 뒤를 이었어. 제후 아래에는 경, 대부, 사 등의 순서로 제후를 위해 일하는 사람들이 있었단다.
>
> 그러니 춘추 시대가 되면서 이미 옛날의 주나라가 아니었어. 신분 질서가 흔들려 경이나 대부 중에서 하극상을 일으키는 사람들이 나오기 시작했거든. 대부가 제후를 몰아내고 그 지역을 차지하는 현상이 일어나고, 도시 국가끼리 싸움을 벌여 하루아침에 나라를 잃기도 했어. 도시 국가의 제후들은 어떻게 하면 나라의 경제력을 튼튼하게 하고, 국방을 강화할까 고민하게 되었지. 이때 각 지역을 돌면서 각자가 생각하는 방법을 설파하는 지식인들이 등장했는데, 이들의 파가 여럿이어서 '제자백가'라고 부른 것이란다.

authority ⓝ the power to control other people

authority는 author에 명사형 접미사 -ity가 붙은 것이다. author는 '뭔가를 처음 만드는 사람, 성장하게 만드는 사람'을 뜻하는 라틴어 auctor에서 유래했다. '저자(author)'의 본질을 잘 말해주는 어원이다. 뭔가를 처음 만들고 성장시키려면 그럴 만한 권위와 힘이 있어야 하므로 authority는 '권한, 권위, 지휘권'을 뜻한다.
Confucius taught his followers that each person should respect the authority of those who are greater. 공자는 추종자들에게 각자 자신보다 더 '큰' 사람들의 권위를 존중해야 한다고 가르쳤다.

analects ⓝ a collection of short literary or philosophical extract

analects는 '어록(語錄), 선집(選集)'을 뜻하는데, 성인이나 철학자가 한 말을 기록하거나 그들이 쓴 글을 모아놓은 책이다. '모아 놓은 것(things gathered up)'을 뜻하는 희랍어에서 온 것이다. The Analects of Confucius는 공자와 그의 제자들의 언행을 정리한, 《논어(論語)》이다.

His sayings were collected together into a book called The Analects of Confucius. 그가 한 말을 《논어》라는 책에 모아 담았다.

> **Q** 공자는 정치가로서는 실패했다면서요?
>
> **A** 공자는 주나라의 '주공 단'의 정치를 이상적으로 생각했어. 꿈에서도 주공이 보이지 않으면 무슨 일일까, 내가 잘못 살고 있는 것일까 고심했다는 일화가 있을 정도로 주공 단을 모델로 생각했단다.
>
> 주공 단은 어린 조카를 대신해 7년간 주나라의 토대를 닦은 다음 조카가 성장하자 정권을 바로 반납해 주변 사람들을 놀라게 했지. 보성 왕은 주공 단에게 노나라를 봉토로 줘서, 그는 노나라의 시조가 되었어. 바로 이런 사연이 있는 노나라에 공자가 태어난 거야.
>
> 공자는 춘추 시대의 노나라 정치를 주공 때처럼 회복하고 싶다는 마음으로 현실 정치에 참여하려고 했으나, 고위 관리들은 공자를 내쳤어. 제대로 정치를 하려는 공자가 부당한 힘을 행사하고 있던 그들에겐 방해자로 보였거든. 공자는 정치가로 실패한 탓에 (혹은 그 덕분에) 제자들과 다른 나라를 떠돌아다녔어. 그러면서 제자들에게 문답 형식으로 바른 정치를 하기 위한 지식을 전했단다. 노나라로 돌아와서도 개인적으로 학교를 열어 제자들을 가르치기도 했지. 공자 자신은 수업 내용을 기록으로 남기지는 않았지만, 후에 제자들이 공사의 가르침을 담아 펴낸 책이 바로 《논어》야.

gratify ⓥ to satisfy a desire or need

gratify는 '부탁을 들어주다'라는 뜻의 라틴어에서 온 것이다. 부탁을 들어준다는 것은 상대를 만족시킨다는 의미이므로 gratify는 '기쁘게 하다, 욕구를 충족시키다'라는 뜻이다. He was gratified by her invitation(그는 그녀의 초대에 기뻤다)처럼 수동태로 감정을 표현하거나 to gratify his appetite(그의 식욕을 충족시키다)처럼 욕구를 채운다는 의미로 쓴다. gratify-gratified-gratified

He who aims to be a man of complete virtue does not seek to gratify his appetite in his food. 온전히 덕을 쌓고자 하는 사람이라면 자신의 식욕을 충족시키려고 하지 않는다.

Q 도가는 어떤 사상인가요?

A 중국인은 관청에서는 유가, 집에 돌아오면 도가라는 말이 있어. 도대체 도가가 무엇이기에 이런 말이 생겨난 걸까? 유가가 평화로운 사회를 위해 사람과 사람 사이의 조화로운 관계를 추구했다면, 도가는 인간과 자연 사이의 조화를 지향하라고 가르친 사상이야.

춘추 시대의 노자, 전국 시대의 장자가 대표적인 사상가인데 두 사람의 사상은 각각 《도덕경》과 《장자》를 통해 알 수 있단다. 《도덕경》에서 노자는 무위자연을 말하고 있는데 아무것도 하지 말라는 뜻이 아니라 자연의 순리에 거슬러서 무리하게 일을 추진하지 말라는 의미란다.

《장자》에서는 내가 좋아하는 것을 상대에게 주는 것이 아니라 상대가 좋아하는 것을 해주는 것이 진정으로 중요하다는 것을 설파하고 있어. 유가에서의 서(내가 싫은 것을 남에게 강요하지 말라)보다 한 단계 높은 경지가 아닌가 감탄하는 사람들이 있었지. 도가의 사상은 나중에 도교라는 종교에 흡수되어 오랫동안 중국인들의 삶에 깊은 영향을 끼쳤어.

The Story of the World

Chapter 34
The Rise of Julius Caesar

1 Caesar Is Kidnapped

영어로 시저(Caesar)라 불리는 율리우스카이사르(Julius Caesar)는 기원전 100년에 로마의 귀족 집안에서 태어났다. 어려서부터 수준 높은 교육을 받으며 정치가로서의 꿈을 키웠기 때문에 대중 선동에 능했고, 정치적인 수완도 뛰어났다. 30대에 이미 재무관과 법무관 등의 직책을 거치며 입지를 다졌고, 40대에는 갈리아 전쟁과 브리튼 섬의 원정을 성공적으로 이끌며 명실상부 로마의 새로운 권력으로 부상한다.

Do you remember the stories we already read about Rome? Rome grew from a small village to a rich, powerful city. Roman builders made roads so people could travel faster, aqueducts to bring water into the city, and apartments so many people could live within the city's walls. Rome also had a strong army. They defeated the Carthaginian general, Hannibal, and even sailed across the Mediterranean Sea to attack Hannibal's home city of Carthage!

The great city of Rome became the richest, strongest city in the world. People from far away knew about Rome. They admired its beautiful buildings and splendid roads. They came from all over to trade in Rome, to watch the gladiator fights, and to admire Roman art. The Romans were the most powerful and prosperous people anywhere.

One day, a baby boy was born to a rich family in Rome. His parents named him Julius Caesar. The Caesars were important people. They claimed to be descended from Romulus, the founder of the city of Rome. Julius's father was a rich nobleman who helped to make the laws of Rome. And Julius's uncle was a consul, one of the two rulers of Rome. "My little boy will accomplish great things!" Julius's father declared. "He will become one of the most famous men in Rome!"

As soon as Julius was old enough, his father sent him to school to learn reading, writing, mathematics, and *rhetoric*—the art of speaking in public. Julius Caesar became very good at speaking in public. He grew up to be tall and strong, with keen black eyes and a deep, powerful voice. Whenever he made a speech, crowds gathered to listen to him.

Soon Julius decided that he wanted to help govern Rome. He threw big parties for the people he needed to vote for him. He did favors for them. He became more and more popular.

But Julius decided that he needed even more lessons in rhetoric, so that he could convince even more Romans to vote for him. And the most famous rhetoric teacher of all lived in an island in the middle of the Mediterranean Sea. So Julius Caesar hired a ship to take him out to the island. "It'll cost you extra," the captain of the ship told him. "There are pirates all over the Mediterranean. Their ships are faster than anyone else's. They steal cargo and kidnap important people. No one can control them. Are you sure you want to go?"

"I'm not afraid of pirates!" Julius answered. He paid the captain of the ship and got on board.

But no sooner was the ship out of sight of land than another ship came into view behind it—a sleek, fast ship. "Pirates!" the captain shouted. He tried to sail faster, but the pirate ship gained on him. All the sailors ran up to the deck to fight, but the pirates boarded the ship and took it over. They stole the cargo—and then they saw Julius Caesar, standing in the middle of the captured sailors. They could tell by his clothing that he was a rich, important man.

"We'll keep you for ransom," the pirate captain said. "Who are your relatives? We'll tell them that we'll send you back as soon as they pay us $100,000!"

Julius Caesar burst out laughing. "Is that all?" he said. "I'm worth at least $250,000!"

"You think you're so important?" the pirate said. "Very well, we'll keep you and see how much money we can make from you!"

"I'm warning you," Caesar said, "as soon as I'm free, I'll return and execute all of you."

The pirates laughed; they didn't take Caesar's threats seriously. They took him back to their ship and kept him for more than a month. But Caesar treated them as though *they* were the prisoners. "Savages!" he would call out. "Be quiet! I'm napping! And be sure that the food I'm served for supper is better than what I had for lunch!"

The pirates thought Caesar was funny. Finally, the government of Rome sent them Caesar's ransom. They took the money and told Caesar goodbye. "Go back to Rome, little boy," they mocked him. "Go back to where it's safe! The sea belongs to us."

But as soon as Caesar got back to Rome, he convinced the Roman navy to lend him three warships and several troops of soldiers. He sailed back out into the Mediterranean. Sure enough, as soon as the warships lost sight of land, the pirates appeared, sailing up fast behind them.

This time Caesar was ready. He told his soldiers, "Get ready to fight!" He circled his warships around and met the pirates head on. The soldiers and pirates fought hand-to-hand, climbing from one ship to another, until the pirates were defeated.

"Now who does the sea belong to?" Caesar said to the pirate captain. He took the pirates back to Rome, and had them all executed!

After this, everyone in Rome knew who Caesar was. They

knew that he was a strong leader and a fierce fighter. Julius Caesar's name was on everyone's lips. The people of Rome were ready to vote for Caesar!

2 The Consuls of Rome

로마 제국의 역사에서 세 명의 지도자가 권력과 역할을 분할해 통치한 것을 '삼두 정치(三頭政治)'라고 하는데, 영어로는 triumvirate라고 한다. 삼두 정치에서 '삼두(三頭)'는 '세 명의 지도자'를 뜻한다. 율리우스 카이사르의 힘이 커지면서 기원전 60년에 폼페이우스, 크라수스, 카이사르 등 세 명의 집정관(consul)이 로마 제국을 운영하는 제1차 삼두 정치를 시행하게 되었다. 제2차 삼두 정치는 카이사르가 죽은 후에 그의 측근이었던 안토니우스와 레피두스, 옥타비아누스에 의해 시행된다.

Once he was back in Rome, Julius Caesar decided that he wanted to be a consul. Do you remember who the consuls were? Rome got rid of its kings because the kings were tyrants who did whatever they wanted. Instead they had two rulers called consuls. Each consul was supposed to keep the other one from getting too much power.

But there was a problem: Rome already had two consuls. There was no room for Caesar.

Instead, Caesar was given the job of governing the Romans who lived all the way over in Spain. Many Romans had settled here, and they needed a Roman leader to run their colony.

Governing Spain was not Caesar's idea of an important job! But he knew that he could not become consul in Rome yet. So in 69 BC/BCE, he gathered together his men and his possessions, and set off for Spain. He traveled up through Italy, over the Alps.

On the way through the Alps, Caesar and his friends came to

a tiny, shabby village high up in the mountains. The streets were made of mud. The people were dressed in rags. Goats ran around between the houses, and the children played barefoot in the dirt.

"What a disgusting place to live!" one of Caesar's friends exclaimed. "Can you imagine spending your life here?"

Caesar turned around to him. "I would rather be the most important man here," he snapped, "than second in command in Rome."

They traveled on to Spain. In Spain, Caesar worked hard and became popular. He drove away the mountain bandits that kept attacking the Roman cities in Spain. But all the time, he longed to go back to Rome and become powerful there, in his home town.

One day, he was sitting in his library reading about the life of Alexander the Great. His friends were there with him, talking

Julius Caesar

about life in Spain and when they might be able to return to Rome. Slowly they noticed that Caesar had stopped reading. He sat with his book on his knee, staring out the window. On the page in front of him was a picture of Alexander the Great, riding his great warhorse Bucephalus, with hundreds of cheering soldiers following him into battle. Suddenly Caesar burst into tears.

His friends had never seen him weep before. "Caesar! Caesar! What is wrong?" they asked.

"Don't you think I have reason to be sad?" Caesar asked them. "By the time he was my age, Alexander the Great was already the king of five or six different countries! And I haven't done anything remarkable yet! I should weep and be sad! When will I have the chance to become famous?"

Finally, Caesar was allowed to return to Rome. He convinced the two consuls who ruled Rome that he should become consul as well. Now three powerful men ruled Rome—and Caesar was one of them! The three rulers were called the *triumvirate*. *Tri* means "three." How many wheels does a tricycle have? Three. How many children are there when triplets are born? Three. Triumvirate means "three leaders."

But Caesar became more and more popular with the people of Rome. They knew that he was a good general and a strong fighter, and they thought that Caesar could keep them safe. Before long, no one paid much attention to the other two consuls. Caesar was the only one who mattered.

3 Caesar and the Senate

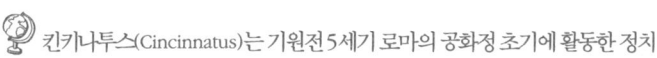 킨카나투스(Cincinnatus)는 기원전 5세기 로마의 공화정 초기에 활동한 정치

가이다. 집정관의 자리에 오르지만, 1년의 임기가 끝난 후 은퇴해 고향으로 돌아갔다. 기원전 458년에 이민족의 침입으로 로마가 위기에 처하자 로마의 귀족들은 킨키나투스를 독재관으로 추대하고 전권을 위임했다. 킨키나투스는 전시 체제로 전환하고 짧은 시간 안에 군대를 양성해 위기에 처한 로마를 구한다. 그리고 임기가 남아 있었음에도 불구하고 다시 권력을 버리고 귀향한다. 킨키나투스는 이상적인 정치인의 표상으로 역사에 기록되어 그의 이름은 '숨어 있는 위인'을 상징하는 용어로도 쓰인다.

Julius Caesar was popular with the people of Rome. But he wasn't popular with the Senate.

The Senate was a group of rich, powerful men who had most of the power in Rome. The Senate helped to take care of Rome. The consuls were supposed to listen to what the Senate said. But Caesar didn't pay very much attention to the Senate. He did what he pleased.

The Senate was unhappy about this. They were suspicious of Caesar. "What if he wants to become king?" they asked each other. "What will happen to Rome? What will happen to us? One man should not rule Rome. We should govern Rome together, so that no single man has all the power in Rome! *If only Caesar were like Cincinnatus!"

Who was Cincinnatus? He was a legendary Roman who represented the ideal ruler of Rome. Here is the story of Cincinnatus:

Once upon a time, Cincinnatus was a consul of Rome. But he lost his wealth, retired from his high position, and became a farmer instead. He spent his days planting wheat and tending grapes. But he was so wise and well-loved that Romans came to him from all over to ask his advice.

Now, Rome was the strongest city in the world. But one day, Rome heard disturbing news: A tribe of barbarians was headed towards Rome, burning and plundering everything in their path. They had sworn to conquer Rome and kill its people.

The Romans weren't afraid—yet. After all, the Roman army was the most powerful in the world. So they sent out their most skillful soldiers to stop the barbarians. The soldiers rode out of Rome, splendid in shining armor and scarlet cloaks. The women and children cheered and waved. "Come back in glory and triumph!" they called out. "Come back in victory!"

They waited day after day after day. Finally, they saw dust in the distance: horsemen were approaching the city. But what had happened to the Roman army? Only five dirty, bloodstained soldiers were returning. They galloped through the gates into the center of the city and told their story, gasping with pain and weariness. "The barbarians are too strong for us!" they said. "They attacked us at a narrow mountain pass! They came at us from behind and from ahead. And meanwhile they threw rocks at us from the hills above us. Send help to our army at once, or Rome will fall!"

The Senate was terrified. "All our strongest soldiers have already gone!" the senators said to each other. "We only have boys left. Who can lead them into battle?"

Suddenly one senator said, "Cincinnatus! Let us send for Cincinnatus. He is our only hope!"

Cincinnatus was out working in his fields when the senators arrived at his house. He washed the dirt off his hands and listened to their pleas. "If you will lead the reinforcements into battle," they promised him, "we will make you the king of Rome."

So Cincinnatus returned to the city with them and became the leader of the reinforcements. He armed the boys and taught them how to fight, and then led them out towards the mountains to rescue the Roman army. Cincinnatus was so wise and crafty that this troop of boys beat off the barbarians, drove them back to the mountains, and brought the rest of the Roman army home! They marched back into Rome with trumpets blaring and people cheering.

"Be our king, Cincinnatus!" the people of Rome begged. "We will give you all power! You can do whatever you want!"

But Cincinnatus took off his armor and gave his banner back to the Senate. "No," he said, "Rome does not need a king. I give all my power back to the senators. They should make your laws." And he went back to his fields and his grapes, leaving the Senate in charge of Rome.

Cincinnatus was the ideal Roman. He served his city when he was needed, but then he gave his power back to the Senate. But Caesar wouldn't behave like Cincinnatus. He kept on gathering power. He became more and more popular.

"One day," the senators said to each other, "Caesar will try to become king of Rome. Then what will we do?"

Note to Parent: Caesar was born in 100 BC/BCE.

The Story of the Words

Chapter 34 The Rise of Julius Caesar

1 Caesar Is Kidnapped

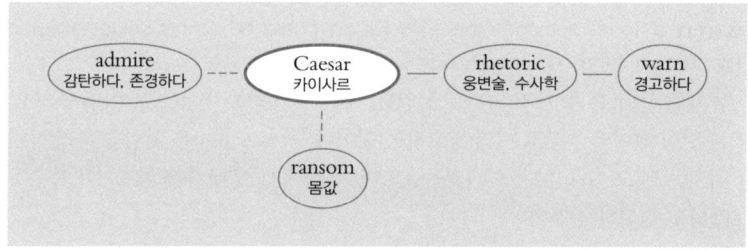

admire ⓥ to respect or approve of someone or something
admire에서 ad는 at(~에)이고, mire는 to wonder(놀라다)를 뜻한다. 즉 '~을 보고(ad) 놀라다(mire)'라는 의미이다. 즉 admire는 '감탄하다, 칭찬하다, 존경하다'라는 뜻이나. '감탄, 칭찬, 존경'을 뜻하는 명사형은 admiration이다.
They admired its beautiful buildings and splendid roads. 그들은 로마의 아름다운 건물들과 멋진 도로를 보고 감탄했다.

rhetoric ⓝ the art of speaking or writing to persuade or influence people
rhetoric은 '말이나 글로 사람의 마음을 움직이는 기술'을 뜻한다. 흔히 '웅변술, 수사학(修辭學)'을 말한다. 고대 그리스 시대부터 존재하는 의미였으나 형태만 바뀌었을 뿐, 의미는 예나 지금이나 똑같다. 민주 정치를 하려면 대중을 설득해야 하고, 적극적으로 소통해야 하기 때문에 rhetoric은 고대 그리스 시대부터 대단히 중요한 능력 중 하나였다.
As soon as Julius was old enough, his father sent him to school to learn reading, writing, mathematics, and *rhetoric*—the art of speaking in public. 율리우스가 어느 정도 나이가 들자, 그의 아버지는 그를 학교에 보내 읽기, 쓰기, 수학, 수사학(대중 앞에서 연설하는 기술)을 배우게 했다.

ransom ⓝ money that is paid to free someone who is captured or kidnapped

ransom은 원래 '대가를 치르고 속죄하는 것'을 뜻하는 말이었다. 예를 들어 다른 사람을 다치게 했다면 치료비와 배상금을 물어주고 죄를 면하는 것이다. 그런데 지금은 '납치되거나 억류된 사람을 풀려나게 하려고 지불하는 돈', 쉽게 말해 '몸값'을 의미한다.
"We'll keep you for ransom," the pirate captain said. 해적 선장이 말했다. "우리가 몸값을 받아내기 위해 너를 붙잡아두겠다."

warn ⓥ to tell someone that they will be punished or that something bad will happen if they do something

동사형 warn은 두 가지 의미로 쓰인다. 우선 '걱정하는 마음'으로 어떤 좋지 않은 일이 일어날 거라고 미리 경고하는 것이다. 즉 warning은 위험을 미리 상기시키는 '경고'이다. 다른 의미로는 잘못된 행동에 대해 대가를 치르거나 복수하겠다고 경고하는 것이다.
"I'm warning you," Caesar said, "as soon as I'm free, I'll return and execute all of you." 카이사르가 말했다. "경고하는데, 내가 풀려나자마자 다시 돌아와 너희 모두를 처형할 거야."

2 The Consuls of Rome

possession ⓝ something that you own

possess는 '점유한, 보유한'을 뜻하는 라틴어에서 유래하여 '소유하다, 갖추다'라는 뜻이다. possession은 possess의 명사형으로, 소유하는 행위나 소유한 물건, 즉 '재산, 소유물'을 뜻한다. 부동산이든 동산이든 자기 것으로 소유한 것은 모두 possessions에 해당한다.
So in 69 BC/BCE, he gathered together his men and his possessions, and set off for Spain. 그래서 기원전 69년에 카이사르는 자신의 하인과 재산을 모두 모아서 스페인으로 출발했다.

> **Q** 원로원 의원들은 왜 카이사르를 싫어했나요?
> **A** 당시 로마에는 귀족파와 평민파가 있었어. 원로원 의원들의 대부분은 귀족파였단다. 그들은 공화정의 이상인 '모든 시민에게 골고루 이익이 보장되는 사회'를 더는 추구하지 않았어. 확보한 재산을 더 늘리고, 노예들의 시중을 받는 삶에 익숙해질수록 그들은 더 보수적으로 되었거든.
> 기원전 60년 집정관에 취임한 카이사르는 쿠리아(원로원 의원들이 모여서 회의하는 장소)의 첫 회의에서 분열을 끝내고 공화정을 위해 일하자고 말했어. 이 말에 원로원 의원들은 기분이 상했겠지? 카이사르는 말로만 끝내지 않고, 실제로 로마의 가난한 사람들의 생활을 개선하기 위해 노력했단다. 사람들이 '올해는 율리우스 집정관과 카이사르 집정관의 해였어'라고 할 정도로 열심히 일했어. 문제는 집정관은 1년밖에 할 수 없다는 것이었지.

snap ⓥ to suddenly speak to someone in an angry way
땅콩이나 얼음을 입에 넣고 씹으면 '바삭, 와작' 하고 큰 소리가 나면서 깨진다. snap은 이렇게 딱딱한 음식을 소리 내며 씹는 행동을 뜻한다. 엄지 검지를 맞대고 비틀어 '딱' 소리를 내는 것도 to snap one's fingers라고 표현한다. 말할 때 갑자기 화가 난 듯 언성을 높이는 경우가 있는데, 이때도 He snapped at me(그는 내게 갑자기 언성을 높였다)처럼 쓴다.
"I would rather be the most important man here," he snapped, "than second in command in Rome." 그가 언성을 높이며 말했다. "난 로마에서 2인자가 되느니 차라리 이곳에서 가장 중요한 사람이 되겠다."

long ⓥ to want something very much
오랫동안(for a long time) 먹고 싶은 것을 먹지 못하면 무척 생각난다. 이처럼 욕구가 채워지지 않은 채 시간이 오래 지날수록 그 욕구의 크기가 점점 더 커진다. 이때 long은 '간절히 바라다, 갈망하다'라는 뜻이다.
But all the time, he longed to go back to Rome and become powerful there, in his home town. 그러나 그는 언제나 로마로 돌아가서 고향인 그곳에서 힘센 사람이 되기를 갈망했다.

burst ⓥ to suddenly begin to make a sound, especially to start crying or laughing

burst는 갑자기 뭔가를 터뜨리거나 터지는 것을 나타낸다. The balloon burst while I was blowing it은 풍선을 불고 있는데, 갑자기 풍선이 터진 것이다. 참고 있던 감정이 북받쳐 밖으로 표출될 때도 burst를 쓰는데, The audience burst into laughter(관객들이 웃음을 터뜨렸다)처럼 갑자기 웃음이나 울음이 나올 때 쓴다. burst-burst-burst
Suddenly Caesar burst into tears. 카이사르는 갑자기 울음을 터뜨렸다.

remarkable ⓐ unusual or surprising in a good way

remarkable은 '계속(re) 주목받다(mark)'라는 뜻의 remark에 형용사형 접미사 -able이 붙은 말이다. 그래서 '주목할 만한, 놀라운, 뛰어난'을 뜻한다. a remarkable talent는 '놀랄 만한 재능'이고, He was a truly remarkable king 이라고 쓰면 '그는 정말 뛰어난 왕이었다'라는 뜻이다.
And I haven't done anything remarkable yet! 그런데 나는 아직도 주목받을 만한 일을 전혀 하지 못했어!

matter ⓥ to be important

matter는 '어머니(mother)'를 뜻하는 라틴어 mater에서 유래했다. 어머니는 '탄생시키는 존재'이다. 그래서 '대자연'을 Mother Nature라고 부르고, 대자연이 낳은 '물질'도 matter라고 한다. 또한 어떤 원인으로부터 '태어난 문제나 상황'을 나타내 It's an important matter(그건 중요한 문제야)처럼 쓴다. 이런 의미에서 발전하여 '중요하다, 문제가 되다'라는 뜻의 동사형으로도 쓰인다.
Caesar was the only one who mattered. 중요한 건 카이사르 한 사람뿐이었다.

3 Caesar and the Senate

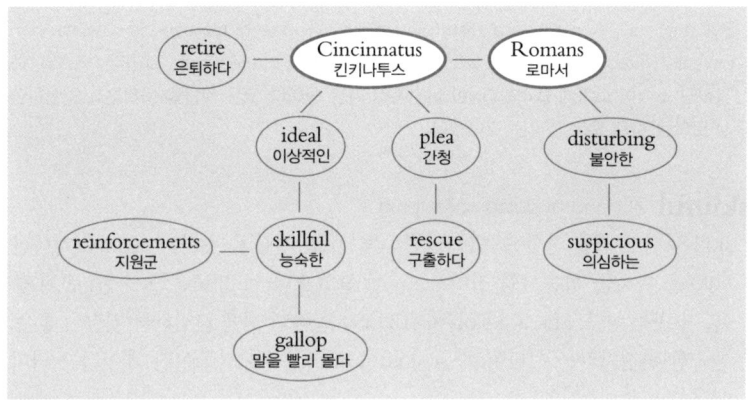

suspicious ⓐ not willing to trust someone or something
suspicious에는 '불신임(mistrust)'의 뜻이 담겨 있다. 믿지 못해 '아래위로(sub-) 훑어보는(spicio)' 것이다. 동사 suspect(의심하다)와 명사형 suspicion(의심, 의혹)도 같은 의미이다. suspicious는 a suspicious death(의문의 죽음)처럼 수식어로 쓸 수 있고, The police was suspicious of me(경찰은 나를 의심했다)처럼 쓸 수 있다.
They were suspicious of Caesar 그들은 카이사르를 의심했다.

retire ⓥ to stop working, usually because you have reached a certain age
retire는 '뒤로(back)'를 뜻하는 re-와 '당기다(draw)'를 뜻하는 tire가 합쳐진 것이다. 뒤로 당기니까 후퇴하여 결국 자리에서 물러나게 된다. 즉 '은퇴하다, 퇴직하다'라는 뜻이다. He retired from his high position(그는 고위직에서 물러났다), 자기 의지와 관계없이 '은퇴를 당할' 경우에는 He was retired due to his illness(그는 병 때문에 은퇴했다)처럼 수동태로 쓴다. 명사형은 retirement(은퇴, 퇴직)이다.
But he lost his wealth, retired from his high position, and became a farmer instead. 그러나 그는 재산을 잃었고, 고위직에서 물러나 농부가 되었다.

disturbing ⓐ making someone feel worried or upset
disturbing은 '불안하게 하다, 흩뜨리다, 방해하다'라는 disturb의 형용사형이다. 혼란과 무질서 상태에 빠뜨릴 만큼 '충격적인, 불안감을 주는, 우려스러운'

chapter 34 The Rise of Julius Caesar 213

상태를 disturbing으로 표현한다. 야만족의 침입 소식에 로마인들이 불안하고 충격에 빠졌으니 그 소식은 disturbing news인 것이다.

But one day, Rome heard disturbing news: A tribe of barbarians was headed towards Rome, burning and plundering everything in their path. 그러나 어느 날, 충격적인 소식이 로마에 들려왔다. 한 야만족이 가는 곳마다 모든 것들을 불태우고 약탈하면서 로마로 향해 오고 있다는 것이었다.

skillful ⓐ good at doing something

skill은 어떤 일을 잘 할 수 있는 능력, 즉 '기술, 기량'을 뜻한다. skill에 '가득한 (full)'을 뜻하는 형용사형 접미사 -ful이 붙었으니, skillful은 '능숙한, 솜씨 좋은, 잘 만든'이다. She is a skillful editor라고 하면 책을 편집하는 기술이 좋은, 능숙한 편집자라는 의미이고, a skillful book은 '잘 만들어진 책'이라는 의미이다.

So they sent out their most skillful soldiers to stop the barbarians. 그래서 그들은 야만족을 막기 위해 전투 기술이 가장 뛰어난 병사들을 내보냈다.

gallop ⓥ to drive a horse to run very fast

갤로퍼(Galloper)라는 이름의 국내 자동차 브랜드가 있었는데, galloper가 '질주하는 말'을 뜻하므로 힘 좋고 잘 달리는 자동차를 표현한 것이다. gallop은 '말이 전속력으로 질주하다' 또는 '말을 전속력으로 몰다'라는 뜻이다.

They galloped through the gates into the center of the city and told their story, gasping with pain and weariness. 그들은 말을 타고 전속력으로 달려서 성문을 통과해 도심으로 들어왔고, 고통과 피로 때문에 숨을 헐떡이며 이야기를 전했다.

plea ⓝ a request that is urgent or full of emotion

plea는 철자에서 짐작할 수 있듯이, plead나 please와 사촌지간이다. 모두 '간절히 청하다'는 의미를 담고 있다. '긴급하게 애원하듯 하는 부탁'이 plea이다.

He washed the dirt off his hands and listened to their pleas. 그는 손을 씻고 나서 그들의 간청을 들었다.

reinforcements ⓝ more soldiers that are sent to a battle, to make their group stronger

inforce는 '힘(force)'을 불어 '넣다(in)'라는 뜻이다. 그 앞에 '다시(again)'를 뜻하는 접두사 re-가 붙으면, reinforce(다시 힘을 불어넣다)가 된다. 명사형 접미사

-ment를 붙이면 reinforcement, 즉 '다시 힘을 불어넣는 것'이다. 전쟁 상황에서 복수형 reinforcements를 쓰면 이미 전투 중인 자기편 군대에 힘을 보태기 위해 파견하는 '중원군, 지원군'을 뜻한다.
"If you will lead the reinforcements into battle," they promised him, "we will make you the king of Rome." 그들은 그에게 약속했다. "만일 당신이 지원군을 이끌고 전투에 나간다면, 우리가 당신을 로마의 왕으로 만들어 주겠소."

rescue ⓥ to save someone from danger
rescue에서 re-는 강조의 역할을 하고, scue는 to pull away(당겨 꺼내다)를 뜻한다. 힘들게[세게] 당겨서 벗어나게 한다, 즉 rescue는 '구조하다, 구출하다'라는 뜻의 동사형이나 '구조, 구출'을 뜻하는 명사형으로 쓰인다.
He armed the boys and taught them how to fight, and then led them out towards the mountains to rescue the Roman army. 그는 그 소년들을 무장시키고 싸우는 법을 가르친 다음, 로마 군대를 구출하기 위해 그들을 그 산으로 이끌고 갔다.

ideal ⓐ perfect; the best or most suitable
ideal은 '이상적인, 가장 알맞은'을 뜻하는 형용사이다. '보다(to see)'를 뜻하는 희랍어 id에서 유래하여, idea는 '보이는 것, 형상, 존재'를 뜻했다. 그런데 고대 그리스 철학자 플라톤(Plato)의 '이데아(Idea)론'에 영향을 받아 ideal이 현재의 뜻으로 쓰이게 되었다. ideal은 '이상, 이상적인 것'을 뜻하는 명사형으로도 쓰인다.
Cincinnatus was the ideal Roman. 킨키나투스는 이상적인 로마인이었다.

The Story of the World

Chapter 35
Caesar the Hero

1 Caesar Fights the Celts

로마 제국의 카이사르가 브리튼 섬을 침입할 당시, 그 섬의 주인은 켈트족(Celts)이었다. 카이사르는 기원전 55년 8월에 대규모 병력과 함대를 거느리고 브리튼 섬에 상륙한다. 그러나 브리튼 전사들의 강력한 저항과 기상 악화로 인해 곧 철수할 수밖에 없었다. 그로부터 1년 후 카이사르는 다시 브리튼 섬을 침공해 템스 강 북쪽까지 진격했다. 그러나 켈트족은 여러 소왕국을 이루고 있었기 때문에 로마군은 계속 여러 왕국의 군대를 상대해야 했고, 결국 전투력이 고갈되었다. 로마가 브리튼 섬에 정착촌을 세운 것은 그로부터 약 90년이 지난 후였다.

Caesar didn't have any intention of going back to his fields, like Cincinnatus. But he knew that the Roman people wouldn't make him king yet. Before he could be king, the Romans would have to love him and trust him even more.

So Caesar set out to be the greatest war hero ever. If he won many battles and conquered a great deal of land for Rome, maybe he could convince the people of Rome that he would make a good king.

Caesar took good care of his army. He trained them to fight. He paid them well and gave them plenty to eat. The soldiers weren't used to being treated so well. Soon they were completely loyal to Caesar. They followed him into battle against Rome's neighbors. Caesar didn't always win his battles, but he didn't let the people of Rome know that. Instead, he only sent them messages about his victories! He pretended that he never lost a fight.

The country Caesar wanted to conquer most was called Britain. Caesar thought that Britain would be easy to conquer. But he had to build ships and sail his army across the water to get to Britain's shores.

He built the ships, and put the soldiers onto them. The ships set out for Britain. But some of them got lost on the way. And the soldiers who did make it to Britain were cold, wet, and tired. They were sick of the ocean and ready to get back to dry land.

"Look!" one of them shouted at last. "Land!"

The soldiers clustered at the side of the boat, anxious to see Britain for the first time. They saw a misty green island—with an army waiting for them on its shore.

The people who lived in Britain were called Celts. They were tall, muscular, warlike men. They were so proud of their height and strength that they went into battle naked! They wore only metal collars and tall metal helmets that made them look even bigger. They carried heavy iron swords and wooden clubs. And they painted their bodies blue all over, because they thought that the blue lines would magically protect them from swords and arrows.

The Romans stared up at these huge, painted warriors. They began to murmur among themselves: "We can never beat them! They are too big and fierce!"

When the boy who held Caesar's flag heard the soldiers murmuring, he jumped out of his ship, into the shallow water near the beach. He started to wade ashore, holding the flag high. The other soldiers didn't want to see Caesar's flag captured, so they leaped in after him. The Celts attacked. They fought there, ankle-deep in the water, for hours. Finally the Celts retreated. The Romans landed triumphantly on the beaches of Britain.

But the Romans only stayed in Britain three weeks. A huge storm wrecked many of the Roman ships. More Roman soldiers were ambushed and defeated. Finally Caesar decided to leave Britain and come back with a bigger army.

He came back a year later with more soldiers. This time he

was able to stay in Britain longer. He forced some of the Celts to pay money to the Roman army as tribute. But the other British tribes remained free of Roman control.

Caesar hadn't exactly conquered Britain. But he didn't tell the people in Rome about his defeats! Instead, he kept sending messages of victory back to Rome. He even wrote a book about his wars in Gaul and Britain, called *The Gallic Wars*. In his book, Caesar hardly even mentioned the times when he was defeated. He only talked about his successes. He didn't exactly tell lies, but he certainly talked about his battles in a way that made him sound even more victorious and successful than he was.

2 Caesar Crosses the Rubicon

기원전 58년부터 51년까지 카이사르는 로마군을 이끌고 갈리아 지역을 정복하는데, 이 정복 전쟁을 갈리아 전쟁(The Galic Wars)이라고 부른다. 갈리아는 현재의 프랑스와 벨기에, 스위스와 독일의 서쪽 지역을 일컫는다. 카이사르는 갈리아를 정복한 후에도 계속 그곳에서 지방 장관으로 지내며 갈리아인들의 반란을 진압했다. 결국 그들은 로마의 속민이 되었고, 카이사르는 로마의 영웅으로 부상하게 된다. 이후 로마의 귀족들로부터 시기와 견제를 받게 된 카이사르는 기원전 49년에 군대를 이끌고 루비콘 강을 건너 로마로 진격한다.

Caesar's victories made him a hero to the people of Rome. But the senators were afraid of Caesar.

"If he comes back to Rome now," the senators said to each other, "the people will want him to be king of Rome! And then what will happen to us? We won't be able to run Rome any more!"

Two of the senators decided that they would try to make

one of the other consuls, Pompey, turn against Caesar. This was hard to do, because Pompey had married Caesar's daughter. But Pompey was jealous of Caesar. He knew that Caesar was much more popular than he was.

So Pompey agreed to listen to the senators. "Listen," they said to him. "Tell the people of Rome that Caesar is a traitor! Tell them that he isn't loyal to Rome. Take away Caesar's position of consul before he gets back to Rome. Then you will be the strongest man in the whole city!"

So Pompey agreed. He sent a message to Caesar, telling him that he would be arrested when he returned to Rome. He told Caesar to give up command of his army. And all the people of Rome were told that Caesar was a traitor.

Far away in Britain, Caesar got the bad news. His own city was calling him a criminal and a traitor! And the Senate wanted to arrest him and put him on trial! What should he do?

Caesar knew that the Senate didn't like him. But he was convinced that the Roman people still thought of him as a great hero. So he took his army and marched back towards Rome.

Soon Caesar came to the Rubicon River. The Rubicon was the border of Roman land. Caesar knew that as soon as he crossed over the Rubicon, he would be in the land controlled by the senators. The senators would try to arrest him, and he would have to fight them. His army would end up fighting against other Romans! If he crossed over the Rubicon, he would start a civil war—a war that a country fights against itself. Should he do it?

He stood at the river for a long time, staring at the bridge. "Even yet," he said to the captain of his army, "we may turn back. But once we cross that little bridge ... we will have to settle this with our swords."

Finally Caesar drew his sword and stepped onto the bridge.

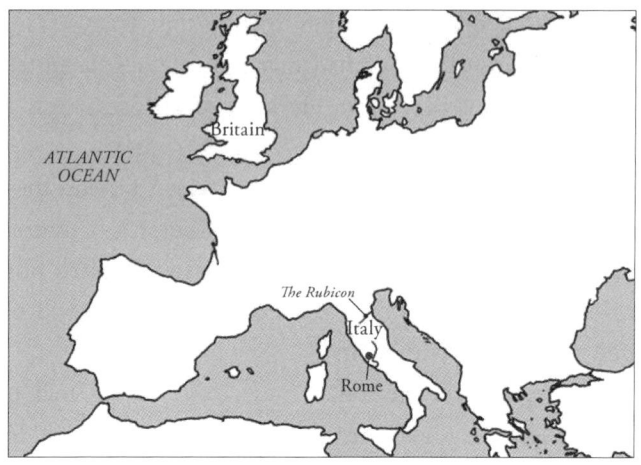

Caesar, Britain, and the Rubicon

"My enemies have forced me to do this!" he announced. "We will march into Rome. Let the die be cast!" He crossed the Rubicon on January 10, 49 BC/BCE. His army followed him towards Rome.

Back in Rome, Pompey and the senators were trying to raise an army of their own. But no one wanted to fight against Caesar's soldiers. After all, Caesar's army had spent years fighting in foreign countries. They were tough, strong, and loyal to their leader. When Caesar and his army came in sight of Rome, all of Pompey's soldiers ran away. And before Caesar could enter the city, Pompey fled as well.

Caesar marched triumphantly into Rome. No one dared to arrest him. Now the Senate had to admit that Caesar was too powerful to drive away. Caesar wasn't king yet, but he was the strongest man in Rome.

Today, when someone has to make an important decision, people still say "You're about to cross the Rubicon." *Crossing the Rubicon* means that you're about to do something that you can't undo. We get this expression from the story of Julius Caesar's return to Rome.

3 Caesar and Cleopatra

클레오파트라(Cleopatra)는 지금도 절세미인의 대명사처럼 기억되는 이름이다. 그런데 사실 클레오파트라의 장점은 지성미와 정치력에 있었다. 그녀는 '세계의 도서관'이라 불릴 만큼 책이 많았던 이집트 왕실의 도서관에서 학식을 쌓았고 여러 언어에도 능통했다고 전해진다. 남동생인 프톨레마이오스 13세와의 권력 다툼에서 이기기 위해 로마의 권력자인 카이사르와 연애를 했고, 그의 사후에는 이집트의 존립을 도모하기 위해 안토니우스의 연인이 된다. 결국 이집트 정벌에 나선 옥타비아누스에게 패해 그녀와 안토니우스는 자결하고 만다.

Caesar now ruled all of Rome and all of Rome's territories. The army obeyed him. The people loved him. And the Senate couldn't drive him out.

But Caesar still wanted to get rid of Pompey. He knew that Pompey had run away to Egypt. And down in Egypt, Pompey was trying to convince the Egyptians to help him attack Caesar and take Rome back.

"I can't leave him down there!" Caesar thought to himself. "He'll come marching back up here with a whole army of Egyptians and attack me again. As long as Pompey is free, this civil war will never end. I'll have to go down to Egypt and arrest Pompey and put him in jail before I can have any peace."

So he started down to Egypt. But the Egyptians were having troubles of their own. They had two pharaohs—a queen named Cleopatra and her brother. Cleopatra and her brother were supposed to rule Egypt together. *But they didn't get along with

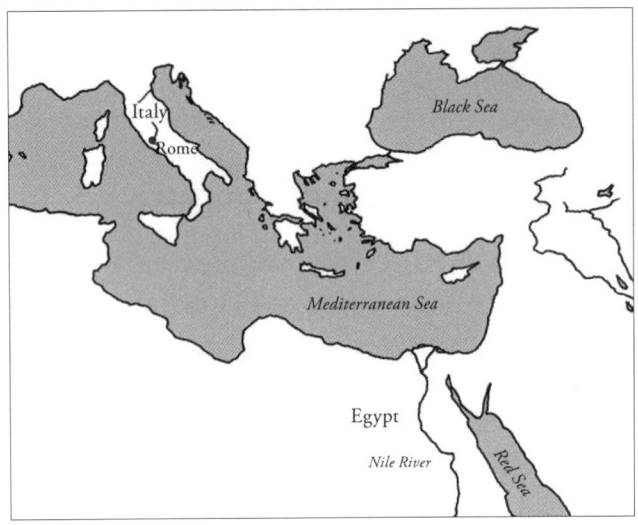

Caesar in Egypt

each other. They fought constantly, because each one wanted to rule Egypt alone.

But when Cleopatra and her brother heard that Caesar was coming, they stopped quarrelling with each other. They were terrified. The whole world had heard of Caesar. The Egyptians were sure that Caesar was coming to conquer them. "What will we do?" Cleopatra and her brother asked each other. "We've got to make friends with him quickly, or else he will attack us with his invincible army!"

"I know," Cleopatra's brother exclaimed, suddenly. "Caesar's old enemy Pompey is living in Egypt. Let's arrest him and send him to Caesar as a prisoner. Then Caesar will know that we want to be his allies."

"I have a better idea," Cleopatra answered. "Let's cut off Pompey's head and send that to Caesar instead."

So that is what they did. Caesar was startled to get Pompey's head in a bag. And he was sad, too. He and Pompey had once been friends. They had been consuls together for years. And Pompey had been his son-in-law! He hadn't intended to kill Pompey. He just wanted to put him in prison where he couldn't cause any more trouble.

Caesar marched the rest of the way to the Egyptian palace, intending to tell the pharaohs of Egypt how unhappy he was. Meanwhile, though, Cleopatra had an idea. "If I can get Caesar to like me," she thought, "maybe he will help me get rid of my brother! Then I will be the only pharaoh of Egypt!"

So she arranged to meet Caesar all alone. She put on her prettiest clothes and surrounded herself with beautiful treasures of Egypt: gold, spices, monkeys, slaves, and jewelry. When Caesar was shown into Cleopatra's room, he was dazzled by her beauty, and by the riches all around her!

"Caesar," Cleopatra said sweetly, "if you'll help me get rid of my brother, so that I can rule Egypt all by myself, I will share Egypt's riches with you."

Caesar was overcome by Cleopatra. He fell madly in love with her and agreed to do everything she said. He told his army to fight against the Egyptians who were loyal to Cleopatra's brother. The Roman soldiers did as they were told. Cleopatra's brother was killed in the battle, and Cleopatra became the sole ruler of Egypt.

It was time for Caesar to go back to Rome, but he delayed. He didn't want to leave Cleopatra. Instead he stayed in Egypt, keeping his new love company.

But the senators back in Rome still wanted to get rid of Caesar. "This is our last chance," they said to each other. "Let's raise an army of Romans who are loyal to the Senate and try to defeat Caesar, one last time!"

So they gathered together an army and marched down

towards Egypt, ready to attack Caesar. Caesar hadn't forgotten how to fight, though. He got his own soldiers together and defeated the Senate army in record time.

Caesar was known for his fast victories. In fact, after one victory, when a friend asked him to describe the battle, he answered, "I can do it in three words: *Veni, Vidi, Vici.*" In Latin, the language of the Romans, this meant, "I came, I saw, I conquered!"

4 The Death of Caesar

카이사르는 루비콘강을 건너 폼페이우스를 비롯한 정적들을 몰아내고 명실상부 로마 제1의 권력자가 되었다. 이후 형식상 공화정은 유지되었지만, 사실상 카이사르의 독재가 펼쳐졌다. 대다수 로마 시민들은 카이사르의 정치를 지지했지만, 귀족들의 불만은 쌓여갔고 카이사르가 왕이 되려고 한다는 의심은 깊어갔다. 결국 원로원의 의원들은 기원전 44년 3월 15일에 카이사르를 무참히 살해한다. 카이사르는 폼페이우스 동상 옆에 쓰러진 채, 원로원 무리에 섞여 있던 브루투스(Brutus)를 보고는 "브루투스, 너마저!"라고 말했다고 한다. 카이사르가 과거에 폼페이우스의 부하였던 브루투스를 살려주고 아껴주었음에도 불구하고, 은혜를 저버리고 그를 죽였기 때문에 한 말이었다.

Caesar finally left Egypt and came back to Rome. No one could fight against him any more! And the people loved him. So when he came back to Rome, Caesar was made dictator for life.

A dictator can do whatever he wants. And once Caesar was dictator, he took power away from the Senate. Now, only Caesar could declare war, pass laws, and raise taxes. He started to make money with his own picture on it. He paid for gladiator fighting and chariot racing to amuse the people of Rome. Everything seemed to be going his way.

But then Caesar did two things that made many people angry. First, he called the Senate together. "I am the dictator of Rome," he told them, "but the kings of other countries will respect me more if you call me 'King Caesar.' So from now on I want you to call me 'king.' Second, I want my nephew Octavian to be king after me. I'm going to adopt him to be my son. I want him to inherit my power too."

The Senate was horrified. They wanted to choose the next leader of Rome. They didn't want another Caesar on the throne, and they didn't want kings of Rome to keep on passing their power on to their sons.

"We have to get rid of Caesar once and for all," said one senator, named Brutus. He had been a friend of Caesar's, but now he too was worried about Caesar's power in Rome. "Tomorrow is the fifteenth of March. We'll attack him as he enters the Senate and stab him to death!"

Other senators agreed, and the plans were made. Caesar was doomed!

Caesar didn't know anything about the plot to kill him. But a Roman writer named Suetonius tells us that many strange things happened to Caesar leading up to that day. He went out to visit his favorite herd of horses, and found that the horses weren't eating. Instead, they were crying. This made Caesar so nervous that he went to the temple, to ask the gods why his horses were so sad. But while he was in the temple, a fortuneteller came up to him and whispered, "Caesar! Caesar! Beware the fifteenth of March!"

When he got home, Caesar told his wife all about the strange things that had happened that day. During the night, she had a terrifying dream. She dreamed that she was holding her husband in her arms, and that he had been stabbed to death. She cried out, "Caesar! Caesar!" and woke up. She sat straight up in bed, and the door of their room flew open—all by itself. When Caesar got up the next morning, his wife pleaded with him, "Don't go to the Senate today. It's the fifteenth of March. Stay home where it's safe."

"Nonsense!" Caesar said. "Nothing will happen to me." He dressed and headed for the Senate building. He walked up the smooth marble steps. The sun shone on the white stone, and the sky was blue and peaceful overhead. "How silly of me to be nervous!" he thought. "Nothing will go wrong today!"

He went into the room where the Senate met and sat down in his special chair.

"Caesar," said one of the senators, "today I want to ask you to bring my brother back to Rome. He was banished several years ago."

"Let's talk about that later," Caesar said, still thinking about his wife's dream.

The senator leaped to his feet. "Friends!" he shouted, "what are we waiting for!" He ran forward and grabbed Caesar by his purple robe. Brutus and two other senators leaped at him with knives drawn. Caesar fought back, but they stabbed him. He staggered, and fell down at the feet of a statue of Pompey. When he looked up, he could hardly believe that his old friend Brutus had helped plot against him.

"*Et tu, Brute?*" he gasped. In Latin, this meant, "You, too, Brutus?" And then Caesar died, there on the marble floor of the Senate building. His slaves came and carried his body home. Caesar, the greatest Roman, had been killed by his own friends and countrymen. 📖

Note to Parent: Caesar's campaigns in Britain took place 55–54 BC/BCE. Cleopatra was born in 69 BC/BCE; she was twenty-one when Caesar arrived in Egypt in 48 BC/BCE (Caesar was fifty-two). Caesar was assassinated on March 15, 44 BC/BCE.

The Story of the Words

Chapter 35 Caesar the Hero

1 Caesar Fights the Celts

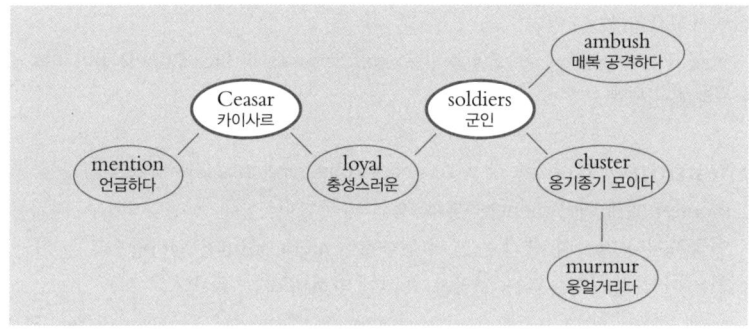

loyal ⓐ faithful; always supporting your country
'충성(忠誠)'은 동서 고금을 막론하고 군주와 상관 사이에 대단히 중요한 필수 덕목이었다. 이런 '충성심'이 loyalty이고, '충성스러운, 신뢰될 수 있는'을 뜻하는 형용사가 loyal이다.
Soon they were completely loyal to Caesar. 곧 그들은 카이사르에 완전히 충성했다.

cluster ⓥ to form a small close group
우리말에 '옹기종기 모여 있다'는 표현이 있다. 서넛, 대여섯 정도의 사람들이 한 곳에 모여 있을 때 쓰는데, 이 상황에 꼭 맞는 단어가 cluster이다. 명사형으로 a cluster of stars(별 무리)처럼 '무리'를 뜻한다.
The soldiers clustered at the side of the boat, anxious to see Britain for the first time. 병사들은 난생 처음 브리튼 섬을 보고는 불안해하며 뱃전에 옹기종기 모여 있었다.

murmur ⓥ to say something in a soft quiet voice
전화 통화할 때 상대방의 소리가 잘 들리지 않으면 그냥 '뭐라 뭐라' 하는 것 같은데, 이렇게 소리가 작고 '웅얼'거리는 듯한 의성어가 murmur이다. '속삭이

chapter 35 Caesar the Hero 229

다, 웅얼거리다'라는 뜻이다.
They began to murmur among themselves: "We can never beat them! They are too big and fierce!" 그들은 작은 소리로 자기들끼리 웅성거렸다. "우린 절대 그들을 이기지 못할 거야! 너무 크고 사나워!"

ambush ⓥ to suddenly attack someone after hiding and waiting for them
ambush는 숨어 있다가 적이 오면 갑자기 나타나 공격하는 것이다. ambush에서 am-은 '속에, 안에(in)'를 뜻하고, bush는 '잡목, 수풀'을 뜻한다. 즉 수풀에 숨어서 기다리다가 적이 오면 기습 공격한다는 의미이다. ambush는 동사형과 명사형으로 쓸 수 있다.
More Roman soldiers were ambushed and defeated. 더 많은 로마 병사들이 매복 공격을 받고 패했다.

mention ⓥ to speak or write about something in a few words
mention에서 어근 ment는 '생각, 정신'을 뜻한다. 상대가 '생각'하도록 뭔가를 언급하거나 자신의 '생각'을 드러내는 것이 mention이다. 명사형으로는 '언급, 거론'이고, 동사형으로는 '언급하다, 짧게 말하다'라는 뜻이다.
In his book, Caesar hardly even mentioned the times when he was defeated. 자신의 책에서 카이사르는 자신이 패했을 때에 관해서는 거의 언급조차 하지 않았다.

2 Caesar Crosses the Rubicon

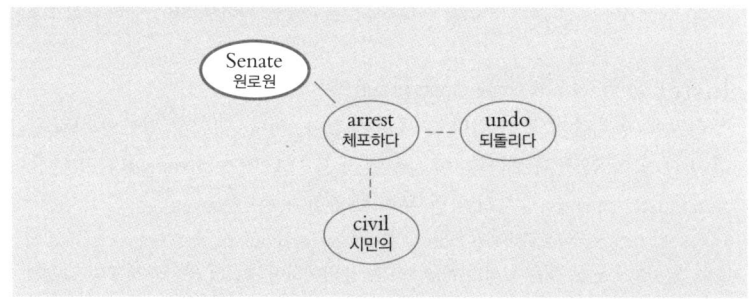

arrest ⓥ to catch and take someone away because he or she has done something wrong
'막다, 중지시키다(to stop)'를 뜻하는 라틴어에서 온 것으로, 불법적인 행동을

'막기 위해' 사법 기관이 개인을 '체포하다'라는 뜻이다. '체포'를 뜻하는 명사형 으로도 쓰인다. 경찰이 범인에게 You are under arrest!라고 하면 '당신을 체포 하겠다!'라는 의미이다.

He sent a message to Caesar, telling him that he would be arrested when he returned to Rome. 그는 카이사르에게 전갈을 보내서 로마로 돌아가면 체포될 것이라고 했다.

civil ⓐ relating to the people of a country

civil은 '도시에 사는 사람'이라는 의미에서 유래했다. 근대에 '국가(nation)' 개념이 확립되기 전까지 유럽에서 도시는 국가와 비슷한 개념이었기 때문에 civil은 '한 나라 안에 사는 사람들'을 의미한다. civil war는 같은 나라 안에 사는 사람들끼리 편을 나눠 싸우는 '내전(內戰)'이다. 미국의 남북 전쟁은 the Civil War이고, 한국 전쟁도 civil war로 표현할 수 있다.

If he crossed over the Rubicon, he would start a civil war—a war that a country fights against itself. 그가 루비콘 강을 건너면, 내전을 일으키게 될 것이다. 내전은 한 나라가 스스로에 대항해 싸우는 것이다.

> **Q** 카이사르는 어떻게 루비콘 강을 건너게 되었나요?
>
> **A** 루비콘 강은 갈리아 키살피나와 이탈리아를 가르는 강이야. 갈리아 키살피나는 이미 로마 속주였지만, 원래의 로마는 아니었어. 군대 지휘자라도 루비콘 강은 군대를 두고 건너야 한다는 규칙이 있었어. 왜냐고? 군사를 동반한 군지휘자는 그 힘으로 나라에 해를 가할 수도 있었거든. 그런데 카이사르의 입장에서 군대 없이 혼자 로마로 가면 체포될 우려가 있고, 군대를 이끌고 가자니 반역자가 되는 상황이니 이러지도 저러지도 못했겠지?
> 카이사르가 망설이고 있던 중, 한 사내가 피리를 불기 시작했어. 그의 연주를 들으러 근처 양치기들과 병사들도 함께 모였는데, 트럼펫을 들고 있는 병사도 있었단다. 그러자 그 사내는 트럼펫을 빌려 행진곡을 불면서 강을 훌쩍 넘어버렸다는거야. 이 광경을 본 카이사르는 신의 뜻으로 받아들이고, '주사위는 던져졌다'라는 역사에 남을 유명한 말을 하면서 루비콘 강을 건너게 되었어. 어디까지가 꾸며진 이야기이고, 어디까지가 사실인지 모르지만 그가 루비콘 강을 건너자 로마는 내전 상태가 되었지.

undo ⓥ to try to remove the bad effects of something

undo는 보다시피 '반대, 부정'을 뜻하는 접두사 un-과 '행동하다'를 뜻하는 do가 붙은 형태로, '한 행동의 반대'를 뜻한다. 쉽게 말해 '원위치!'의 개념이다. 세상에는 원위치가 안 되는 일들이 훨씬 더 많다. 그래서 What is done cannot be undone(이미 저지른 일은 되돌릴 수 없다)이라는 표현도 있다. undo-undid-undone

Crossing the Rubicon means that you're about to do something that you can't undo. '루비콘 강을 건너기'라는 말은 여러분이 어떤 되돌릴 수 없는 일을 하려고 한다는 의미이다.

3 Caesar and Cleopatra

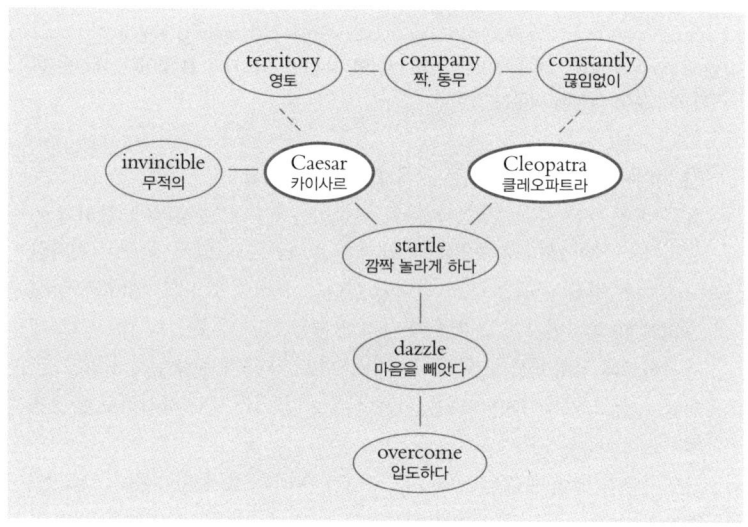

territory ⓝ land that is controlled by a government

territory에서 terr는 '땅(land)'을 의미하는 라틴어 어근이다. territory는 원래 '도시 경계의 땅'을 의미했으나 지금은 '영토, 영역'을 뜻한다. 카이사르가 통치하게 된 영토를 all of Rome's territories처럼 복수형으로 표현한 것은 로마가 제국이라서 식민지 영토가 여러 곳에 있었기 때문이다.

Caesar now ruled all of Rome and all of Rome's territories. 이제 카이사르는 로마 전체와 로마의 땅 전부를 통치하게 되었다.

constantly ⓐᵈ always or regularly
constantly는 형용사형 constant의 부사형이다. constant에서 라틴어 어근 sta는 '서 있다(stand)'를 뜻하고, 접두사 con-은 '함께(with)'를 뜻한다. '같이 계속, 변함없이 서 있다'라는 의미에서 '끊임없는, 거듭되는'이 되었다. 즉 constantly는 '끊임없이, 지속적으로'를 뜻한다.
They fought constantly, because each one wanted to rule Egypt alone. 그들은 계속 싸웠는데, 각자 혼자서 이집트를 지배하고 싶어 했기 때문이다.

invincible ⓐ too strong to be defeated
invincible은 '부정(not)'을 뜻하는 in-과 '극복할[이길] 수 있는(able to overcome)'을 뜻하는 vincible이 합쳐져 '이길 수 없는'라는 뜻이 되었다. 너무 강해서 대적할 상대가 없는 상태를 의미한다. 본문에서 his invincible army는 '카이사르의 무적 군대'를 뜻한다.
"We've got to make friends with him quickly, or else he will attack us with his invincible army!" "우리는 속히 그와 친구가 되어야 한다. 그렇지 않으면 그가 무적 군대로 우리를 공격할 것이다."

startle ⓥ to make someone suddenly surprised or shocked
startle은 '갑자기, 빨리 움직이다(to move suddenly or quickly)'를 뜻하는 의미에서 왔다. '출발하다, 시작하다'를 뜻하는 start와 어원이 같다. 깜짝 놀라면 갑자기 후다닥 움직이므로 startle은 '깜짝 놀라게 하다'라는 뜻이다.
Caesar was startled to get Pompey's head in a bag. 카이사르는 자루에 든 폼페이우스의 잘린 머리를 받고서 깜짝 놀랐다.

dazzle ⓥ to impress someone a lot
dazzle은 '강한 빛으로 눈앞이 안 보이게 하다'이다. 예를 들어 태양을 보면 눈이 부신 것과 같은 느낌이다. 화려한 것, 아름다운 것을 보고서 마음이 황홀해질 때는 be dazzled라는 수동태로 쓴다.
When Caesar was shown into Cleopatra's room, he was dazzled by her beauty, and by the riches all around her! 카이사르는 클레오파트라의 방에 들어갔을 때 클레오파트라의 미모와 그녀 주위에 가득한 보물에 마음을 빼앗겼다.

overcome ⓥ to make someone very emotional or weak
overcome은 '극복하다, 이기다'라는 뜻인데, 수동태로 쓰면 '정복되다, 패하다라는 의미가 된다. Caesar was overcome by Cleopatra 문장은 '카이사르가 클레오파트라에게 졌다'라는 뜻도 되지만, '카이사르가 클레오파트라에게 넘어갔다(마음을 빼앗겼다)'라고 이해할 수도 있다. overcome-overcame-overcome

Caesar was overcome by Cleopatra. 카이사르는 클레오파트라에게 압도되었다.

company ⓝ a person or people you are with

company에서 com-은 접두사로 '함께(together)'를 뜻하고, pan은 포르투갈어에서 프랑스어로 넘어온 '빵(bread), 식사'를 뜻한다. 우리말 '빵'이 바로 pan에서 왔다. '빵(pan)'을 얻기 위해 '함께(com)' 일하는 곳이 '회사(company)'이고, 함께 어울리는 사람들이 '일행, 동무(company)'이다.

Instead he stayed in Egypt, keeping his new love company. 대신, 그는 새로운 사랑의 짝을 지켜주면서 이집트에 머물렀다.

4 The Death of Caesar

amuse ⓥ to make someone laugh or smile

'재미있게 하다, 즐겁게 하다'라는 뜻이다. 카이사르도 로마인들을 즐겁게 하기 위해(to amuse the people of Rome)' 돈을 많이 썼던 모양이다. 아이들을 놀이동산에 데려가면 즐거워하기 때문에, 놀이동산을 amusement park라고 한다.

He paid for gladiator fighting and chariot racing to amuse the people of Rome. 그는 로마인들을 즐겁게 하기 위해 검투사 대결과 전차 경주에 돈을 썼다.

adopt ⓥ to take someone else's children into your family and treat them as if they were your own

'입양하다'라는 뜻으로, to choose(선택하다)의 라틴어에서 왔다. 입양한 자식은 나의 의지에 의해 '선택된' 아이라는 의미이다. 명사형으로 '입양'은 adoption이다. '맞추다, 조정하다, 적응하다'라는 뜻의 adapt와 혼동하지 않도록 유의하자.
I'm going to adopt him to be my son. 그 아이를 입양해 내 아들로 삼겠다.

stab ⓥ to push a sharp object into someone or something using force

stab은 '날카로운 물체로 찌르다'를 뜻한다. 비유적으로 '배신하다'를 '뒤통수를 치다'라고 표현하면 to stab someone in the back(뒤에서 칼로 찌르다)으로 표현한다.
We'll attack him as he enters the Senate and stab him to death! 우리는 카이사르가 원로원에 들어서면 그를 공격해서 칼로 찔러 죽일 것이다!

> **Q** 카이사르의 적수가 된 폼페이우스는 왜 달아났나요?
> **A** 카이사르가 루비콘 강을 건넌 날, 병사들은 '카이사르 만세'를 외치면서 환호했단다. 그들은 서로 앞다투어 강을 건넜고, 바로 그날 밤 아드리아해 연안의 아리미눔을 점령했어. 이 소식을 듣고 누구보다 놀란 사람은 폼페이우스였어. 그는 이렇게 빨리 카이사르가 움직일 줄은 몰랐던 거지. 더구나 그가 소집 명령을 내려도 카이사르 군대의 위력을 알고 있는 병사들은 대장의 명령을 따르지 않았어.
> 시민들은 겁을 먹고 시골로 도망가기 바빴고, 결국 폼페이우스도 그리스로 도망을 갔어. 그곳에서 병사를 모아 싸우려고 했거든. 실제로 폼페이우스는 10만 명의 군사를 모을 수 있었지만, 처음부터 훈련을 시켜야 하는 미숙한 군사들이었단다. 반면 추격전을 시작한 카이사르 군대의 규모는 수적으로 반에 불과했지만, 오랜 세월 카이사르와 호흡을 맞춘 군사들이었지. 그리스의 테살리아 지방 파르살루스 근처에서 맞붙은 군대는 기습 작전으로 카이사르 쪽이 대승리를 거두었지.

plot ⓝ a secret plan to do something wrong

소설이나 시나리오에서 plot은 '줄거리, 구성'을 의미한다. 그 외에 몰래 거사를 도모하는 '음모'라는 의미도 있다. 동사형으로 '모의하다, 구성하다, 플롯을 짜다'라는 뜻으로도 쓸 수 있다.

Caesar didn't know anything about the plot to kill him. 카이사르는 자신을 죽이려는 음모에 대해 아무것도 몰랐다.

beware ⓥ to be careful of something because it is dangerous

beware에서 ware는 '알고 있는, 의식하는(aware)'을 뜻하고, be-는 형용사를 동사로 만들어주는 역할을 한다. 즉 beware는 '알다, 의식하다'라는 뜻이다. 주로 명령형으로 '조심하라, 주의하라!'라는 의미로 쓰인다.

Beware the fifteenth of March! 3월 15일을 조심하시오!

banish ⓥ to send someone away from their country or a region as an official punishment

banish에서 ban은 '금지'를 뜻한다. 사형 다음으로 무거운 형벌은, 조선의 역사에도 있었던 '유배'를 보내는 것이다. 자기 터전에서 살지 못하게 '금지'하는 것이다. 그래서 banish에는 '국외로 추방하다, 유배를 보내다'라는 뜻도 있다. 로마 제국에도 중죄를 지은 사람이나 국가에 해를 끼칠 수 있는 위험 인물을 국외로 추방하는 제도가 있었다.

He was banished several years ago. 그는 몇 년 전에 추방되었다.

stagger ⓥ to walk in an unsteady way, as if you are going to fall

stagger는 몸이 많이 불편하거나 술에 취해 비틀거리며 걷는 모습을 표현한 동사이다. '비틀거리며 걷다, 휘청거리다'라는 뜻으로, totter와 stumble에도 비슷한 의미가 있다.

He staggered, and fell down at the feet of a statue of Pompey. 카이사르는 비틀거리다가 폼페이우스 동상의 발치에 쓰러졌다.

> **Q** '왔노라, 보았노라, 이겼노라'는 누가 어느 전투에서 남긴 말인가요?
>
> **A** 이집트에서 프톨레마이오스 왕조의 분쟁을 해결하려던 카이사르는 클레오파트라 7세를 편들게 되었다. 알렉산드리아에서 내전이 일어났고, 마지막 승리자는 카이사르의 도움을 받은 클레오파트라였단다. 원래는 분쟁을 해결하고 바로 로마로 돌아가야 했지만, 카이사르는 이집트에서 로마의 지배력을 확립하면서 한동안 남아 있었어. 그동안 클레오파트라와 나일 강을 따라 여행을 하면서 이집트 문명과 그곳의 권력자가 갖는 절대적인 힘에 매료되었어.

그러던 중 시리아 지방에서 반란이 일어났다는 소식이 전해졌어. 그 지역은 폼페이우스가 지배했던 보스포루스 왕국이 있던 곳인데, 파르나케스가 정세가 달라진 틈을 타 영토를 확장하려던 중이었거든. 카이사르 군대가 출동하자 파르나케스는 카이사르와 협상하려고 황금으로 된 왕관까지 바치면서 노력했지만, 카이사르는 협상을 거부했지. 두 군대는 기원전 47년 8월 2일, 젤라에서 전투를 벌였는데 파르나케스의 군대는 완패했어. 이때 카이사르가 한 말이 바로 '왔노라, 보았노라, 이겼노라'야.

The Story of the World

Chapter 36
The First Roman Prince

1 Augustus Caesar

카이사르가 암살된 후 그의 양아들인 옥타비아누스(Octavian)는 악티움 해전에서 안토니우스와 클레오파트라의 연합군을 격파하고 이집트를 손에 넣은 후 로마 최고의 권력자가 되었다. 그는 카이사르처럼 권력을 휘두르지 않고 '동등한 시민'으로서 정치를 하겠다는 의미로 자신을 '제1시민(Princeps)'이라 불렀다. 그러나 권력을 독점하고, 원로원도 그에게 '존엄한 위대한' 자라는 의미의 '아우구스투스(Augustus)' 칭호를 바침으로써 사실상 1인 지배 체제를 구축하게 되었다. 그래서 역사는 그를 '제1시민'이 아니라 '로마 최초의 황제'로 기록하고 있다.

*After Caesar died, Rome was in an uproar! Who would be in charge of Rome now? The people had loved Caesar. They were angry about his death. Some of the senators were angry about Caesar's death too. Other senators were glad that Caesar was gone. The senators quarreled with each other. The people of Rome were restless. Fights broke out. Rome was a mess, and no one was in charge.

Caesar's nephew, Octavian, was only nineteen when Caesar died. But he had inherited all of Caesar's money, because he was Caesar's adopted son. He took Caesar's money and threw a big party in memory of Caesar. The party lasted ten days, and the whole city of Rome was invited. Then Octavian gave presents and money to every poor family in Rome. Suddenly Octavian was very popular! The people of Rome loved him because he was generous. The army loved him because he was Caesar's adopted son.

When he saw how popular he was, Octavian went to the Senate and demanded to be made a consul. The Senate didn't want to make Octavian a ruler of Rome. He was too young. And he was too much like Caesar. Once he had power as consul, he could start to work towards becoming a king.

But the people of Rome and the army wanted Octavian to be a consul, and the Senate was afraid to say no. So Octavian became a consul of Rome. Just like Julius Caesar, he led the army into nearby countries and conquered them for Rome. Just like Julius Caesar, he made the Roman Empire bigger and richer.

But Octavian didn't make the same mistakes that Caesar had made. He knew that Caesar had made the Senate angry when he demanded to be called "king." Octavian wanted to be like Cincinnatus instead. We read the story of Cincinnatus a few days ago. He was taking care of his grapes when the Senate asked him to be head of the army. But when all the Romans asked him to be king, he gave his power back to the Senate and went back to taking care of his grapes.

One day, Octavian called the whole Senate together. "I have made Rome bigger and wealthier than ever," he said. "Now

Octavian, Rome's "First Citizen," was renamed Augustus Caesar

there is peace, all over the Roman Empire. No one is fighting. No enemies are attacking us. Rome is strong and healthy. So I have decided to quit my job. I don't need to be consul any more. I won't lead the army any more. You can be in charge from now on."

The senators should have been pleased by this. But Octavian had become popular with the people, and they knew that the people would protest if he left the government. They might even riot. And then other ambitious Romans would begin to fight for power. A civil war might break out.

So they protested, "But you brought peace to Rome. If you stop being consul, Rome will fall apart again! Please, stay on and be consul."

"No, no," Octavian said. "Rome shouldn't have a king, and if I stay people will want me to be king. I'm just a Roman citizen like everyone else."

"We won't call you king, then," the senators promised him. "We'll call you the 'First Citizen' instead."

Then the whole Senate met together and voted to make Octavian the "First Citizen" of Rome. In Latin, the word for "first citizen" is *princeps*. Our English word "prince" comes from the word *princeps*. A prince is the most important citizen in his country. And even though Octavian was called "First Citizen," he acted like a prince. He ruled Rome, led the army, and had complete control over the whole Roman Empire. He was actually the first emperor of Rome.

The Senate also gave Octavian a new name. His old name was "Octavian Caesar," because he was Caesar's adopted son. But his new name was "Augustus Caesar."

Augustus means "Blessed" and "Majestic." To show how much they honored Augustus Caesar, the Senate even decided to name a month of the year after him! Can you guess which month of the year is named after Augustus Caesar? The month of August.

They also agreed to name a month of the year after his adopted father, Julius Caesar. Can you guess which month is named after Julius Caesar? The month of July. Julius Caesar and Augustus Caesar lived a very long time ago. But every time we look at a calendar, we are reminded of them.

Note to Parent: Octavian became a consul in 43 BC/BCE, one year after Caesar's death. He remained a consul until 27 BC/BCE, when he assumed the position of emperor and continued to rule until 14 AD/CE.

> # The Story of the Words
>
> Chapter 36 **The First Roman Prince**

1 Augustus Caesar

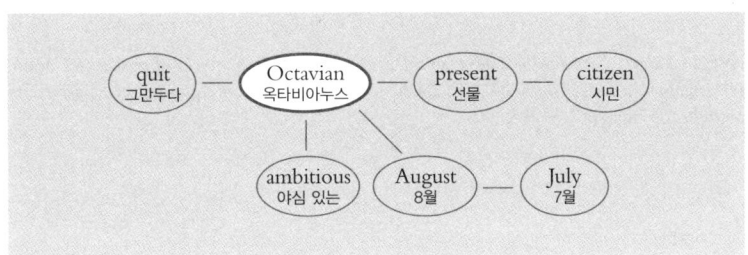

present ⓝ something that you give someone

present는 '앞에 놓다(place before)'라는 뜻의 라틴어에서 온 것이다. 누군가에게 뭔가를 줄 때 그 사람 앞에 놓거나 내밀게 된다. 바로 present는 '주다, 내놓다, 선물'을 의미한다.

Then Octavian gave presents and money to every poor family in Rome. 옥타비아누스는 로마의 모든 가난한 집에 선물과 돈을 주었다.

quit ⓥ to stop doing something

quit은 '조용한(quiet)'을 뜻하는 라틴어에서 왔다. 하던 행동이나 일을 '그만두고' 가만히 있으면 조용하다는 의미에서 quit은 '그만두다, 중지하다'라는 뜻이 되었다. I have decided to quit my job(나는 일을 그만두기로 결심했다)은 직장을 그만두고 사표를 쓸 때 하는 말이다.

So I have decided to quit my job. 그래서 나는 일을 그만두기로 결심했다.

ambitious ⓐ wanting very much to be successful

정치인으로 출세하려는 꿈이 있었기 때문에 ambition은 '야망, 꿈, 포부'이고, 형용사형 ambitious는 '야망이 있는, 포부가 큰'을 뜻한다. Boys, be ambitious!(소년들이여, 야망을 품어라!)는 19세기 말에 일본에서 교육가로 잠깐 활동했던 미국인 윌리엄 클라크(William Clark)가 일본 학교를 떠나면서 했던 말이다. 그로부터 약 50년 후에 일본은 '야망'을 품고서 미국 진주만을 폭격했다.

And then other ambitious Romans would begin to fight for power. 그러면 다른 야심 있는 로마인들이 권력을 쥐기 위해 싸우기 시작할 것이다.

> **Q 아우구스투스 칭호를 받았던 옥타비아누스 시대를 왜 원수정이라고 하나요?**
>
> **A** 아우구스투스는 살아 있는 동안 황제라고 불리지 않았기 때문에 그의 치세를 '원수정'이라고 불러. 반면에 역사가들은 사실상 첫 황제를 '아우구스투스'로 꼽는단다. 그가 첫 황제인지 아닌지 하는 사실보다 더 중요한 것은 그가 어떤 정치를 했는가야. 그가 다스린 시기를 '팍스 로마나(로마의 평화)'라고 부를 정도로 로마의 정치는 안정되었어. 사회 질서를 확립하기 위해 원로원 의원, 기사, 평민의 세 신분 자격과 직능을 정했으며, 혼인법을 마련해 도덕적인 해이를 바로잡으려고 했어. 또한 군제도를 정규군, 보조군, 근위대로 구분하였으며 근위대로 하여금 로마 방위를 하게 했고, 경찰대와 소방대를 두어 시민의 안전을 지켰지. 그 외에 벽돌로 된 로마를 물려받아 대리석으로 만들었다는 말이 있을 정도로 로마의 도시 미관을 아름답게 하는 일에 힘을 기울인 것도 아우구스투스의 중요한 업적이었단다. 모든 신의 신전이란 뜻인 판테온과 포럼을 건설한 것도 바로 이 시기였어. 기원전 27년부터 시작된 아우구스투스의 시기는 그가 죽은 기원후 14년까지 이어졌단다.

citizen ⓝ a person who lives in a particular city or country and has special rights there

citizen 역시 civilization이나 civil처럼 '도시(city)'에서 유래한 단어이다. '도시에 사는 사람(city dweller), 즉 시민'을 뜻한다. 과거에는 도시의 개념이 국가 개념이었기 때문에 citizen은 '국민'을 지칭하는 말로도 쓰인다. 인터넷(Internet) 사용자를 뜻하는 '네티즌(netizen)'도 citizen에서 유래한 것이다.

I'm just a Roman citizen like everyone else. 다른 모든 사람들과 마찬가지로 나 역시 로마의 시민일 뿐이다.

August ⓝ the eighth month of the year

본문에 설명되어 있듯이, '8월'의 영어 이름인 August는 로마의 초대 황제인 '아우구스투스(Augustus)'에서 온 것이다. Augustus는 라틴어로 '신성한, 축복받은'을 뜻한다.
The month of August 8월

July ⓝ the seventh month of the year

'7월'의 이름인 July는 율리우스(Julius) 카이사르에서 온 것이다. 아이러니하게도 율리우스 카이사르의 이름을 7월에 붙이자고 제안한 사람은 클레오파트라의 또 다른 연인으로 잘 알려진 안토니우스였다. 카이사르가 암살당한 해에 붙여졌다.
The month of July 7월

The Story of the World

Chapter 37
The Beginning of Christianity

1 The Birth of Jesus

🌏 기독교 신약 성서의 기록과 이 책의 내용에서 볼 때, 예수(Jesus Christ)가 '하느님의 아들(Son of God)'이라는 세 가지 결정적인 증거를 꼽을 수 있다. 첫 번째는, 처녀인 마리아(Mary)의 몸에서 태어났다는 점이다. 두 번째는, 하나님의 상징인 십자가에 못 박혀(crucified) 죽음을 맞았다는 점, 마지막으로는 부활했다(resurrected)는 점이다. 예수의 등장으로 '야훼교'는 '기독교(Christianity)'로 거듭나게 되었다.

Augustus Caesar may have been called "First Citizen," but he was actually an emperor. He ruled over Rome and all the land that Rome had conquered. No one questioned his decrees. He was in charge.

Augustus Caesar became famous for keeping the peace all over the Roman Empire. Everywhere in the Roman Empire, Roman law was followed. Roman soldiers kept villages and cities safe from enemy attack. There were no wars anywhere within the Roman Empire.

This time of peace and safety had a name—the *Pax Romana*. In Latin, this means "The Roman Peace." All across the Roman Empire, people could live in safety, without worrying about invasion. They could work out in their fields, raise their animals, travel back and forth between Roman cities, and even sail on the Mediterranean Sea without being attacked.

During the time of this Roman peace, a baby was born in Judea, the land that was once called Canaan, and was now under Roman control. This baby would grow up to start a whole new *religion*. The Bible tells us about this baby in four books called "the *Gospels*." Here is the story as it is told in the Gospel of Luke:

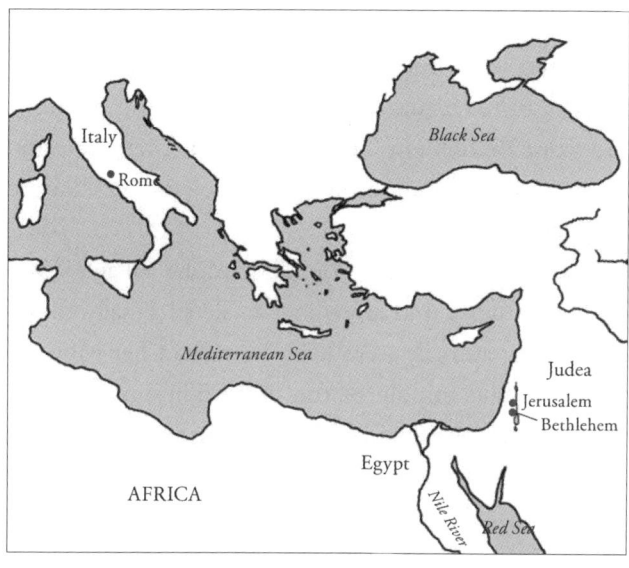

Judea

In the days when Augustus Caesar ruled over Rome, a girl named Mary lived in Nazareth. Mary was a Jewish girl who worshipped the God of Abraham. She was engaged to be married to a man named Joseph, but the wedding was still months away.

One day, God sent an angel to Mary to give her a message.

"Mary, God is with you!" the angel said. "You will have a baby, and you will name him Jesus!"

"But I can't have a baby," Mary said. "I don't even have a husband yet!"

"God will send the baby," the angel answered. "He will be called the Son of God."

When Mary told Joseph about the angel's visit, he was amazed! But he agreed to marry her and help her raise the baby.

Just before Mary's baby was born, Augustus Caesar ordered

that everyone in the Roman Empire should be counted. He wanted everyone to go back to the place where their ancestors came from, to make the counting easier. Joseph came from Bethlehem. So, even though Mary was about to have her baby, Joseph and Mary traveled from Nazareth to Bethlehem.

When they arrived in Bethlehem, the village was so full that they couldn't find anywhere to sleep! Finally, they found a cave where animals were kept. Mary had her baby there, in the cave, in the middle of the night. They named the baby "Jesus," just as the angel had said. Joseph wrapped the baby in clean linen cloths, and laid him in the feeding trough where the animals ate.

Now, just outside Bethlehem, there were shepherds spending the night out in the fields, watching over their sheep. When Jesus was born, an angel appeared to the shepherds. The angel shone with light, and the shepherds were afraid. But the angel said, "Don't be afraid! I bring you good news of great joy. Today, a Savior has been born to you. He is Christ the Lord! You will find him wrapped in linen cloth, lying in a feed trough." Then a great company of angels appeared in the sky over the field where the shepherds were sleeping. "Glory to God in the highest!" they sang. "Peace on earth, good will to men!"

The shepherds were astounded! They hurried to the cave where the baby had been born. And after they saw him, they went out and told everyone what they had seen and heard.

Today, many people celebrate the birth of Jesus on December 25. We call this day "Christmas."

Jesus Crucified and Resurrected.

2 Jesus Crucified and Resurrected

🌐 기독교 신약성서의 마태복음에는 예수가 갈릴리에 있는 작은 산에서 제자들과 군중에게 행한 설교가 기록되어 있다. 이 가르침을 우리말로는 '산상수훈(山上垂訓)'이라고 하고 영어로는 Sermon on the Mount라고 한다. '~한 자는 복이 있다(Blessed are ~)'란 말로 여덟 가지 복(福)에 대해 규정하고, 기독교의 기본적인 교리와 하느님을 믿는 자들의 윤리와 삶의 태도를 설교한 것이다. '원수를 사랑하라'나 '오른쪽 뺨을 맞으면 왼쪽 뺨을 대라'는 등의 유명한 말들도 이 산상수훈에서 나온 것이며 기독교인들이 예배에서 항상 외는 '주기도문'도 산상수훈의 내용을 담고 있다.

After Jesus was born, he lived in Judea for thirty years. Then he started to travel around Judea, teaching people what God wanted them to do. His most famous teaching was given on the side of a mountain, so today, people call it the "Sermon on the Mount." Here are some of the things that Jesus taught:

Blessed are the poor,
for the kingdom of God belongs to them.

The Death of Jesus

chapter 37 The Beginning of Christianity

Blessed are the merciful,
for they will receive mercy.

Blessed are peacemakers,
for they will be called the children of God.

If someone strikes you on the cheek, don't fight
back. Turn the other cheek instead.

Love your enemies, and pray for
*those who are **mean** to you.*

Do not judge other people,
or you will be judged.

The "Gospels," in the New **Testament**, record these and many other teachings of Jesus.

Jesus was very popular with the people of Judea. He was so popular that the leaders who were **governing** Judea began to worry. The Jewish leaders were afraid that Jesus might begin a rebellion against the Romans. If that happened, Roman soldiers might march into Judea and kill hundreds of Jews.

When the Roman official who was supposed to keep the peace in Judea heard about Jesus, he got worried too. If he didn't get rid of Jews who might start rebellions against Rome, he could get into trouble with the Roman "First Citizen"—a man named Tiberius, who had inherited the job of running Rome from Augustus Caesar. He might lose his job as a Roman official, or even be executed.

So the Romans helped some of the leaders of Judea arrest Jesus. They put him on trial for treason. The **penalty** for treason was death! Jesus was convicted of treason and put to death near Jerusalem, the capital city of Judea.

The Gospels tell the story of what happened after Jesus' death. Here is what the Gospel of Luke says:

> After Jesus died, he was put in a tomb that was like a cave, carved into rock. •A huge stone was rolled into place across the entrance to the tomb. His followers and the people who loved him were very sad. They mourned and wept.
>
> Three days after Jesus died, some of the women who followed him went to the tomb where he had been buried. But when they got there, they found that the huge stone at the entrance had been rolled away! And the tomb itself was empty.
>
> "What has happened here?" they asked each other. "What has happened to the body of Jesus?"
>
> Then two angels, dressed in shining clothes, appeared to them. "Why are you looking for Jesus here?" one of them asked. "He is not here. He has risen from the dead!"
>
> The women were terrified! They ran back to tell Jesus' other followers what had happened. But no one believed them!
>
> While his followers were talking about the story the women told, Jesus himself appeared to them. "Peace be with you!" he said. "I am not a ghost! I have risen from the dead." Then he blessed them and said, "Go and tell all nations what you have seen."

The followers of Jesus told this story all around Jerusalem. Then they spread it all the way to Rome itself! More and more people believed that Jesus had been *resurrected*, or brought back to life from the dead. They were careful to follow the teachings of Jesus. They believed that Jesus was the son of God. Soon, these people were called "Christians." 📖

Note to Parent: The actual year of Jesus' birth is probably closer to 3 BC/BCE than to the year 1.

The Story of the Words
Chapter 37 The Beginning of Christianity

1 The Birth of Jesus

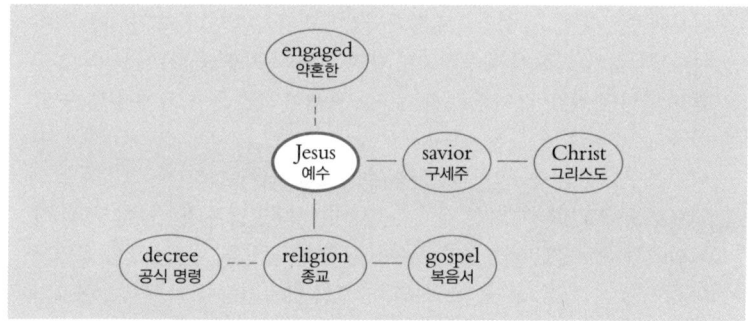

decree ⓝ an official order or decision by the ruler of a country
'결심한[결정된] 것(something decided)'을 뜻하는 라틴어에서 유래한 단어로 '명령, 결정, 칙령'의 의미이다. 흔히 '명령'을 뜻하는 order는 개인적인 명령과 공식적인 명령을 표현할 때 모두 쓰인다. decree는 공식적인 명령으로 널리 공표되는 것을 의미하여 지배자나 법원의 명령을 나타낼 때 쓰인다.
No one questioned his decrees. 아무도 그의 공식적인 명령에 대해 의문을 제기하지 않았다.

religion ⓝ belief in one or more gods
religion은 to bind tightly(단단히 묶다)를 뜻하는 라틴어에서 왔다. 신과 인간을 단단히 묶어주는 것이 바로 religion이며, 이것이 '종교'의 본질이기도 하다.
This baby would grow up to start a whole new religion. 이 아기가 자라서 완전히 새로운 종교를 창시하게 된다.

gospel ⓝ one of the stories about Christ's life in the Bible
gospel은 '좋은(good)'을 뜻하는 gōd와 '소식(news)'을 뜻하는 spell이 합쳐진,

고대 영어에서 온 것이다. 말 그대로 '좋은 소식'을 의미하는데, 한국 기독교에서는 '복음(福音)'이라고 표현한다. 예수의 탄생과 가르침에 관한 내용이 담긴 성경의 '복음서'를 지칭하기도 하다. four books called 'the Gospels'에 해당하는 것은 마태복음, 마가복음, 누가복음, 요한복음이다.

The Bible tells us about this baby in four books called "the Gospels." 성경은 '복음서'라고 부르는 네 권의 책에서 이 아기에 대해 말해준다.

> **Q 예수는 유대인이지만 유대교를 믿지 않았나요?**
> **A** 예수는 나사렛 사람 '마리아'에게서 태어났어. 《성서》에서는 가브리엘 천사의 방문을 받고, 성령으로 잉태되었다고 나와 있단다. 그가 자란 곳이 나사렛이라서 '나사렛 예수'라고도 불려. 예수가 자란 곳은 마리아와 결혼한 요셉의 집이었어. 어린 시절 예수도 요셉이 하는 일을 곁에서 볼 수 있었겠지?
> 예수는 유대인의 종교인 유대교에 대한 지식도 많았다고 해. 그러나 결정적으로 유대교인들과 다른 점이 있었단다. 유대인들은 자신들이 '야훼' 하느님에게 선택받았다는 선민의식이 강했고, 율법을 지키는 일을 무엇보다 중시했어. 반면 예수는 율법보다 중요한 것은 사랑이고, 야훼는 유대인만을 선택한 것이 아니라고 본 거야. 이 점에서 예수는 유대교인이면서도 유대교와는 다른 생각을 갖고 있었던 것이지.

engaged ⓐ having promised to marry someone
engaged는 '맹세하다(to pledge)'라는 뜻이 담겨 '약혼한, 혼인을 약속한'의 의미이다. '약혼하다'라는 표현은 항상 수동형 형용사를 써서 be[get] engaged라고 써야 쓴 점에 주의하자.

She was engaged to be married to a man named Joseph, but the wedding was still months away. 그녀는 요셉이라는 이름의 사내와 결혼하기로 혼인 약속이 되어 있었지만, 결혼식은 아직 여러 달 남아 있었다.

Jesus ⓝ the man on whose life and teachings Christianity is based
'예수'라는 뜻으로, 원래 '구원자'를 뜻하는 히브리어 Yeshua가 희랍어로 넘어오면서 Jesus로 변형되었다. 성경의 복음서에 기록된 바에 의하면, 이 이름은 하느님이 정해서 천사를 통해 전해준 것이다.

They named the baby "Jesus," just as the angel had said. 그들은 그 천사가 일러준 대로 아기의 이름을 '예수'라고 정했다.

savior ⓝ someone who saves you from difficulty or danger

savior는 '구하다(to save)'를 뜻하는 라틴어에서 온 것으로, '구해주는 사람'이라는 뜻이다. saver와는 완전히 다른 말이다. saver는 은행의 직원들이 '고객님!'이라고 부르는 '예금주'를 의미한다. Savior처럼 첫 글자를 대문자로 쓰면 기독교에서 말하는 '구세주, 구원자'를 뜻한다.
Today, a Savior has been born to you. 오늘 너희에게 구세주가 태어나셨다.

Christ ⓝ the man who is worshipped by Christians as the son of God

Christ의 어원은 '기름 부은(anointed)'를 뜻하는 희랍어이다. Christ는 히브리어 '메시아(Messia)'를 번역한 것인데, '하느님의 선택을 받은 자'라는 의미이다. 예수를 칭할 때 영어로 Jesus Christ라고 한다. Christian(기독교인), Christmas(크리스마스)도 모두 Christ에서 나온 것이다.
He is Christ the Lord! 그는 주 예수 그리스도이다!

2 Jesus Crucified and Resurrected

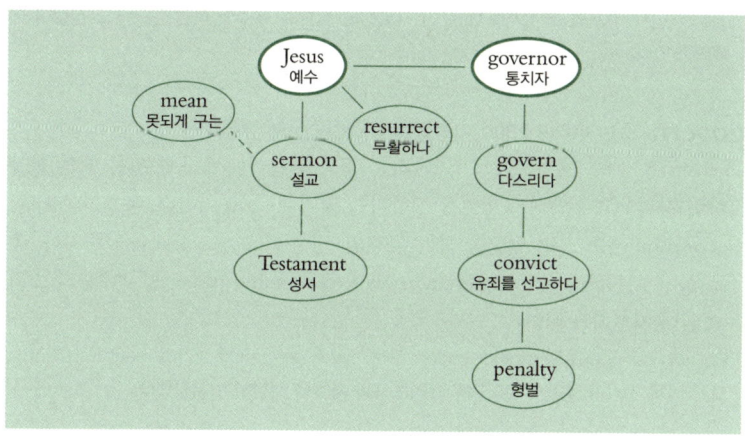

sermon ⓝ a speech made by a religious leader

sermon은 교회에서 목사나 신부가 하는 '설교'를 뜻한다. Sermon on the Mount는 마태복음에 기록된 예수님의 설교로, 산에서 행했기 때문에 우리말 성경에는 '산상설교, 산상수훈(山上垂訓)'으로 번역되었다. sermon은 '이야기(talk), 담화(discourse)'를 뜻하는 라틴어에서 왔다.

His most famous teaching was given on the side of a mountain, so today, people call it the "Sermon on the Mount." 그의 가장 유명한 가르침은 산비탈에서 전해졌기 때문에, 오늘날 사람들은 그 가르침을 '산상수훈'이라고 부른다.

mean ⓐ not nice; cruel

다른 사람에게 못되게 굴거나 야비한 성격을 표현하는 것이 mean이다. She is always mean to me라고 하면 '그녀가 나한테 항상 못되게 군다'라는 뜻이다. 즉 형용사형 mean은 '못된, 심술궂은, 사나운'이라는 뜻이다.
Love your enemies, and pray for those who are mean to you. 원수를 사랑하라. 너희에게 못되게 구는 자들을 위해 기도하라.

Testament ⓝ a division of the Bible

testament는 원래 '약속, 유언(will)'을 뜻하는 라틴어에서 온 것인데, 기독교의 성경을 분류할 때 쓴다. the Old Testament는 '구약 성서'이고, the New Testament는 '신약 성서'이다. 연대기적 서술 방식을 쓰고 있기 때문에, 예수 탄생을 기점으로 내용을 나눈 것이다.
The "Gospels," in the New Testament, record these and many other teachings of Jesus. 신약 성서의 '복음서들'에는 이 가르침을 비롯해 예수의 다른 많은 가르침들이 기록되어 있다.

govern ⓥ to control and rule a country and its people

govern은 '배를 조정하다(to steer)'라는 뜻의 희랍어에서 유래했다. 배의 선장처럼 지휘하고 통제하고 항로를 정한다는 의미에서, '통치하다, 다스리다'이다. government는 그런 역할을 하는 조직인 '정부'이고, governor는 '주지사, 총독' 등을 지칭한다. the leaders who were governing Judea는 '유대를 다스리고 있던 지도자들'이다.
He was so popular that the leaders who were governing Judea began to worry. 그가 너무 인기가 많아서 유대를 다스리는 지도자들은 걱정하기 시작했다.

penalty ⓝ a punishment for not obeying a law or rule

penalty에는 '고통(pain)'이라는 뜻이 담겨 있다. 고통을 느껴서 반성을 하게 한다는 의미로 '형벌'을 주는 것이다. punishment는 누구나 주고받을 수 있는 '벌'인 반면에 penalty는 법과 규칙에 따라 정해진 '형벌'을 뜻한다. 스포츠 경기에서도 반칙을 하면 penalty가 주어진다.

The penalty for treason was death! 반역죄에 대한 형벌은 죽음이었다!

convict ⓥ to decide in a law court that someone is guilty of something
convict에서 vict는 '정복하다, 제압하다'라는 뜻으로, victory(승리)의 vict와 같은 어근이다. 재판관이 피고인을 '이기면' '유죄가 선고'되었다. 그래서 convict는 '유죄를 선고하다, 유죄 판결을 내리다'라는 뜻이 되었다. 명사형은 conviction이다.
Jesus was convicted for treason and put to death near Jerusalem, the capital city of Judea. 예수는 반역죄로 유죄를 선고받고 유대의 수도인 예루살렘 인근에서 처형되었다.

resurrect ⓥ to bring someone back to life after death
resurrect에서 re-는 '다시'를, surrect는 '일어서다(to rise)'를 뜻한다. 쓰러졌다가 다시 벌떡 일어난다, 즉 '부활'을 의미한다. 명사형은 resurrection(부활)인데, 이 단어는 기독교에서 대단히 중요한 의미를 갖는다.
More and more people believed that Jesus had been *resurrected*, or brought back to life from the dead. 점점 더 많은 사람들이 예수가 부활했거나 죽은 자들 가운데에서 다시 살아났다고 믿었다.

The Story of the World

Chapter 38
The End of the Ancient Jewish Nation

1 The Destruction of the Temple

로마 제국의 지배를 받을 당시 예루살렘(Jerusalem)은 유대인들의 중심 도시여서 기독교 성전들이 즐비했다고 한다. 그러나 기독교인들의 반란을 진압한다는 명목으로 서기 70년에 로마 황제의 아들인 티투스가 예루살렘을 공격해서 성전을 파괴했고, 135년에도 로마군들이 쳐들어와 다시 성전을 파괴하고 유대인들을 예루살렘에서 몰아냈다. 로마 제국에서 기독교가 공식적인 종교로 인정을 받기 전까지 예루살렘과 기독교인들의 시련은 계속되었다.

Earlier, we read about Jesus, the founder of Christianity. The Romans put Jesus to death, because they were afraid that the Jewish people would follow Jesus and obey him, instead of obeying the rulers of Rome. They were always worried that the countries Rome ruled would rebel against the "First Citizen," who was now known as *imperator*, or "emperor." And the Jews hated Roman rule. They wanted to be free again!

The Jews had been ruled by other countries for many years. Do you remember who was the father of the Jewish people? Abraham left Haran and went to Canaan. There, he had a son named Isaac and Isaac had a son named Jacob. Jacob had twelve sons. And each one of Jacob's sons had a family of their own. Now Abraham's family was as big as a whole nation! And they were called "Israelites" or "Jews."

Jacob loved his son Joseph more than his other sons. The other eleven brothers were jealous, and they sold Joseph as a slave. Joseph was taken to Egypt, and soon the rest of the Israelites came down to join him, because a famine had wiped out all their crops—and there was only grain in Egypt.

The Israelites lived in Egypt for a long time. But the pharaoh made them into slaves, until Moses came along and led them out of Egypt, back up to Canaan. The Israelites lived in Canaan until the Assyrians came along, captured them, and took them away, back to Assyria. The Assyrians were then conquered by the Babylonians—who took the Israelites from Assyria and moved them to Babylon. Then the good king of Persia and Babylon, Cyrus the Great, gave the Jews permission to move back to their own land—back to Canaan.

The Jews had been moved around the ancient world for hundreds of years. After Cyrus allowed them to go home, they hoped that they would finally get to stay in their own country and live in peace.

But now they were being ruled by Rome. The Romans were telling them what to do. The Romans were forcing them to pay high taxes.

Finally, the Jews refused to obey any longer. They set fire to the house of the Roman ruler of Judea. Armed groups of Jewish men attacked Roman soldiers. Fighting between the Jews and the Romans in Jerusalem grew worse and worse.

When the emperor in Rome heard what was happening, he sent more Roman soldiers with orders to destroy Jerusalem, the capital city of the Jews.

Jerusalem was an important city to the Jews. Inside the city was the Temple, the place where they worshipped God. But when the Roman soldiers attacked, they burned down the Temple. Inside the temple were many beautiful decorations made of gold and silver. *One ancient historian writes that, when the Temple burned down, the gold and silver melted and ran into the cracks between the huge stones of the Temple's foundation. The Roman soldiers, anxious to get at this wealth, pried the stones apart with crowbars. This completely destroyed the Temple, all the way down to its foundation. And then the Romans drove the Jewish people away from Jerusalem.

Now the Jews had no Temple to worship God in, no capital city, and no country of their own. *They were scattered throughout all the countries of the ancient world. The Jews didn't return to the land of Canaan until just a few years ago. 📖

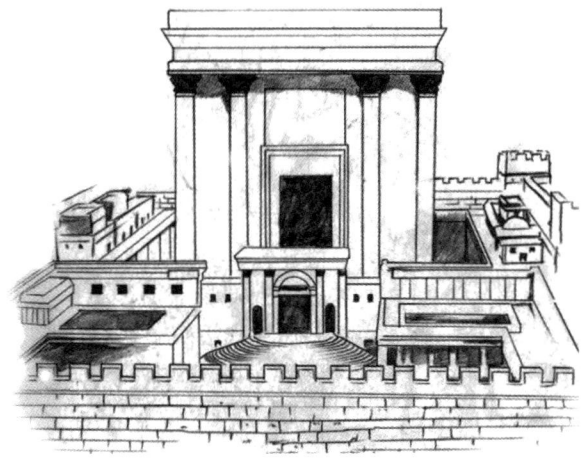

Roman soldiers destroyed the Temple in Jerusalem

Note to Parent: *The Temple was destroyed in AD/CE 70.*

264

The Story of the Words

Chapter 38 The End of the Ancient Jewish Nation

1 The Destruction of the Temple

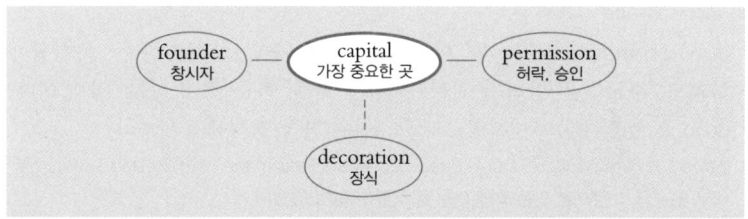

founder ⓝ someone who starts a organization, business or school
found는 '토대, 기초(bottom, base)'를 뜻하는 라틴어에서 유래했기 때문에 동사형 found는 '설립하다, 창립하다, 처음 만들다[세우다]'라는 뜻이다. 여기에 -er을 붙여 founder로 쓰면 '설립자, 창립자'가 된다.
Earlier, we read about Jesus, the founder of Christianity. 앞에서 우리는 기독교의 창시자인 예수에 대해 읽었다.

permission ⓝ the act of allowing someone to do something
동사형 permit의 명사형으로, permit에서 per-는 '통과(through)'를 뜻하고, mit는 '보내다(send), 가게 놔두다(let go)'이다. 즉 통행을 허락한다는 의미이다. 그래서 permit는 '허락하다'이고, permission은 '허락, 허가, 승인'을 뜻한다.
Then the good king of Persia and Babylon, Cyrus the Great, gave the Jews permission to move back to their own land—back to Canaan. 그러다가 페르시아와 바빌론의 선한 왕인 키루스 대제가 유대인들이 고향인 가나안으로 다시 이주할 수 있게 허락했다.

capital ⓐ the most important place
cap, capt, capit 등은 모두 '머리(head)'를 뜻하는 어근이다. '머리'는 가장 중요하고, 높은 것을 의미한다. 그래서 capital(capit + al)도 '수도, 자본, 대문자의, 사형의'처럼 중요한 의미를 담고 있다. Jerusalem, the capital city of the Jews(유대인들의 수도인 예루살렘)에서 capital city는 현재의 '수도(首都)'와는 개념이 다르지만, 그만큼 '중요한 도시'로 이해할 수 있다.

When the emperor in Rome heard what was happening, he sent more Roman soldiers with orders to destroy Jerusalem, the capital city of the Jews. 로마의 황제는 어떤 일이 벌어지고 있는지 들었을 때 유대인들의 중심 도시인 예루살렘을 파괴하라는 명령과 함께 더 많은 로마 병사들을 보냈다.

decoration ⓝ an attractive thing that is added to something to improve its appearance

decoration에서 decor-는 '아름다움, 영예, 꾸밈'을 의미한다. '아름답게 하려고, 누군가를 기리기 위해, 꾸미기 위해' 하는 것이 바로 '장식'이다. decorate(장식하다)의 명사형 decoration은 '장식, 장식물'을 뜻한다.

Inside the temple were many beautiful decorations made of gold and silver. 신전 내부에는 금과 은으로 만든 아름다운 장식물이 많이 있었다.

Q 유대인 중에 여러 나라 사람이 있는 이유가 '디아스포라'와 관련이 있나요?

A 2차 디아스포라 이후 유대인들은 여러 나라로 흩어졌어. 유대인들은 지금의 러시아, 독일, 프랑스, 영국, 폴란드, 네덜란드 등 어디라도 발붙일 곳이 있다면 정착해서 살았지. 오랜 세월 그들은 나라 없는 백성으로 살았지만, 토라(구약 성서의 앞 5장, 흔히 모세 오경이라고 함)와 그들의 삶의 규범인 탈무드를 중심으로 뭉쳐서 생활했어. 각 지역에 그들의 정신적인 지주 역할을 하는 랍비가 있었고, 그들을 중심으로 율법을 지키는 삶을 고수했지.

로마 제국이 기독교를 정식 국교로 채택하게 되면서 유대교인은 묘한 상황이 되었단다. 왜냐고? 기독교인들은 유대교인이 예수를 죽음으로 몰아넣은 장본인이라고 생각했기 때문이야. 그래서 살던 지역에서 박해를 받기도 하고, 심지어는 쫓겨나는 경우도 있었어. 각지에 흩어져 살던 유대인들은 그들의 선조들이 약속의 땅으로 다시 돌아가 나라를 세우게 되었어. 그러니 유대인 중에는 다양한 나라 사람들이 모일 수밖에 없었던 거야.

The Story of the World

Chapter 39
Rome and the Christians

1 Nero, the Evil Emperor

지금도 역사상 최악의 폭군(暴君)으로 기억되고 있는 네로(Nero)는 서기 54년에 제5대 로마 황제의 자리에 올랐다. 초기에는 어머니의 섭정과 스승인 세네카(Seneca)의 지도 덕분에 내치와 외치 모두 성공적으로 수행할 수 있었다. 그러나 스무 살이 넘으면서 서서히 광기를 드러내기 시작했다. 경쟁 관계에 있던 의붓동생을 살해했고, 결혼을 반대하는 어머니와 아내도 살해했다. 로마에 대화재가 발생하자 새로운 왕궁을 건설하는 계획을 무리하게 실행하다가 시민들의 원성을 샀고, 기독교도들을 화재의 범인으로 몰아서 300여 명을 학살했다. 결국 68년에 히스파니아의 총독인 갈바(Galba)가 원로원과 로마 시민에 대한 충성을 명분으로 군대를 이끌고 로마로 들어와 황제를 축출한다. 네로는 로마 근교 하인의 집에 숨어 있다가 자살한다.

Augustus Caesar was a good and fair ruler of Rome. His people loved him, and his army obeyed him. His reign was a good time for the city of Rome, and for all of the lands that Rome controlled.

But after Augustus Caesar died, Rome had other emperors who weren't fair and just. They were cruel to their subjects. They got richer and richer and spent more and more money on themselves, while the people of Rome got poorer and poorer. The emperor of Rome was supposed to tell the army how to fight, but the emperors after Augustus Caesar were such bad generals that the army refused to obey them! One Roman emperor even made his horse a consul, and told all the people of Rome to do whatever the horse said.

The worst Roman emperor of all was named Nero. Nero had everyone who disagreed with him murdered. His favorite pastime was playing the lyre; he was a very bad lyre player, but everyone was afraid to tell him so. So they all praised his terrible music. "When I die," Nero used to say, "what a loss I shall be to the art of music!" And the Romans in the royal court all agreed with him, because they were afraid for their lives.

After Nero had been emperor of Rome for ten years, he decided to take a vacation from Rome. He went out to his house in the country and invited his favorite friends to go with him. They had a party that went on for days and days.

Meanwhile, Rome was burning.

The fire began late at night, in a rickety wooden building in a dark and dirty Roman street. No one knows exactly how it started. But the poor families who lived in that part of town often built small fires to keep warm. Perhaps a coal fell out of one of these fires, onto the dry wooden floor. It smoldered away until the floorboard caught fire. The fire spread to a wall, and then to the entire building. And then the flames leapt to the building next door.

Soon a whole section of Rome was on fire. The fire roared along until it came up against a stone wall. The rich people of Rome had built the wall to keep fires from spreading into the wealthy part of town. But this fire was stronger than the wall. The flames leapt right over the wall and kept on burning.

The people of Rome realized that this was the worst fire in Roman history. They sent a messenger to Nero to tell him what was happening. The messenger galloped hard until he reached the country house where Nero and his friends were celebrating.

"Your Majesty!" the messenger cried. "Your city is burning!"

But Nero didn't even answer the messenger. He ordered him taken away, before he ruined the party. And he didn't return to Rome for days more.

When he finally did come back to Rome, he found his people waiting for him. Hundreds of families had been driven out of their homes. Everything they owned had been burned. They were cold and hungry. They begged Nero for help. "Remember your great ancestor, Augustus Caesar!" they cried. "He gave money to every poor family in Rome! Surely you can help us out of your great wealth!"

Nero did give some money to the poor and the homeless. But he made a big mistake. He announced, "The fire has cleared away ugly, broken-down houses and left space for my new building projects! I will take the land where those houses used to stand and build myself a new and bigger palace."

The people of Rome were furious. Nero had been unpopular even before the fire. Now they hated him even more. Soon, Nero realized that the Romans were on the edge of rebelling and taking his throne away. He had to find someone to blame for the fire—right away.

"I know who set the fire to Rome!" he told the Romans. "It was those Christians! They set the fire on purpose!

Of course, the Christians hadn't set the fire. But many people

Nero was an unpopular emperor

believed Nero's lies. The Romans began to persecute the Christians. Christians were arrested and executed. Some of them were forced to fight in gladiator shows. Others were killed by wild animals. *Nero's cruelty to the Christians drew attention away from his own selfishness.

2 Christians in the Catacombs

예수의 등장 이후 로마 제국의 기독교인들은 수난의 길을 걷게 된다. 본거지인 예루살렘은 로마군에 의해 파괴되었고, 로마를 비롯한 이탈리아 대도시에 살던 기독교도들도 반란 세력으로 낙인 찍혀 박해를 받았다. 이들에게 신앙의 자유를 준 것은 밀라노 칙령(Edict of Milano)이었다. 밀라노 칙령은 313년, 서로마 제국의 황제인 콘스탄티누스 1세와 동로마 제국의 황제인 리키니우스가 지금의 '밀라노(Milano)'에서 공동으로 발표한 황제의 명령을 말한다. 로마 제국의 모든 사람이 기독교를 포함해 자신이 원하는 종교를 믿고 종교 의식을 행할 수 있다는 내용이었다. 그 칙령 덕분에 기독교는 사교(邪敎)의 꼬리표를 떼고 로마의 정식 종교가 되었으며 기독교인들도 박해에서 벗어날 수 있었다.

The Romans punished runaway slaves, criminals, and Christians by making them fight wild animals. But what was wrong with being a Christian?

In the Roman Empire, it was a crime to be a Christian, because Christians would not sacrifice to the emperor. *The Roman emperors kept control over their people by saying, "Obey us, because we are gods!" The emperors claimed to be descended from Jupiter, the king of the gods. Special feast days were held every year in honor of the emperors. At these celebrations, all Romans were supposed to worship the emperor and promise to obey only him.

But Christians refused to do this. "We only worship our God!" they told other Romans. "We refuse to bow down to someone who is only a man! The emperor is not God. We will pray for him, but we will not worship him."

The Roman emperors were furious. If the Christians disobeyed them, other Romans might be brave enough to do the same. So the emperors ordered Christians arrested and put in jail. Many Christians were put in prison. Others were forced to fight lions.

The Christians were frightened by this persecution. So they stopped holding their meetings in public. Instead, they dug underground passages beneath Rome and beneath other cities in the Roman Empire. They held their religious meetings in these underground passages, in secret. The passages were called *catacombs*. Down in the catacombs, the Christians also buried their dead. The underground tunnels were dark and damp. Stones lined the floors. They were lit only by torches. Shadows lurked in every corner. But when the Christians were underground, they were safe.

This secrecy soon made people even more suspicious of the Christians. What were they doing down there, underground? Rumors started to fly around. Maybe the Christians were calling down floods and famine on the rest of the Roman Empire. Maybe they were planning to overthrow the government! "We must wipe out this new and harmful religion," one Roman senator wrote to another. "Otherwise, Romans will cease to worship the emperor."

Of course, the Christians weren't calling down famines or trying to overthrow the government. They were just meeting peacefully together to talk about Jesus and his teachings. They protested to the emperors that they were doing nothing wrong.

But the Roman emperors kept right on throwing them in jail. Soon Christians were even afraid to say to people they didn't know, "I am a Christian! Are you?" If they told the wrong person they were a Christian, they might end up in jail.

*So they decided on a secret symbol. It looked like a fish. When a Christian met someone she didn't know, she might draw a fish on a wall, or in the sand at her feet, or on the edge of a piece of paper. If the other person was a Christian, he would draw a fish too. Then both Christians knew that it was safe to talk to each other.

Today, you can still see the catacombs that the Christians dug below the cities of the Roman Empire. Some of the catacombs have tombs of ancient Christians in them. Others have pictures that the Christians drew of Jesus. Archaeologists have found fish carved on the walls as well—secret messages that the Christians sent to each other.

3 The Emperor Is a Christian!

콘스탄티누스(Constantine)는 전쟁을 통해 분열되어 있던 로마 제국을 평정한 후 312년에 원로원으로부터 '위대한 인물'이라는 뜻의 '막시무스(Maximus)'라는 호칭을 얻으며 황제의 자리에 올랐다. 관료제와 세제를 정비해 정치를 안정시켰고, 이민족의 침략도 성공적으로 막아내며 로마의 재건에 힘썼다. 313년에는 그동안 박해받아 온 기독교를 로마의 종교 중 하나로 정식 인정하는 '밀라노 칙령'을 공표함으로써 기독교의 성장과 팽창의 계기를 제공했다.

The Roman emperors kept on persecuting Christians until an emperor named Constantine came to the throne. Constantine was a fair man. He worshipped the Roman god Apollo, but he didn't think it was right to put people in jail because of the god they worshipped. So he ordered all persecution to stop. No one was to arrest Christians for being Christians any more.

Constantine himself went on worshipping Apollo—until something strange happened to him. Different ancient writers tell us different stories about Constantine. Some say he had a dream. Others say he had a vision. But whatever Constantine saw, everyone agrees about what happened next: The emperor himself became a Christian!

So what did Constantine see?

One Roman writer tells this story about Constantine's vision:

Constantine was marching towards the most important battle of his life. He had fought the enemy for months now, and had not been able to triumph. The coming battle was his last hope. Would he win? Would the Roman Empire remain safe? Or would his soldiers be defeated, driven backwards by the enemy and forced to surrender? He would know tomorrow, when they met the enemy at the Milvian Bridge.

He looked behind him at his army. They had fought hard against invaders and won. But now they were so tired they could barely drag themselves along. Their feet hurt; their heels were blistered in their shoes, and their armor was heavy on their shoulders.

Constantine glanced up at the gray, cloudy sky. On top of everything else, he thought, it was going to rain on them. They would be tired, discouraged, and soaking wet. They would have to set up camp in the pouring rain, and no one would sleep well before the next morning's battle.

"Look," the soldier beside him said. "The sun is coming out."

Constantine squinted at the sky. It did look brighter. But —

"That's not the sun," he said. "What is it? It … it looks like a cross!"

Constantine and his soldiers stared with open mouths. Above them in the sky hovered a cross of light, growing larger and brighter by the moment. The golden light from the cross fell across their weary faces until they were forced to blink and shield their eyes with their hands. The grass around them glittered with light!

Underneath the cross, fiery letters burned themselves across the sky. Constantine read them out, one by one: *By this sign you will be victor.*

"It is the cross of Christ!" Constantine gasped.

"What does it mean?" the soldiers asked.

"It means that we must fight for God," Constantine answered. "The God of the Christians!"

When they set up camp that night, Constantine sent out an order to his men. "Every soldier must have the sign of Christ on his shield!" he ordered. "Until that is done, we will not go into battle!"

So each soldier painted onto his shield the Greek letters standing for Christ's name. When they went into battle, Constantine led the charge under a banner bearing the name of the Christian God. And Constantine's army won the Battle of Milvian Bridge. When he stood victorious on the bridge, Constantine raised his sword to the sky. "The God of the Christians gave me this victory!" he announced. "From now on, I will always fight under his banner. And I will only worship him!"

After he won this battle, Constantine became a Christian. He claimed that the Christian God had helped him to beat the

Rome and Constantinople

enemy. He made Sunday a holiday all over Rome, so that people could go to church. Soon, many more people in the Roman Empire became Christians, following the example of their emperor.

After he became a Christian, Constantine decided that the new center of the Roman Empire should no longer be in Rome. After all, Rome was an old city, beginning to look shabby and run-down. Constantine moved the capital of the empire to another city that he named after himself: Constantinople. From now on, Constantinople, not Rome, would be the center of Roman power.

But that power would not last long! 📖

Note to Parent: Nero ruled from AD/CE 54–68. Constantine ruled from AD/CE 312–337. The emperors between Nero and Constantine had varying policies towards Christianity, but Christians were rarely tolerated for long.

The Story of the Words

Chapter 39 Rome and the Christians

1 Nero, the Evil Emperor

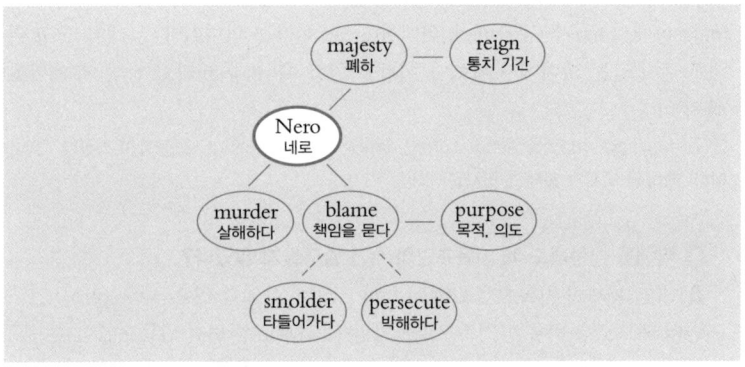

reign ⓝ the time when a king or queen rules a country

reign은 '왕국(kingdom)'을 뜻하는 라틴어에서 유래했다. '왕국'에서 '왕의 통치'나 '왕의 통치 기간'의 의미로 확장되었다. 지금은 '통치 기간, 치세'를 뜻하는 명사형으로 쓰인다.

His reign was a good time for the city of Rome, and for all of the lands that Rome controlled. 그의 통치 기간은 로마에게, 그리고 로마가 지배한 모든 땅에게도 좋은 시절이었다.

murder ⓥ to kill someone on purpose

murder에는 원래 '죽음(death)'이라는 의미가 있다. 다른 사람을 죽음에 이르게 한다는 의미에서, '죽이다, 살해하다'라는 뜻으로 쓰이게 되었다. to have A murdered는 'A가 살해되도록 만들다'이다. '살인자'는 murderer이다.

Nero had everyone who disagreed with him murdered. 네로는 자신에게 반대하는 사람들은 모조리 살해되도록 했다.

smolder ⓥ to burn slowly without a flame but with some smoke
과학 시간에 돋보기로 먹종이에 불을 붙여본 적이 있을 것이다. 돋보기로 한곳에 햇빛을 모아 기다리면 한참 동안 연기가 나다가 결국 불이 붙는다. 불꽃이 보이기 전, '연기가 나면서 타는' 모습을 표현한 동사가 바로 smolder이다. '그을다, 연기만 나면서 서서히 타들어가다'라는 의미이다.
It smoldered away until the floorboard caught fire. 뜨거운 석탄이 연기를 내며 천천히 타들어가다가 결국 마룻바닥에 불이 붙었다.

majesty ⓝ the title used when talking to or about a king or queen
majesty에서 maj-는 '큰(large), 위대한(great)'이라는 의미이다. 그래서 '크고 위대한 존재'라는 의미에서 왕이나 여왕을 칭할 때 majesty라고 한다. 우리말로 '폐하'이다.
"Your Majesty!" the messenger cried. "Your city is burning!" 전령이 소리쳤다. "황제 폐하! 폐하의 도시가 불타고 있사옵니다!"

> **Q** 박해를 받는데도 왜 기독교인의 수가 줄어들지 않았나?
> **A** 네로 황제의 기독교도 박해는 로마 시내의 화재로 더욱 촉발되었어. 그런데 베드로를 비롯한 기독교인들의 순교 이후로 오히려 기독교인의 수가 늘어나는 놀라운 현상이 벌어졌단다. '팍스 로마나'라고 불린 시대였지만, 사실은 아우구스투스 황제 이후로 모든 것이 순조롭게 진행된 것은 아니었거든. 군인이 황제가 되어 50년 동안 황제가 26명이나 바뀔 정도로 혼란스러운 시대였으니까. 이 세상에서 살아가는 일이 힘겹게 느껴지는 사람들에겐 예수를 믿고 회개하면 죽어서 좋은 세상으로 갈 수 있다는 교리가 마음속에 스며들게 되지 않았을까? 그렇게 해서 점차로 로마 제국 내에서 기독교인의 숫자가 늘어나게 되었어.

blame ⓥ to say that someone is the cause of something bad
blame은 어떤 잘못된 일에 대해 책임을 묻는 것이다. '~을 탓하다, ~의 책임으로 여기다'라는 뜻이다. 자신의 책임이 아니라고 항변할 때 흔히 Don't blame me. It's not my fault(내 탓 하지 마. 내 잘못 아냐)'라고 말한다.
He had to find someone to blame for the fire—right away. 그는 그 화재에 대해 책임을 물을 누군가를, 당장, 찾아야만 했다.

purpose ⓝ the intention of doing what you do

purpose에서 pur-는 '앞(before, front)'이고, pose는 '놓다, 두다(to place)'를 뜻한다. '앞에 두는 것'이 바로 '목적'이다. purpose는 항상 앞에 있어서 전진하는 것이다. 외국에 나갈 때 공항 출입국 관리소에서 자주 들을 수 있는 질문이 What's the purpose of your visit?으로 방문의 '목적'을 묻는 질문이다. on purpose는 '목적[의도]을 갖고, 고의적으로'라는 표현이다.
They set the fire on purpose! 그들이 고의로 불을 질렀다!

persecute ⓥ to treat someone very badly or unfairly because of their religion, race or political beliefs

persecute는 '완전히, 끝까지(utterly, through)'를 뜻하는 접두사와 '따라다니다(follow), 쫓다(pursue)'를 뜻하는 secute가 합쳐진 것이다. 계속 따라다니며 괴롭히고, 끝까지 쫓아내려고 하는 것이 persecute의 의미이다. 종교, 인종, 정치적 신념이 다르다는 이유로 '박해하다'라는 뜻으로 쓰인다. '박해(迫害)'라는 말도 '괴롭히고 해친다'는 뜻이다. 명사형은 persecution이다.
The Romans began to persecute the Christians. 로마인들은 기독교인들을 박해하기 시작했다.

Q 로마 황제들은 왜 유독 기독교인을 박해했나요?

A 로마는 다신교의 나라였어. 그리스 신만 받아들인 것이 아니고, 이집트의 신을 비롯해 그들이 정복한 나라의 신까지 수용했거든. 그러니 로마 제국에서 기독교인이 박해를 당한 것은 교리 때문만이 아니었단다. 그렇다면 무슨 이유로 박해를 당한 것일까?
키케로가 카이사르를 신으로 격상시킨 사건 기억나지? 그때부터 로마 황제는 죽어서 신으로 숭배받았고, 나중에는 심지어 살아 있는 황제를 신으로 숭배하기도 했지. 그러나 로마 제국의 기독교인들은 우상을 숭배하지 말라는 그들의 교리에 따라 황제 숭배를 거부했어. 게다가 병역도 거부했으니 로마 황제의 입장에서는 점점 증가하는 기독교인들을 그대로 두기 어려웠던 것이지.

2 Christians in the Catacombs

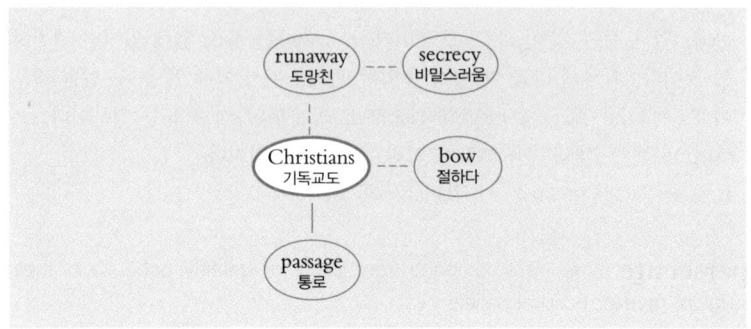

runaway ⓐ escaped from somewhere
'달려서(run) 멀어지다(away)'라는 의미에서 동사구 to run away는 '도주하다, 도망치다'라는 뜻이다. 형용사 runaway는 '도망친'을 뜻한다. '가출 청소년'은 runaway teenagers이고, 군대 '탈영병'은 a runaway soldier라고 한다. 명사형 runaway는 '도망자'인데, '가출자, 가출 청소년'의 의미로도 쓰인다. runaway slaves는 '도망친 노예, 도망치다 잡힌 노예'를 말한다.
The Romans punished runaway slaves, criminals, and Christians by making them fight wild animals. 로마인들은 사나운 동물들과 싸우게 함으로써 도망치다 잡힌 노예, 범죄자, 기독교인을 처벌했다.

bow ⓥ to bend your head or the top part of your body forward to show respect
bow의 기본적인 의미는 '둥글게 구부러진(curved, arch)'이다. 비 온 뒤 하늘에 뜬 '무지개'가 rainbow인 것은 그 형태가 '둥글게 구부러졌기' 때문이고, 무기인 '활'도 둥글게 구부러졌기 때문에 bow이다. 우리가 배꼽인사나 절을 할 때도 몸을 굽히기 때문에 bow라고 한다. 즉 '몸을 굽혀 인사하다, 절하다, 활처럼 휘어지다'라는 뜻이다.
We refuse to bow down to someone who is only a man! 우리는 인간에 불과한 자에게 절을 하지 않는다!

passage ⓝ a narrow place in a building that connects one room to another
passage는 말 그대로 '지나가는(pass) 곳' 또는 '지나가는 행동'이다. 즉 '통로, 복도, 통행, 통과'의 명사형이다. 책의 내용 중에 일부분을 passage라고 하는 것도 그 부분이 앞뒤의 내용과 '통로'처럼 연결되기 때문이다. 기독교인들이 로마인들의 눈을 피해 지하에 판 catacomb도 '통로' 모양이었기 때문에 passage 라고 할 수 있다.

Instead, they dug underground passages beneath Rome and beneath other cities in the Roman Empire. 대신에 기독교인들은 로마 시의 밑과 다른 로마 제국의 도시 밑에 지하 통로를 팠다.

secrecy ⓝ the act of keeping something secret, or the state of being kept secret

secrecy에서 se-는 '멀리, 따로(away)'이고, 어근 cre는 '분리하다, 떼어내다(separate)'를 뜻한다. 뭔가를 '떼어내어' 다른 사람들이 보지 못하게 '치워 놓는' 것이다. 그렇다면 나만 알고 다른 사람은 모르는 것이므로 secrecy는 '비밀 유지, 비밀 상태'를 뜻한다. '비밀, 비밀의, 남 몰래 하는'을 뜻하는 secret은 명사형이나 형용사형으로 쓰인다.

This secrecy soon made people even more suspicious of the Christians. 이 비밀스러움 때문에 사람들은 더욱더 기독교인들을 의심하게 되었다.

3 The Emperor Is a Christian!

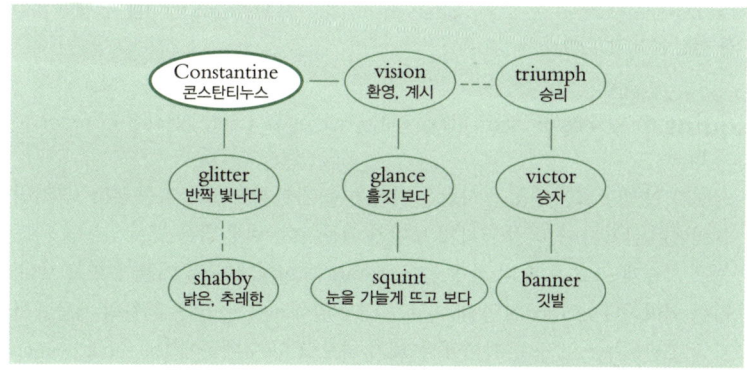

vision ⓝ something that you seem to see as part of a powerful religious experience

UFO나 외계인을 봤다고 주장하며 존재를 믿는 사람들이 있다. 그런데 그중 대부분은 엉뚱한 것을 잘못 보고 오해했거나 '헛것'을 본 것으로 판명되었다. 이렇게 봤다고 믿는 이미지, '환영(幻影), 환각'을 vision이라고 한다. 종교에 심취하면 이런 환영을 볼 수도 있기 때문에 '종교적 계시'라는 의미도 있다.
Others say he had a vision. 어떤 작가들은 그가 환영[신의 계시]을 보았다고 말한다.

triumph ⓥ to win a great victory

triumph는 '술의 신인 바쿠스(Bacchus)에 대한 찬가(讚歌)'를 뜻하는 희랍어에서 유래한 것으로 추정된다. 전쟁에서 이기고 돌아와 '술을 달라고 노래'한다는 것은 '승리'를 축하한다는 의미이다. 그래서 triumph는 '승리, 대성공'과 '승리하다'라는 동사형으로도 쓰인다. 부사형 triumphantly는 승리한 사람의 태도를 표현하는, '의기양양하게, 우쭐대며'를 뜻한다.
He had fought the enemy for months now, and had not been able to triumph. 그는 지금 여러 달 동안 적과 싸워 왔으나 승리할 수 없었다.

glance ⓥ to look quickly at someone or something

멋진 이성이 옆으로 지나가면 눈길이 가는데, 뚫어지게 쳐다보지는 못하고 그냥 한번 흘긋 본다. 이렇게 뭔가를 '흘긋 보다, 한번 훑어보다'라는 뜻에 딱 맞는 영어 동사가 glance이다. look at처럼 보는 대상 앞에 at이 붙는다. 서로 쳐다봤다면 They glanced at each other라고 할 수 있다. to glance up at은 '위를 올려다보다'이다.
Constantine glanced up at the gray, cloudy sky. 콘스탄티누스는 구름 낀 잿빛 하늘을 한번 올려다보았다.

squint ⓥ to look at something with your eyes partly closed in order to see better

근시가 있거나 노안이 있는 사람은 가끔 눈을 가늘게 뜨고 글자를 본다. 그러면 흐릿했던 글자가 좀 더 뚜렷하게 보이기 때문이다. 너무 밝은 곳에 있는 물체도 눈을 가늘게 뜨고 보면 더 잘 보인다. squint는 이렇게 '눈을 가늘게 뜨고 보다'라는 의미이다. glance처럼 대개 보는 대상 앞에 at을 붙인다. 본문의 예문에서도 콘스탄티누스도 구름 사이에서 '해가 나오고 있기 때문에(The sun is coming out) 눈을 가늘게 뜨고 하늘을 본 것이다.
Constantine squinted at the sky. 콘스탄티누스는 눈을 가늘게 뜨고서 하늘을 보았다.

glitter ⓥ to shine brightly with a lot of flashes of light

햇빛을 받은 금, 다이아몬드, 바다의 물결은 '반짝반짝' 빛이 난다. 빛의 가루가 뿌려진 듯하다. 이렇게 눈부시게 빛나는 것을 glitter로 표현한다. All that glitters is not gold(반짝인다고 다 금인 것은 아니다)라는 유명한 속담이 있다.
The grass around them glittered with light! 그들 주위의 풀이 빛으로 반짝였다!

victor ⓝ the winner of a battle or competition
victor는 앞에서 다룬 victory와 마찬가지로 '정복하다(conquer)'를 뜻하는 라틴어에서 온 것이다. '정복한 사람'이라는 의미에서 '승자'를 뜻한다. 그런데 victor는 일상에서 잘 쓰지 않는 표현으로, '승자, 우승자'는 보통 winner라고 한다. By this sign you will be victor(이 상징으로 인해 너는 승자가 될 것이다)에서 victor 앞에 관사(a, the)를 쓰지 않은 것은 십자가(cross)만 있으면 영원한 승자가 된다는 의미를 표현하고자 한 것이다.
Constantine read them out, one by one: By this sign you will be victor. 콘스탄티누스는 큰소리로 한 단어 한 단어씩 읽었다. "이 상징으로 너는 승자가 될 것이다."

banner ⓝ a long piece of cloth on which something is written or drawn
인터넷 서핑을 하다 보면 각종 사이트에서 배너 광고(banner ads)를 보게 된다. 이 광고에 banner라는 이름을 붙인 것은 '큰 깃발'처럼 생겼기 때문이다. 왕, 군주, 군대를 상징하는 깃발에는 상징적인 문양이나 글자가 쓰여 있었다. 배너 광고도 대개 네모 모양에 광고 문구가 적혀 있다. 과거에는 banner를 앞세우고 전쟁에 나가는 것이 관행이었다. banner는 band와 어원이 같은데, '하나로 묶고 결속시키는' 역할을 하기 때문이다.
When they went into battle, Constantine led the charge under a banner bearing the name of the Christian God. 그들이 전투에 나갈 때, 콘스탄티누스는 기독교 신의 이름이 적힌 깃발을 들고서 공격을 이끌었다.

shabby ⓐ old, dirty and in bad condition
shabby는 몸에 생긴 '상처의 딱지, 긁힌 자국'을 뜻하는 말에서 왔다. 다친 당사자는 '그 자리'가 아프고 가렵겠지만, 모르는 사람이 보면 좀 지저분해 보인다. 그런 이미지에서 shabby는 '낡은, 허름한, 추레한' 모습을 표현하는 형용사이다.
After all, Rome was an old city, beginning to look shabby and run-down. 어차피 로마는 낡고 추레해 보이기 시작하는 오래된 도시였다.

The Story of the World

Chapter 40
Rome Begins to Weaken

1 The British Rebellion

로마 제국이 브리튼 섬을 침략해 정착촌을 건설한 후에도 켈트족의 저항은 계속되었다. 특히 동남부에 근거지를 둔 이케니족의 저항이 심했는데, 네로 황제의 재임기인 서기 60년경에 이케니족의 여왕인 보아디케아(Boadicea; '부디카'라고도 불림)가 주변 부족들을 규합한 후 로마군과 정착촌을 공격해 막대한 타격을 입힌다. 그러나 그 저항도 결국 진압되었고, 이후 로마군은 브리튼 섬의 절반 이상을 점령해 로마의 땅으로 만든다. 로마의 브리튼 점령은 300년 이상 지속되다가 410년에 갈리아 지역의 반란을 진압하기 위해 브리튼 섬의 로마군을 모두 철수시키면서 브리튼 섬은 해방을 맞게 된다.

When Julius Caesar and Caesar Augustus were in charge of the Roman Empire, Rome was strong and prosperous. But bad emperors like Nero started to weaken Rome. Even worse, some of the countries that Rome had conquered began to resist Roman rule. They wanted to be free again.

The Celts who lived in Britain had never liked Roman rule. And the Romans had never managed to control all of the British islands. Some of the Celts obeyed Roman laws and paid taxes to the Romans. But others rebelled.

One of these disobedient Celtic tribes was particularly annoying to the Romans—because their leader was a woman! In ancient times, women weren't considered to be brave or strong. Men thought it was very embarrassing to be beaten by a woman.

But the leader of this Celtic tribe was no ordinary woman. She was a powerful warrior queen named Boadicea. A Roman writer named Cassius described Boadicea: She was very tall, taller than a man, and her voice was strong and powerful, loud enough to echo from mountain to mountain. She had fierce, piercing eyes, and long, thick, red-brown hair that hung down past her waist. She wore a billowing tartan cloak and a thick gold collar around her neck.

Boadicea refused to make her tribe part of the Roman Empire. Instead, she led the Celts in raids on the Roman settlements. The Romans seemed powerless to stop them! They even raided the biggest Roman settlement in Britain—Londinium. Later, this Roman settlement became the city of London.

Soon, the Romans in Britain were terrified of Boadicea and her warriors. The Roman citizens who lived in the settlements started telling each other that they had seen strange things, signs that Rome was doomed to be defeated by the Celts. *The statue of Victory fell face down without being pushed! *A woman claimed that she had seen the sea turn as red as blood. Other people said that they saw a ghost town in ruins near Londinium. And a man insisted that he had heard strange shrieks and yells coming from an empty Roman theater.

Did these strange things really happen? Probably not. But the stories show how nervous the Romans were about Boadicea.

Boadicea collected more and more Celtic warriors around her. Soon there were a hundred thousand British marching down on ten thousand Romans. That means that there was one Roman for every ten British fighters. Just before the final attack, Boadicea rode around and made a famous speech to all her warriors. "We British are accustomed to having women in command!" she shouted. "The gods will grant us revenge against the Roman invaders! I plan to win this battle—or die trying! Let the men live as slaves to the Romans if they want to—but I refuse to live in slavery!"

Then the Celts attacked. They rode into battle without any plan. They charged in at top speed, each soldier doing exactly what he wanted. But the Romans stayed together. They did what their general said. Even though they were outnumbered, they won!

The victory in Britain was only temporary, though. Soon the Romans were forced to leave Britain altogether. Today, in Britain, you can still see the ruins of Roman walls and roads. Those ruins are all that is left of the Roman settlements in Britain.

2 Rome Divided in Two

로마 제국이 서로마 제국과 동로마 제국으로 분할 통치된 계기는 284년 황제의 자리에 오른 디오클레티아누스(Diocletian)의 개혁 정치였다. 전임 황제들의 폭정과 실정으로 제국 내부가 혼란스러웠고, 식민지인들의 반란과 이민족의 침입이 빈번했기 때문에 제국을 근본적으로 개혁하고자 했던 것이다. 디오클레티아누스는 막시미아누스가 서로마를 다스리게 했고, 그 밑으로 각각 부황제를 두어 제국의 동쪽과 서쪽의 영토를 통치하게 했다. 이후 오랫동안 권력 투쟁이 전개되었고, 100여 년 후에 로마 제국은 완전히 둘로 나뉘게 된다.

The Roman Empire didn't last forever. Today, if you go to Italy, you will see ruins of old Roman buildings. You will see the remains of old Roman roads. But you won't see any ancient Romans.

What happened to the Roman Empire? The Roman Empire got too big. Its borders were too long for one army to protect. The soldiers of Rome couldn't possibly keep all invaders out of Rome's territory. And more and more invaders started to wander into the Roman Empire.

Ruling Rome was a little bit like having the biggest candy bar in a group of very hungry people. Everyone wanted to take it away. The emperors of Rome had to fight constantly against invaders. These invaders wanted Roman land and Roman wealth. They wanted to use the Roman roads and live in the Roman villages. But they didn't want to obey the Roman emperor or pay taxes to the Roman government. So they attacked Rome's borders with armies, hoping to take Rome's countries away. The Roman emperors had a difficult time keeping invaders out. There was so much Roman land that they couldn't protect all of it at once.

If ruling Rome was like having the biggest candy bar in a group of hungry people, ruling the entire empire was like having a candy bar as big as a car. How could you keep the whole candy bar safe? While you were protecting one side of it, a hungry person could sneak up and take a bite out of the other side. And if you ran around to protect the other side, you would leave the first side without anyone to guard it.

How could you protect such a big candy bar? Do you have any ideas? Here's one idea: You could break the candy bar in half and give the other half to someone you trusted to guard for you. That's exactly what happened to the Roman Empire. A wise emperor named Diocletian realized that no one ruler could keep all of Rome safe.

"This empire is too big for one man!" he exclaimed. "I will break it into two pieces, and ask someone else to rule the other half."

So Diocletian asked another Roman leader to be his partner. This partner, Maximian, ruled the western part of the Roman Empire. Diocletian ruled the eastern half.

Now Rome had two emperors! Diocletian and Maximian worked hard to protect Rome. Each one had an army, and they recruited more and more soldiers to make their armies bigger.

For a while, the Romans held off invaders. The Roman Empire seemed to be doing well. Eventually, Rome became the capital of the western half of the empire. And Constantinople, the city named after Constantine, became the capital of the eastern half of the empire.

But something strange began to happen to Rome. The Western Roman Empire grew poorer and poorer, while the Eastern Roman Empire became richer and richer. The people of the West even had trouble finding enough food for themselves. They had to buy food from the East. And Rome, which had once been the greatest city in the world, was looking rundown. But Constantinople was a shining beautiful city full of marble buildings with gold trim.

The Western Roman Empire had other problems, too. Invaders from the north kept attacking its borders, and the Western army was too weak to keep these invaders away. The people of the Western Roman Empire called the invaders barbarians, because they could not understand their language. And they were frightened of the barbarians, who seemed able to conquer anything in their path.

The armies of the Western Roman Empire tried to fight the barbarians off, but they just kept on coming. They invaded Britain. They invaded Gaul. They invaded Spain. And soon, they invaded Italy itself.

Note to Parent: Boadicea's revolt against Rome was in AD/CE 61–63; it is presented slightly out of chronological order in order to introduce the idea that Rome was weakening. Diocletian came to the throne in AD/CE 284 and divided the empire in 286. He ruled jointly with Maximian from 286–305.

The Story of the Words
Chapter 40 Rome Begins to Weaken

1 The British Rebellion

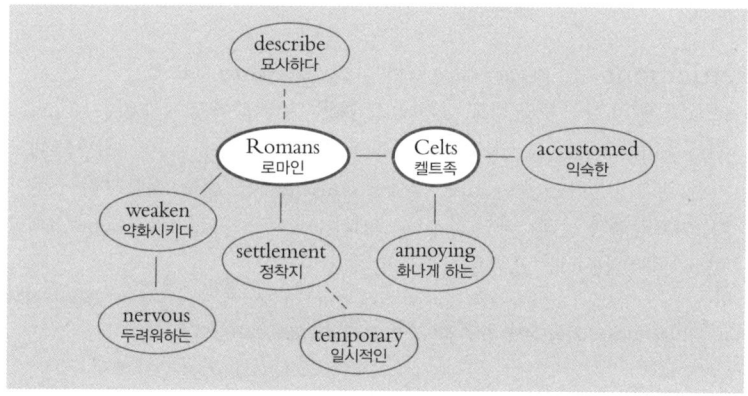

weaken ⓥ to make something or someone less strong
형용사에 -en이 붙으면 동사형으로 변하는 단어들이 있다. '약한'을 뜻하는 형용사형 weak에 -en을 붙여 weaken을 만들면 '약하게 하다, 약화시키다'라는 뜻의 동사형이 된다. weaken의 반대말은 명사형 strength(힘)에 -en을 붙인 strengthen(강하게 만들다, 강화하다)이다.
But bad emperors like Nero started to weaken Rome. 그러나 네로 같은 나쁜 황제들이 로마의 힘을 약화시키기 시작했다.

annoying ⓐ making someone feel angry
annoying은 동사형 annoy에 -ing가 붙은 형용사형이다. annoy는 '몹시 싫어하는(hateful)'을 뜻하는 말에서 유래했다. annoy는 '짜증 나게 하다, 화나게 하다'이고, annoying은 '짜증 나게 하는, 열 받게 하는'을 뜻하는 형용사형이다.
One of these disobedient Celtic tribes was particularly annoying to the Romans—because their leader was a woman! 이 반항적인 켈트족들 중 하나가 특히 로마인들을 화나게 하고 있는데, 그 이유는 그들의 대장이 여자였기 때문이다!

describe ⓥ to say what someone or something is like

고대 로마인들이 뭔가를 describe하려면 필기구가 필요했다. 왜냐하면 describe는 '밑에(down)'를 뜻하는 de-와 '쓰다(write)'를 뜻하는 scribe가 합쳐진 라틴어에서 유래했기 때문이다. 글로 표현하면 말로 할 때보다 더 정확하고 상세하게 설명하고 묘사할 수 있다. 그래서 지금도 describe는 글이나 말로 '상세하게 묘사하다, 자세히 설명하다'라는 뜻으로 쓰인다. 명사형은 description이다.
A Roman writer named Cassius described Boadicea. 로마의 역사가 카시우스(Cassius)는 보아디케아에 대해 이렇게 묘사했다.

settlement ⓝ a place where a lot of people newly settled

settle은 여러 가지 뜻을 갖고 있는데, 그중에는 여러분이 앞에서 읽은 Nomads who settled in the Fertile Crescent(비옥한 초승달 지대에 정착한 유랑민들)에서처럼 '정착하다'라는 뜻이 있다. 명사형 settlement는 '정착, 정착지'라는 뜻이다. 이스라엘과 팔레스타인 분쟁 뉴스에서 Jewish[Israeli] settlements(유대인[이스라엘] 정착촌)라는 표현을 자주 접할 수 있다.
They even raided the biggest Roman settlement in Britain—Londinium. 그들은 심지어 브리튼 섬에서 가장 큰 로마인 정착지인 론디니움까지 습격했다.

nervous ⓐ worried or afraid

nerve는 '힘줄'을 뜻하는 라틴어 nerbus에서 왔다. '아킬레스건'이라고 말할 때의 '건(腱)'이 힘줄이다. 뼈와 근육을 연결하는 조직인데, 힘줄이 강하면 힘이 세고, 힘줄이 약하면 힘도 약하다. 그래서 사전에서 nerve라는 단어를 찾아보면, '긴장, 불안'과 '용기'라는 상반된 의미가 실려 있다. nerve는 인체의 '신경'을 말하며 형용사형 nervous는 '신경이 약한' 상태를 의미하여 '불안해하는, 두려워하는'을 뜻한다.
But the stories show how nervous the Romans were about Boadicea. 그러나 그 이야기는 로마인들이 보아디케아에 대해 얼마나 두려워했는지 보여준다.

accustomed ⓐ familiar with something and accepting it as normal

accustom의 어근인 custom은 앞에서 배웠듯이 '매우 익숙해지다'라는 뜻을 담고 있다. 자주 접하고 행동해서 관습, 습관처럼 된 것이다. 앞에 붙은 ac-는 '~에(to, at)'를 뜻한다. 그래서 동사형 accustom은 '~에 익숙하게 하다, 길들이다'라는 뜻이 된다. I have to accustom myself to the new environments(나는 새로운 환경에 익숙해져야 한다)처럼 쓸 수 있다. 'to accustom oneself to 명사형' 은 'be accustomed to 명사형'으로 바꿔 쓸 수 있다. 'be used to 명사형'과 같은 의미이다.
"We British are accustomed to having women in command!" she shouted. 그녀가 외쳤다. "우리 브리튼 사람들은 여성을 지휘관으로 두는 것에 익숙하다!"

temporary ⓐ existing or happening for a short time only
템포(tempo)가 너무 빠른 노래는 따라 부르기 힘들다. 도시에서는 시골에서보다 삶의 속도가 빠르다. 이처럼 tempo는 '속도, 빠르기, 박자'를 뜻하는 단어이다. tempo는 temporary의 어근으로 '시간(time)'을 뜻하는 라틴어 tempus에서 왔다. tempo에 접미사 -ary가 붙어 '잠깐, 짧은'의 의미가 더해진 형용사형 temporary는 '일시적인, 임시의'라는 뜻이다. 그래서 영구 고용된 직장이 아닌 '임시직, 비정규직'을 a temporary job이라고 한다.
The victory in Britain was only temporary, though. 그러나 브리튼 섬에서의 승리는 일시적인 것이었다.

2 Rome Divided in Two

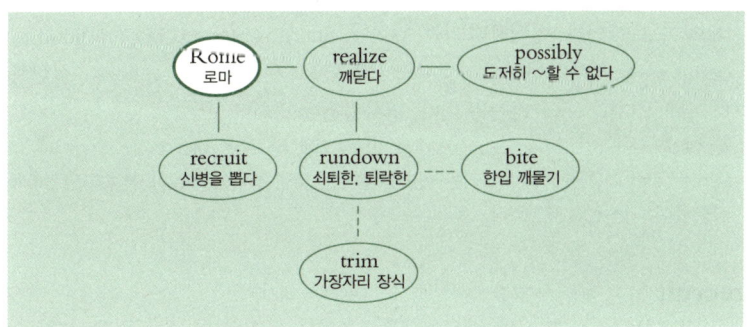

possibly ⓐ likely to happen or be true
possibly는 '가능한'을 뜻하는 형용사 possible의 부사형이다. possibly가 들어간 문장은 '일어날 수 있는 가능성'을 표현하는데, 축구팀이 상대에게 10:0으로 졌으면, It was possibly their worst game ever(아마 그들이 한 경기 중 최악이었을 것이다)라고 표현할 수 있다. maybe, perhaps의 의미이다. How could a wolf possibly raise a human baby(도대체 어떻게 늑대가 인간의 아기를 기를 수

가 있어)?처럼 '어떻게 그게 가능해?'라는 의미를 표현할 수도 있다. 부정문에 쓰면 '불가능'을 의미한다. 이때 possibly는 '도저히, 아무리 해도' 정도로 이해하면 해석이 매끄러워진다.

The soldiers of Rome couldn't possibly keep all invaders out of Rome's territory. 로마 병사들은 아무리 해도 모든 침략자들을 로마 영토 밖에 묶어 둘 수는 없었다.

bite ⓝ the act of cutting something with your teeth
bite는 '물다'로 이로 깨무는 동작이나 '깨물기, 깨문 한입'을 뜻하는 명사형으로도 쓰인다. to take[have] a bite는 '한입 깨물다, 한번 물어뜯다'라는 뜻이다. 예를 들어 You can take a bite of my cookie(내 과자 한입 먹어도 돼)나 Don't bite your nails!(손톱 깨물지 마!)처럼 쓴다.

While you were protecting one side of it, a hungry person could sneak up and take a bite out of the other side. 막대사탕의 한쪽을 지키고 있는 동안에 배고픈 사람이 몰래 다가와 다른 쪽을 한입 깨물 수 있었다.

realize ⓥ to know or understand something that you did not know before
realize는 '현실[사실]의, 진짜의'를 뜻하는 real의 동사형이다. realize는 '현실[사실]을 이해하다'와 '현실이 되게 하다'라는 두 가지 뜻이 있다. He realized that it was false(그는 그것이 거짓이었다는 사실을 깨달았다)에서 realize는 전자의 의미로 '깨닫다, 인식하다'라는 뜻이다. She has realized her ambition of being an actress(그녀는 배우가 되고자 한 꿈을 실현했다)에서 realize는 '실현하다, 달성하다(achieve)'라는 뜻이다. 명사형은 realization이다.

A wise emperor named Diocletian realized that no one ruler could keep all of Rome safe. 디오클레티아누스라는 현명한 황제는 어떤 통치자도 로마 전체를 안전하게 지킬 수 없다는 점을 깨달았다.

recruit ⓥ to find new people for an organization
recruit에서 re-는 '다시(again)', cruit는 '늘이다, 증가하다(grow)'를 뜻한다. 다시 수와 양, 규모를 증가시키는 것이 recruit이다. 회사에서 직원 수가 줄면, 다시 늘이기 위해 신입사원을 뽑는다. 군대에서는 제대한 군인 수만큼, 다시 신병을 뽑아야 한다. 이처럼 recruit는 '인원을 뽑다, 모집하다'와 '신입 사원[회원], 신병'을 뜻한다.

Each one had an army, and they recruited more and more soldiers to make their armies bigger. 각자 군대를 보유해서 더욱더 많은 병사들을 뽑아 군대를 증강시켰다.

rundown ⓐ being in very bad condition

rundown, run-down은 원래 너무 오래 심하게 '달려서(run)' 지쳐 '땅에 주저앉은(down)' 모습을 표현한 것이다. 건물이나 도시에 적용하면, '가꾸거나 수리하지 않고 계속 사용하기만 해서 여기저기 낡거나 고장 난 상태'이다. rundown은 '쇠퇴한, 퇴락한, 황폐한, 추레한'을 뜻한다.

And Rome, which had once been the greatest city in the world, was looking rundown. 그리고 한때 세계 최고의 도시였던 로마는 퇴락해 보이고 있었다.

trim ⓝ decoration on something, especially on the edges of something

trim은 모발을 손질할 때 자주 쓰는 단어이다. 수염을 기르는 사람은 거의 매일 수염 끝을 자르며 다듬는다. 미장원에 가면 I want my hair just trimmed(머리를 다듬어만 주세요)라고 말한다. 이렇게 trim은 '끝을 정돈해서 말끔하게 보이게 하다'라는 뜻이다. 명사형으로 쓰면 '다듬기'나 '가장자리나 끝의 장식'을 뜻하기도 한다.

But Constantinople was a shining beautiful city full of marble buildings with gold trim. 그러나 콘스탄티노플은 가장자리가 금으로 장식된 대리석 건물들이 가득한 빛나는 아름다운 도시였다.

> **Q** 디오클레티아누스와 콘스탄티누스 이야기 순서가 바뀌었다고요?
>
> **A** 이 책에서는 기독교 박해와 공인 이야기를 이어서 하느라 콘스탄티누스의 체험과 밀라노 칙령, 이어지는 수도 이전까지의 이야기를 한꺼번에 설명했어. 그러나 사실은 이번 장에서 나오는 디오클레티아누스가 먼저이고 그 다음이 콘스탄티누스란다.
>
> 디오클레티아누스는 군인 황제 시대의 혼란을 끝낸 황제였어. 그는 넓은 로마 제국을 둘로 나누어 동로마, 서로마라는 이름을 낳게 한 황제였지. 그런데 강력한 리더십이 없었다면 두 명의 황제, 두 명의 부제로 통치력이 나뉘는 것이 좋지 않았지. 그가 황제 자리에서 물러난 이후 벌어진 싸움을 보면 바로 알 수 있지 않니? 막센티우스와의 싸움에서 승리한 콘스탄티누스가 동로마 황제 리키니우스와 공동으로 밀라노 칙령을 발표한 것은 이미 상당수의 로마인이 기독교를 믿고 있었기 때문이란다. 이미 무시할 수 없는 세력으로 성장한 기독교인들을 포용하는 것이 정치적으로 필요하다고 판단한 것이겠지?

The Story of the World

Chapter 41
The Attacking Barbarians

1 Attila the Hun

4세기 말에 '낯선 야만인'들이 유럽으로 들어오기 시작했다. 생김새도 유럽인들과는 달랐으며 생활 모습도 많이 달랐다. 식물의 뿌리와 생고기를 먹는 이들은, 곧 유럽의 동쪽을 휩쓸며 로마인들을 공포에 떨게 했다. 이들은 서아시아의 산악 지역에 살던 기마 민족으로 추정되는 훈족(Huns)이었다. 중국 한(漢)나라에 쫓겨난 '흉노족'의 후손이라는 설이 있지만, 현실적으로 흉노족으로 보기에는 이동 거리가 너무 멀다. 아무튼 로마 제국은 한때 훈족에게 조공을 바치는 치욕을 감내해야 했다. 지금도 영화 속에서 훈족은 무서운 사람들로 등장하기도 한다.

The barbarians called Huns swept down on the Roman Empire on strong, fast warhorses, wearing strong armor and shooting deadly arrows from horseback. They came from the north, from Central Asia.

They drove all their enemies into retreat. All along the borders of the Roman Empire, people told terrible stories about the savage Huns. One Roman historian wrote, "•They are uglier than any other men on earth. They eat roots that they find in the fields. And they don't even cook their meat. Instead, they put the raw meat between their saddles and the backs of their horses, and ride on it all day. Then they eat it!" The Huns taught their babies to ride horseback even before they could walk. And Hun children didn't go to school; instead, they learned how to shoot arrows at a full gallop.

The most terrifying barbarian of all was Attila, the greatest Hun war leader. Attila led his Hun army in attacks against both Roman Empires—the East *and* the West. He was so powerful that the Romans began calling him "The Scourge of God." •They thought that God was punishing them by sending Attila the Hun to attack their borders!

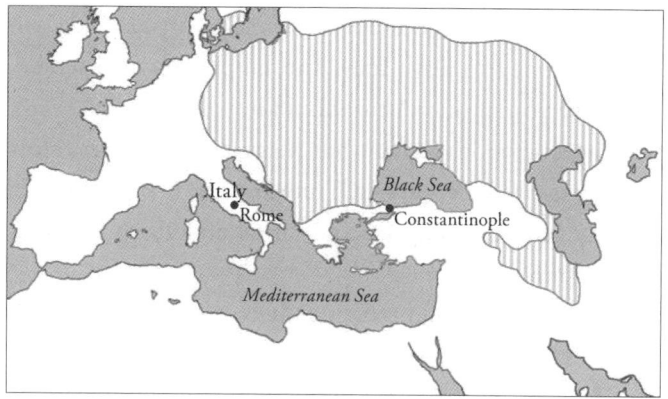

The Area of Attila the Hun's Rule, Before His Attack on Rome

The Western Roman emperor and his advisors tried to think of a way to keep Attila away. But the emperor's sister, Honoria, had different ideas. Honoria was bored with life at the Roman court. She was tired of being a great lady. And her brother, the emperor, wanted her to marry a weak, ugly man whom she didn't love. "If you don't marry him," he told her, "I'll throw you in jail!"

So Honoria wrote a letter to Attila the Hun. "Come and rescue me!" she wrote. "If you do, I will marry you!" She paid a servant to take this letter and her favorite ring to Attila.

The servant rode for days and days to reach Attila's army, which was camped at the borders of the Western Roman Empire. When Attila read Honoria's letter, he thought, "This is my chance to invade the Empire and take it for myself!" So he sent a message back to the emperor. The message was: "I am engaged to be married to your sister Honoria. I want half of your empire as a wedding present. And I'm coming to claim it—now!"

Attila and his men fought their way through Gaul and finally marched down into Italy. They conquered and burned the cities in their path. Finally, the emperor offered to pay Attila a huge amount of money to leave Italy. And he promised to send Attila money every year, if only Attila would leave Italy alone.

Attila agreed to leave Italy, but he warned, "I want Honoria sent to me as my wife, or I will return." He marched the Huns back out of Italy, planning to come back and claim his wife and his new empire.

But before Attila could return to Italy, he died of a nosebleed. And he never did marry Honoria, the sister of the emperor. Attila's followers put his body into a golden coffin. They put the golden coffin into a silver coffin, and the silver coffin into an iron coffin. They buried the iron coffin in the dead of night, and then killed all of the slaves who had helped to dig the grave, so that no one would know where Attila was buried. To this day, the grave of Attila the Hun has not been found.

2 Stilicho, Roman and Barbarian

스틸리코(Stilicho)는 반달족 출신으로, 서로마 제국의 황제 테오도시우스 1세의 신임을 받아 로마군의 지휘관이 되었다. 각지에서 반란을 일으킨 이민족들의 침입을 성공적으로 막아내며 서서히 권력의 중심에 서게 되었는데, 특히 자신의 사위인 호노리우스를 새로운 황제로 세우면서 로마의 '실세'가 되었다. 스틸리코는 동로마의 아르카디우스 황제가 사망하자 군대를 동원해 동로마의 수도인 콘스탄티노플을 장악해야 한다고 주장했다. 반대 세력은 그가 자신의 아들을 동로마 황제로 옹립하기 위해 로마 전체를 위험에 빠뜨린다고 생각했다. 결국 408년에 스틸리코는 반대파에 의해 축출되고 반역죄로 참수되었다.

The Huns were a powerful barbarian tribe. But so were the Visigoths, barbarians who lived around the Danube River. The armies of the Western Roman Empire fought with the Visigoths, the Huns, and other barbarian tribes for years and years. Some barbarians grew to like the Roman way of life. They stopped fighting and settled down in Roman villages. Sometimes, the barbarians even switched sides and fought for Rome.

One barbarian chief who switched sides married a Roman girl and settled down with her. We don't know his name, but we do know the name of his son: Stilicho.

Stilicho grew up with a barbarian father and a Roman mother. But Stilicho thought of himself as all Roman. He was a patriotic man who wanted to fight for Rome and protect Rome's lands from the barbarian invaders. When he was old enough, he traveled to the city of Rome itself and joined the Roman army. He was a brave fighter and a loyal servant of the emperor.

Soon the emperor himself took notice of Stilicho. He sent Stilicho on important errands to other countries. And Stilicho fell in love with the emperor's daughter, Serena. Finally, they were married. The half-barbarian boy had become part of the emperor's family.

The emperor put Stilicho in charge of the whole Roman army. "Stilicho," he said, "the Visigoths have decided to try and invade Rome. I give you the job of keeping them away. Go and destroy the Visigoths! Keep Rome safe."

Stilicho accepted the job. He marched his army out to meet the invading Visigoths. Time after time, the Visigoths and the Romans clashed in battle. Each time, the Visigoths backed away. But the Roman soldiers were never able to destroy the Visigoths completely. After each battle, the barbarians went away, rested, found fresh horses and men, and returned to fight again. Soon the Roman army was exhausted.

Stilicho returned to Rome. "We can never beat the Visigoths," he told the people of Rome. "But if we send them four thousand pounds of gold, they will leave us in peace."

"Four thousand pounds!" the people protested. "We will become even poorer."

"But if we don't send the money," Stilicho said, "the Visigoths will continue to fight us—and soon they will win."

Finally the Roman people agreed. The Visigoths took their gold and retreated from Roman land. But now the Romans were poorer and hungrier than ever. They were angry with Stilicho, because he had not defeated the Visigoths. They resented him because they had been forced to pay gold to drive the Visigoths away.

Soon people began to whisper about Stilicho. "He didn't try hard enough to conquer the barbarians!" they murmured. "He allowed them to escape on purpose! If he really wanted to, he could wipe them out. But he spared them, because he's part barbarian himself! Stilicho is a traitor to Rome! It's his fault that we had to send all that gold to the barbarians!"

Stilicho tried to defend himself. "I did my best," he said. "I am a faithful, loyal servant of Rome. But our armies are weaker than they were in ancient times. No general could defeat the Visigoths. Paying them gold was our only hope!"

But the people of Rome paid no attention. They turned against Stilicho and demanded his execution. Even Stilicho's own army mutinied. Stilicho was afraid for his life. He ran to a nearby church to hide.

"Come out!" his army told him. "We promise that you will be safe."

So Stilicho came out of the church. But as soon as he appeared, his own soldiers grabbed him and said, "The emperor has ordered you to be executed."

Stilicho's servants were still loyal to him. "We will fight for you!" they cried. But Stilicho refused to allow this. "Let us have no more bloodshed," he said. "I will abide by the emperor's command."

So Stilicho was beheaded. After his death, many Romans regretted his execution. "He was a faithful Roman," they said, "and he was our best defense against the barbarians."

3 The Coming of the Visigoths

서고트족(Visigoths)은 서로마 제국을 멸망의 길로 이끈 역사의 주역이었다. 서고트족은 스칸디나비아에서 남하한 게르만족의 일파로, 오랫동안 다뉴브 강 북쪽에 터를 잡고 살았다. 그러나 370년경에 서쪽에서 쳐들어온 훈족에게 쫓기자 로마에게 복종을 맹세하고서 로마 변방에 거주하게 된다. 이때 이동한 서고트족의 수는 약 100만 명에 이를 것으로 추정된다. 그러나 로마의 압제에 시달리면서 반란을 일으키게 된다. 서고트족은 이탈리아 전역을 휩쓸며 약탈했고, 410년에는 로마까지 점령했다. 그로 인해 서로마 제국은 수도를 라벤나로 옮겨야 했고, 쇠망의 길을 걸어야 했다.

Stilicho, the half-barbarian, half-Roman general, did his best to protect Rome from the barbarian invaders. He fought the Visigoths for years. But the Romans executed him because they thought he wasn't doing his best for Rome.

They shouldn't have! Stilicho was the only general who could keep the Visigoths away from Rome. Only two years after Stilicho's execution, the Visigoths finally marched all the way down through Italy to the city of Rome itself.

When the emperor and his court heard that the Visigoths were coming, they packed up all their belongings and left the city of Rome. They traveled to a much smaller city that sat in the middle of a swamp. The Visigoths couldn't get through the soft, muddy ground of the swamp with their horses, so the emperor was safe. From now on, this tiny, dirty, damp city would serve as the capital of the Western Roman Empire.

The people who stayed in Rome were terrified. For eight hundred years, the city of Rome had been safe from attack. Its thick walls and world-famous army had protected it from invasion. But now, the army was weak and frightened, and the walls were unprotected. The people of Rome sent desperate messages to the Eastern Roman Empire. "The Visigoths are coming!" they wrote. "Please, come and help us!"

But the army of the Eastern Roman Empire was afraid to fight the Visigoths. And the Eastern Roman emperor didn't dare send his army away from Constantinople, all the way to Rome. If he did, other barbarians might attack his city while it was unprotected.

So no one came to help Rome. The Visigoths poured over the walls and overwhelmed the soldiers who had remained on duty. The Visigoth commander, Alaric, ordered, "Gather up all the gold you can find! Take Rome's treasures! Now they belong to us!"

The Visigoths were happy to obey! They ripped down Rome's

The Visigoths invaded Rome

beautiful golden statues and melted them. They stole coins and jewelry.

But the Visigoths didn't kill the unarmed people of Rome. And because many of the Visigoths had converted to Christianity, they didn't destroy Rome's churches. They took everything valuable that they could put their hands on, and then marched away.

When they heard the news, people all over the old Empire mourned. Over in the Eastern Roman Empire, a monk named Jerome wrote, "Terrifying news has come to us from the West. Rome has been taken by assault. *Sobs disturb my every word. The city has been conquered which had once ruled the whole world."

Rome would never again be a great world power. Some Romans still lived in the city. But forty-five years after the Visigoth attack, another barbarian tribe invaded the city again. This tribe, called the Vandals, took everything valuable that the Visigoths had left behind. They were even worse than the Visigoths. They captured the frightened people of Rome and led them off to be slaves and hostages. They burned buildings made from wood, and tore bricks and stones out of walls that wouldn't burn. They even peeled the gold decorations off the roofs of Rome's temples! Today, we call someone who destroys things for fun a "vandal," after the Vandals who destroyed what was left of the city of Rome.

*The Western Roman Empire still survived, but just barely. *Its capital city was gone, and its emperor was ruling in the middle of a swamp. Soon, the Western Roman Empire would be gone forever.

Note to Parent: Attila's birthdate is unknown; he died in AD/CE 52. Stilicho became regent for the Western Roman Empire in 395, after Theodosius. Stilicho drove Alaric away in 397 but fell from favor and was executed in 408. The Visigoths sacked Rome in 410.

The Story of the Words

Chapter 41 The Attacking Barbarians

1 Attila the Hun

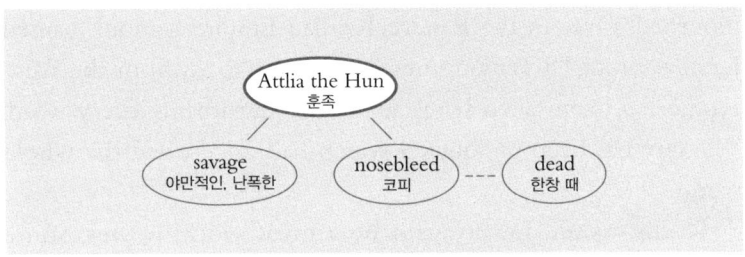

savage ⓐ wild and violent

savage는 '숲에 있는, 숲에서 온(of or from woods)'의 의미에서 유래했다. 문명화된 도시의 사람들과 가축들은 대개 점잖고 순해졌다. 반면에 숲속은 약육강식의 원칙이 존재하는 무서운 곳이었다. 동물들도 사납고, 숲속에 사는 사람들도 잔인했다. 이러한 이미지 때문에 savage는 '야만적인, 미개한, 난폭한' 성향을 의미하는 형용사로 쓰인다.

All along the borders of the Roman Empire, people told terrible stories about the savage Huns. 로마 제국의 국경을 따라 모든 곳에서 사람들이 야만적인 훈족에 대한 끔찍한 이야기들을 했다.

nosebleed ⓝ blood flowing from your nose

nosebleed는 형태 그대로 nose(코)와 bleed(피 나다)가 합쳐진 것이다. 바로 '코피'가 nosebleed이다. nosebloo드라는 말은 영어에 없다. 아틸라의 사망 원인에 관한 정확한 기록은 없다. Attila died of nosebleed는 하나의 '설'일 뿐이다.

But before Attila could return to Italy, he died of nosebleed. 그러나 이탈리아로 돌아가기 전에 아틸라는 코피가 나서 죽었다.

dead ⓝ the middle (of night or winter)

어둠과 겨울은 '죽음'을 상징해서 dead를 night과 winter에 쓸 수 있다. in the dead of night은 '한밤중에', in the dead of winter는 '한겨울에'를 뜻한다. in the middle of night[winter]와 같은 의미이다.

They buried the iron coffin in the dead of night, and then killed all of the slaves who had helped to dig the grave, so that no one would know where Attila was buried. 그들은 한밤중에 그 철제 관을 묻고 나서 무덤을 파는 일을 도운 노예들을 모두 죽여서 아무도 아틸라가 어디에 묻혔는지 모르도록 했다.

2 Stilicho, Roman and Barbarian

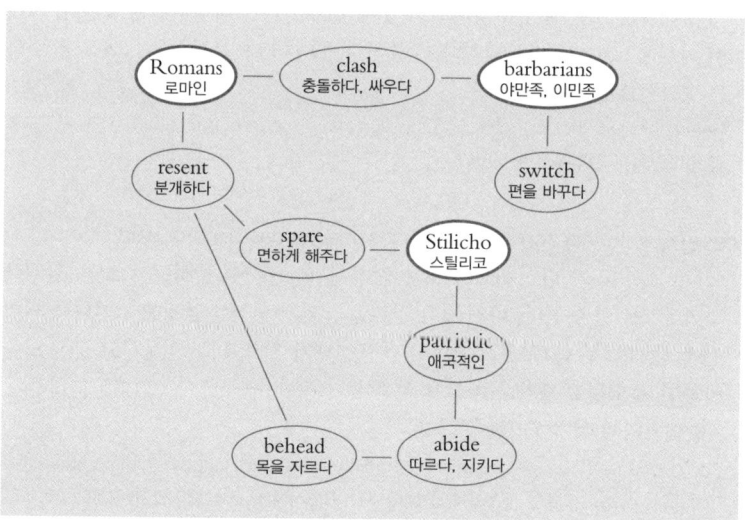

switch ⓥ to change from one thing to another

전등의 '스위치를 켜면(switch on)' 불이 켜지고, '스위치를 끄면(switch off)' 불이 꺼진다. 이렇게 스위치는 A에서 B로 '바꾸는' 역할을 한다. 그래서 switch가 '바꾸다, 전환하다, 바뀌다, 전환되다'라는 뜻이다. 원래 switch는 말 엉덩이를 '이쪽저쪽' 때리는 '회초리'를 가리키는 단어였다.

Sometimes, the barbarians even switched sides and fought for Rome. 때때로 이민족들은 편[입장]을 바꾸어 로마를 위해 싸우기까지 했다.

patriotic ⓐ showing great love for your country

patriotic은 '애국자'를 뜻하는 patriot의 형용사형으로, '애국적인'을 뜻한다. '조국(fatherland)'을 뜻하는 희랍어 patris에서 유래했다. 조국을 걱정하고, 조국을 위해 행동하는 것이 애국이기 때문에 patriot가 '애국자', patriotic이 '애국의, 애국적인', patriotism이 '애국, 애국심'을 뜻한다.

He was a patriotic man who wanted to fight for Rome and protect Rome's lands from the barbarian invaders. 그는 로마를 위해 싸우고 이민족의 침입으로부터 로마의 땅을 지키고자 했던 애국자였다.

clash ⓥ to fight

clash는 원래 뭔가 '쨍강! 쾅! 와장창!' 부딪히거나 깨지는 소리, 즉 의성어이다. 영어 만화를 보면 뭔가 부딪히고 깨질 때 'Clash!'라는 의성어가 등장한다. 그래서 의성어 clash가 '맞부딪히다, 충돌하다, 싸우다'나 '충돌, 대립, 싸움'을 뜻하는 명사형으로 쓰인다.

Time after time, the Visigoths and the Romans clashed in battle. 여러 차례 서고트족과 로마인들은 전투에서 부딪혔다.

resent ⓥ to feel angry about what someone has done or said

resent에서 re-는 '다시(again)' 또는 '강하게(strongly)'를 뜻하고, sent는 '감정을 느끼다(feel)'를 뜻한다. 다시 같은 감정을 느끼거나 격한 감정을 느낀다는 의미인데, 대개 너무 화가 났을 때 이런 감정 상태가 된다. 너무 억울하고 분한 일을 당하면, 두고두고 생각나고 화가 치민다. 그래서 resent는 '~에 대해 분개하다, ~을 억울하게 여기다'라는 뜻이다.

They resented him because they had been forced to pay gold to drive the Visigoths away. 그들은 서고트족을 몰아내기 위해서 금을 지불해야만 했기 때문에, 스틸리코에 대해 분개했다.

spare ⓥ to not harm or kill someone

스페어 타이어(spare tire)나 스페어 키(spare key)라는 말을 들어봤을 것이다. 스페어 타이어는 자동차 트렁크 깊숙이 '모셔져' 있다. 열심히 달려서 마모되고 있는 네 바퀴와는 달리 쓰지 않고 아껴두는 타이어이다. 스페어 키도 지금 사용하는 열쇠를 잃어버렸을 때를 대비해 쓰지 않고 있는 열쇠이다. 전쟁에서 자국의 병력을 spare하면 전투에 투입하지 않고 아껴둔 병력이 된다. 반대로 적의 군대를 spare하면 '해치지 않고 살려둔다'라는 의미이다. spare는 '아껴두다'라는 기본적인 의미에서 확장되어 '피하게[면하게] 해주다'라는 뜻이다.
But he spared them, because he's part barbarian himself! 그러나 그는 그들을 해치지 않았다. 왜냐하면 자신의 반이 야만족이기 때문이다!

abide ⓥ to accept and obey a decision, rule or agreement

고대 영어에서 온 abide에는 to live with(~와 함께 살다)나 to live by(~에 따라 살다)라는 뜻이 담겨 있다. 그래서 I can't abide those people. They lie all the time(난 저런 사람들 딱 싫어. 만날 거짓말만 해)와 같은 문장이 가능하다. '같이 살 수 없을 만큼 싫다'라는 의미이다. 또한 abide의 단골 문구인 to abide by A는 'A에 따르다, 복종하다, 지키다'라는 뜻이다.
I will abide by the emperor's command. 나는 황제의 명령에 따를 것이다.

behead ⓥ to cut someone's head off

behead는 '머리(head)' 앞에 붙은 be 때문에 정말 살벌한 말이 되었다. 여기서 be-는 '절단, 단절(off)'을 뜻한다. 머리가 떨어져 나간다니 끔찍하다. behead는 '목을 베다, 참수하다'라는 뜻이다. 옛날에는 사람 머리를 자르는 것이 형벌과 복수의 방법이어서 살인자나 반역자는 참수형에 처해졌고, 적장은 목을 베어 복수했다.
So Stilicho was beheaded. 그래서 스틸리코는 참수되었다.

3 The Coming of the Visigoths

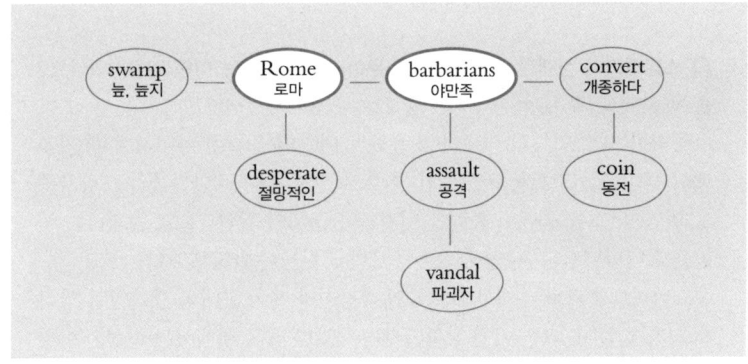

swamp ⓝ land that is always soft and very wet

swamp는 '물을 머금고 있는 땅'을 의미하여 '습지, 늪'이다. wetland와 비슷한 단어이다. 서로마 황제가 이민족을 피해 이주한 곳은 아드리아 해변에 위치한 '라벤나(Ravenna)'로, 땅이 질고 습한 곳이어서 swamp로 표현한 것이다.

They traveled to a much smaller city that sat in the middle of a swamp. 그들은 습지 한가운데에 자리한 훨씬 더 작은 도시로 이주했다.

desperate ⓐ extremely urgent and serious

desperate에서 de-는 '~로부터 멀어진(away from)'이고, sperate는 '희망(hope)'이다. 즉 희망으로부터 멀어졌다는 의미인데, 이런 상황에서 사람들은 필사적이고, 극단적으로 변하여 뭐든지 희망의 끈이 되기를 간절히 소망한다. 그래서 desperate은 '절망적인, 필사적인, 간절히 원하는, 다급한'을 뜻한다.

The people of Rome sent desperate messages to the Eastern Roman Empire. 로마 사람들은 동로마 제국에 다급한[절망적인] 메시지를 보냈다.

coin ⓝ a piece of money made of metal

coin은 '쐐기(wedge)'를 뜻하는 라틴어에서 온 것이다. 로마 제국에서 처음 쓰인 금속 화폐의 모양이 '쐐기' 모양이었기 때문에 '동전'이라는 뜻으로 쓰이게 되었다. 희한하게도, 춘추전국 시대 중국에도 쐐기 모양의 금속 화폐가 있었다. 또한 동전 앞뒤 면에는 양각과 음각으로 마치 '요철(凹凸)'처럼 문양이 그려져 있고, 옆에는 마치 '쐐기'로 찍은 듯 홈이 촘촘히 패어 있다. '동전'은 coin일 수밖에 없다. 참고로 로마의 동전은 금이나 은으로 만들었다.

They stole coins and jewelry. 그들은 동전들과 귀금속들을 훔쳤다.

> **Q** 스틸리코가 상대한 서고트족의 우두머리 알라리크는 어떤 인물이었나요?
> **A** 발렌스 황제, 테오도시우스 황제가 게르만족을 이탈리아 영토 안에 받아들였어. 게르만족의 이주를 허용하자 이주의 물결이 이어졌지. 조약을 맺어 들어온 서고트족도 있지만, 힘으로 밀고 들어온 반달족과 프랑크족도 있었지. 그들 중에서 능력을 인정받아 군대의 지휘관으로 승격하는 사람들도 나타났단다. 당연히 기존의 로마 군인들이 반발했겠지?
> 콘스탄티노플의 군대에서 고트족의 족장이자 제국 군대의 장교였던 '알라리크'가 있었어. 그는 이런 상황에서는 동로마 제국 내에서는 자신의 야망을 실현하기 어렵다고 판단하여 부하들을 이끌고 이탈리아로 들어갈 결심

을 했지. 알라리크가 조용히 살았던 것은 아니었어. 그는 로마군을 분열시키는 일에 주력했고, 아탈루스를 지원해 황제 자리를 억지로 빼앗도록 돕기도 했단다.

convert ⓥ to change to a different religion
convert는 '강조'의 의미가 있는 접두사 con-과 '돌다, 돌리다(turn)'를 뜻하는 vert가 합쳐진 것이다. 즉 '완전히' 방향을 틀어 '돌거나 돌리는' 것이다. 그래서 '바꾸다, 개조하다, 변환하다'의 뜻으로 쓰인다. 종교는 자신과 세계를 규정하는 틀로 종교를 바꾸면 다 바뀔 수 있는 것이므로, convert는 '종교를 바꾸다, 개종(改宗)하다'라는 뜻이다. 명사형은 conversion이다.
And because many of the Visigoths had converted to Christianity, they didn't destroy Rome's churches. 많은 서고트인들이 기독교로 개종한 상태였기 때문에, 그들은 로마의 교회들을 파괴하지 않았다.

assault ⓝ an attack
assault는 to leap toward(~쪽으로 뛰어오르다)라는 뜻의 라틴어에서 왔다. 호랑이나 사자는 사냥을 할 때 '풀쩍 뛰어' 먹잇감을 덮친다. 자기 것으로 만들기 위해 공격하는 것이다. 그래서 assault는 '점령을 위한 공격', 형법상의 '폭행'을 뜻하기도 한다.
Rome has been taken by assault. 로마가 공격을 받아 함락되었다.

vandal ⓝ someone who damages or destroys public property intentionally
Vandals, 반달족은 5세기 무렵 반달 왕국을 세우고 지중해를 무대로 활동했던 게르만족을 말한다. '로마 문화의 파괴자'라는 역사적 낙인이 찍혀, 지금도 공공기물이나 문화재 등을 이유 없이 파괴하는 사람을 vandal, 그런 행위를 vandalism이라고 한다.
Today, we call someone who destroys things for fun a "vandal," after the Vandals who destroyed what was left of the city of Rome. 로마 도시에 남아 있던 것을 파괴한 반달족의 이름을 따서, 지금도 우리는 (재미로) 물건을 부수는 사람을 '반달'이라고 부른다.

The Story of the World

Chapter 42
The End of Rome

1 The Last Roman Emperor

권력을 장악하고 이민족의 침입을 막아내던 스틸리코가 처형된 후, 서로마 제국은 극심한 혼란에 빠졌다. 각지에서 황제를 자임하는 자들이 난립해 권력 투쟁이 치열해졌고, 군사력은 더욱 약해져 곳곳에서 이민족들이 기승을 부렸다. 410년에는 서고트족이 로마를 점령했고, 455년에는 반달족이 로마를 약탈했다. 결국 475년에 게르만족의 용병대장인 오도아케르가 서로마 황제인 로물루스를 폐위시킴으로써 서로마 제국은 멸망하고, 이후 제국은 해체의 길을 걷게 된다.

What happened to the Roman Empire?

The Romans used to rule dozens of other countries. They were the most powerful people in the world.

But then the empire was divided, and the barbarians came. The Western Roman Empire grew weaker and weaker, and the Eastern Roman Empire refused to help the West out. As a matter of fact, the Eastern Roman Empire wasn't even called "Rome" anymore. Instead, it became known as "the Byzantine Empire."

The Western Roman Empire still existed. But barbarians took over most of its land. And although the Western Roman Empire still had an emperor, he didn't live in Rome, because Rome had been destroyed. He lived in a small, swampy city, hiding from the barbarians.

Finally one of the invaders, named Orestes, decided to drive the Roman emperor out of hiding. He collected an army and marched towards the small, swampy city where the emperor lived. When the emperor heard that Orestes and his men were coming, he ran away. By the time Orestes arrived, the emperor was long gone.

Orestes decided to make his son emperor. There was only one problem—his son was six years old!

But that didn't stop Orestes. He ordered all his men to obey the six-year-old emperor. And he gave his son a new name, Romulus Augustus. He called him Romulus, because an old legend said that a man named Romulus was the first king of Rome, long, long ago. And he called him Augustus after Caesar Augustus, Rome's most famous emperor.

That was a big name for a little boy! And when the people who were left in the Western Roman Empire heard it, they laughed. "Romulus Augustus!" they said. "What a silly name for a child! We won't call him Romulus—we'll call him Momyllus!"

Momyllus meant "Little disgrace." The Romans felt insulted, because they were expected to obey the child of a barbarian. But Momyllus didn't get to be emperor very long. Another barbarian captured Momyllus and his father Orestes. Momyllus, now seven years old, was sent off to live in another city. He was given plenty of money to pay for food and clothes, but he wasn't allowed to rule any more. His crown and scepter were taken to Constantinople.

And that was the end of the Western Roman Empire. It was full of barbarian kings, each one ruling his own little kingdom. The lands that used to belong to Rome now belonged to them.

The new settlers still used the wide, beautiful Roman roads. Rome's huge buildings still stood, although many were beginning to crumble away. Many people still spoke Latin, the language of the Romans. And the barbarians had begun to learn Roman ways and Roman customs. But the Roman Empire itself was gone forever.

Over in the Eastern Roman Empire (now called the Byzantine Empire), people mourned. Rome had been a great and beautiful city, but now it was in ruins. As long as an emperor still ruled, there was hope that Rome might be great again. But now the last Roman emperor, a little boy just your age, had lost his throne. Rome would never again rule the world.

2 The Gifts of Rome

로마 제국은 오랫동안 유럽을 지배하며 번영을 누린 '부자'였기 때문에 유산도 많았다. 그중 주목할 것은 언어에 미친 영향이다. 특히 영어에 미친 라틴어(로마 제국의 말)의 영향은 지대했다. 로마가 한때 브리튼 섬을 점령했기 때문이 아니다. 그때는 영어의 원래 '주인'인 게르만족이 브리튼에 정착하기 전이다. 노르만족이 오랫동안 영국을 지배했고, 라틴어에 많은 영향을 받은 그들의 언어가 영어에 대거 융합되었기 때문이다. 영어에 유입된 유럽의 다른 언어들도 라틴어의 영향을 받은 것이었다. 또한 16세기에 영어로 쓴 성경이 보급되기 전까지 아주 오랫동안 영국인들은 라틴어로 쓰인 성경을 들고 교회에 다녔다.

The Roman emperor is gone; the ancient city of Rome was destroyed; the Roman Empire has disappeared. But the Romans gave us words and inventions that we use every single day. You're using one of them right now! How many books do you have in your house? How often do you use a book?

The Romans were the first people to use books with pages. They figured out how to sew pages together along one side so that you can turn the pages and read both the front and back of each one. Before the Romans, people used *scrolls*—long, long pieces of paper or animal skin, that you had to unroll to read and roll back up whenever you were finished. Can you imagine reading a scroll in bed? Or in the car? Every time you read a book, you're using a Roman invention.

The words you're reading came from the Romans too. We use the Roman alphabet to write our words. Whenever you sing *The*

Alphabet Song or write a word, you are using the letters that the Romans used.

Do you know the twelve months of the year? Most of those months have Roman names. *January* is named after the Roman god Janus. *March* is named after Mars, the god of war. *June* is named after Juno, the most important Roman goddess. *July* and *August* are both named after Roman heroes: July is named after Julius Caesar, the famous Roman general, and August is named after Augustus, Rome's first emperor.

Do you like to go swimming in the summer? If so, thank the Romans. The Romans built big bathtubs, big enough for twenty or thirty people to wash in at once. These bathtubs were the first swimming pools.

If you look at a US penny, you'll see that it has the picture of a head on it. The portrait is of Abraham Lincoln, one of the United States' greatest presidents. The Romans began the custom of putting the heads of great leaders on coins. They put pictures of their emperors on their coins. Today, we put pictures of our leaders on coins—copying the Romans.

Now look at a dime. On one side of the dime, you can see some tiny words: *E pluribus unum.* Those words are in Latin, the language that the ancient Romans spoke. They mean "Out of many, one." This means that America has many different states in it, but all of the states are united together into one country. The Romans gave us these words to write on our coins.

We live on the Earth, but there are eight other planets in our solar system: *Mercury, Venus, Mars, Jupiter, Saturn, Uranus, Neptune, Pluto.*

All of our planets have Roman names. They are named after Roman gods and goddesses. Jupiter was the king of the gods. He was a big, important god, and Jupiter is a very big planet.

Mars is named after the god of war; Mercury is named after the messenger of the gods, and Venus is named after the goddess of love and beauty. Saturn is Jupiter's father. Neptune is the god of the sea, and Uranus the god of the sky.

Finally, even our words come from Rome! The English language borrowed many, many words from Latin, the language of the Romans. Can you figure out what English words come from these Latin words?

The *frigidarium* was the room where Roman bathers jumped into very cold water. What word sounds like frigidarium and keeps things cold? The refrigerator!

A Roman child lived in a *familia* with his mother, father, sisters, and brothers. What is a familia? A family.

The Latin word for book was *liber*. What word sounds like liber and is a place where books are kept? A library.

In Latin, a ship is a *navis*. Do you know what word comes from navis? It means "many ships that sail together." That's right—navy.

Have you ever written "P.S." at the end of a letter? If so, you've used Latin words. "P.S." stands for the Latin words "*post scriptum*," or "after the writing." A "P.S." goes *after* the main *writing* of the letter.

In Rome, a *floris* was a beautiful plant that smelled good. Can you think of a beautiful plant that smells good and sounds like floris? Our word "flower" comes from the Latin *floris*.

Even though the ancient Roman Empire is gone, we use the words, inventions, and ideas of the Romans all the time. So, in a way, Rome will never completely disappear. The gifts that the Romans gave to us are still with us today.

Note to Parent: Romulus Augustus ruled 475–476.

> # The Story of the Words
>
> ---
> Chapter 42 The End of Rome

1 The Last Roman Emperor

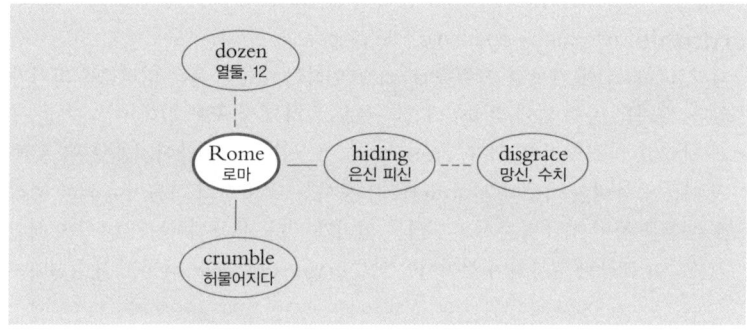

dozen ⓝ twelve

dozen의 어원은 라틴어 duodecim인데, duo는 '둘(two)'이고, decim은 '열(ten)'이다. 10이 둘 있다는 의미가 아니라, 그냥 '2+10'이다. 그래서 dozen은 '열둘, 12'가 된다. '연필 한 다스'라는 말을 들어봤을 텐데, 연필 12개 묶음을 말한다. '다스'는 dozen의 일본식 발음이다. 복수형 dozens는 '수십 개'를 말한다.
The Romans used to rule dozens of other countries. 로마는 한때 수십 개의 나라를 지배했다.

hiding ⓝ the state of being hidden

죄를 짓고 도망가 어딘가에 숨어 있는 것이나 적을 피해 숨어 있는 것을 hiding이라고 한다. '숨다, 숨기다'라는 뜻의 동사형 hide에 -ing를 붙여 명사형 '은신, 피신'이 된 것이다.
Finally one of the invaders, named Orestes, decided to drive the Roman emperor out of hiding. 마침내 침입자들 중 한 명인 오도아케르가 로마의 황제를 은신 상태에서 몰아내고자 결심했다.

disgrace ⓝ someone that makes people feel ashamed

그러면 안 되겠지만, 부모의 뜻에 따르지 않고 잘못을 저지르고 다니는 자식에게 '넌 우리 가문의 수치야!'라고 마음 아프게도 말하는 경우가 있다. 이 말을 영어로 옮기면 You are a disgrace to our family!가 된다. dis-는 '반대, 부정(not)'을 뜻하는 접두사이고, grace는 '품위, 우아함, 선행'을 뜻한다. 인품이 떨어지고 상스러운 사람에게는 '망신, 수치, 불명예'의 꼬리표가 붙는데, 바로 disgrace가 그런 의미이다.

Momyllus meant "Little disgrace." '모밀루스'는 '어린 망신[수치]'이라는 의미이다.

crumble ⓥ to break apart into little pieces

제과점(bakery)에 가보면 '크럼블(crumble)'이라는 이름이 붙은 디저트용 과자가 있다. 밀가루 반죽 위에 과일이나 견과류를 올려 바삭 구운 건데, 이 과자는 세게 만지면 '바스러지기' 쉽다. crumble이 '바스러지다, 허물어지다' 등을 뜻하기 때문에 붙여진 이름이다. crumble을 동사로 쓰면 '풍화 작용이나 외부 충격으로 건물 등이 조금씩 부서지다'라는 의미가 된다. 본문에서는 로마의 오래된 건물들이 조금씩 부서지며 없어지는 모습을 to crumble away라고 표현했다.

Rome's huge buildings still stood, although many were beginning to crumble away. 로마의 큰 건물들은, 비록 상당수가 허물어지기 시작했지만, 여전히 그 자리에 서 있었다.

Q 서고트족의 로마 침공을 왜 서로마의 몰락이라고 하나요?

A 408년 서고트 족의 왕인 알라리크는 아탈루스가 황제 자리를 빼앗는 일에 힘을 더했어. 그러나 막상 황제가 되자 아탈루스는 알라리크의 공을 제대로 인정해주지 않아 둘 사이에 틈이 생겼단다. 알라리크는 이미 아리우스파 기독교(예수의 신성을 부정하는 기독교의 일파)를 믿고 있어서 로마 침공 당시 교회는 파괴하지 않았어. 그럼에도 당시 관행으로 승리한 군대는 약탈이 허락되어 로마 사람들은 공포에 빠졌지.

서고트족은 로마 시내를 약탈한 후에 이베리아 반도에 정착했어. 반달족은 이베리아 반도에 정착했으나 이곳에 온 서고트족에 밀려 아프리카 북쪽에 자리잡았지. 갈리아 지방에는 프랑크족이 앵글족, 색슨족은 브리타니아 지방으로 갔어. 브리타니아 지방은 로마의 속주라서 로마군이 주둔하고 있었어. 그들은 켈트족의 반란을 막느라 힘겨워도 그곳을 계속 지키고 있는 상황이었어. 그러나 410년 로마 시내가 침략당하자 브리타니아

> 주둔군은 로마로 갔단다. 이렇게 되면 로마 제국은 허울에 불과했지. 역사가들은 사실상의 몰락은 이미 410년에 시작되었다고 평가해.

2 The Gifts of Rome

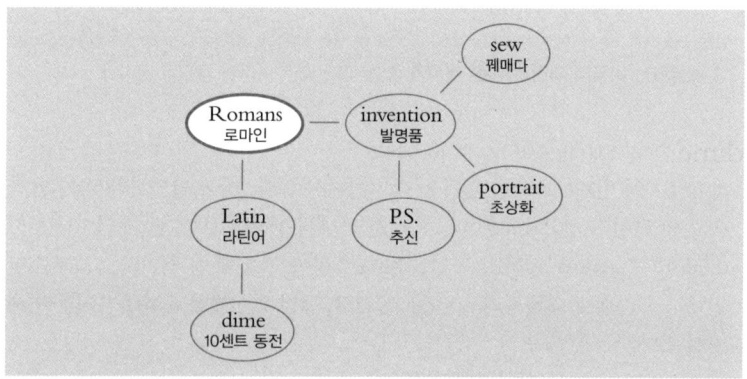

invention ⓝ something completely new that is made for the first time
invention은 invent의 명사형이다. invent는 '안으로(into)'를 뜻하는 접두사와 '오다(come)'를 뜻하는 vent가 합쳐진 것이다. 어떤 것이 눈에 들어오면 발견하게 되고, 머릿속으로 들어오면 아이디어가 된다. 그래서 invent가 '발명하다'라는 뜻이다. 부정적인 의미로 '사실이 아닌 것을 지어내다'라는 뜻도 있다. invention은 '발명, 발명품'이고, inventor는 '발명가'이다.
But the Romans gave us words and inventions that we use every single day. 그러나 로마인들은 우리가 매일 사용하는 단어와 발명품을 우리에게 주었다.

sew ⓥ to join pieces of cloth or paper together using a needle and thread
sew는 바늘과 실로 '꿰매다, 바느질하다'라는 뜻이다. '재봉틀'은 sewing machine이다. 흔히 재봉틀을 '미싱'이라고 부르는데, 이 말은 sewing machine에서 machine만 따와 일본식으로 발음한 것이다. 철자도 비슷하고 발음도 같은, '씨뿌리다'라는 sow와 혼동하지 않도록 주의해야 한다.
They figured out how to sew pages together along one side so that you can turn the pages and read both the front and back of each one. 그들은 한쪽 면을 따라 페이지를 함께 꿰매는 법을 고안함으로써 페이지를 넘기며 앞면과 뒷면을 모두 읽을 수 있게 했다.

portrait ⓝ a painting, drawing or photograph of a person

portrait는 동사형 portray의 명사형이다. portray에서 por-는 '밖으로, 앞으로 (forth)'를 뜻하는 접두어이고, tray는 '당기다, 끌다(to drag)'를 뜻한다. 가려져 있거나 숨어 있는 존재를 '밖으로, 앞으로 끌어내면' 그 실체가 드러난다. 그런 의미에서 portray는 '묘사하다, 구체적으로 표현하다'라는 뜻이다. portrait는 사람을 그린 것, 즉 '초상화'이다.

The portrait is of Abraham Lincoln, one of the United State's greatest presidents. 그 초상화는 미국의 가장 위대한 대통령 중 한 명인 에이브러햄 링컨의 것이다.

dime ⓝ a coin that is worth 10 cents

dime은 '열 번째(tenth)'를 뜻하는 라틴어에서 왔다. 미국 달러화에서 가장 작은 돈의 단위가 '센트(cent)'이다. cent를 하나씩 셈하다 보면 '열 개'의 10센트가 dime이다. 그래서 '10센트' 동전을 dime이라고 이름 붙인 것이다. dime의 앞면에는 루스벨트 대통령의 portrait가 있고, 뒷면에는 횃불과 나뭇가지들이 새겨져 있다.

Now look at a dime. 이제 10센트 동전을 보자.

Latin ⓝ the language that people spoke in ancient Rome

고대 로마인들이 사용한 언어를 Latin이라고 한다. 로마인들이 처음 정착하고 번성한 이탈리아 반도의 중서부 지역을 '라티움(Latium)'으로 부른 데에서 유래했다. 또한 Latin은 로마 제국에 속해서 라틴어 영향을 직접적으로 받은 '이탈리아, 스페인, 포르투갈, 프랑스 등의 언어권이나 그 언어의 사용자'를 뜻하는 말로도 쓴다. 중남미를 왜 '라틴아메리카(Latin America)'라고 부르는지 짐작할 것이다.

The English language borrowed many, many words from Latin, the language of the Romans. 영어는 로마인들의 언어인 라틴어에서 아주 많은 단어들을 빌려왔다.

P.S. ⓝ 'postscript,' a word used for introducing an additional information at the end of a letter

분문에 나와 있듯이 P.S.는 '글 쓴 후(after the writing)'를 뜻하는 라틴어 post scriptum에서 왔다. 이 말은 영어로 postscript가 되었다. 편지나 책을 다 쓰고 나서 본문의 내용과 다른 새로운 내용을 첨가할 때 쓴다. 우리말로 '덧붙이는 말, 추신(追伸), 후기'에 해당한다.

Have you ever written "P.S." at the end of a letter? 편지의 말미에서 'P.S.'를 읽은 적이 있는가?

Q 서로마 제국은 어떻게 멸망했나요?

A 410년 로마가 약탈당한 후 황제는 로마를 지킬 엄두를 내지 못했어. 오히려 도망을 갔지. 어디로? 게르만족이 쳐들어오기 어려운 늪지대 라벤나로 갔단다. 그러나 라벤나에서도 역시 황제 지위를 찬탈하는 일이 벌어졌어. 이제 위용을 자랑하던 로마 제국은 흔적도 없이 사라져가는 중이었단다.

로마인으로 아틸라의 고문 노릇을 했고, 나중에는 라벤나 군대의 대장이었던 인물이 황제 자리를 빼앗아 아들에게 물려주었어. 바로 그가 '오레스테스'로, 그때 아들의 나이가 겨우 여섯 살이었어. 거창한 이름 로물루스 아우구스투스를 받았는데, 너무 어려 통치를 할 수는 없어서 아버지가 대신 정치를 했지. 이때가 475년이었는데, 이듬해 용병 대장 '오도아케르'가 라벤나에 쳐들어와 어린 황제를 다른 도시로 쫓아냈단다. 그는 더 이상 황제가 아니었어.

오도아케르도 스스로 서로마 황제를 칭하지는 않았어. 그는 당시의 동로마 황제인 제노에게 편지를 보내 이탈리아에는 황제가 필요 없다고 밝히면서 동로마 황제의 명령을 받들어 로마 제국을 지키겠노라 맹세했단다. 서로마 황제의 왕권도 동로마로 보냈어. 이런 의미에서 476년 서로마 제국의 몰락을 로마 제국의 멸망으로 보는 것이 타당한지를 묻는 역사가들도 많단다.

진의행(등명중학교 1학년), 진달래(등명중학교 3학년)

Sentence Review 구문은 직접 두 명의 학생이 문장을 선정하고, 저자 지소철이 해설하였다. 구문을 선정한 진의행은 평소 '깊이 읽기 독서'를 즐긴다. 영어 과목은 좋아하지 않았으나 《the Story of the World》 역사 지식을 통해 영어라는 언어와 친해지게 되었다. 진달래는 《the Story of the World》를 시작으로 원서 리딩의 매력에 빠져, 현재 100명의 영향력 있는 인물을 소개하는 《the 100》을 만나고 있다.

The Story of the World

Sentence Review

Chapter 22 Sparta and Athens

20   The Greeks were horrified by the thought of obeying one, single, powerful ruler.
   ▶ 동사 horrify는 '충격을 주다, 두렵게 하다'라는 뜻이다. 그래서 '충격을 받다, 두려워하다'라고 표현하려면 'be horrified by ~' 형태로 써서 '~에 대해 끔찍하게 생각하다, 몸서리치다'로 해석한다.

21   Instead, when they were seven, they were sent away to special camps where they learned how to be obedient, disciplined fighters.
   ▶ obedient는 '복종하는, 순종적인'이고, disciplined는 '잘 훈련된, 규율을 따르는'을 뜻한다. 따라서 obedient, disciplined fighters는 '명령에 복종하고, 규율과 훈련에 충실한 전사들'을 의미한다.

21   He suffered without showing it until the soldiers went away.
   ▶ suffered는 '고통을 참았다'라는 뜻이다. without showing it에서 it은 pain이므로 '고통을 드러내지 않고, 아픈 내색을 하지 않고'라고 해석할 수 있다.

21   All Spartan boys were supposed to be this brave and silent.
   ▶ suppose는 '~을 사실이라고 생각하다, 당연하게 여기다'라는 의미이다. 그래서 were supposed to be this brave and silent는 '이 정도로 용감하고 과묵한 것이 당연하다고 여겼다'라고 해석한다.

21   Even if they got married, they weren't allowed to live with their families.
   ▶ even if는 even though와 의미가 같은 절로, 'even if + 문장'은 '비록 ~하더라도, 설령 ~일지라도'라는 표현이다. Even if they got married는 '비록 그들이 결혼을 하더라도'라고 해석한다.

21   Instead, they lived with the other soldiers in barracks.
   ▶ barracks은 군대에서 병사들이 생활하는 집, 즉 '막사, 병영'을 뜻한다. 항상 복수형으로 쓴다.

22   Spartan mothers were supposed to praise their sons for warlike behavior, and reward them for bravery.
   ▶ warlike behavior는 '공격적이고 거친 행동'이다.
   ▶ reward them for bravery는 '용감한 행동에 대해 상을 주다[칭찬하다]'라는 의미이다.

22
Come back with your shield, or on it!
▶ 전투에 나갔다가 승리하고 '방패를 들고(with your shield)' 돌아온다. 죽거나 심한 부상을 입으면 '방패에 실려서(on it)' 돌아온다. 즉, '이기든가, 죽든가'라는 의미이다.

22
Sparta wasn't known for its art or storytelling, but the Spartan army was known and feared all over the world for its bravery and toughness.
▶ 'be known for ~'는 '~로 알려지다[유명하다]'이고, 'be feared for ~'는 '~로 인해 두려움의 대상이 되다'라는 의미이다. for가 겹치므로 하나만 써서 for its bravery and toughness(용맹함과 강인함으로)를 뒤에 쓴 것이다.

23
Everyone who lived in Athens had a say in how the city was run, because Athens was a *democracy*.
▶ have a say in ~은 '~에 대해 발언권을 갖고 있다'라는 의미이다.
▶ democracy는 국민이 국가의 주인인 '민주주의'를 뜻하는데, 이 문장에서는 '민주주의 국가'라는 의미로 쓴 것이다.

23
Whenever it was time for the citizens to vote about something, they would gather in the middle of the city, at a special meeting place called a *forum*.
▶ 'Whenever + 문장'은 '~할 때마다, ~할 때에는 언제나'라는 표현이다. Whenever it was time for the citizens to vote about something은 '어떤 일에 대해 시민들이 투표를 할 때마다'로 해석한다.

23
There, they would argue about whether to vote yes or no.
▶ would argue about은 '~에 대해 논쟁하곤 했다'라는 의미이다.
▶ whether to vote yes or no는 '찬성에 투표할지 반대에 투표할지'라고 해석한다.

23
So that they could understand how to vote properly, the citizens had to be educated.
▶ properly는 '올바르게, 적절하게'인데, '이치와 원리에 맞게'라는 의미이다.

23
If they were ignorant, they wouldn't be able to argue properly about the government of the city.
▶ 'be able to 동사'는 '~할 수 있다, ~할 능력을 갖고 있다'라는 의미이다.

24
They learned mathematics, so that they could count and add and subtract.

▶ add는 '숫자를 더하다, 덧셈을 하다'이고, subtract는 '숫자를 빼다, 뺄셈을 하다'라는 의미이다.

25 So you hand over your money, and your neighbor walks off with it.
▶ hand over your money는 '너의 돈을 (이웃에게) 넘겨주다[건네주다]'라는 의미이다.
▶ walk off with it은 '그 돈을 갖고서 걸어가 버리다'를 뜻하는데, 바로 it이 your money이다.

Chapter 23 The Greek Gods

36 Zeus was standing innocently by the punch bowl.
▶ 이 문장에서 stand by는 '~옆에 서 있다'라는 의미이다. stand와 by 사이에 '천진난만하게, 아무 것도 모르는 척'을 뜻하는 innocently가 끼어든 것이다.
▶ punch bowl은 파티에서 여러 사람이 떠서 마실 수 있게 '음료(punch)'를 부어 놓은 커다란 '사발(bowl)'이다.

Chapter 24 The Wars of the Greeks

42 Athens and Sparta fought battle after battle against the Persian invasion.
▶ fought battle and battle은 '여러 차례[연거푸] 전투를 치렀다'라는 의미인데, 이어진 against the Persian invasion은 '페르시아의 침략에 맞서'라고 해석한다.

43 They were sailing from Asia Minor across the Aegean Sea, straight for the village of Marathon.
▶ straight for the village of Marathon에서 for는 앞에 있는 동사 sailing과 연결되는 것으로, '마라톤이란 마을을 향해 항해하고 있다'라는 의미이다.

44 The Athenians were outnumbered.
▶ outnumber는 '수(number)가 더 많다, 수적으로 우세하다'를 뜻한다. 이 문장은 The Athenians were outnumbered by the Persians를 줄인 것으로, '아테네인들은 페르시아인들보다 수가 더 적었다'라는 의미이다.

44 There were too many Persian soldiers for the army of Athens to defeat alone.
▶ 'too ~ for A to 동사'는 '너무 ~해서 A가 …할 수 없다, A가 …하기에는 너무 ~하다'라는 표현이다. 이 문장은 '페르시아의 병사들이 너무 많아서 아테네 군대가 홀로 물리칠 수는 없

었다'라고 해석한다.

44 They were forced to retreat.
- 'be forced to 동사'는 '(힘에 밀려서) 어쩔 수 없이 ~할 수밖에 없다'라는 표현이다. 이 문장은 '그들은 후퇴할 수밖에 없었다'라고 해석한다.

44 When the Athenians saw that they had won the battle, they sent a runner back to Athens, to tell the people who were anxiously waiting at home that the Persian threat had been driven back.
- 'to tell A that 문장'의 형태는 'A에게 that 이하를 말하다'라는 의미이다. A에 해당하는 the people who were anxiously waiting at home은 '집에서 애태우며 기다리고 있던 사람들'을 뜻한다.
- that the Persian threat had been driven back은 '페르시아의 위협을 물리쳤다고'라는 의미이다.

44 The runner, Pheidippides, ran over twenty-six miles, up steep hills and through rough country, to reach Athens.
- up steep hills and through rough country는 동사 ran과 연결되어 '가파른 산을 오르고 험준한 지역을 헤치며 (달렸다)'라는 의미이다.

44 It is run in the Olympics in honor of the brave Athenian who ran from Marathon to Athens with the good news of victory.
- It is run in the Olympics는 '마라톤은 올림픽에 있는 경주이다'라는 의미이다.
- in honor of는 '~을 기리는'으로, the brave Athenian ~ victory는 '승리의 희소식을 갖고서 마라톤에서 아테네까지 달렸던 그 용감한 아테네 사람'을 뜻한다.

44 The Persians and Greeks went on fighting until the Greeks finally defeated the Persians, once and for all, in a great sea battle at a place called Salamis.
- once and for all은 '완전히, 최종적으로'이다.
- in a great sea battle at a place called Salamis은 '살라미스라고 불리는 곳에서 벌어진 큰 해전에서'라는 의미이다.

45 They became famous for their architecture—the way they designed and built buildings.
- the way they designed and built buildings는 their architecture를 설명하는 말로, '그들이 건물들을 설계하고 짓는 방식'을 의미한다.

45   Inside the Parthenon were pictures, carved in marble, of different Greek battles.
▶ 파르테논 신전 안에 그림들이 carved in marble, 즉 '대리석에 조각되어 있었는데', 그 그림들이 어떤 그림이냐면 of different Greek battles(그리스인들의 치른 여러 전투)의 그림이었다.

45   The Greeks tried very hard to make their pictures and statues look like real people.
▶ tried very hard는 '매우 공을 들였다, 노력을 많이 했다'라는 의미이다. to make their pictures and statues look like real people는 '그들의 그림과 동상이 진짜 사람처럼 보이게 만들려고'라고 해석한다.

45   It is hard to believe that they are carved from stone.
▶ It is hard to believe that은 'that 이하를 믿기 힘들다'라는 뜻으로, 대단히 놀랍다는 의미를 담고 있다.
▶ that they are carved from stone은 '돌로 조각되어 있다는 사실은'을 뜻하는데, 문장의 실제 주어에 해당한다.

46   With the Persians defeated, Athens and Sparta no longer had to fight.
▶ With the Persians defeated는 '페르시아인들이 패배한 상황에서'라는 의미로, '페르시아인들을 물리쳤기 때문에'라고 해석할 수 있다.

46   The Greeks could have gone on making their beautiful buildings and creating their statues in peace.
▶ 'could have 동사 완료형'은 과거에 '~할 수도 있었을 것이다'라고 가능성을 추측하는 표현이다.
▶ 'go on 동사의 –ing'는 '계속 ~하다'이므로 '그리스인들은 계속 평화롭게 아름다운 건물들을 만들고 동상들을 창조할 수 있었을 것이다'라고 해석한다.

46   So instead of remaining on friendly terms, Sparta and Athens began to fight with each other again.
▶ remaining on friendly terms은 '우호적인 관계에 계속 머무르다'라는 의미이다.

46   Instead of fighting with swords, they would let the strong walls of the city protect them.
▶ instead of fighting with swords는 '칼로 싸우기보다는'을 뜻한다. swords는 '무력'을 상징한다.
▶ let the strong walls of the city protect them은 '그 도시의 튼튼한 성벽이 그들을 보호하게 하다'라는 뜻이다.

46

Maybe their strategy would have worked—if something terrible hadn't happened.
▶ 이 문장에서는 옆줄(–)을 빼도 된다. 뒤의 문장 if something terrible hadn't happened는 '만약 끔찍한 일이 발생하지 않았더라면'이고, 앞 문장은 '아마도 그들의 전략이 통했을 것이다'라고 해석한다.

47

The survivors straggled back into Athens, angry and embarrassed.
▶ The survivors straggled back into Athens는 '생존자들은 뿔뿔이 흩어져서 아테네로 돌아왔다'라는 의미이다.
▶ angry and embarrassed는 그 생존자들의 마음 상태를 표현한 것으로, '화가 나 있고, 수치심을 느꼈다'라는 의미이다.

47

But Alcibiades was nowhere to be found.
▶ 이 문장은 '앨키비아데스는 어느 곳에서도 찾을 수 없었다'라는 것이다. 사람들이 그를 찾으려고 했지만 실패했다는 의미이다.

48

Now Greece no longer had the men they needed to keep other invaders away.
▶ they needed to keep other invaders away는 the men을 설명하는 말로, '그리스인들이 다른 침략자들을 막기 위해 필요한'을 뜻한다.

48

The Greeks had spent all their energy fighting each other; they had none left to defend themselves.
▶ they had none left to defend themselves는 '그들에게는 자신들을 방어할 만한 힘이 전혀 남아 있지 않았다'라는 의미이다. 여기에서 none은 no energy를 나타낸다.

Chapter 25 Alexander the Great

56

If the Greek cities had stayed friends and allies, like they were when they fought against the Persians, Greece would have been a strong country.
▶ allies는 공동의 목적을 위해 힘을 합치는 '동맹, 연합국, 협력자'를 뜻한다.
▶ If the Greek cities had stayed friends and allies는 '만약 그리스의 도시들이 친구와 동맹 관계를 계속 유지했다면'으로 해석한다.

56

They were like brothers who were too busy arguing with each other to notice that a bully is coming.

▶ too busy ~ to notice that은 '너무 바빠서 that 이하를 알아채지 못하다'라는 의미이다. 바쁜 이유는 arguing with each other(서로 말다툼을 하느라고)이다.

57　The horse, a huge black stallion named Bucephalus, bucked and kicked constantly.
▶ buck은 '말이 껑충 뛰다, 날뛰다'로, bucked and kicked constantly는 '계속 날뛰고, 발길질을 했다'라는 뜻이다.

57　When Alexander met the Persian army in Asia Minor, he used his cavalry—soldiers riding on horseback—to push the Persians back.
▶ cavalry는 '말을 탄 군인(soldiers riding on horseback)', 즉 '기병'이다.
▶ to push the Persians back은 '페르시아인들을 뒤로 밀어냈다, 물리쳤다'라는 뜻이다.

60　But the men were firm: They would not fight in India any longer.
▶ the men은 알렉산더의 '부하들'을 의미한다.
▶ firm은 '흔들리지 않는, 변하지 않는'라는 뜻으로, 결정을 바꾸지 않았다는 의미이다.

62　Others say that he probably died of malaria—a fever caused by mosquitoes who carry certain kinds of germs.
▶ 'to die of 질병'은 '그 질병으로 죽다'라는 표현이다. malaria는 '말라리아'인데, 특정한 종류의 병균을 옮기는 모기(mosquitoes who carry certain kinds of germs)에 의해 발생되는 열병으로 설명되어 있다.

 Chapter 26　The People of the Americas

74　But the people of the Americas did leave artifacts behind them—ancient buildings, ruined villages, and mysterious earth mounds.
▶ artifact는 사람이 만든 물건을 통칭하는 말인데, 고고학에서는 '사람이 만든 유물'을 의미한다.

74　And if you keep going across the Atlantic Ocean, you'll come to two continents (big masses of land) linked together in the middle by a narrower strip.
▶ a narrow strip은 '좁은 해협'을 뜻하는데, 비교급 narrower를 쓰면 '점점 좁아지는'이다.

74　They ate cassava, just like the people of ancient Africa.
▶ cassava는 '카사바 나무의 뿌리'인데, 고구마나 밀처럼 녹말 성분이 있어서 식용으로 쓴다.

▶ just like the people of ancient Africa는 '고대 아프리카의 사람들처럼'을 뜻한다.

75　The lines of the drawing were scraped into the earth.
▶ scrape는 '긁어서 파내다'를 뜻하고, the earth는 '땅'을 뜻한다. were scraped into the earth는 '흙을 긁어 파내서 땅에 새겨졌다'라는 의미이다.

75　The lines just looked like old roads, or gashes in the ground.
▶ gashes in the ground는 '땅에 생긴 틈, 땅이 갈라진 자국'을 뜻한다. 원래 gash는 '상처 자국'을 의미한다.

75　Making a line drawing on the ground must have been like drawing with your eyes closed.
▶ Making a line drawing on the ground(땅에 선 그림을 그리는 것)이 문장의 주어이다.
▶ like drawing with your eyes closed는 '눈을 감은 채 그림을 그리는 것과 같은'이다.

76　It probably wouldn't look much like a bird when you were finished.
▶ look much like a bird는 '별로 새처럼 보이지 않다'라는 뜻이다. 부정문에서 much는 '별로, 그다지'로 해석한다.
▶ when you were finished는 '당신이 (그리기를) 마쳤을 때'라는 의미이다.

77　The platform was so high that it could be seen by someone standing miles away.
▶ 이 문장에서 platform은 '피라미드의 끝, 단상(壇上)'을 말한다. 단상이 '너무 높아서(so high)' '몇 마일 떨어진 곳에서 서 있는 사람(someone standing miles away)'의 눈에도 보였다는 의미이다.

78　That's taller than the biggest person you know, and probably higher than your ceiling.
▶ taller than the biggest person you know는 '당신이 알고 있는 가장 큰 사람보다 더 키가 큰'을 뜻한다.
▶ higher than your ceiling은 '당신 (집의) 천장 높이보다 더 높은'이다.

78　The eyes of the heads are bigger than your whole head.
▶ the eyes of the head는 '그 두상의 눈들'을 뜻한다.
▶ bigger than your whole head는 '당신의 머리 전체보다 더 큰'인데, whole head는 머리끝부터 턱까지를 의미한다.

78　You could put your entire hand up their noses!

- ▶ put your entire hand up은 '손을 위로 최대한 쭉 펴서 올리다'라는 뜻이다. 그래야 그 두상의 코(their noses)에 손이 닿을 수 있다는 것이다.

78 If you were standing next to one, your head would only come up to its cheek.
- ▶ If you were standing next to one은 '두상 하나의 옆에 서 있다면'이라고 해석한다.
- ▶ your head would only come up to its cheek은 '당신의 머리가 겨우(only) 그 두상의 뺨 정도밖에 오지 않을 것이다'라는 의미이다.

80 They followed the huge herds of buffalo that roamed around from meadow to meadow.
- ▶ the huge herds of buffalo는 '큰 버팔로 무리'이다. roamed around from meadow to meadow는 '이 목초지 저 목초지로 돌아다녔다'라는 의미이다.

80 They moved from place to place, eating whatever the land could give them.
- ▶ moved from place to place는 '이곳저곳 이동했다'이다.
- ▶ whatever는 '무엇이든'을 뜻하는데, give의 목적어로 쓰여서 eating whatever the land give them은 '땅이 그들에게 주는 것은 무엇이든 먹으면서'를 의미한다.

82 At once, the arrow ripped a great hole in the Sun.
- ▶ ripped a great hole은 '찢어서 거대한 구멍을 냈다'는 의미인데, 태양이 찢어질 수 있다는 상상을 했기 때문에 이런 표현이 가능하다.

82 Fire poured out all over the world.
- ▶ poured out은 '쏟아져 나왔다'이고, all over the world는 '온 세상 위로'를 뜻한다. 그래서 이 문장은 '불이 쏟아져 나와 온 세상을 뒤덮었다'라고 이해할 수 있다.

82 The tree above Rabbit's head began to smoke and crackle.
- ▶ crackle은 나무가 불에 탈 때 나는 '탁탁' 소리를 말하는데, 여기에서는 '탁탁 소리를 내다'라는 뜻의 동사로 쓰였다.

82 The grass at his feet went up into flames.
- ▶ at은 '붙어 있는 상태'를 의미한다. 그래서 the grass at his feet은 '그의 발치에 있는 풀'을 뜻한다.
- ▶ flame은 '불길, 불꽃, 화염'으로, went up into flames는 '활활 타오르다, 화염에 휩싸이다'로 해석할 수 있다.

82 In a panic, he threw down his bow and arrow and ran away.
▶ in a panic은 '공황 상태에 빠진'이다.
▶ threw down his bow and arrow는 '자기 활과 화살을 밑으로 던졌다' 즉, '내팽개쳤다'라는 의미이다.

Chapter 27 The Rise of Rome

92 Alexander the Great built his own huge kingdom, but then he died and his generals broke the kingdom up into pieces.
▶ to break up은 '나누다, 분해하다'이다. 따라서 broke the kingdom up into pieces는 '그 왕국을 여러 조각으로 나누었다'라는 의미이다.

92 One king comes along, wins battles, and builds a big empire.
▶ comes along은 '나타나다, 생기다'이어서, One king comes along은 '한 명의 왕이 나타나서'라고 해석한다.

92 It grew to be bigger than Alexander's empire, and it lasted much longer.
▶ It grew to be bigger than Alexander's empire는 '그 제국은 성장해서 (결국) 알렉산더의 제국보다 더 커졌다'라는 의미이다.
▶ last는 동사로 '계속 존재하다, 존속하다'이므로 it lasted much longer는 '(알렉산더의 제국보다) 훨씬 더 오래 존속했다'라는 의미이나.

93 But she felt sorry for them, and put them into a basket and pushed it out into the current.
▶ to feel sorry for someone은 '그 사람에 대해 안쓰러움을 느끼다, 불쌍히 여기다'라는 뜻 표현이다. 여기에서 sorry는 '미안함'이 아니라 '안쓰러운, 딱한'을 뜻한다.

94 One day a shepherd, out looking for a lost lamb, heard a coo and then a gurgle from the brush surrounding the wolf's den.
▶ out looking for a lost lamb에서 out은 '밖에 나와 있는 상태'를 의미한다. looking for a lost lamb은 '잃어버린 양 한 마리를 찾아서'이다.

95 What does this story remind you of?
▶ 'to remind A of B'는 'A에게 B를 생각나게 하다, A에게 B를 상기시키다'이다. 따라서 이 문장은 '이 이야기가 여러분에게 무엇을 생각나게 하는가?' 또는 '여러분은 이 이야기를 통해

무엇을 떠올리는가?'라고 해석한다.

96 The Etruscans also grew crops, made weapons and jewelry out of metal, and sailed back and forth between Greece and Italy, trading with the Greeks.
  - ▶ 'to make A out of B'는 'B를 사용해서 A를 만들다'라는 뜻의 표현이다. made weapons and jewelry out of metal은 '금속으로 무기와 보석류를 만들었다'이다.

96 The purple showed everyone how important the king was.
  - ▶ 'to show A B'는 'A에게 B를 보여주다'를 뜻한다. 이 문장에서 B에 해당하는 것이 how important the king was인데, '왕이 얼마나 중요한지'라는 뜻이다.

97 Soon Roman kings, like Etruscan kings, wore special purple-bordered togas and carried fasces.
  - ▶ border는 '옷의 가장자리, 테두리'로, purple-bordered는 '옷의 테두리가 보라색인'이다.

97 But in Rome, only rich and powerful men called patricians were allowed to have a say in the government.
  - ▶ say를 명사로 쓰면 '발언권, 결정권'이므로 to have a say는 '발언권을 갖고 있다'를 뜻한다. were allowed to have a say in the government는 '정부 안에서 발언권을 갖도록 허용되었다'라고 해석한다.

97 The Romans thought that having two leaders, instead of one king, would keep any one man from getting too much power.
  - ▶ 'to keep A from 동사의 -ing'는 'A가 ~하지 못하게 막다'를 뜻하는 표현이다. keep any one man from getting too much power는 '어느 한 사람이 너무 많은 권력을 갖지 못하게 막다'라는 의미이다.

97 The two consuls were supposed to keep an eye on each other!
  - ▶ 'be supposed to 동사'는 '~하도록 정해져 있다'라는 표현이다.
  - ▶ to keep an eye on A는 'A를 감시하다, 계속 지켜보다'를 뜻한다. 따라서 이 문장은 '두 명의 집정관들은 서로를 감시하도록 (임무와 역할이) 정해져 있었다'라고 해석한다.

97 Neither one could do exactly what he pleased.
  - ▶ neither는 not either가 합쳐진 말로, '둘 다 아닌'을 의미한다.
  - ▶ what he pleased는 '그가 기뻐하는[만족하는] 것'이므로, 이 문장은 '아무도 자기 마음대로 할 수는 없었다'라고 해석할 수 있다.

Chapter 28 The Roman Empire

104 And when they came back to Italy, they passed these stories along to the Romans.
▶ to pass A along to B 표현은 'A를 B에게 전하다'라는 뜻이다. along은 '연속성'을 의미하므로, 여러 사람에게 연이어 전한다는 의미를 담고 있다. 그래서 '그들은 이 이야기들을 로마인들에게 계속 전했다'라고 이해할 수 있다.

105 Wherever Ceres stepped, ripe grain sprang up; whenever she touched a tree, fruit blossomed beneath her hands.
▶ spring은 스프링처럼 '위로 튀어 오르다, 솟아 나오다'라는 뜻이므로, ripe grain sprang up은 '잘 익은 곡식이 위로 나왔다'이다.

105 As she bent down to pick them, the ground suddenly opened beneath her and she disappeared!
▶ 바닥에 있는 물건을 줍거나 신발 끝을 묶기 위해 '몸을 밑으로 굽히는' 동작이 to bend down이다.
▶ pick은 '꽃을 꺾거나 열매를 따다'는 의미이므로 As she bent down to pick them은 '백합을 꺾기 위해 몸을 굽혔을 때'라고 해석한다.

105 When he saw her, he fell in love with her, and the ground opened up beneath her so that she could walk through it into the land underground.
▶ to fall in love with A는 'A를 깊이 사랑하게 되다'라는 뜻이다.

105 In great rage, Ceres turned and climbed up into the heavens, all the way to the palace of Jupiter, king of the gods.
▶ rage는 몹시 화가 난 상태, 즉 '분노'이다. 앞에 great가 붙으면 '엄청난 분노'가 되어 in great rage는 '대단히 분노해서'이다.

106 But Ceres refused to give in.
▶ to give in에는 자신의 의지나 고집을 꺾는다는 의미가 있다. 그래서 '항복하다, 굴복하다'와 이 문장에서처럼 '(자기 고집을 꺾고) 다른 의견에 동의하다, 받아들이다'라는 뜻으로도 쓰인다.

107 The bigger the city got, the more land the Romans wanted.
▶ 'the 비교급 ~, the 비교급 ~' 구조의 문장은 '~할수록 더 ~하다'라고 해석한다. 이 문장은 '그 도시가 커질수록, 로마인들은 더 많은 땅을 원했다'로 해석할 수 있다.

107　Now that Rome ruled all of Italy, the Romans needed to be able to travel easily from one end of the peninsula to the others.
- ▶ from A to B는 'A에서 B까지, A에서 B로'라는 뜻으로 자주 쓰이는 표현이다.
- ▶ the others는 'the other ends of the peninsula(반도의 다른 끝)'를 줄여 쓴 것이다. 그래서 '반도의 한쪽 끝에서부터 (여러) 다른 쪽 끝으로'라고 해석한다.

109　Through these aqueducts, the Romans could bring water into the cities from springs thirty miles away.
- ▶ bring water into the cities는 '도시 안으로 물을 가져오다'이고, from springs thirty miles away는 '30마일 떨어진 곳에 있는 샘들에서'라는 의미이다. 1마일이 약 1.6킬로미터이므로 30마일은 약 4.8킬로미터이다.

110　He looked up, wondering if it were about to rain.
- ▶ 'be about to 동사' 표현은 '~할 때가 되다, 곧 ~하려고 하다'이다.
- ▶ 사실이 아닌 가정의 의미로 문장을 썼기 때문에 주어가 it이지만, was가 아니라 were로 쓴 것이다. if it were about to rain은 '곧 비가 내리려고 하는지'라고 해석한다.

110　Around the corner of the peaceful village rode a group of men with swords, shields and spears.
- ▶ A group of men with swords, shields and spears rode around the corner of the peaceful village(칼과 방패, 창을 든 사내들이 말을 타고서 평화로운 마을의 모퉁이를 돌아 나타났다) 문장을 '마을 모퉁이→말을 탄 사람들→무장한 사내들'의 이미지 순서로 표현하기 위해 도치시킨 것이다.

110　It was the highest wall he had ever seen.
- ▶ the highest wall은 '가장 높은 성벽'이다.
- ▶ he had ever seen은 '그가 이제껏 본 것 중에'라는 뜻으로 the highest wall을 수식한다.

111　A man standing on another man's shoulders couldn't even see over it.
- ▶ a man standing on another man's shoulders는 '다른 사람의 어깨를 밟고 올라선 사람'이다.
- ▶ see over it은 '그 성벽 너머를 보다'라는 의미이다.

111　When they came out the other side, Servius found himself in a narrow, crowded street full of people.
- ▶ to find oneself 표현은 '자신이 ~의 상태에 있음을 깨닫다'라는 의미로, 어떤 장소나 상황에 처해 있음을 인식하게 되었다는 뜻이다.
- ▶ in a narrow, crowded street full of people은 '사람들이 가득한 좁고 붐비는 거리에'이다.

111 You'll make a great fighter, once the trainers at the school have taught you what to do.
- ▶ make a great fighter는 '뛰어난 전사가 되다'라는 뜻이다. 이때 make는 노력을 통해 '변하다'라는 의미이다.
- ▶ once는 '일단 ~하면'의 의미로, 조건이나 가정의 말을 이끌어서 '일단 학교의 훈련관들이 무엇을 할지 가르친다면'으로 해석한다.

111 Servius felt his mouth go dry with fright.
- ▶ his mouth go dry는 '입이 마르다'를 뜻한다. go는 점점 변한다는 의미를 담고 있다. 입이 마르는 이유가 with fright(두려움으로 인해)이다.

112 If this was just the training camp, what would it be like to fight a real gladiator fight, in the arena?
- ▶ If this was just the training camp는 '이것이 단지 훈련소에 불과하다면'이라는 뜻이다.
- ▶ to fight a real gladiator fight, in the arena는 '경기장에서 진짜 검투사의 시합을 싸우는 것은'을 뜻한다. 문장의 주어인데 너무 길어서 앞에 가짜주어 it을 두고, 뒤로 간 것이다.

113 By night, he was covered with sweat and mud, and was so tired he could hardly drag himself back to his cell.
- ▶ tired와 he 사이에 that이 생략되어 있다고 보면 된다. 'so 원인 that 결과'의 표현이다.
- ▶ hardly는 '거의 ~않다, 못하다'란 뜻으로 쓰는데, 이 문장에서는 그만큼 힘들었다는 의미로 썼다. 즉 drag himself back to his cell은 '자기 몸을 끌듯이 움직여 방으로 들어가다'라고 해석한다.

113 I undertake to be burnt by fire, to be bound in chains, to be beaten by rods, and to die by the sword.
- ▶ undertake는 '~을 감내하다. ~하는 데 무조건 동의하다'라는 뜻이다. 이 문장은 '나는 불에 타고, 쇠사슬에 묶이고, 몽둥이로 얻어맞고 칼에 찔려 죽어도 좋다'로 해석할 수 있다.

114 Servius felt like he could barely breathe.
- ▶ 이 문장에서 barely는 '가까스로, 힘들게'이고, breathe는 '숨을 쉬다. 호흡하다'를 뜻하므로 he could barely breathe는 '그는 숨을 쉬기도 힘들었다'라는 의미이다.

115 Some even killed themselves so that they would not be forced to kill other men.
- ▶ 'to kill oneself'는 '자살하다, 자결하다'이다.
- ▶ be forced to kill other men은 '강제로 다른 사람들을 죽이게 되다'라는 의미이므로, 이 문장은 '심지어 어떤 이들은 자살을 하기도 했는데, 그래야 다른 사람들을 어쩔 수 없이 죽이

지 않을 것이기 때문이다'라고 해석할 수 있다.

115 The show was even better to watch when this happened—because the men in the audience learned that it is more decent to die than to kill."
- 이 문장에서 the show는 검투사의 시합을 말하고, decent는 '인간적으로 훌륭하다'라는 의미이다. 그래서 이 문장은 '그 구경거리는 이런 일이 일어나는 것을 볼 때가 훨씬 더 좋다. 다른 사람을 죽이는 것보다 스스로 죽는 편이 더 훌륭하다는 것을 구경하는 남자들이 배웠기 때문이다'라고 해석할 수 있다.

Chapter 29 Rome's War With Carthage

126 Rome took over all of Italy.
- 여기에서 Rome은 '로마 시(city)'가 아니라 '로마 제국(empire)'을 뜻한다.
- to take over A는 'A를 차지하다, 점령하다'라는 의미이다. '로마 제국은 이탈리아 전부를 점령했다'라고 해석한다.

126 They wanted to keep on trading with these cities, and they didn't want Rome to get in the way!
- to get in the way는 가고 있는 길에 들어온다는 의미로, '방해하다, 끼어들다'를 뜻한다. 그래서 they didn't want Rome to get in the way는 '그들은 로마가 방해하는 것을 원하지 않았다'라고 이해할 수 있다.

126 But when a Carthaginian ship wrecked on the coast of Italy, the Romans took it apart and figured out how to copy it.
- it은 a Carthaginian ship(카르타고의 배)이다.
- to take apart A는 'A를 분해하다'이고, figure out A는 'A를 알아내다'이다. 그래서 이 문장은 '로마인들은 그 배를 분해해서 똑같이 만드는 법을 알아냈다'라고 해석한다.

128 They bolted, carrying the Roman soldiers off into the dark.
- bolt는 '말이 놀라서 달아나다'라는 뜻이다.
- off는 '멀어짐'을 의미한다. 즉 이 문장은 '말들이 놀라서 로마의 병사들을 태운 채 어둠 속으로 달아나 버렸다'라는 의미이다.

129 But his soldiers were so worn out from burning and sacking towns in Italy that they were defeated!
- 이탈리아에 있는 마을들을 불태우고 파괴하느라 '너무 지쳐 있었다(so worn out)'가 원인이

고, '그들은 패배했다(defeated)'가 결과이다.

Chapter 30 The Aryans of India

We'll never know for sure.
▶ know for sure는 '확실히 안다'를 뜻한다. 그래서 이 문장은 '우리는 결코 (앞으로도) 확실히 알지는 못할 것이다'라고 이해할 수 있다.

But India didn't just sit empty!
▶ 이 문장은 '그러나 인도는 그저 비어 있는 채로 존재하지는 않았다'라고 해석할 수 있다.

Without the Ganges River, the people of India wouldn't have been able to survive.
▶ 앞에 있는 Without the Ganges River는 '가정'의 의미로 쓴 것이다. '만약 갠지스 강이 없었다면'이라고 해석한다. 그래서 뒤의 문장에 가정법 형태로 wouldn't have를 썼다. '인도의 사람들은 생존할 수 없었을 것이다'로 해석한다.

She balanced on the top of a cloud, ready to throw herself down to the earth with such violence that water would flood the entire surface of the ground.
▶ 'such 원인 that 결과'의 표현이다.
▶ violence는 '피해를 줄 만큼 강한 힘'을 의미한다. '강가 신이 너무 격렬하게[난폭하게] 땅으로 뛰어들어 물이 온 땅 위에 넘쳐 홍수가 났다'라는 의미이다.

And the Ganges River brought life and plenty to all the people who lived along its banks.
▶ brought life and plenty는 '부와 풍요를 가져다주었다'이다.
▶ to all the people who lived along its banks는 '그 강의 둑을 따라 살았던 모든 사람들에게'라는 의미이다.

At dusk, they float lighted candles on the water and pray to the river-goddess, Ganga.
▶ at dusk는 '해가 질 무렵, 황혼녘에'를 뜻한다.
▶ lighted candles는 '불을 붙인 초들'로, they float lighted candles on the water는 '그들은 불을 붙인 초들을 물에 띄웠다'라는 의미이다.

140　They too had good food and fine clothing, but not quite as fine as that of the priests.
▶ 'not quite as fine as ~'는 '~만큼 아주 좋지는 않다'를 뜻한다.
▶ that of the priests에서 that은 food and clothing을 의미하는데, '받은 것'이라고 지칭하여 복수형 those가 아닌 that으로 쓴 것이다.

141　But the poorest people in India were those who didn't belong to the caste system at all.
▶ 이 문장에서 those는 '그 사람들(those people)'을 뜻하는데, 앞에 이미 people이 나왔기 때문에 those만 쓴 것이다. those who didn't belong to the caste system at all은 '카스트 제도에 전혀 속하지 않은 사람들'이다.

143　He gave Siddhartha a thousand servants to wait on him hand and foot.
▶ to wait on someone hand and foot은 '손발이 되어 지극 정성으로 ~의 시중을 들다'라는 표현이다. 그렇게 시중드는 '하인이 천 명(a thousand servants)'이었다는 의미이다.

Chapter 31　The Mauryan Empire of India

156　They made people who were quarrelling and fighting with each other be friends and allies.
▶ to make A be B는 'A를 B가 되게 만들다'를 뜻한다. 이 문장에서는 A에 해당하는 것이 people who were quarrelling and fighting with each other(서로 말다툼하고 싸우는 사람들)이고, B에 해당하는 것은 friends and allies(친구들과 협력자들)이다.

157　But when Asoka visited the defeated cities after his great victories, he saw the suffering that his soldiers had caused.
▶ the suffering that his soldiers had caused는 '그의 병사들이 야기한 고통'이다. 그가 본(saw) 시점보다 앞서 일어난 일이기 때문에 that절의 동사를 had caused로 쓴 것이다.

157　Instead, I will draw people into my empire through honesty, truthfulness, and mercy.
▶ draw의 기본적인 의미는 '잡아당기다'이므로 draw people into my empire는 '내 제국 안으로 사람들을 끌어들이다'라는 뜻이다. 그런데 그 방법이 through honesty, truthfulness, and mercy(정직함, 신뢰, 자비를 통해서)이다.

158　He tried to reason with his subjects, rather than giving out strict,

harsh commands.
> 이 문장에서 reason은 '이성으로 대하다'를 뜻하는 동사형이다. 그래서 reason with his subjects는 '자신의 백성들을 이성으로 대하다'이다.

159 Many travelers walked along the path, traveling to the village on the forest's other side.
> walked along the path는 '그 오솔길을 따라 걸었다'이다.
> the village on the forest's other side는 '그 숲의 다른 쪽에 있는 마을'을 뜻한다.

Chapter 32 China: Writing and the Qin

170 Chinese calligraphers put these lines together to form Chinese characters.
> Chinese calligraphers는 '중국의 서예가들'이다.
> put these lines together는 '이 선들을 조합해서'이고, 그 결과로 '중국 글자들을 만든 것이다(to form Chinese characters).

171 It is supposed to look like a mother with a baby on her lap.
> 'It is supposed to ~'는 '~하도록 이미 정해져 있다'라는 의미이다.
> a mother with a baby on her lap은 '무릎 위에 아기를 앉힌 어머니'를 뜻한다.

171 In ancient China, calligraphy was done with a special sharp paintbrush, made out of animal hairs.
> with a special sharp paintbrush는 '특별한, 끝이 뾰족한 붓'인데, 그 붓은 '동물의 털로 만들어졌다(made out of animal hairs)'이다.

171 Then, a craftsman would carve away the wood from around the character, so that it stood out.
> it은 the character(글자)이다.
> stand out은 '도드라지다, 튀어나오다'를 뜻하는 표현이다. 글자 주위의 나무를 파서 글자가 도드라지게 만드는 '양각(陽刻)' 기법을 설명하고 있다.

173 So he forced all the warlords and former rulers of the Warring States to move into his capital city.
> 'force A to 동사'의 표현이 쓰인 문장이다. 이 문장에서는 all the warlords and former rulers of the Warring States(전국들의 모든 군벌들과 이전의 통치자들)가 A에 해당한다. forced ~ to move into his capital city는 '강제로 그의 수도로 이주하도록 만들었다'라는

의미이다.

173 As long as they lived near him, he could keep an eye on them and make sure they weren't planning to overthrow him.
- ▶ As long as they lived near him은 '그들이 그와 가까이 사는 한'을 의미한다.
- ▶ make sure they weren't planning to overthrow him은 '그들이 그를 타도하려고 계획하지 않고 있음을 확인하다'라는 의미이다.

175 The Mongols rode swift horses, and shot arrows with deadly precision.
- ▶ 이 문장에서 swift와 fast는 동의어로 쓰였다. swift horses는 '속도가 빠른 말'이다.
- ▶ precision은 '정확성'인데, '명중률'로 이해하면 된다. 앞에 붙은 deadly는 '지극히, 굉장히'를 뜻해 with deadly precision은 '굉장히 정확하게'로 해석할 수 있다.

176 "But, Emperor," the architects and builders protested, "there is not enough stone in the far reaches of your kingdom to build a Great Wall!"
- ▶ there is not enough stone to build a Great Wall(만리장성을 짓기에는 돌이 충분하지 않다) 문장에 stone을 꾸며주는 in the far reaches of your kingdom이 삽입되어 있는데, 여기에서 the far reaches는 '멀리 떨어져 있는 그 외곽', 즉 '그 변방'을 의미한다.

176 They lifted the frame up, set it on top of the packed dirt, and filled it again.
- ▶ lifted the frame up은 '그 틀을 들어 올렸다'이고, set it on the packed dirt는 '쌓아 놓은 흙 위에 놓았다'이며, filled it again은 '그 틀을 다시 채웠다'라는 의미이다. 흙벽돌을 계속 찍어 내는 과정을 묘사하고 있다.

178 We're bound to hit water soon.
- ▶ 'be bound to 동사'는 '~할 가능성이 매우 크다, 결국 ~하게 되어 있다'라는 표현이다.
- ▶ hit water는 '물을 찾아내다'라는 의미로, 이 문장은 '우린 곧 물을 찾아내게 될 거야'이다.

178 Soon their shovels began to turn up pieces of broken pottery.
- ▶ to turn up something은 '(숨겨진) 뭔가를 찾아내다[발견하다]'라는 뜻이다. '곧 그들의 삽이 깨진 질그릇 조각들을 찾아내기 시작했다'라는 해석은 '그들이 삽질을 하자 곧 깨진 질그릇 조각들이 나타났다'라고 이해할 수 있다.

179 And all the soldiers were facing east, as though they were guarding something behind them.
- ▶ were facing east는 '동쪽을 바라보고 서 있었다'라는 의미이다.

▶ as though they were guarding something behind them은 '마치 그들이 뒤에 있는 무언가를 지키고 있는 것처럼'을 뜻한다. 동쪽에는 적이 있고, 서쪽에는 지켜야 할 존재가 있는 듯 서 있었다는 의미이다.

Rivers and seas in miniature were dug and filled with mercury, made to flow by mechanical devices.
▶ 주어인 Rivers and seas in miniature는 '축소 크기로 만든 강과 바다'를 뜻한다.
▶ were dug and filled with mercury는 '땅을 파서 수은을 채웠다'라는 의미이고, made to flow by mechanical devices는 '기계 장치에 의해 물이 흐르도록 만들어졌다'라는 의미이다.

Chapter 33 Confucius

Confucius taught his followers that each person should respect the authority of those who are greater.
▶ authority는 '권위, 권한'을 뜻하고, those who are greater에서 great는 '나이가 많은, 지위가 높은, 중요한'의 의미를 포괄한다. 그래서 respect the authority those who are greater는 '자기보다 더 큰[중요한] 사람들의 권위를 존중하다'라고 해석한다.

Children ought to listen to and obey their parents.
▶ 동사 listen to와 obey의 목적어가 their parents로 같다. 그래서 listen to and obey their parents(자기 부모님의 말을 잘 듣고 복종하다)로 their parents를 뒤에 한 번만 쓴 것이다.
▶ ought to는 '~해야 한다, ~하는 게 합당하다(should)'를 뜻하는 조동사이다.

Husbands should do whatever the rulers tell them to do.
▶ whatever는 '무엇이든, 전부 다(any or all of the things)'이므로 이 문장은 '결혼한 성인 남자들은 통치자들이 하라고 시키는 것은 뭐든지 해야 한다'라고 해석한다.

Chapter 34 The Rise of Julius Caesar

Soon Julius decided that he wanted to help govern Rome.
▶ 율리시스가 마음먹은 것은 '로마를 혼자 다스리는 것'이 아니라, 다스리는 것을 돕고자(help) 함이다. 즉 공무원이나 정치가가 되어 '정부의 일을 하고 싶다는 생각을 갖게 되었다'는 의미이다.

All the sailors ran up to the deck to fight, but the pirates boarded the

ship and took it over.
- ▶ board는 '배나 비행기에 오르다[타다]'라는 동사이므로, took it over는 '배를 장악했다[차지했다]'이다.

202 Very well, we'll keep you and see how much money we can make from you!
- ▶ 이 때 keep은 '가지 못하게 붙잡아 두다'라는 뜻이다. 목적은 '몸값을 뜯어내는' 것이다.
- ▶ see how much money we can make from you는 '우리가 너에게서 얼마나 많은 돈을 벌 수 있을지 보자'는 의미이다.

202 And be sure that the food I'm served for supper is better than what I had for lunch!
- ▶ what I had for lunch는 '내가 점심으로 먹은 것(food)'을 뜻한다. 그것보다 더 나아야(better than)하는 것은 the food I'm served for supper(저녁 식사로 내게 갖다 바칠 음식)이다.

204 He drove away the mountain bandits that kept attacking the Roman cities in Spain.
- ▶ He drove away the mountain bandits는 '그가 산적들을 멀리 몰아냈다'라는 의미이다.
- ▶ that kept attacking the Roman cities in Spain은 the mountain bandits가 어떤 산적들인지 설명하는 말로, '스페인에 있는 로마 제국의 도시들을 계속 공격하는'을 뜻한다.

204 But all the time, he longed to go back to Rome and become powerful there, in his home town.
- ▶ 'to long to 동사'는 '~하기를 열망하다'라는 표현이다. 그가 열망하는 것은 두 가지, '로마로 돌아가는 것(go back to Rome)'과 '자신의 고향에서(in his home town) 강해지는 것(become powerful), 즉 권력을 쥐는 것'이다.

206 If only Caesar were like Cincinnatus!
- ▶ 'If only + 문장'은 '~하기만 한다면 좋을 텐데'라는 의미로 '소망, 기대'를 표현한다. 이 문장은 '카이사르가 킨키나투스와 같다면 좋을 텐데!'라고 해석한다.

Chapter 35 Caesar the Hero

219 The soldiers clustered at the side of the boat, anxious to see Britain for the first time.
- ▶ at the side of the boat는 배의 측면, 즉 '배 갑판 위 난간'을 의미한다.
- ▶ anxious to see Britain은 '브리튼 섬을 보고 불안했다'라는 의미가 아니라 '브리튼 섬을 무

척 보고 싶어 했다'라는 것이다.

220 We won't be able to run Rome any more!
▶ 이 문장에서 run은 '운영[경영]하다, 관리하다'라는 뜻으로, 이 문장은 '우리는 더는 로마를 다스릴 수 없을 것이다'로 해석할 수 있다.

220 Two of the senators decided that they would try to make one of the other consuls, Pompey, turn against Caesar.
▶ 'to make A 동사'는 'A가 ~하도록 만들다[시키다]'를 뜻한다. 이 문장에서 A에 해당하는 one of the other consuls와 Pompey는 동격으로, '다른 집정관들 중 한 명인 폼페이'라는 의미이다.
▶ turn against Caesar는 '카이사르에게 등을 돌리도록'을 뜻한다.

221 And all the people of Rome were told that Caesar was a traitor.
▶ be told는 '다른 사람이 하는 말을 듣다'를 뜻한다. 말을 한 사람을 밝힐 수 없거나 밝힐 필요가 없을 때 수동태로 쓴다.

221 "Even yet," he said to the captain of his army, "we may turn back. But once we cross that little bridge ... we will have to settle this with our swords."
▶ even yet은 '아직까지도'를 뜻한다. 뒤의 we may turn back을 연결하면 '아직까지도 우리는 돌아갈 수 있다'라는 의미이다.
▶ to settle this with our swords는 '우리의 칼로 이것을 해결하다'라는 의미인데, this는 '이 상황, 이 문제'를 나타낸다.

222 Let the die be cast!
▶ 주사위(die)는 누군가 던져야 움직인다. 그래서 cast(던지다)가 아니라, be cast(던져지다)로 쓴 것이다. '주사위는 던져졌다!'는 카이사르가 남긴 유명한 말이다.

223 But they didn't get along with each other.
▶ to get along with A는 'A와 계속 잘 어울리다, 사이좋게 지내다'의 표현이다. 이 문장은 '그러나 그들은 서로 사이가 좋지 않았다'로 해석한다.

225 Caesar was overcome by Cleopatra.
▶ overcome이 수동태인 be overcome으로 쓰면 '지다, 압도되다'라는 의미가 된다. 이 문장은 '카이사르는 클레오파트라에게 압도되었다'라고 해석한다.

226 So when he came back to Rome, Caesar was made dictator for life.

▶ Caesar was made dictator for life는 '카이사르가 종신 독재자가 되었다'라는 의미이다. 카이사르가 스스로 독재자가 된 것이 아니라, 다른 사람들이나 상황에 의해서 '만들어졌다'라는 의미를 were made로 쓴 것이다.
▶ dictator for life는 '종신[평생] 독재자'이다.

226　Everything seemed to be going his way.
▶ to go one's way는 '~가 가는 길[방향]로 가다'라는 뜻인데, '~가 원하는 방향으로 일이 이루어지다'라는 의미도 있다. 이 문장은 '모든 것이 그가 원하는 방향으로 이루어지는 듯했다'라고 해석할 수 있다.

228　"How silly of me to be nervous!" he thought.
▶ It was silly of me to be nervous(내가 불안해한 것은 어리석은 짓이었다)라고 말해도 되지만, '어리석었다'는 후회가 확 밀려온다면 감탄문을 써서 How silly of me to be nervous!(나는 얼마나 어리석은가, 불안하다니!)라고 표현해야 느낌이 산다.

228　"Friends!" he shouted, "what are we waiting for!"
▶ 원래 의문문인 What are we waiting for?(우리는 무엇을 기다리는가?)를 느낌표(exclamation mark)를 붙여서 감탄문처럼 쓴 것은 대답을 하라고 묻는 것이 아니라, '뭘 기다리란 말인가! 기다릴 필요가 없잖아!'의 의미로 행동을 촉구하기 위함이다.

Chapter 36　The First Roman Prince

240　After Caesar died, Rome was in an uproar!
▶ uproar는 '고함(roar)이 가득(up)하다'는 의미이다. '큰소란, 시끄러운 논쟁, 대규모 항의' 등을 뜻해서, 이 문장은 '카이사르가 죽은 뒤에 로마는 대단히 소란스러웠다'라고 해석한다.

242　Rome shouldn't have a king, and if I stay people will want me to be king.
▶ if I stay는 '내가 머문다면(이 자리에 그대로 있으면)'을 뜻하고, people will want me to be king은 '사람들은 내가 왕이 되기를 원할 것이다'라는 의미이다.

Chapter 37　The Beginning of Christianity

248　No one questioned his decrees.
▶ question은 명사 '질문, 물음'이 아니라, '이의를 제기하다, 의심하다'라는 뜻의 동사로 쓰였다.

348

250
When they arrived in Bethlehem, the village was so full that they couldn't find anywhere to sleep!
▶ 이 문장에서 full은 '사람들로 가득 차 있다'는 의미이다. 베들레헴 출신 사람들이 한꺼번에 몰렸기 때문에 빈집이 없는 것이다. 사람들이 너무 많아서(so full) '그들이 잠을 잘 곳을 찾지 못했다(that they couldn't find anywhere to sleep)'라는 의미이다.

250
Today, a Savior has been born to you.
▶ '낳다'라는 의미인 bear는 주로 be bron(태어나다)의 형태로 쓰이는데, 이 문장은 '오늘, 구세주가 당신들에게 태어났다'라고 해석한다.

252
If he didn't get rid of Jews who might start rebellions against Rome, he could get into trouble with the Roman "First Citizen"—a man named Tiberius, who had inherited the job of running Rome from Augustus Caesar.
▶ to get into trouble with A는 'A와 마찰을 일으키다, A와 갈등을 겪게 되다'이다.
▶ the Roman "First Citizen"은 로마의 '일등 시민' 즉 황제인 티베리우스(Tiberius)이다.

253
A huge stone was rolled into place across the entrance to the tomb.
▶ A huge stone was rolled into place는 '커다란 바위가 굴러서 자리를 잡다'라는 의미이다. 사람들이 돌을 굴렸기 때문에 was rolled로 썼다. into place는 '자리에 꼭 맞게'를 뜻한다.
▶ across the entrance to the tomb은 '그 무덤 입구를 가로질러'라는 의미이다.

Chapter 38 The End of the Ancient Jewish Nation

263
One ancient historian writes that, when the Temple burned down, the gold and silver melted and ran into the cracks between the huge stones of the Temple's foundation.
▶ to burn down은 '불에 타서 무너지다, 전소하다'이고, ran into the cracks는 '틈으로 흘러 들어갔다'를 뜻한다.
▶ between the huge stones of the Temple's foundation은 the cracks가 있는 위치로, '그 사원 기단의 커다란 돌들 사이에 있는'을 의미한다.

264
They were scattered throughout all the countries of the ancient world.
▶ scatter는 '흩어지게 하다'인데, 이 문장에서 They(유대인들)가 '타의에 의해 강제로 흩어졌기' 때문에 were scattered로 표현했다.
▶ throughout all the countries of the ancient world는 '고대 세계의 모든 나라 여기저기로'를

Chapter 39 Rome and the Christians

269 "When I die," Nero used to say, "what a loss I shall be to the art of music!"
- ▶ I shall be a loss to the art of music(난 음악이란 예술에 손실이 될 것이다)이라는 말로는 부족해서, '엄청난 손실'이라고 허풍을 치고자 감탄문으로 표현한 것이다. '내가 죽는다면, 음악이란 예술에 그 얼마나 엄청난 손실이란 말인가!'라는 의미이다.

269 It smoldered away until the floorboard caught fire.
- ▶ smolder는 '연기를 내며 천천히 타들어가다'라는 뜻의 동사이고, away는 '점점 번져간다'라는 의미를 담고 있다.
- ▶ until the floorboard caught fire는 '마룻바닥에 불이 붙을 때까지'를 의미한다.

270 I will take the land where those houses used to stand and build myself a new and bigger palace.
- ▶ I will take the land는 '내가 그 땅을 가지겠다'라는 말이다. '그 땅'을 설명하는 말이 where those houses used to stand(그 집들이 서 있던 곳)이다.
- ▶ build myself a new and bigger palace는 '자기가 새로운, 더 큰 궁전을 짓겠다'라는 의미이다.

271 Nero's cruelty to the Christians drew attention away from his own selfishness.
- ▶ 주어인 Nero's cruelty to the Christians는 '기독교도들에 대한 네로의 학대'를 뜻한다. drew attention away from his own selfishness는 '자신의 이기적인 행동으로부터 (사람들의) 주의를 다른 곳으로 돌리게 했다'라는 의미이다.

271 The Roman emperors kept control over their people by saying, "Obey us, because we are gods!"
- ▶ to keep control over A는 'A에 대한 통제를 유지하다, 계속 A를 통제하다'를 뜻하는 표현이다. 따라서 이 문장은 '로마 황제들은 "우리에게 복종하라. 왜냐하면 우리는 신이기 때문이다"라고 말함으로써 계속 백성들 통제했다'라고 해석할 수 있다.

272 If the Christians disobeyed them, other Romans might be brave enough to do the same.
- ▶ 이 문장에서 might는 '아마도(maybe)'라는 추측의 의미를 담고 있다.
- ▶ brave enough to do the same은 '똑같은 행동을 할만큼 용감한'을 뜻하는데, 여기에서 the same은 '그들에게 복종하지 않는(disobeyed them) 행위'를 의미한다.

272 This secrecy soon made people even more suspicious of the Christians.
▶ secrecy는 '비밀스러움'이고, suspicious of A는 'A를 의심하는'이다. 이 문장은 '이런 비밀스러움은 곧 사람들이 기독교인들을 훨씬 더 의심하게 만들었다'라는 의미이다.

273 So they decided on a secret symbol.
▶ to decide on A는 'A를 정하다, A에 대해 결정하다'의 표현이다. '그래서 그들은 (다른 사람들은 모르는) 비밀스러운 표시[기호]를 하나 정했다'라고 해석한다.

275 So each soldier painted onto his shield the Greek letters standing for Christ's name.
▶ the Greek letters는 '그리스 글자'이다.
▶ to stand for A는 'A를 나타내다, 상징하다, 대표하다'라는 뜻으로, 이 문장은 '그래서 병사들은 각자 자신의 방패 위에 예수의 이름을 나타내는 그리스어 글자들을 그려 넣었다'라고 해석할 수 있다.

276 After all, Rome was an old city, beginning to look shabby and run-down.
▶ shabby는 '낡은, 허름한, 추레한'이고, run-down은 '점차 무너지고 있는'이라는 의미로, '쇠퇴한, 황폐한'이라고 해석한다.

Chapter 10 Rome Begins to Weaken

286 One of these disobedient Celtic tribes was particularly annoying to the Romans—because their leader was a woman!
▶ 주어인 One of these disobedient Celtic tribes는 '이 반항하는 켈트 부족들 중 하나는'을 뜻한다.
▶ annoying은 '짜증나게 하는, 성가신'을 뜻하는 말이다. 따라서 was particularly annoying to the Romans는 '특히 로마인들을 짜증 나게 했다'라는 의미이다.

286 Men thought it was very embarrassing to be beaten by a woman.
▶ to be beaten by a woman은 '여자에게 매를 맞다'가 아니라, '여자에게 지다[패하다]'라는 의미이다. 따라서 이 문장은 '남자들은 여자에게 지는 것은 수치스러운 일이라고 생각했다'로 해석한다.

287 The statue of Victory fell face down without being pushed!
▶ to fall face down은 '얼굴이 땅에 부딪히게 앞으로 넘어지다, 앞으로 고꾸라지다'라는 뜻의 표현이다. without being pushed는 '밀리지도 않았는데, 누가 밀지도 않았는데'를 뜻한다.

287 A woman claimed that she had seen the sea turn as red as blood.
- claim은 '~이 사실이라고 주장하다'라는 뜻이다.
- turn as red as blood는 '피처럼 붉게 변하다'이므로 '한 여인은 바다가 피처럼 붉게 변하는 것을 자신이 봤다고 주장했다'라고 해석한다.

Chapter 11 The Attacking Barbarians

298 They are uglier than any other men on earth.
- uglier는 '추한, 못생긴'을 뜻하는 ugly에 −er이 붙은 비교급이다. 이 문장은 '그들은 세상 다른 어떤 사람들보다 더 못생겼다'라고 이해할 수 있다.

298 They thought that God was punishing them by sending Attila the Hun to attack their borders!
- God was punishing them은 '하느님이 그들을 벌하고 있다'라는 의미이다.
- 벌하는 방법이 by 이하에 나온다. by sending Attila the Hun to attack their borders는 '훈족의 아틸라를 보내어 그들의 국경들을 공격하게 함으로써'라고 해석한다.

305 Sobs disturb my every word.
- my every word는 '내가 하는 모든 말'이라는 의미로, '계속 흐느껴 울 수밖에 없어서 말 한 마디 제대로 할 수 없다'라는 의미이다.

305 The Western Roman Empire still survived, but just barely.
- barely는 '가까스로, 힘들게'이므로 이 문장은 '서로마 제국은 여전히 살아남았지만, 그저 가까스로 존재할 뿐이었다'라고 해석한다.

305 Its capital city was gone, and its emperor was ruling in the middle of a swamp.
- Its capital city was gone은 '그 제국의 수도는 없어졌다'로, 즉 '로마는 더는 수도가 아니다'라는 의미이다.
- in the middle of a swamp는 '늪의 한가운데'를 뜻한다.

Chapter 12 The End of Rome

315 *Momyllus* meant "Little disgrace."
- 이 문장에서 little은 '작은' 또는 '어린'을 뜻한다. disgrace는 '망신스러운 사람, 수치거리'를 뜻하므로, 이 문장은 'Momyllus(모밀루스)는 "어린 망신거리"를 의미한다'라고 해석한다.

세계 역사 연대표 · 고대

BC / BCE Date

7000 BC/BCE	Nomads roam the Fertile Crescent
6800	Stone walls built at Jericho
3500	Climate changes in the Sahara
3000	King Narmer unites Upper and Lower Kingdoms of Egypt
3000-2100	Era of the Old Kingdom of Egypt
3000-1200	Gilgamesh Myth composed
2690	Huang Di rules China
2550	Great Pyramid built (burial place of Cheops)
2334	Sargon becomes king of the city-state of Kish
2200-1450	Peak of Minoan civilization
2040-1720	Middle Kingdom of Egypt
2000-1750	Harappan civilization is at its peak strength
1980-1926	Amenemhet becomes pharaoh of Egypt
1792	Hammurabi inherits the throne of Babylon
1766	T'ang becomes King of China
1766-1122	Shang Dynasty rules
1750	Exodus of Indus Valley
1567	Ahmose expels Hyksos from Egypt
1524	Thutmose I becomes pharaoh
1500	Aryan people enter India
1493-1481	Thutmose I rules Egypt as pharaoh
1473-1458	Hatshepsut rules as pharaoh
1450	Mycenaeans settle in Crete
1357	Tutankhamen born
1352-1336	Amenhotep IV rules Egypt as pharaoh
1339	Tutankhamen dies at age 18
1300-1200	Spread of Assyrian Empire

1200–900	Olmec civilization flourishes
1200–700	Height of Phoenician civilization; Greek "Dark Ages"
mid-800s	Greek city-states begin to arise
814	Carthage is first settled
800	Homer lives during this time
745–727	Reign of Tiglathpileser III
700	Time of the earliest Persians
668–627	Ashurbanipal's reign as king of Assyria
605–561	Nebuchadnezzar rules as king of Babylon
563–483	Siddhartha Gautama (the Buddha) lives
559–525	Cyrus the Great rules over Medes and Persians
551–479	Confucius lives
539	Babylon falls to the Persians
500	War against Persia by Greece begins
500	Aryan civilization in India reaches high point
500	"Period of the Warring States" begins in China
490	First marathon run by Athenian to announce victory over Persia
480	Battle of Salamis
431–404	War between Sparta and Athens (Peloponnesian War)
338	King Philip of Macedonia conquers Greek city-states
336–323	Alexander the Great rules
321–233	The Mauryan Empire of India
268–233	Asoka rules India; Mauryan empire disintegrates following his death
264–241	First Punic War fought
264–146	Punic Wars
230	Shi Huangdi (Qin Zheng) begins uniting Warring States of China
221	First united Chinese empire, under Shi Huangdi
218	Hannibal's invasion of Italy
218–202	Second Punic War takes place
214	Construction of Great Wall of China begins

212	Qin Zheng orders book burning
200	Nazca civilization flourishes
100	Julius Caesar born
69	Cleopatra born
55-54	Caesar's campaigns in Britain take place
48	Caesar arrives in Egypt
March 15, 44	Caesar is assassinated
43	Octavian becomes a consul in Rome
27	Octavian becomes Caesar Augustus, emperor of the Roman Empire
3 BC/BCE	Probable year of Jesus' birth

AD / CE Dates

14	Caesar Augustus dies
52	Attila the Hun dies
54-68	Nero's reign
61-63	Boadicea revolts against Rome
70	The Temple in Jerusalem is destroyed
284	Diocletian comes to the throne in Rome
286	Diocletian divides the Roman Empire
286-305	Diocletian rules jointly with Maximian
312	The Battle of Milvian Bridge
312-337	The reign of Constantine
395	Stilicho, following Theodosius, becomes regent for the Western Roman Empire
397	Stilicho drives Alaric away
408	Stilicho falls from favor and is executed
410	Visigoths sack Rome
475-476	Romulus Augustus rules

저자의 말

영어로 만나는 역사,
역사로 배우는 영어

우리는 왜 역사를 알아야 하는가? 우리는 왜 영어를 공부해야 하는가? 우리에게 중요한 이 두 가지 질문에 대한 답이 《The Story of the World》 안에 들어 있다.

인간이 만들어온 세상을 이야기하는 것이 역사이다. 변하지 않는 인간의 본성과 그에 따른 행동으로 인해 원인과 결과가 끊임없이 연결되어 지금 우리가 사는 세상이 만들어졌다. '역사란 과거와 현재, 미래의 대화'라는 영국 역사가 토인비(Arnold Toynbee)의 말처럼, 역사를 알아야 과거와 현재를 직시하며 더 나은 미래를 개척할 수 있는 것이다. 그럼에도 우리는 세계사를 힘들게 암기해야만 하는, 굳이 공부하지 않아도 상관없는, 하나의 선택 과목쯤으로 여겨 왔다.

역사에 대한 이런 인식은 《The Story of the World》의 책장을 넘기면서 자연스럽게 바뀌게 된다. 이 책은 제목에서 알 수 있듯이 역사를 이야기 형식으로 풀고 있다. 저자는 부모가 자녀와 함께 읽을 수 있는 역사 이야기, 누구든 신나게 역사 속으로 첫걸음을 내디딜 수 있는 이야기를 쓰고자 했고, 수많은 독자들이 저자의 의도에 고개를 끄덕였다. 이 책 덕분에 많은 독자들이 역사에 관심을 갖게 되었고, 역사에 눈을 뜨게 되었다. 지난 10여 년간 미국은 물론 한국에서도 많은 사랑을 받으며 역사 부문의 베스트셀러로 자리매김한 것은 우연이 아니다.

이제 여러분은 이 책을 원서로 읽고자 한다. 이 시점에서 여러분은 '과연 영어 학습에 도움이 될까? 너무 어렵지 않을까?'라는 의문을 품을 수 있다. 해설서를 쓰면서 먼저 원서를 읽은 독자로서, 나의 대답은 영어 학습에 '대단히 유용한 책'이며 '독해 실력을 확실하게 향상시킬 수 있는 책'이라는 것이다.

우선 중고등학교 과정의 필수 영어 어휘들이 생생한 역사적 상황과 문맥 속에

녹아 있다. 그래서 정확한 의미와 용법을 자연스럽게 익힐 수 있는 것이다. 또한 그 어휘들은 반복되는 역사의 흐름에 따라 빈번하게 등장하기 때문에 머리에 각인되는 효과가 있다. 뿐만 아니라 저자는 미국의 초등학교 저학년부터 성인 독자들까지 모두 쉽게 읽을 수 있게 문장의 난이도를 고려해서 책을 썼다. 영어 수준이 대체로 우리의 중고등학교 수준과 맞다. 독해 실력 향상을 위해 필요한 문법이 총망라되어 있기 때문에 이 책을 일독하면 영어 문장에 대한 자신감이 생길 것이다.

원서를 읽는 과정에서 해설이 힘이 될 것이다. 각 장마다 내용에 맞게 역사적 배경 지식을 덧붙여 원서의 이해를 돕고자 했다. The Story of the Words에서는 영어 학습을 위해 독자들이 반드시 알아야 하는 단어, 내용의 핵심어, 어려운 개념어 등을 선별해 의미를 완전히 이해하고 활용할 수 있도록 했다.

역사와 영어, 이 두 마리 토끼가 이 책 속에서 뛰어다니고 있다. 세계 곳곳을 누비며 시간 여행을 하다가 마지막 책장을 덮을 때, 두 마리 토끼가 여러분의 두 손에 모두 들려 있길 바란다.

지소철

저자의 말

이야기로
이해하는 역사

현재 저는 아이들, 엄마들과 《The Story of the World》를 영어로 읽는 수업을 하고 있어요. 사실 수업이라기보다는 영어를 함께 읽고 역사를 이해하는 나눔의 시간을 갖는 것이지요. 처음에는 영어는 물론 역사에도 관심 없던 아이들이 한 챕터씩 함께 읽어가면서 '피라미드를 직접 보고 싶어요', '스파르타와 아테네 중에 어느 쪽이 더 좋은지' 등 질문을 통해 영어를 읽는 힘과 역사를 보는 힘, 더불어 생각하는 힘이 커가는 것을 보며 보람을 느낍니다.

이 책의 장점을 꼽으라면 크게 세 가지를 말할 수 있어요.

우선 표현력이 뛰어납니다. 기초 단어와 쉽고 간결한 문장으로 역사적 내용을 명쾌하게 설명해내고 있어요. 언어적 측면에서 볼 때 사실 영어는 익히기 쉬운 언어에 속해요. 효과로 보자면 최대한 단순한 문장으로 쓰인 영어책을 많이 읽는 편이 어려운 문장으로 쓰인 책을 힘들게 읽는 편보다 외국어 습득에서는 훨씬 효율적이지요. 꾸준히 읽어가다 보면 읽는 속도도 빨라지고 원서를 읽는다는 부담이 차차 사라지는 것을 아이들을 통해 확인할 수 있었어요.

그 다음은 역사를 바라보는 관점이 어느 한쪽으로 치우침이 없이 균형 잡혀 있다는 것입니다. 고대를 다룬 역사책에서 메소포타미아 문명, 수메르인들의 역할, 아프리카 구전 신화까지 짚어주는 책은 사실상 찾아보기 힘들거든요. 역사란 인류의 발자취이므로 인류가 있던 곳이면 어디에서나 역사가 시작되고 지속되었다고 볼 수 있어요. 동양과 한국의 역사를 좀 더 다뤄주었으면 하는 아쉬움이 남기는 하지만, 나름의 균형 감각을 가지고 써내려간 훌륭한 책이라고 말할 수 있어요.

마지막으로 이야기 중심의 글쓰기입니다. 흔히 역사라고 하면 연대와 사건,

어려운 용어, 왕들의 이름과 각종 지명을 외워야 하는 암기 과목으로 여기지요. 하지만 수잔은 완전히 다른 역사의 세계를 보여줍니다. '아, 역사가 이렇게 재미있구나'라는 생각이 들게 하는 것은 바로 이야기로 풀어썼기 때문이에요. 마치 우리가 그 시대로 날아가 그 시대를 함께 사는 듯한 착각이 들 정도예요. 이야기로 역사를 이해하니 역사 자체에 대한 친근감이 절로 생겨납니다.

훌륭한 한 권의 책은 어떤 선생님보다 배울 점이 많지요. 하지만 문제는 영어로 된 원문을 혼자 힘으로 읽어낼 수 있을까 하는 의문이 들지요. 그래서 이 책이 나오게 되었어요. 영어가 모국어가 아닌 아이들도 단어와 구문을 익히고 나서 원문을 읽을 수 있도록 도와주는 책이에요. 이 책에서 제가 쓴 부분은 Q&A인데요, 실제로 아이들과 함께 공부하며 설명이 부족하거나 놓친 부분들을 선별하여 질문과 대답 형식으로 해설을 달았습니다. 이외에도 더 많은 질문들이 나올 수 있어요. 호기심을 가지고 다른 책을 찾아보기를 권합니다. 공부란 자기가 궁금한 것들을 하나씩 해결하며 지의 세계로 나아가는 과정이거든요.

나아가 아이들뿐만 아니라 어른들도 이 책의 일독을 권합니다. 왜냐하면 영어를 새로 시작하는 어른들에게 영어와 역사를 동시에 공부할 수 있는 거의 유일한 책이거든요. 사실상 어른들과 공부를 해보면 의외로 수준 문제로 적당한 교재를 찾기가 힘든데, 이 책은 우리가 알아야 할 역사 교양을 알려주면서도 영어가 쉬워서 어른들의 지적 호기심을 충분히 만족시킬 수 있어요. 먼저 시작한 사람들이 이웃과 친구에게 권하고 그렇게 입에서 입으로 전해지며 역사 읽기의 재미가 퍼져나가는 상상을 하는 것만으로 마음이 즐겁습니다.

심금숙

지소철

성균관대학교 영어영문학과를 졸업하고 Sungkyunkwan-Georgetown University의 TESOL 과정을 이수하였다. 영어를 보다 재미있게 공부하는 학습법, 영어를 효과적으로 가르치는 교수법 둘 다에 몰두하면서 영어책 저자, 번역가, 도서 기획자로서 영어와 함께하는 삶을 살아왔다. 《플로이드의 오래된 집》《내 인생의 다이아몬드》《해적과 제왕》《제국의 몰락》 등 100여 권의 책을 번역했고 《징글리시가 잉글리시로》《행복한 영어 초등학교》《수능과 직결되는 최정예 영단어 마지노999》《보카 출생의 비밀》 등 다수의 영어학습서를 저술하였다. 인문서 번역 경험과 영어학습서 집필 노하우를 살려 이 책의 영단어와 구문을 초보자 눈높이에 맞춰 해설하였다. 관심 있는 분야의 원서를 많이 읽는 것, 이것이 그가 제안하는 영어 정복의 지름길이다.

심금숙

대학과 대학원에서 영문학을 전공하였고 《소설 목민심서》를 기점으로 역사책 읽기에 빠져들었다. 책이 좋아 늘 책과 함께 살던 어느 날 급기야 '행복한 왕자'라는 이름의 도서관을 열고 운영한 지 어느덧 18년째다. 책을 권하다 보니 암기식 공부가 아닌 진짜 공부의 즐거움을 찾으러 오는 아이들에게 선생님이 되어 있었고 현재는 영어, 일본어와 역사를 가르치고 있다. 공부가 생활인 삶 속으로 자연스럽게 어른들도 찾아왔고 그들과 인문학 공부를 함께 하며 매일을 바쁘게 보낸다. 인문주의가 삶에 미치는 영향을 아이들과 엄마들을 통해 확인하며 최근에는 그동안 쌓인 내공을 독자들에게 나눠줄 저술에 힘쓰고 있다.

- 초판 발행 2015년 3월 31일 • 초판 20쇄 발행 2025년 4월 7일
- 지은이 수잔 와이즈 바우어, 지소철, 심금숙
- 펴낸이 이주애, 홍영완 • 편집 김진희, 장정민 • 디자인 오필민디자인 • 마케팅 김진겸
- 펴낸곳 ㈜윌북 • 출판등록 제2006-000017호 • 주소 10881 경기도 파주시 광인사길 217
- 전화 031-955-3777 • 팩스 031-955-3778 • 홈페이지 willbookspub.com
- 블로그 blog.naver.com/willbooks • 인스타그램 @willbooks_pub
- ISBN 979-11-5581-039-2(14740)

이 도서의 국립중앙도서관 출판시도서목록(CIP)은 서지정보유통지원시스템 홈페이지(http://seoji.nl.go.kr)와 국가자료공동목록시스템(http://www.nl.go.kr/kolisnet)에서 이용하실 수 있습니다.

책값은 뒤표지에 있습니다. 잘못 만들어진 책은 구입하신 서점에서 바꿔드립니다.